CW01066517

Springer Series in Language and Communication   24

Editor W.J.M. Levelt

Springer Series in Language and Communication

Editor: W.J.M. Levelt

(continued after Index)

Gisela E. Speidel
Keith E. Nelson

Editors

The Many Faces
of Imitation
in Language Learning

With 18 Figures

Springer-Verlag New York Berlin Heidelberg
London Paris Tokyo

Gisela E. Speidel
Center for Development of Early Education
Kapalama Heights, Honolulu, HI 96817, USA

Keith E. Nelson
Department of Psychology
Pennsylvania State University
University Park, PA 16802, USA

Series Editor

Willem J.M. Levelt
Max-Planck-Institut fur Psycholinguistik
Wundtlaan 1
6525 XD Nijmegen
The Netherlands

Library of Congress Cataloging-in-Publication Data
The Many faces of imitation in language learning/Gisela E. Speidel,
  Keith E. Nelson, editors
      p. cm.—(Springer series in language and communication:
  24)
    Bibliography: p.
    Includes index.
    ISBN 0-387-96885-7 (alk. paper)
    1. Language acquisition. 2. Imitation. I. Speidel, Gisela E.
  II. Nelson, Keith E. III. Series
  P118.M354   1989
  401'.9—dc19   88-31822

Printed on acid-free paper.

Typeset by Publishers Service, Bozeman, Montana.
Printed and bound by Edwards Brothers, Inc., Ann Arbor, Michigan.
Printed in the United States of America.

9 8 7 6 5 4 3 2 1

ISBN 0-387-96885-7 Springer-Verlag New York Berlin Heidelberg
ISBN 3-540-96885-7 Springer-Verlag Berlin Heidelberg New York

Preface

In this book we take a fresh look at imitation. With the knowledge of some 20 years of research after Chomsky's initial critique of the behavioristic approach to language learning, it is time to explore imitation once again. How imitation is viewed in this book has changed greatly since the 1950s and can only be understood by reading the various contributions. This reading reveals many faces, many forms, many causes, and many functions of imitation – cognitive, social, information processing, learning, and biological. Some views are far removed from the notion that an imitation must occur immediately or that it must be a perfect copy of an adult sentence. But the essence of the concept of imitation is retained: Some of the child's language behavior originates as an imitation of a prior model.

The range of phenomena covered is broad and stimulating. Imitation's role is discussed from infancy on through all stages of language learning. Individual differences among children are examined in how much they use imitation, and in what forms and to what purposes they use it. The forms and functions of parent imitation of their child are considered. Second-language learning is studied alongside first-language learning.

The juxtaposition of so many views and facets of imitation in this book will help us to study the commonalities as well as differences of various forms and functions of imitative language and will help us to discern the further dimensions along which we must begin to differentiate imitation.

Honolulu, Hawaii
University Park, Pennsylvania

Gisela E. Speidel
Keith E. Nelson

Contents

CHAPTER 10

The Phylogenetic Processes of Verbal Language Imitation
Roland G. Tharp and Caleb E.S. Burns

CHAPTER 11

Observational Learning and Language Acquisition: Principles of
Learning, Systems, and Tasks
Grover J. Whitehurst and Barbara D. DeBaryshe

Contributors

Lutfi A. Abuelhaija, Department of English, Yarmouk University, Irbid, Jordan

John N. Bohannon III, Department of Psychology, Butler University, Indianapolis, IN 46208, USA

Susan Broome, Pathfinder Research Group, Boxborough, MA 01719, USA

Caleb E.S. Burns, Gresham Psychology Clinic, Gresham, OR 97030, USA

Barbara D. DeBaryshe, Department of Child Development and Family Relations, University of North Carolina at Greensboro, Greensboro, NC 27412, USA

Alison Gopnik, Department of Psychology, University of California, Berkeley, CA 94720, USA

Mikael Heimann, Goteborgs Universitet, Psykologiska Institutionen, 400 20 Goteborg, Sweden

Madeleen J. Herreshoff, Center for Development of Early Education, Kapalama Heights, Honolulu, HI 96817, USA

Jan C. Kruper, Department of Psychiatry and Behavioral Sciences, University of Washington School of Medicine, Seattle, WA 98105, USA

Elise Frank Masur, Department of Psychology, Northern Illinois University, DeKalb, IL 60115, USA

Andrew N. Meltzoff, Department of Psychology, University of Washington, Seattle, WA 98195, USA

Ernst Moerk, Department of Psychology, School of Natural Sciences, California State University at Fresno, Fresno, CA 93740, USA

Keith E. Nelson, Department of Psychology, Pennsylvania State University, University Park, PA 16802, USA

Catherine E. Snow, Human Development and Psychology, Graduate School of Education, Harvard University, Cambridge, MA 02138, USA

Gisela E. Speidel, Center for Development of Early Education, Kapalama Heights, Honolulu, HI 96817, USA

Laura Stanowicz, Department of Psychology, Virginia Polytechnic Institute and State University, Blacksburg, VA 24061, USA

Roland G. Tharp, Department of Psychology, University of Hawaii at Manoa, Honolulu, HI 96822, USA

Ina Č. Užgiris, Department of Psychology, Frances Hiatt School of Psychology, Clark University, Worcester, MA 01610, USA

Grover J. Whitehurst, Department of Psychology, State University of New York at Stony Brook, Stony Brook, NY 11794, USA

Roberta Wroblewski, Department of Psychology, Pennsylvania State University, University Park, PA 16802, USA

CHAPTER 1

A Fresh Look at Imitation in Language Learning

Gisela E. Speidel and Keith E. Nelson

> I make childish remarks, they are remembered, they are repeated to me. I learn to make others. I make grown-up remarks. I know how to say things "beyond my years" without meaning to. These remarks are poems. The recipe is simple: you must trust to the Devil, to chance, to emptiness, you borrow whole sentences from grown-ups, you string them together and repeat them without understanding them. In short, I pronounce true oracles, and each adult interprets them as he wishes.
>
> Jean-Paul Sartre, 1964

In reminiscence at least, Sartre displays a clear awareness of others' imitations of his utterances and of his own production "recipe" that includes whole borrowed sentences. Moreover, Sartre seems to reach back and in autobiographical reconstruction show deferred imitation and reworking of particular verbal productions from his childhood language-learning days. So, Sartre has done us the favor of introducing this book on young children who are learning language and their conversational partners. Its concerns are who imitates whom, when, with what awareness, with what purpose, and with what impact.

In this book we and our colleagues examine the many faces of imitation. A central thesis is that *imitation* in language learning can be understood only if due care is taken to classify the various types of imitations and their many consequences and many roots. Accordingly, the authors of each chapter were free to adopt their own operational definitions of imitative behavior. At the same time, in this opening chapter and throughout the book there is considerable emphasis on discussing how the data yielded from diverse research strategies can be integrated.

We begin the process of analyzing imitation by identifying four levels that explicitly or implicitly come into play whenever imitation occurs:

(1) Imitation can be a skill, a tendency, an intent, a process, an achieved match, or all of these.
(2) The interpretation of the above aspects of imitation will vary by the *timing delay* observed between *models* and imitations—for example, immediate, delayed by minutes, or delayed by hours or weeks.
(3) The interpretation of the above aspects of imitation also will be modulated by differences in nonverbal *contexts* and by the *individuals* (children and adults) who do the imitation. For example, the same very highly accurate "model-to-imitation match" may represent different intents and different processes for the parent and the child.
(4) Imitation has *consequences*. Sartre treated his imitation productions as interesting and profound, as "poems." But in other instances adults may treat frequent imitations as uninteresting, as contributing little to discourse.

The fact of an obvious imitation by child or adult does not reveal the impact of the imitation on learning; this needs to be inferred from additional evidence of what happens in the immediate context and across successive levels of language mastery. By searching through such evidence, we hope to understand when imitation has the face of facilitator of language progress, when it has the face of mere place holder in conversation, when it has the face of jesting and mocking, when it has the face (as for young Sartre) of illusory competence beyond one's true level, and when it wears still other faces.

1.1 A Brief Overview of This Book

Meltzoff and Gopnik (Chapter 2) summarize the most recent findings on nonverbal infant imitation. Their chapter reflects the importance of imitation, particularly deferred imitation, in nonverbal cognitive development. The evidence that 9-month-old infants are capable of imitating motor acts 24 hours after a single modeled presentation is of great relevance for the onset of speech. The authors present evidence that the nature of deferred imitation shifts at about the age of 18 months. Deferred imitations seem to become less tied to immediate contexts and show more pretend-acting. This suggests the development of an ability to represent hypothetical relationships and behaviors. The authors begin to explore how this shift in the nature of deferred imitation could affect the nature of language learning.

The next three chapters are empirical chapters describing naturally occurring imitative interchanges between mothers and their infants. The remarkable variability in the use of imitation is noted in all three chapters. Masur (Chapter 3) asks several questions of her cross-sectional data: What is the consistency of imitation across the domains of verbal, gestural, and object-related imitation? Are there developmental shifts in imitation from one behavioral domain to the next? Are there recognizable patterns of imitation between mother and child? Are more imitative children better at particular linguistic tasks? In Chapter 4 Snow also looks at the question of domain specificity of imitation and the question of whether imitativeness is a general trait or whether it is domain specific. Snow, furthermore, addresses the issue of the relationship between imitativeness and language development and includes fascinating data on whether verbally imitative children have more developed phonological systems. Užgiris, Broome, and Kruper (Chapter 5) look at their longitudinal data on imitative interchanges from the mother's perspective. By using identical categories of imitation for both mother and child, these authors are able to show how imitation changes with the infant's development from 12 months to 24 months and how in tune the mother's use of imitation is with her child's changes. Užgiris et al.'s description of the varied pragmatic functions of verbal imitation reveals the rich potential that imitation has for human communication.

Bohannon and Stanowicz present in Chapter 6 an information-processing model for language and show how the functions and determinants of various child and adult imitations can be understood within this model. They address the question of negative evidence in language acquisition and provide data to show that certain adult imitations of the child, particularly recasts, can be construed as negative evidence for speech errors and that children make use of such information. Speidel, in Chapter 7, also presents a language-processing model and the implications this model has for understanding different kinds of verbal imitation and their function in learning to speak. She describes how certain cognitive operations on imitated chunks could be the means whereby imitation leads to spontaneous speech. In Chapters 8 and 9 she applies this language-processing model to the finding that imitation helps to generate longer utterances and to individual differences in learning to speak.

Tharp and Burns (Chapter 10) look at vocal imitation from a phylogenetic perspective. They point out the futility of the "innate versus learned" debate in language acquisition. Language development in the individual, according to these authors, is the joint result of phylogenetic, cultural/historical, and specific processes affecting the individual. They look for precursors to human vocal imitation in other mammals and in birds. One concept they present to support the phylogenetic hypothesis of vocal imitation is that of *neoteny*, or "stretching youth." They suggest that vocal imitation does not occur until about the age of 9 months because of the neoteny process. Nine months is also the age at which Meltzoff and Gopnik have found that deferred imitation becomes established, a most intriguing coincidence.

Whitehurst and DeBaryshe (Chapter 11) take a broad view of imitation that incorporates both deferred imitation and selective imitation (Whitehurst & Vasta, 1975). Emphasizing the observational and associational components of imitation, they prefer to use the term *observational learning* rather than *imitation*. They present a unified conception of how the observational variables interact with individual differences and language-structure variables in the course of language learning. Their viewpoints are substantiated with findings from numerous studies by Whitehurst and his associates. Moerk (Chapter 12) shows how imitation can be viewed as the intersection of different domains of learning: perceptual, observational, and learning by doing. He analyzes the fuzziness of the concept of imitation, which results from this overlap of domains, discussing observational and production components of imitation, processing levels of imitation, and ways in which the imitated behavior can vary from the original model.

Nelson, Heimann, Abuelhaija, and Wroblewski (Chapter 13) overlap with Whitehurst and DeBaryshe in discussing factors influencing lexical acquisition. They place both lexical and syntactic acquisition into a theoretical framework that incorporates individual differences in imitativeness and temperament from infancy onward. They give an explicit information-processing account of how different children use available language input. Across cultures it is argued that the effective processing opportunities set up for children by mothers' recasts and exact imitations vary by the children's developmental stage and style.

Together the chapters provide a new look for imitation and throw light on the integral part imitation plays in language acquisition. The topics and issues discussed by the different authors overlap and interweave. We will now briefly describe some of the major issues with which the chapters deal.

1.2 The "New Look" for Imitation

1.2.1 Imitation: A Complex Behavior

One assumption has been that imitation is a rather primitive, simple kind of behavior requiring minimal skill and no thought or understanding. Verbal imitation, however, entails many complex transformations. Speech sounds are transformed from sound waves traveling through the air into physical energy at the eardrum and thence into neural signals in the brain. The neural signals are transformed several times until they reach the auditory projection areas of the cortex. They then interact in complicated ways with representational processes to produce comprehension. The re-production phase begins with the selection and activation of the neural networks necessary for the complex movements of the speech musculature: Many fine muscle movements must be performed in correct sequence to duplicate the sounds of the model.

One indication of the high level of cognitive involvement in some kinds of verbal imitation is that bilinguals will often on elicited imitation tasks *translate* what they hear into their more preferred language. Thus, translation, a high-level cognitive skill, can be easier than imitation under some circumstances! In short, far from being simple, imitation is the result of many transformations of energy and the activation of many neural patterns. It is the result of new incoming information meshing with information already in memory. The diverse contributions in this book reveal this complexity of imitation.

1.2.2 Imitation and Observational Learning

Imitation can be viewed as consisting of two components: (1) the observation of the modeled behavior and (2) its reproduction. The reproduction of speech requires the observation and analysis of the model, but to what extent can language learning be purely observational and without motor representation? The answer to this question is obviously critical for the role attributed to verbal imitation in language learning. This issue is part of the more general one for theories of learning: What is the role of neuromuscular and motor processes in learning? It was the question already asked in the historical debate between *sign* learning (e.g., Tolman, Ritchie, & Kalish, 1946) and the more accepted *response* learning theories: Is it stimulus-stimulus relationships or is it stimulus-response relationships that are learned? (See Kimble, 1961, for a succinct review of the issues and outcomes of the research.) The question exists today in cognitive psychology in the tension between schema and production theories (e.g., Anderson, 1983). "One serious question about schema theories is how one gets any action from them" (Anderson, 1983, p. 37). Anderson's ACT theory emphasizes learning by doing. For Piaget, too, behavior was an integral part of learning as reflected in his basic building blocks for learning: the sensorimotor schemata.

One strategic approach to this issue is to recognize several complex overlaps in the terms. Observational learning has been so broadly defined that imitative processes make up a subset in its domain (see Moerk, Chapter 12). Another approach is to place observation and imitation on a continuum with respect to the *degree* of activation and elaboration of the central representational networks involved in the reproduction of the response. This approach is consonant with the definition of imitation given by Bandura, an influential observational learning protagonist (see Bandura, 1969). Bandura defined observational learning as the "symbolic coding and central organization of modeling stimuli, their representation in memory, in verbal and imaginal codes, and their subsequent *transformation from symbolic forms to motor equivalents*" (italics added; Bandura, 1969, p. 127). In other words, his broad definition includes covert or symbolic motor acts in observational learning. It seems artificial to draw the line between observational and imitational learning in terms of the degree of overtness of the behavior, particularly since observational learning is typically studied by looking at the reproduction of the model by the learner, that is, by deferred imitation (see Whitehurst & DeBaryshe, Chapter 11). The strategy of recognizing overlapping terms and overlapping processes between observational and imitative learning is also consonant with the view proposed by Liberman and Mattingly (1985) that speech perception involves motor representation.

The distinction between observational and motor aspects of learning in language development is addressed to some extent by Moerk in Chapter 12. It is, however, most clearly portrayed by Whitehurst and DeBaryshe in Chapter 11 and by Speidel in Chapter 7. Although both parties distinguish between comprehension and production in language learning, Whitehurst emphasizes the comprehension and the observational components, whereas Speidel emphasizes speaking and the motor components of language learning. A comprehensive model of language learning would probably need to integrate these two positions.

1.2.3 Child and Adult Imitation

The pervasiveness of mutual imitation in interactions between infant and care-taker has been recognized for some time in the field of infant cognitive development (e.g., Užgiris, 1984). In the field of language development this picture of mutuality has been muddied by calling adult imitations of children's utterances expansions, recasts, extensions, etc., whereas children's imitations of adults' utterances have been called immediate, reduced, exact, and expanded imitations. In this book, however, this mutuality of verbal imitation is explicitly studied by Masur and by Užgiris et al. By using the same category definitions for both child and mother, Užgiris et al. show how finely tuned the mother–child use of imitation can be: As the child becomes older and more skilled, the types of imitation used by the child and the mother develop correspondingly. This mutual imitation in mother–child interactions appears to have critical social and motivational functions according to Užgiris et al. The findings reported by Bohannon and Stanowicz (Chapter 6) suggest that adult imitation of children can also be a rich source of information and input for language learning.

Observation and imitation are central to communication. The very definition of communication (*Webster's New World Dictionary*) implies imitation: "To impart, pass along, transmit," literally, "to make common." What better way to make language "common" than through verbal interchanges that rely on imitation by both partners. Repeating each other's words would appear to be an efficient and effective way by which mothers and their toddlers can begin to establish shared knowledge and to construct the meanings of the speech sounds that initially are meaningless for the child.

1.2.4 Multiple Dimensions of Imitation

The field of imitation has been hounded by definitional problems (cf. Snow, 1981; Oksaar, 1982). As Moerk writes in his chapter, imitation is a very "fuzzy" concept. One possibility is simply to drop the term because it is so ubiquitous, something at which Moerk and Whitehurst and DeBaryshe hint. Another possibility is to begin with a very broad, inclusive definition of imitation and use it to devise category systems and dimensions along which the phenomenon can be studied more precisely. Moerk's chapter deals explicitly with this attempt.

The difficulty we have in attempting to classify the speech of toddlers as imitated or spontaneous is actually very instructive. It tells us something about language development—that it is a continuum ranging from speech closely tied to a few modeled words to spontaneous speech along a number of different dimensions. Some of the dimensions along which imitation can be studied developmentally and which are a focus for the chapters in this book are the following.

1.2.4.1 Time Interval Between the Model and the Imitation

The process of imitation can differ in terms of the length of the time interval between the model and the imitated utterance. If the imitation is preceded within a short period of time by its model, it is called an *immediate imitation*; if there is a longer time interval (typically a day or more), it is a *deferred imitation*. The distinction between the two is one of degree rather than of dichotomy.

The time dimension is explored by several authors: Meltzoff and Gopnik (Chapter 2) discuss the developmental progression from immediate imitation to deferred imitation in gestural behaviors. According to Moerk, the prevalence of immediate over deferred imitation may not only be a function of the stage of a child's *general* level of cognitive development, but may also be a function of his or her stage of learning of a *particular* item or skill.

The possible functions of immediate and deferred imitations are also discussed. Bohannon and Stanowicz (Chapter 6), Moerk (Chapter 12), and Speidel and Herreshoff (Chapter 8) suggest that immediate imitation may have a priming function as well as a rehearsal function: It may help to bring new forms available in short-term memory into long-term memory. In contrast, deferred imitations, as Snow (1983) and Moerk and Moerk (1979) have pointed out, are already in long-term memory and are available without any prompting. Indeed Meltzoff and Gopnik (Chapter 2) suggest that deferred imitation is a necessary ability for learning to speak. In order to say a word, like *book*, in the appropriate context, one must be able to remember another person's utterance as well as the corresponding context. Their finding that infants of 9 months of age are cognitively capable of deferred imitation is critical for the view that learning to speak is based on deferred imitation. In Chapter 7 Speidel elaborates upon this view and shows how creative, spontaneous speech could result from a variety of cognitive operations on units of deferred verbal imitation. Moerk, in his discussion of the temporal dimension includes the additional factor of number of practice trials and raises the issue of massed versus distributed practice as a variable in imitation and its role in learning. Most of the variables that Whitehurst and DeBaryshe describe as affecting observational learning could be viewed as *determinants* of deferred imitation. The methodology they use to study the effects of verbal models on a child's verbal behavior by testing the child at a later point in time is similar in some respects to the one used by Meltzoff and Gopnik to study deferred imitation in the nonverbal domain.

1.2.4.2 Accuracy of the Match Between Model and Reproduction

The process of imitation, we have said, involves many steps and transformations. Much can be lost or altered between the model and its imitation. How accurately the imitation matches the model can be examined on several planes — of which the articulatory and the word levels are two.

Until now, a poorly articulated repetition of words has often been viewed by researchers of normal language acquisition as a methodological nuisance rather than as a source of insight into language learning. An exception to this view has been the work of Leonard and his colleagues on the impact of individual differences in children's articulatory production systems on word acquisition (e.g., Schwartz & Leonard, 1985). In this volume several chapters address the accuracy of articulation in imitation. Snow (Chapter 4) distinguishes between the accuracy of articulation during imitation and the tendency or willingness to imitate. Her findings suggest that the relationship of these two variables to progress in speaking may not be the same. Moerk's description of Adam's and Eve's progressive attempts to articulate words they have just heard are valuable examples of the microgenesis of speech—snapshots of how new information is coupled with motor responses already in the speech repertoire. In Chapter 9 Speidel suggests that individuals differ widely in their ability to imitate speech sounds accurately. These differences, which may have a neurological basis, could affect the different ways in which children go about learning to speak.

The match between model and its reproduction at the word level has received a thorough description by Snow (1981). In *exact* imitation all the words and morphemes of the adult's utterance are imitated with no additions or changes. In *reduced* imitation there is a reproduction of only a portion of the model's words, and no new words are added. *Expanded* imitation consists of utterances that include at least one stressed content word from the model and at least one new morpheme supplied by the child.

These different types of imitations seem to be operative at different stages in language development. For example, Snow (1981), Kucjaz (1982), and Nelson and Bonvillian (1978) have shown that initially children use more reduced and exact imitations and gradually, as they become more skilled in speaking, they begin to use more expanded imitations. In the present volume, Užgiris et al. add to our knowledge on this course of development. Not only toddlers but also their mothers show a progressive change from reduced to expanded imitation. Moreover, the type of imitation most frequently used by mothers correlates significantly with the pattern of imitation used by the child. This finding is consistent with a view that the mother's speech is indeed finely tuned and responsive to her child's development.

The progression from reduced and exact imitations to expanded imitations in the child is very likely the result of changes in the child's processing capacity. The language-processing models by Bohannon and Stanowicz, Nelson et al., and Speidel provide us with conceptual frameworks for further understanding the processing demands of the different kinds of matches between model and imitation and the roles these forms of imitation may play at various stages of learning to speak.

Which features of the model are selected for imitation is not only a function of processing capacity, but also a function of a child's focus of attention. Whitehurst and DeBaryshe discuss factors that determine a child's attention, which in turn determines what becomes stored as a deferred imitation.

1.2.5 Developmental Changes in Imitation

We saw already in the previous section that the nature of verbal imitation changes with the development of the child's cognitive skills. Several authors address in greater detail the developmental progression of imitation: Masur (Chapter 3), Meltzoff and Gopnik (Chapter 2), Moerk (Chapter 12), Snow (Chapter 4), Speidel (Chapter 7), and Užgiris et al. (Chapter 5). Moerk suggests that there is a curvilinear relationship of the match between an imitation and its model as a function of time and practice. During the first phase, the imitation comes to resemble the model more and more. Then there is a period in which the imitation is a very close copy of the verbal model, followed by the final phase, in which there is less and less resemblance between model and imitation. This intriguing conception, however, must be further differentiated according to the kinds of imitation and particular dimensions of variation from the model. Thus, this view of change may hold for the contexts in which particular words are used and for the use of specific sentence patterns, but not for the articulation of words. Articulation of a word may continue the closest match to the prototypical model the child achieved.

Tharp and Burns (Chapter 10) raise a provocative question about the onset of verbal imitation: Because some kinds of nonverbal imitation are already present in the newborn (see Bjorklund, 1987, for a review), why does it take so long for verbal imitation to develop? Does it have something to do with the process of neoteny and the fact that neurologically the child may not be ready for the development of the very complex integration required for the production of speech sounds? Once the neuronal substrate of the speech musculature is ready, is there a critical echoic period in which it is easier for the child to imitate? Speidel points out the wide range of individual differences in onset of intelligible speech and asks whether these differences are not related to differences in the development of the cortical areas responsible for the planning and coordinating of the speech musculature.

1.2.6 Biological Foundations of Imitation

Even Skinner, the great behaviorist, contrary to his previous conclusions, now thinks that the tendency to imitate is innate in origin. The possibility that echoic behavior, like other imitative behavior, may have a phylogenetic basis is fascinating. This idea is studied by Tharp and Burns, in Chapter 10, who explore the evidence for vocal imitation in other mammals and in birds. Meltzoff's research findings, described in Chapter 2, also bear on the phylogenetic view of vocal imitation. Moreover, the concept of innate echoic behavior can be connected to the idea, discussed in Chapter 9, that speech perception and the motor representation of speech production are closely linked neurologically and are perhaps even identical (Liberman & Mattingly, 1985). In other words, Liberman's notion of neuromuscular speech perception can be viewed as covert echoic behavior. Speidel suggests that constitutional factors may affect the ease of producing speech sounds (i.e., articulation), which in turn affects the ease of imitation. The notion that we have one form of a biological *language acquisition device* in our ability to imitate speech sounds is not all that farfetched.

1.2.7 Sources of Individual Differences in Imitativeness and Imitation Skill

The three empirical chapters on verbal imitation during natural interactions between mothers and their toddlers all reveal remarkable differences in the amount of imitation. Snow finds little consistency in frequency of imitation across various behavioral domains and concludes that verbal imitativeness is not an underlying trait, but rather a strategy acquired in a particular skill domain. Masur's findings are in agreement with Snow's conclusion. Užgiris et al. are able to look at the consistency of imitation in individual children across time. Finding little consistency in imitation within the same individuals between two time periods, they suggest that imitation is used selectively by mothers and children depending upon the situation. In Chapter 9 Speidel looks at possible biological causes of variation in ability to imitate speech accurately. Snow's findings suggest that these individual differences in imitative skill may only be moderately related to differences in imitative tendencies.

Individual differences in imitative skill and imitative strategy in the presyntactic child may be direct or indirect contributors to later imitation differences. The chapters by Meltzoff and Gopnik and Nelson et al. bear on these questions.

1.2.8 Verbal Imitativeness and Language Acquisition Rate

Just as the sources of differences in imitation are of interest, so is the question whether these individual differences have any bearing on language learning. If verbal imitation helps in learning to speak, then one would predict that children who imitate more should show faster language growth. The relationships reported by Snow, Užgiris et al., and Masur are consonant with this view. There are, however, two aspects to imitation that may work against finding a strong positive relationship between amount of imitation and advances in language learning.

First, there is the observation mentioned earlier that the relationship between verbal imitation and speech development changes as mastery of speech progresses. After a certain level of mastery has been attained, exact imitation should decrease, and one should actually find a progressively negative relationship between imitation and growth in language. Such a curvilinear relationship can disguise in correlational studies the initial relationship between imitation and rate of language acquisition—even in studies comparing children who are of the same age, but at different levels of speech development.

Second, speech and therefore verbal imitation can be covert or "soundless, invisible, reduced movements of the speech mechanism" (English & English, 1958). Speidel, in Chapter 9, suggests that individual differences in ability to babble and to articulate may reflect differences in the ease with which speech sounds are acquired. The faster a child learns to make overt speech sounds, the faster she may be able to use covert speech. The implication is that children who constitutionally are more skilled in making speech sounds may use covert speech earlier and may much sooner show a negative relationship between overt imitation and progress in speaking than their less-skilled peers.

1.2.9 Imitation and Memory

There is an intimate relationship between imitation and memory that until now
has been given minimal attention in the field of language acquisition. The relationship can be viewed from many angles, of which only a few are discussed in
this book. First, there appears to be the phenomenon of *priming*, which suggests
that a word just heard is more likely to be used (cf. Bohannon & Stanowicz,
Chapter 6; Speidel & Herreshoff, Chapter 8). This priming effect seems to help
children make longer utterances (Speidel & Herreshoff, Chapter 8) and may have
a rehearsal function (Moerk, Chapter 12; Speidel, Chapter 7).

Then there is the intriguing relationship between short-term verbal memory, as
measured by elicited imitation, and difficulties in acquiring syntax, suggesting
perhaps that children need to be able to store verbal strings of significant length
in order to abstract syntactic rules (Speidel, Chapters 7 and 9). Furthermore,
spontaneous speech can be construed as the result of novel ways of combining
speech units stored in long-term memory, that is, novel ways of combining
deferred imitations (Speidel, Chapter 7).

Another area in the development of memory (suggested by the work of Meltzoff and Gopnik and of Tharp and Burns) that would appear to be a rich source
of information is the study of nonverbal deferred imitation and (1) its relationship
to the onset of speech and (2) the change in the nature of deferred imitation at
18 months and its effects on the learning of different kinds of words and syntactic
structures.

1.3 Specific Contributions of Children's Imitations to the Children's Language Growth

Despite the neglect of imitation in the mainstream research of language acquisition, information has been amassed on how children may use imitation in learning to speak (e.g., Bloom, Hood, & Lightbown, 1974; Brown & Fraser, 1963;
Clark, 1977; Moerk, 1977; Moerk & Moerk, 1979; Ramer, 1976; Reger, 1986;
Snow, 1981, 1983; Stine & Bohannon, 1983; Whitehurst and Vasta, 1975). In
this book, Užgiris et al., Snow, and Masur bring further correlational evidence
on the relationship between imitation and language development, while Moerk,
Bohannon and Stanowicz, and Speidel describe mechanisms by which a child's
imitation can be progressive and can lead to spontaneous speech. Whitehurst and
DeBaryshe describe how variables of the observational component affect language learning.

Together these various sources strongly indicate that the social and cognitive
functions of imitation are interwoven, and although one may have to separate the
various functions in order to understand how imitation works, in reality they are
different sides of the same coin (cf. Moerk). An example of the multiple functions
of the same imitative act is shown in the following excerpt of Adam talking with
his mother (from Slobin, 1968):

MOTHER.   It fits in the puzzle someplace.
ADAM.   Puzzle? Puzzle someplace?
MOTHER.   Turn it around.
ADAM.   Turn it around?
MOTHER.   No, the other way.
ADAM.   Other way?
MOTHER.   I guess you have to turn it around.
ADAM.   Guess turn it round. Turn it round.

Keenan described this excerpt: "Adam appears first to be using repetition as a vehicle for querying a prior utterance, and then as a vehicle for informing himself and/or agreeing with the mother's comment" (Keenan, 1977, p. 128). The excerpt also illustrates another function of imitation suggested by Keenan: "satisfying his obligations as a conversational partner." Without the mother's relatively complex models, he possibly would not have been able to converse as skillfully. This kind of imitation could be viewed as a bootstrap for making conversation, allowing children to speak at a level that is beyond their independent speaking level (compare with Sartre at the beginning of this chapter). At the same time, imitations may function as rehearsal by helping the child remember the words and the sentence patterns provided by the mother's input.

At this point, we will turn to some important past work and then to some possible future work on this central question of what contributions children's use of imitation can make to their linguistic progress.

1.3.1 The Past

During the late 1950s and early 1960s, when behaviorism was extended to the analysis of verbal behavior, imitation was thought to be a major process by which children acquired language (Brown & Fraser, 1963; Fraser, Bellugi, & Brown, 1963; Jenkins & Palermo, 1964; Skinner, 1957; Staats, 1968, 1971a,b). In Skinner's (1957) model of language learning, imitation, or as Skinner called it, "echoic behavior," was seen as a quick way to get the speech sounds into the toddler's speech repertoire because it short-circuited the "process of progressive approximations." Brown and Fraser (1963) proposed that remembered exact and reduced imitations of adult utterances formed a storehouse of information from which children would be able to induce the grammatical rules of their language.

Chomsky's (1959) critique of Skinner's book *Verbal Behavior*, however, seriously questioned the behavioristic approach to language learning. Chomsky (1968) proposed specialized linguistic structures in the child's mind that guide the analysis of language input; his theoretical concepts soon supplanted the behavioristic research orientation, including the concept of imitation (see Slobin, 1971). The following quotes indicate the fate of imitation in language acquisition research. Slobin wrote, "There are circumstances when imitation is grammatically progressive, but these are special cases and do not reflect a general didactic role for imitation" (1971, p. 32). Ervin-Tripp (1971) concluded, "Imitations, even if they were reinforcing, could not be a route to learning since they are not more advanced than where the child is already syntactically." Gleitman (1981) argued, "The first mechanism that comes to mind to explain language learning is imitation. But it is also the first hypothesis that has to be discarded" (p. 383).

What has been the case against imitation? Ervin-Tripp (1971) has summarized four kinds of evidence: First, "motoric output is not necessary to language acquisition." The evidence cited to substantiate this conclusion was the report of a congenital quadriplegic spastic child with a hearing loss (Fourcin, 1975). He spoke only with the greatest difficulty. However, when as a young adult he was given a typewriter he was able to communicate in fluent English. The case suggests that overt imitation of speech sounds may not be necessary for learning to read and write. However, one must be cautious in making generalizations from children who are very different in their neurological processing and ways of learning language. We do not know exactly how the child learned to comprehend language and how he learned to read, though it is told that his mother spent very much time in teaching him and he used his body movements as signs of recognition. Rather than arguing against the usefulness of vocal imitation in learning to speak, this case suggests that the nervous system is amazingly pliable and that, with extensive teaching of the right kind, such a child can circumvent the usual sequence in learning to read and write. Moreover, the case does not rule out the observational component of imitation (see Chapter 7, section 1.2.2, this volume).

A second piece of evidence against imitation was that speech development appears to be discontinuous. Forms that have been correctly used are supplanted by forms never heard by the child. Often these errors are regularizations of the language, or overgeneralizations as they have also been called (e.g., Slobin, 1971). Neither the most frequently heard sequences nor the most frequently produced forms remain dominant. Children will say "'handses' after months of use of the plural form 'hands'. Such forms overthrow well-practiced items, frequently heard items" (Ervin-Tripp, 1971, p. 196). At first blush, this may seem to be strong evidence against imitation. But imitation, like many other cognitive processes, can be *highly selective*, rather than driven blindly by the highest frequency of input exemplars. Thus, the model attended to and imitated by the child may change; the child may first attend to whole words (in this case *hands*), then become sensitive to the meanings of morphemes (in this case, *es*). More broadly speaking, a sudden qualitative change need not be contrary to a quantitative explanation: When water comes to a boil, it undergoes a *qualitative* change, but this change is due to a *quantitative* increase in its temperature. Over time, the child will have heard many plural words ending in *es*. The representation of these words together with the representation of plurality will slowly accumulate until the *es* becomes a separate representation denoting plurality that competes with *hands*. Rumelhart and McClelland (1987) present a parallel distributed processing model that gives one account of overgeneralization of the past tense as a function of different response strengths of regular and irregular verbs over trials.

A third point against imitation was the observation that children do not seem to accept parental corrections readily. This example from McNeill (1966) is often cited:

CHILD.   Nobody don't like me.
MOTHER.   No, say "nobody likes me."
CHILD.   Nobody don't like me.

This interchange is repeated several times. Then the following discourse occurs:

MOTHER.   No, now listen carefully; say "nobody likes me."
CHILD.   Oh! Nobody don't likeS me.

Actually, the demand for imitation was in some way effective, because the child did change *like* to *likes*, showing the selectivity of imitation at work. Once again, this piece of evidence against imitation can be countered. First, the example above is an elicited imitation: The mother is asking the child to imitate. Chapter 8 by Speidel and Herreshoff shows that elicited imitation is something very different from self-selected imitation. When we look at the function of imitation in language acquisition, we need to look at imitations to which the child *attends*, that is, self-selected imitation. Second, corrections given by the parent in the form of recasts and expansions *are* at times imitated. For instance, Slobin (1968) and Hirsh-Pasek, Treiman, and Schneiderman (1984) showed that when parents recast those child sentences that have a grammatical error, the children will often adopt the correction in the next turn. In Chapter 6 Bohannon and Stanowicz provide further data showing that parents use this form of correction and that children, in turn, utilize their parents' corrections. In some cultures the explicit instruction of repeating the adult's phrase is used very systematically for developing the toddler's language (Ochs & Schieffelin, 1982; Watson-Gegeo & Gegeo, in press).

Finally, evidence against imitation as a source of specific language advancement came from findings that children's imitated sentences were not more complex than their non-imitative speech (Brown and Fraser, 1963; Ervin, 1964; Moerk, 1977). However, these findings could result from the methodology used. Bohannon and Stanowicz explain with reference to their language-processing model how these negative findings might come about. Looking at self-selected imitation and at utterances that are at or beyond the child's mean length of utterance (MLU), Speidel and Herreshoff find that utterances containing imitated portions are longer, on the whole, than utterances produced without any imitated words.

It is of historical interest to note that two players whose writings helped to bring about imitation's temporary fall from grace actually did argue, at least in their early writings, that imitation had a place in language learning. Chomsky (1959) in his critique of Skinner's position wrote, "*Children acquire a good deal of their verbal and non-verbal behavior by casual observation and imitation of adults and other children*" (p. 49, italics added). Ervin (1964) in her study that came to be the classic citation as evidence *against* the usefulness of imitation, wrote, "*The shift from one (grammatical) system to another may be initiated from several sources: One is the comprehension of adult speech, another is imitation*" (p. 186, italics added).

Since the mid-1970s a handful of language researchers have begun to take a closer look at imitation. The newer studies were more extensive, had more sophisticated methodologies, and argued for more differentiated definitions of imitations (e.g., Bloom et al., 1974; Clark, 1977; Kucjaz, 1982; Moerk, 1977; Reger, 1986; Snow, 1981, 1983; Whitehurst & Vasta, 1975). These studies, which varied in their methods and in the kinds of imitation studied, showed that imitation could not simply be dismissed from the process of language learning. In the field of nonverbal cognitive development, the concept of imitation is very much alive, and research on infant imitation has mushroomed (see Bjorklund, 1987). Deferred imitation is a central concept in Piagetian theory (Piaget, 1946/1962). The methodologies and conceptual frameworks of researchers like Užgiris (1984) and Meltzoff and Moore (1983) have much to offer the research on imitation in language learning.

1.3.2 The Future

Future work can be expected to draw upon refined methodologies for specifying individual differences in how and when children use imitative processes to achieve specific steps forward in language. The wide variation in the frequency with which different children use imitation shown throughout this volume and in past work (e.g., Bates, Bretherton, & Snyder, 1988; Bloom, Hood, & Lightbown, 1974; K. Nelson, 1981; K. E. Nelson, Baker, Denninger, Bonvillian, & Kaplan, 1985) needs to be integrated theoretically with accounts of the processing steps through which new language structures come about in a child's system. An essential source for achieving such integrated theoretical accounts will be highly detailed "case histories" that describe the manner in which children's particular language interactions contribute to the acquisition of particular structures. (cf. K. E. Nelson, 1980, 1987, 1988; Speidel, 1987, Chapter 7). New work needs to *go beyond clues* about the role of imitation derived from very limited samples of language interactions to *tests* of how imitative processes and other processes contribute together to particular language advances.

Even when children seem to have instantly learned a new structure in that they have imitated exactly a preceding adult utterance containing that structure, only further evidence across time will reveal whether they can use it flexibly rather than just as an echo from episodic memory. We need to determine when imitated chunks aid language growth, when they merely aid smooth interaction with adults who expect, demand, or reward productions of such chunks, or when they serve both functions simultaneously. The aim is to bring together varied but converging evidence that will help us make reasonable interpretations of children's imitations as well as of adults' imitations.

The study of language learning has much to gain from cognitive psychology. When concepts such as schema, co-occurrence of events in learning, automatic and nonautomatic processes, working memory, pattern analyzers, declarative and procedural knowledge, and parallel distributed processes are applied to language learning, they will throw new light on the possible uses of imitation.

1.4 Specific Contributions of Adult Imitations to Children's Language Growth

Several chapters deal directly with how imitation by the adult can help the language learning of the child. Bohannon and Stanowicz provide data on the feedback function of parents' imitations, recasts, and expansions of their child's verbal expressions. Užgiris et al. propose an indirect route between a mother's verbal imitation and her child's language development: The mother's imitation may signal recognition and thereby reinforce the child's general verbalization. Nelson et al. in their chapter look at longitudinal data as well as data from an experimental intervention to see how specific adult verbal variations of children's utterances can influence the children's language progress. As Nelson et al. point out, the same questions arise for imitative skill and imitative strategies when sign language rather than speech is acquired (cf. Bonvillian, Nelson, & Charrow, 1976).

Just as we have seen in the case of children's imitations of adult language, so individual differences are rampant in adults' imitations of children's language. And, just as in the case of imitations by children, we need to draw distinctions and ask questions about the *kinds* of imitations that adults make and how they may influence the child's language growth (Speidel, 1987). If different kinds of imitations have contrasting effects, then pooling these together under very broad imitation analysis may obscure a whole range of effects. It would be very helpful to theoretical progress if questions like the following were addressed in a coordinated fashion in language-imitation research:

(1) Does the imitation by the adult carry any new syntactic structures relative to the child's language performance?
(2) Are there any clues to suggest that the child processed the imitation?
(3) Did one imitation or a series of imitations by an adult affect the child's acquisition of particular structures?

1.5 The Need for Differentiation: Intents, Processes, and Impacts

Understanding development in one domain is often facilitated by comparison with another domain. The course of art development raises some interesting parallels with that of language development because the role of copying has been hotly debated in art education and art history. Consider the following passages from a review of an art exhibit called *Creative Copies*:

Appropriately, Rubens and Rembrandt are the heroes of the show, for, more than any other major artists, they seem to have understood the way that the act of copying produces change, and to have made it a voracious principle of creation. But there is no guarantee of progress in this process; it can lead to dead ends. One of the truths that the show makes uncannily vivid, for instance, is that Michelangelo is almost impossibly hard to transform through copying. There are two Rubens drawings after Michelangelo, and though both are as compelling as a Medusa's head, they also seem somehow sterile. In Rubens' copy of the compacted action within the "Brazen Serpent" spandrel from the Sistine ceiling – an inverted pyramid of agonized bodies – the pathos of the Michelangelesque composition becomes mere Jacobean horror.

Until the middle of the nineteenth century, artists depended on copying by hand both to keep tradition alive and to alter it. The appearance of mechanical means of reproduction – photography – obviously changed all that. It has become almost an article of faith that mechanical reproduction is the enemy of art – that photographs make works of art lose their "aura" – but on the evidence of this exhibition one might arrive at a very different view of the relationship between mechanical reproduction and innovation. Even the most mechanical copy, after all, creates variations – in color, scale, framing. Indeed, the very element that is supposed to hurt art most – the overwhelming replication of images – is in itself a powerful and potentially fruitful form of variation. (Gopnik, 1988)

Both these passages on imitation in art serve as reminders for language development. As with imitation in art, imitation in language requires a close analysis of detail, intent, process, and impact to take us beyond the descriptive application of an overbroad category.

We can be certain from the reports in this book that not every adult imitative act will have a teaching goal or impact and that not every child imitative act will have a learning goal or impact. On the other hand, as we saw in the example with Adam, the same imitative act may have a particular intent, but also meet other different pragmatic and learning goals.

Within language we have noted how widely variable imitative tendencies can be in children and their conversational partners. One part of this pattern that needs to be explored is how the same intentions and goals can be served through different actions. One child may hold a place in a conversation by imitating as exactly as possible, and another may achieve the same goal by being extremely novel and adventurous. Similarly, one adult may provide acknowledgment to the child who imitates, whereas another may say "Uh-huh" and proceed immediately to a nonimitative topic continuation.

Intent is an integral part of an imitation. Yet, it is something we have avoided studying because it is extremely difficult to determine reliably in naturalistic studies (cf. Reger, 1986). However, we can gain something by a fresh look at a series of intervention studies conducted by Nelson and his colleagues (Baker & Nelson, 1984; Baker, Pemberton, & Nelson, 1985; Nelson, 1977, 1987; Nelson et al., 1985). In each study we can see that the adult intervenors had the *intent* to imitate in a special way – through producing a "growth recast" that recast the child's meaning and provided challenge to growth through incorporating structures that the child did not yet use. However, imitation by the child was *not* requested or encouraged, thus leaving it up to the child whether to observe/analyze/imitate in the turn following the adult's imitation. Reasonable interpretations were made by obtaining further data over time, data indicating that these kinds of growth-recast-imitations by adults did lead to children's acquisition of new language structures.

To understand how varied imitations fit into the picture of language learning, we will need to look beyond syntax and semantics to include conversational roles and skill. So far, one of the clearest contributions in this area is that by McTear (1985) on developing discourse among playmates. Over many months, cycles of conversation may become rich with the direct and indirect residues of familiar imitated chunks and new language pieces that are responsive to these chunks. Also relevant is the argument that through repeated, intimate conversational cycles, young children acquire much more than language structure: They acquire views about people, the environment, and the culture. These conversational experiences, in turn, will influence the ways in which individual children come to use their language (Cook-Gumperz, 1985; Oksaar, 1982).

Across individuals the recipes for conversation will share many ingredients, yet successful recipes can also be dramatically diverse. And, for the individual child, as for young Sartre in *The Words*, some particular remarks will become important components of the conversational recipe. For him the conversational recipe included a potent dose of verbal pleasure and a spicy sense of open meaning, of poetry achieved through his own brand of imitating words of others. Imitation, indeed, can have many faces in such conversations.

Throughout this chapter we have argued for more differentiated analyses and definitions of imitation. If we study how these different forms of imitation change over time, how they are a function of the developing neural substrate, and how they interweave with other cognitive functions, with memory, with psychological and social needs and motivations, our understanding of language phenomena will become fuller.

1.6 A Final Word

> On the one side, the child's creation is not original, not an invention out of nothing, but on the other side imitation is not a mechanical helpless acceptance. The child creates as it borrows. . . . Every imitation requires a selection, and so, a creative deviation from the model. (Jakobson, cited in E. Oksaar, 1982)

We have touched on many interesting empirical and theoretical explorations of how imitation contributes to children's language acquisition. In spite of all this work, the word *imitation* is used only sparingly in the language-learning field today. Many recent books on language-learning research do not even mention imitation in their indexes. The purposes of this book are to help bring imitation back as a reputable concept, to show that new ways of looking at imitation combined with appropriate research methodologies will reveal its usefulness in understanding language learning, and to place imitative processes in perspective along with other processes that contribute to language development.

Acknowledgment. We thank Janet Cooke for her very helpful editorial comments.

References

Anderson, J.R. (1983). *The architecture of cognition.* Cambridge, MA: Harvard University Press.

Baker, N., & Nelson, K.E. (1984). Recasting and related conversational techniques for triggering syntactic advances by young children. *First Words, 5,* 3–22.

Baker, N., Pemberton, E.F., & Nelson, K.E. (1985, October). *Facilitating young children's language development through stories: Reading and recasting.* Paper presented at the Boston University Conference on Language Development, Boston, MA.

Bandura, A. (1969). *Principles of behavior modification.* New York: Holt, Rinehart and Winston.

Bates, E., Bretherton, I., & Snyder, L. (1988). *From first words to grammar.* New York: Academic Press.

Bjorklund, D.F. (1987). A note on neonatal imitation. *Developmental Review, 7,* 86–92.

Bloom, L., Hood, L., & Lightbown, P. (1974). Imitation in language development: If, when, and why? *Cognitive Psychology, 6,* 380–420.

Bonvillian, J.D., Nelson, K.E., & Charrow, V.R. (1976). Languages and language-related skills in deaf and hearing children. *Sign Language Studies, 12,* 211–250.

Brown, R., & Fraser, C. (1963). The acquisition of syntax. In C. Cofer & B.S. Musgrave (Eds.), *Verbal behavior and learning: Problems and processes* (pp. 158–197). New York: McGraw-Hill.

Chomsky, N. (1959). Review of *Verbal Behavior* by B.F. Skinner. *Language, 35,* 26–58.

Chomsky, N. (1968). *Language and mind.* New York: Harcourt Brace Jovanovich.

Clark, R. (1977). What's the use of imitation? *Journal of Child Language, 4,* 341–358.

Cook-Gumperz, J. (1985, May). *The child's acquisition of languages and world views.* Paper presented to the Georgetown Roundtable on Linguistics, Georgetown University, Washington, DC.

English, H.B., & English, A.C. (1958). *A comprehensive dictionary of psychological and psychoanalytical terms.* New York: David McKay Company, Inc.

Ervin, S.M. (1964). Imitation and structural change in children's language. In E.H. Lenneberg (Ed.), *New directions in the study of language* (pp. 163–189). Cambridge, MA: MIT Press.

Ervin-Tripp, S.M. (1971). An overview of theories of grammatical development. In D.I. Slobin (Ed.), *The ontogenesis of grammar* (pp. 190–212). New York: Academic Press.

Fourcin, A.J. (1975). Language development in the absence of expressive speech. In E.H. Lenneberg & E. Lenneberg (Eds.), *Foundations of language development: A multidisciplinary approach* (Vol. 2, pp. 263–268). New York: Academic Press.

Fraser, C., Bellugi, U., & Brown, R. (1963). Control of grammar in imitation, comprehension and production. *Journal of Verbal Learning and Verbal Behavior, 2,* 121–135.

Gleitman, H. (1981). *Psychology* (1st ed.). New York: Norton.

Gopnik, A. (1988, July 4). *The New Yorker*, 61–65.

Hirsh-Pasek, K., Treiman, R., & Schneiderman, M. (1984). Brown & Hanlon revisited: Mothers' sensitivity to ungrammatical forms. *Journal of Child Language*, *11*, 81–88.

Jenkins, J.J., & Palermo, D. (1964). Mediation processes and the acquisition of linguistic structure. In U. Bellugi & R. Brown (Eds.). *The acquisition of language. Monographs of the Society for Research in Child Development*, *29-1*, 141–169.

Keenan, E.O. (1977). Making it last: Repetition in children's discourse. In S.M. Ervin-Tripp & C. Mitchell-Kernan (Eds.), *Child discourse*. New York: Academic Press.

Kimble, G.A. (1961). *Hilgard and Marquis' conditioning and learning* (2nd ed). New York: Appleton-Century-Crofts.

Kucjaz, S.A. (1982). Language play and language acquisition. In H.W. Reese (Ed.), *Advances in child development and behavior* (Vol. 17, pp. 197–232). New York: Academic Press.

Liberman, A.V., & Mattingly, I.G. (1985). The motor theory of speech perception revised. *Cognition*, *21*, 1–36.

McNeill, D. (1966). On theories of language acquisition. In F. Smith & G.A. Miller (Eds.), *The genesis of language: A psycholinguistic approach* (pp. 15–84). Cambridge, MA: MIT Press.

McTear, M. (1985). *Children's conversation*. New York: Basil Blackwell.

Meltzoff, A.N., & Moore, M.K. (1983). The origins of imitation in infancy: Paradigm, phenomena, and theories. In L.P. Lipsitt (Ed.), *Advances in infancy research* (Vol.2, pp. 265–301). Norwood, NJ: Ablex.

Moerk, E.L. (1977). Processes and products of imitation: Additional evidence that imitation is progressive. *Journal of Psycholinguistic Research*, *6*, 187–202.

Moerk, E.L., & Moerk, C. (1979). Quotations, imitations and generalizations. Factual and methodological analyses. *International Journal of Behavioral Development*, *5*, 95–109.

Nelson, K. (1981). Individual differences in language development. *Developmental Psychology*, *17*, 170–187.

Nelson, K.E. (1977). Facilitating children's syntax acquisition. *Developmental Psychology*, *13*, 101–107.

Nelson, K.E. (1980). Theories of the child's acquisition of syntax: A look at rare events and at necessary, catalytic, and irrelevant components of mother–child conversation. *Annals of the New York Academy of Sciences*, *345*, 45–67.

Nelson, K.E. (1987). Some observations from the perspective of the rare event cognitive comparison theory of language acquisition. In K.E. Nelson & A. van Kleeck (Eds.), *Children's language* (Vol. 6, pp. 289–331). Hillsdale, NJ: Erlbaum.

Nelson, K.E. (1988). *Strategies for first language teaching*. In R. Schiefelbusch & M. Rice (Eds.), *The teachability of language*. Baltimore, MD: Dan Brookes.

Nelson, K.E., Baker, N.D., Denninger, M.M., Bonvillian, J.D., & Kaplan, B.J. (1985). *Cookie* versus *do-it-again*: Imitative-referential and person-social-syntactic-initiating language styles in children. *Linguistics*, *23*, 443–454.

Nelson, K.E., & Bonvillian, J.D. (1978). Early semantic development: Conceptual growth and related processes between 2 and 4 1/2 years of age. In K.E. Nelson (Ed.), *Children's language* (Vol. 1, pp. 467–556). New York: Gardner Press.

Ochs., E., & Schieffelin, B.B. (1982). Language acquisition and socialization: Three developmental stories and their implications. *Sociololinguistic Working Paper*, No. 105. Austin, TX: Southwest Educational Development Laboratory.

Oksaar, E. (1982). *Language acquisition in the early years.* New York: St. Martin's Press. Translated from the German, *Spracherwerb im Vorschulalter* (1977). Stuttgart: Kohlhammer.

Piaget, J. (1962). *Play, dreams and imitation in childhood.* New York: Norton. (Original work published in 1946.)

Ramer, A.L.H. (1976). The function of imitation in child language. *Journal of Speech and Hearing, 19,* 700–717.

Reger, Z. (1986). The functions of imitation in child language. *Applied Psycholinguistics, 7,* 323–352.

Rummelhart, D.E., & McClelland, J.L. (1987). Learning the past tenses of English verbs: Implicit rules or parallel distributed processing. In B. MacWhinney (Ed.) *Mechanisms of language acquisition* (pp. 195–248). Hillsdale, NJ: Erlbaum.

Sartre, J.P. (1964). *The words* (p. 19). New York: Fawcett World Library.

Schwartz, R.G., & Leonard, L.B. (1985). Lexical imitation and language acquisition in language-impaired children. *Journal of Speech and Hearing Disorders, 50,* 141–149.

Skinner, B.F. (1957). *Verbal Behavior.* New York: Appleton/Century Crofts.

Slobin, D.I. (1968). Imitation and grammatical development in children. In N.S. Endler, L.R. Boulter, & H. Osser (Eds.), *Contemporary issues in developmental psychology* (pp. 437–443). New York: Holt, Rinehart & Winston.

Slobin, D.I. (Ed.). (1971). *The ontogenesis of grammar.* New York: Academic Press.

Snow, C.E. (1981). The uses of imitation. *Journal of Child Language, 8,* 205–212.

Snow, C.E. (1983). Saying it again: The role of expanded and deferred imitations in language acquisition. In K.E. Nelson (Ed.), *Children's language* (Vol 4. pp. 187–230). Hillsdale, NJ: Erlbaum.

Speidel, G.E. (1987). Conversation and language learning in the classroom. In K.E. Nelson and A. van Kleeck (Eds.), *Children's language* (Vol. 6, pp. 99–135). Hillsdale, NJ: Erlbaum.

Staats, A.W. (1968). *Learning, language & cognition.* New York: Holt, Rinehart & Winston.

Statts, A.W. (1971a). *Child learning, intelligence and personality.* New York: Holt, Rinehart & Winston.

Staats, A.W. (1971b). Linguistic-mentalistic theory versus an explanatory S-R learning theory of language development. In D.I. Slobin (Ed.), *The ontogenesis of grammar* (pp. 103–150). New York: Academic Press.

Stine, E.L., & Bohannon, J.N. (1983). Imitations, interactions, and language acquisition. *Journal of Child Language, 10,* 589–603.

Tolman, E.C., Ritchie, B.F., and Kalish, D. (1946). Studies in spatial learning: II. Place learning versus response learning. *Journal of Experimental Psychology, 36,* 221–229.

Uzgiris, I.Č. (1984). Imitation in infancy: Its interpersonal aspects. In M. Perlmutter (Ed.), *Minnesota symposia on child psychology* (Vol. 17, pp. 1–32). Hillsdale, NJ: Erlbaum.

Watson-Gegeo, K.A., & Gegeo, D.W. (1986). Some aspects of calling out and repeating routines in Kwara'ae children's language acquisition. In B.B. Schieffelin & E. Ochs (Eds.), *Language socialization across cultures.* New York: Cambridge University Press.

Whitehurst, G.J., & Vasta, R. (1975). Is language acquired through imitation? *Journal of Psycholinguistic Research, 4,* 37–59.

CHAPTER 2

On Linking Nonverbal Imitation, Representation, and Language Learning in the First Two Years of Life

Andrew N. Meltzoff and Alison Gopnik

This book is a collection of research on diverse aspects of imitation with a focus on how imitation contributes to language learning. Most of the chapters are concerned with imitative processes in language itself, with the imitation of syntactic forms or lexical items. A primary aim of this chapter is to discuss a different face of imitation—that of nonverbal imitation, and, in particular, nonverbal deferred imitation. The capacity to use deferred imitation is an integral part of the ability to use words productively. One elementary prerequisite for using a particular form like *chapeu* or *hat*, for example, is that children be able to retain and imitate the specific target word they have heard in their culture. Understanding the ontogenetically prior development of nonverbal deferred imitation may help illuminate a basic cognitive prerequisite of language acquisition.

In fact, at least one influential theorist, namely Piaget, has argued that the roots of language learning can be directly traced to prior developments in nonverbal imitation. A major point in the recent Piaget–Chomsky debate (Piattelli-Palmarini, 1980) was whether nonverbal imitation is a developmental foundation for the emergence of language, as Piaget advocates, or whether the two domains, nonverbal imitation and language, are entirely distinct, as Chomsky argues. We will suggest a compromise position. Unlike the Chomskyan position, we believe there are indeed interesting developmental relations between nonverbal imitation and language, but we will marshal evidence to show that these relations are rather different from the ones Piaget proposed.

Piaget proposed that the onset of deferred imitation and productive word use both reflect a fundamental change in the child's cognitive abilities. According to the theory, this change is also reflected in other milestone achievements, such as deducing the location of hidden objects (object permanence) and inventing new solutions to means–ends problems. The broad synchrony in the emergence of all these different behavioral skills provides evidence for Piaget's hypothesis of a global shift from a purely sensorimotor to a representational cognitive system at 18 months of age—the so-called *Stage 6* shift.

We will first present new experimental results suggesting that the notion of a global Stage 6 shift from a purely sensorimotor infant to a representational child must be amended. In fact, we will see that infants can produce deferred imitation, one integral component of the classic Stage 6 shift, at least as early as 9 months of age. Next we will argue that the examination of this early imitative competence illuminates fundamental issues, methods, and theoretical points that may play a role in verbal imitation and in language learning more generally. Finally, we will suggest that, by taking seriously the new results in nonverbal imitation and by relating them to some recent findings on semantic and cognitive development, we can better understand the important changes that occur in the child's language at about 18 months of age.

Based on new findings about early nonverbal imitation, we make several interlocking proposals. On the one hand, we will argue that the young infant is not a purely sensorimotor being, as is classically suggested, and that the early nonverbal representational system is far richer than Piaget had postulated. On the other hand, we will suggest that this initial representational system itself undergoes a transformation. We will show, contra the Piagetian view of infancy, that the primary representational code can support aspects of language and deferred imitation well before 18 months of age, but that there also seems to be a further shift in the nature and function of the representational system that has consequences for cognitive and linguistic behavior at about 18 months of age.

2.1 Deferred Imitation: A Statement of the Problem

One way in which research on cognitive development in general and nonverbal imitation in particular has influenced theories of language learning is in the assumptions that are made by psycholinguists about the young child's mental capabilities. It is a broadly held belief among cognitive developmentalists that deferred imitation is a late-emerging capacity (Flavell, 1985; McCall, Parke, & Kavanaugh, 1977; Piaget, 1962; Užgiris & Hunt, 1975). This notion is shared by a host of modern psycholinguists (Anisfeld, 1984; Bates, 1976; Bates, Benigni, Bretherton, Camaioni, & Volterra, 1979; Clark & Clark, 1977; Gleitman, 1986; Sinclair, 1970; Smolak, 1986), and it also colored the work of early language researchers.

Traditionally, deferred imitations were excluded, a priori, from the study of language imitation, or at best put into a different or problematic category. For example, in Ervin's (1964) work on imitation in children's language, imitation was operationalized as "overt immediate repetitions" (p. 168), thereby definitionally excluding perfect imitations after a delay. Indeed, many of the original studies that concluded that imitation played little or no role in language development were limited in their focus exclusively to immediate imitation, as noted by Snow (1981, 1983), Moerk (Chapter 12, this volume), and others. In the majority of the studies reviewed by Snow, an utterance was scored as imitative if and only if it occurred as the very next utterance of the child after the model's (Ervin, 1964; Moerk, 1977; Ramer, 1976) or were temporally very close, for example, within five utterances (Bloom, Hood, & Lightbown, 1974; Folger & Chapman, 1978). Imitation may historically have been viewed as playing a more salient role, in at least certain aspects of language development, if there had been some consideration of long-term imitative effects, not simply immediate repetition (Kuczaj, 1987; Moore & Meltzoff, 1978).

Of course, one of the hesitancies in opening up one's study of language to deferred imitation is the problem of whether the child's response is actually an imitation or would have occurred spontaneously. How can we be sure that a behavior or utterance emitted 10 or 20 hours after the model is actually based on this prior exposure? Might not the child have produced the behavior or utterance "on his or her own" at that point? In studies of language imitation, researchers have sought to isolate true imitation by narrowing the temporal window in which response is allowed. The idea is that, if a child duplicates an utterance very soon after the model, the probability of this having occurred by chance is slim. But is narrowing the temporal window the only, or even the best way, of isolating true imitation? Here there may be something to be learned from recent work in nonverbal imitation, for this very same issue confronts researchers in that domain.

Meltzoff's research strategy has been to investigate nonverbal imitation without necessarily confining the definition of imitation to "the very next action" (Meltzoff, 1985a, 1988a,b). As operationalized in this research, the temporal delay is independent of the criteria for imitation itself. One is free to manipulate delay experimentally in order to investigate whether children are constrained to immediate imitation or whether they also can perform deferred imitation. The key is to establish the chance probability for the occurrence of the target behavior or utterance. If the occurrence of a behavior matched to the model is significantly greater after that behavior is demonstrated than in appropriate control conditions, there is reason to infer imitation. But how does one gain sufficient control over the child's behavior in order to manipulate delay? And what are the relevant control conditions for ruling out spurious matching behavior? Three studies from the work on nonverbal deferred imitation are particularly relevant.

In one study, 14-month-old infants were found to represent and subsequently imitate actions they saw performed 24 hours earlier (Meltzoff, 1985a). In a second study, deferred imitation of actions was demonstrated in 9-month-old infants, again after a 24-hour delay (Meltzoff, 1988a). In the most recent study, 14-month-old infants were found to be able to retain and imitate multiple acts, including novel ones, over a very long-term delay interval—a 1-week delay (Meltzoff, 1988b). These studies may be of potential methodological and theoretical interest for language researchers—the former because they suggest a test paradigm that might be used to assess deferred linguistic imitation, the latter because they suggest that a deep revision is needed in Piaget's theory about the ontogenesis of deferred imitation and consequently in its potential role in language development. Rather than deferred imitation emerging at about 18 months of age (Stage 6), the new data indicate that this ability exists well before the child's first birthday.

2.2 Deferred Imitation of Object-Related Acts in 1- to 2-Year-Old Infants

There is an interesting parallel between the research on verbal and nonverbal imitation. The early work on nonverbal imitation also excluded deferred imitation from empirical analysis. Only immediate imitation was measured by Mehrabian and Williams (1971), Užgiris and Hunt (1975), Rodgon and Kurdek (1977), Abravanel, Levan-Goldschmidt, and Stevenson (1976), Masur and Ritz (1984), and others. Yet the imitation of actions can play only a limited role in learning and development if children are constrained to immediate reproduction. The functional significance of nonverbal imitation, at least in older children and adults, derives from the fact that a behavior can be observed at one point in time and can be remembered and used as the basis for action at a later date, when the appropriate situation presents itself.

One basic goal of the study by Meltzoff (1985a) was to expand the empirical study of imitative phenomena to include deferred imitation. A second goal was more methodological in nature. Many of the early researchers of nonverbal imitation had monitored children's responses to a target display and made two inferences: (1) They inferred the *existence of imitation* if the subjects duplicated the target, and (2) they inferred *imitative development* if older infants were more likely to duplicate the behavior than were younger infants. Meltzoff argued that from an experimental viewpoint both of these inferences were unwarranted. With regard to the existence of imitation, he argued that control conditions were necessary to evaluate the spontaneous likelihood of infants emitting the target behavior under test. For example, suppose that infants who see an adult bang two blocks together duplicate the behavior when given the chance to do so. Does this demonstrate imitation? No. Infants who have not seen that adult display might nonetheless engage in this behavior when presented with the two objects. Data that simply show that subjects duplicate the adult's action do not in themselves establish imitation. There may be something in the environmental setting (two blocks) that sparks the infant's performance independently of the adult's behavior.

With regard to claims about imitative development, it is not enough to show that older subjects are more likely to duplicate an adult display than younger ones. For example, if 2-year-olds feed a doll with a bottle after seeing an adult do so, and 1-year-olds do not, this does not in itself demonstrate an improvement in symbolic imitation. It might simply be the case that older children have a higher spontaneous probability of feeding the doll whether or not the model demonstrates this behavior. It might be true even if the experimenter simply put the doll and bottle on the table and left the room without providing anything to imitate whatsoever. For at least some of the activities that have been studied, both verbal and nonverbal, there is an increased likelihood that older infants will engage in the same "script" as the adult even in the absence of seeing/hearing the model, perhaps due to prior learning of the game (adults teaching the child to insert bottlelike things in dolls' mouths) or to a host of other possibilities. If one does not pay heed to these possibilities, an experiment might be interpreted as showing an improvement in symbolic imitation per se while leaving these other factors confounded. This could have untoward effects on theory, and using such an experimental design might lead to erroneous conclusions about the relation between imitative development per se and the emergence of other cognitive and linguistic abilities. (Errors in evaluating developmental progress in one domain, e.g., imitation, would necessarily cause difficulties for studies assessing developmental relations across domains.) In the work described below, procedures have been developed to address these issues.

In the initial study of infant deferred imitation, Meltzoff (1985a) used a simple action on a novel object. The object was a dumbbell-shaped toy that could be pulled apart by grasping the two ends and pulling outward. The infants were tested in the laboratory, and their behavior videotaped for subsequent analysis. Two age groups were used, 24-month-olds and 14-month-olds. In each age group, half the infants were given a test of immediate imitation and half a test of deferred imitation after a 24-hour delay. A large sample, 180 infants, was tested: 60 24-month-olds and 120 14-month-olds.

In the immediate imitation condition, the adult pulled apart and reassembled the object three times. The object was then presented to the infants, and their responses were monitored for a preset response period. A baseline control condition was used to assess the likelihood that infants would spontaneously produce the target act in the absence of a model to imitate. These infants did not see the adult pull the object apart and were simply given the object to play with for the timed response period. It can be argued, however, that a baseline control is not sufficient to assess imitation of either a nonverbal or verbal variety. To take an example relevant to the current experiment (parallels can be imagined for more symbolic or verbal imitation), it is possible that infants who see the adult pick up the test object might become more curious about it and might be induced to manipulate it themselves, thereby leading to the chance discovery that the object can be pulled apart. To control for this, Meltzoff also designed an "adult-manipulation" control. In this condition infants saw the adult pick up the object and move it in a small circle for the same length display period as in the imitation condition. The infants were then presented with the test object for the preset response period. In short, the design provided a direct assessment of the probability that infants might be induced to produce the target display for nonimitative reasons—for example, because they simply saw the experimenter pick up and touch the toy.

The deferred tests followed the identical procedure as that just described, save for the introduction of a 24-hour delay. Infants were shown the target or control displays on a first laboratory visit and then sent home. They were then brought into the laboratory for a second visit a day later and presented with the toy.

The results supported the idea that imitation of object play is a strong phenomenon in 1- to 2-year-old children. Across all test conditions, fully 65% of the 60 infants in the imitation condition produced the target behavior, as compared to 17% of the 120 control infants, χ^2 (1) = 40.24, p < .0001. There was no difference in target production between the two types of controls. Broken down in more detail as a function of age and task, the results showed that the 24-month-olds produce both immediate and deferred imitation, and that the 14-month-olds also imitated immediately. That much was expected by standard theory. More unexpectedly, the results also revealed that the younger group successfully imitated even after the 24-hour delay. After the 24-hour delay, 45% of the 14-month-olds produced a target behavior as compared to only 7.5% of the controls, χ^2 (1) = 9.49, p < .01.

Moreover, the results revealed that the 14-month-olds were not limited to reconstructing what they saw through trial and error, but represented it well enough to duplicate the act quickly and accurately even after the enforced 1-day delay. Indeed, the mean latency to produce the target act, once the infant was given access to the toy after the 24-hour delay, was only 5.02 seconds. The infants apparently retained the relevant information and were able to access it rapidly and use it when presented with the appropriate context, even after the 24-hour delay.

Two points of theoretical interest are to be noted — one social, the other cognitive. From a social viewpoint, the results show that infants will imitate adults with whom they have no established "attachment." The experiment involved a short warm-up period, but basically, the child was presented with a display by no more than a friendly stranger. That the infants would systematically repeat the actions of a stranger up to 24 hours later is a testament to their proclivity to study carefully and absorb adult behaviors. Moreover, judging from the success smiles upon duplication of the activity, infants seem to get some satisfaction out of imitation. Many of the infants would pick up the toy, imitate, and then look up smiling at the experimenter; a large proportion would also hand over the two pieces to the experimenter and indicate that they wanted another go-around. One infant played this same reciprocal imitation game for 20 imitative exchanges, until the experimenter and mother both tired of the interaction and decided to stop the game — much to the visible (and audible) displeasure of the baby. Nonverbal imitation seems to be a particularly compelling social activity for children of this age.

From a more cognitive viewpoint, it is noteworthy that infants were not permitted to imitate on-line and then later to perform the deferred task. Piaget has argued that a strong test of deferred imitation arises only if the infant is not permitted to perform immediate imitation on-line. His claim is that it is cognitively easier to retain an action or utterance one has already duplicated in context than it is to store the event and produce it for the first time after a delay. The current design made use of this theoretical distinction. The children in the deferred condition were simply shown the action but not given access to the toy on Day 1. Thus, they needed to direct their subsequent actions on the basis of a stored representation of the perceived event, and not simply as a retention of their own previous activity.

One conclusion of this study is that we can design an experimental paradigm to assess deferred imitation in a laboratory setting. In order to gain more theoretical leverage, we next wanted to know if still younger infants could also imitate after a 24-hour delay. Furthermore, we wanted to test a wider range of actions. Therefore, a study was designed testing 9-month-old infants on a series of three new actions.

2.3 Deferred Imitation in 9-Month-Old Infants

One hundred twenty 9-month-old infants were tested, half on an immediate and half on a deferred imitation task involving a 24-hour delay (Meltzoff, 1988a). Three simple objects built in our laboratory served as the test stimuli. The first was an L-shaped object composed of two pieces of unpainted wood. The parts were hinged together such that the vertical piece stood upright from the baseplate. In the imitation condition, the action demonstrated was to fold the vertical piece down flat against the baseplate. The second object was a small black box with a button on its top surface. The action demonstrated was to reach out and poke the button, which triggered a beeper inside the box. The third object was a plastic egg into which we had placed a few metal nuts. The action demonstrated was to pick up and shake the egg.

All three target actions were shown to each infant in a randomly determined sequence. At the end of the sequence, infants in the immediate imitation condition were immediately given each toy in turn for a preset period. The responses were videotaped for subsequent analysis. In the deferred imitation condition, infants were sent home after seeing the series of three displays *without having any chance to touch or play with the toys*. They returned to the laboratory on Day 2 and were then given the toys in sequence, identically as in the immediate condition.

In order to assess whether the matching behavior was truly attributable to imitation, three different controls were used. In the baseline control, the experimenter provided no demonstration whatever; he simply presented the three objects in sequence and videotaped the infants' responses. This assessed infants' spontaneous tendency to produce the targets. In the adult-touching control, the subject saw the experimenter reach out and pick up each of the three objects in turn before he presented them one at a time to the subject. This procedure directly mimicked aspects of the imitation condition, complete with the fact that the experimenter touched the toys, but without demonstrating the target displays at issue. This controls for the possibility that infants might be induced to play

Table 2-1. Number of Infants With High Versus Low Test Scores as a Function of Delay and Experimental Condition

Condition	Immediate		Deferred	
	Low	High	Low	High
Baseline control	9	3	8	4
Adult-touching control	12	0	11	1
Adult-manipulation control	12	0	10	2
Imitation	12	12	12	12

with the objects if they see the adult pick them up, and that this alone might lead them to perform the target action. Such response facilitation might be confused with imitation in the absence of this control. Finally, the adult-manipulation control was used to mimic still further distinctive features of the target display. Infants who see that objects have particular consequences when handled, that they rattle or beep, may become especially interested in them and actively run through a wider range of action schemes than infants who are not given this information; phrased differently, it is possible that infants engage in a "button-pushing script" simply if they hear a beeper. This possibility was controlled for by including an adult-manipulation condition in which the experimenter presented such consequences (beeping, rattling), but without demonstrating the critical target actions themselves. For example, the experimenter surreptitiously activated the beeper via a hidden switch, thereby exposing the infant to the sound-emanating-from-the box event, but still without demonstrating the target action under test. (See Meltzoff, 1988a, for further procedural details.) The experimental design thus permits the inference of imitation if differentially more target behaviors are produced by infants in the imitation versus control groups.

Consider first the results of the immediate imitation test. Each infant was presented with three test objects and therefore could duplicate 0 to 3 of the target behaviors. For the purposes of analysis, each infant's response was cast into one of two levels: either low (0 to 1 target behaviors produced) or high (2 to 3 target behaviors produced). These data are displayed in the left side of Table 2-1. A chi-square test assessing the effects of the four experimental conditions on the infants' behavior reached significance, $\chi^2 (3) = 16.00, p < .01$. These same data were also reanalyzed as a 2×2 table contrasting the imitation condition ($n = 24$) with the combined controls ($n = 36$). These results were also highly significant ($p < .001$), with infants in the imitation condition producing more target behaviors than the controls.

These results indicate that 9-month-olds are proficient in immediate imitation tasks. Of more interest are the results showing that 9-month-old infants are capable of imitation after the 24-hour delay (Table 2-1, right side). The 4×2 table assessing the effects of the four experimental conditions on infants' behavior was significant, with infants in the imitation condition producing more target behaviors than the controls, $\chi^2 (3) = 8.01, p < .05$. The data were also reanalyzed as a 2 × 2 table contrasting the imitation condition (n = 24) with the combined controls (n = 36), and this was also significant (p < .05).

Inspection of the left versus right two columns of Table 2-1 reveals that the imitation effect not only replicates, but also that the detailed profile of the results is not affected by the delay. That the results are so similar allows us to combine the two studies, and this larger sample size of 120 subjects in turn affords a further look at the effectiveness of imitation. The data show that about 20% of the subjects in the imitation condition reproduced all three of the target displays. This result is impressive inasmuch as subjects were remembering not one or two events, but all three, and then duplicating them after the delay. The control infants document that the production of all three target behaviors is not a behavior pattern that can be attributable to chance—it is not a high baseline occurrence. Indeed, not a single infant of the 72 controls produced all three targets. The difference between the imitation group and controls is highly significant (p < .0005).

The results have four major implications. First, it is relevant to social-developmental theory that the design involved showing infants first one, and then a second, and finally a third act, and only then allowed them to respond. In a more naturalistic home setting, parents, peers, and siblings do not always allow infants access to one object before showing other potentially competing acts with different toys. The results show that these social realities are not in themselves enough to block the imitation of the now-absent events. Even these young infants can hold in mind more than one event for subsequent reproduction. These findings are thus compatible with the notion that imitation could be functional between young infants and their siblings or other naturally occurring models. Such a finding is also relevant to verbal imitation in a naturalistic setting, in which a large number of different words are produced in different contexts and the child must keep track of which words to imitate in which settings.

Second, the results are relevant to Piagetian theory, for the experiment was designed to be sensitive to three critical distinctions made in this theory. (1) The control groups eliminated the possibility that infants in the imitation condition produced the target behavior on Day 2 solely because they were more comfortable with the toys, laboratory, or experimenter on this second day. The subjects in both the adult-touching and adult-manipulation control conditions were exposed to the same toys for the same length of time, and they, too, were brought back on the second day. Had such controls not been included, few theoretical implications could be drawn from the deferred experiment. (2) About 20% of the subjects in the imitation condition, as opposed to 0% in the controls, reproduced all three of the target actions modeled. This indicates that some 9-month-olds can simultaneously keep in mind three different inputs over the 24-hour delay, and provides evidence for greater representational facility than is commonly supposed within the first year. (3) The design ensured that the infant's reproduction on Day 2 was based on a representation of the adult's behavior, not on a memory of the infant's own previous activity from Day 1, and thus was a strong test of deferred imitation. Many theorists acknowledge that some form of memory is involved in the following sequence of events: Immediate imitation, followed by a delay, and then a reinitiation of this imitation after delay. However, this is not regarded as a pure case of deferred imitation, and its first appearance might well be predicted to occur prior to 18 months of age (sensorimotor Stage 6). The current study was designed to avoid this problem, inasmuch as infants were not given the opportunity for immediate duplication. They were simply shown the actions on Day 1 and not even allowed to handle the toys. Thus, their imitation on Day 2 could not have been due to a memory for their own immediate mimicry and must be rooted in a representation of the now-absent action pattern. As such, the results suggest a downward revision in the age at which clear-cut deferred imitation first emerges in development.

The results also are informative for theories of preverbal memory development, because the imitation effects after the 24-hour delay were similar to those of immediate imitation. On the basis of this and other work, Meltzoff (1985a, 1988a) hypothesized that, once an event is encoded by the infant, the retention interval per se is not a narrowly delimiting factor in early infancy. The strong version of this hypothesis is that any behavior or event infants are capable of imitating immediately can also be imitated under carefully designed delay conditions.

2.4 Long-Term Memory and Imitation: Novel Acts and Multiple Stimuli

To test the hypothesis that young infants can imitate a variety of acts even over exceedingly long delay intervals, a new study was conducted (Meltzoff, 1988b). Thirty-six 14-month-olds were tested. The delay period chosen was 1 week. Six different acts were shown to the infants in the initial visit. They were (1) the three acts described above in the 3-object study, (2) the pull-toy from the previously described study, (3) shaking an object from a short string, and (4) a novel act— one in which the adult bent forward from the waist and with his forehead pressed a small plastic panel mounted on a box. The design of the experiment was essentially the same as that just described; that is, the performance of an imitation group was compared both to baseline and adult-manipulation controls.

The results show that infants produce significantly more of the target behaviors in the imitation ($M = 3.42$) versus control groups ($M = 1.46$) ($p < .05$). Some individual infants imitated as many as five of the six acts, and this never occurred in the controls. That infants can store this many items for "read out" at the appropriate time a week later attests to the power of nonverbal imitation at this age. What is most striking, however, is the aptitude these young infants exhibited for duplicating the novel act. The data show that head touching is indeed a novel action, in that it simply was never performed by any of the control infants; none of the 24 controls leaned forward and touched the panel with his head. Nonetheless, fully 67% of the infants in the imitation condition produced this behavior ($p < .0001$). Imitation of a series of behaviors, including a novel act, was thus firmly demonstrated over a delay interval of 1 week.

In summary, the data from the most recent studies of infant nonverbal imitation suggest that memory skills, in the sense of the ability to recover information about adults' actions after lengthy retention intervals, does not seem to be a tight constraint on infant behavior. (In subsequent studies it was found that infants will even perform deferred imitation from a TV, and not just from "live" models [Meltzoff, 1988c]). This revision of our usual views of the infant's memory capacity has implications for early language learning. A child who was already equipped with a capacity to remember the behaviors of others, including novel ones, over a long period of time would obviously have a much easier time learning language than a child without this ability (cf. Bloom 1973; Bloom & Capatides, 1987; Moerk & Moerk, 1979; K. E. Nelson, 1982, 1987, in press; Speidel & Herreshoff, Chapter 8, this volume).

It must be acknowledged that the study of deferred imitation in 9- and 14-month-olds does not conclusively address the larger idea associated with Piaget's theory and others (Piaget, 1952, 1962; Piattelli-Palmarini, 1980) of a synchronous Stage 6 shift involving deferred imitation, language, object-permanence, symbolic play, and means–ends understanding, because these additional measures were not also taken on these same subjects. However, the results show that at least some capacity for deferred imitation is present under 1 year of age, which is well before the usual age estimate for the emergence of Stage 6 behaviors. This underscores the need for reexamining which cognitive achievements are related to which during late infancy and the transition to early childhood – an issue taken up in Sections 2.6 and 2.7.

2.5 Newborn Imitation of Primary Actions: Roots of Sociality, Reciprocity, and Communication

Piaget has argued that imitative phenomena in infancy are all of one piece – they are developmentally related to one another. Although he would have been surprised at deferred imitation in 9-month-old infants, he would have wanted to know if this was simply an isolated deviation from theory or if there were other examples. We think we have uncovered a second example – the early imitation of elementary facial and manual gestures. According to orthodox developmental theory, the imitation of facial acts emerges at about 8 to 12 months of age. Facial imitation is considered a landmark developmental achievement, for it indicates some primitive ability to recognize analogies between self and other. A series of studies have now been completed indicating that facial imitation does not first emerge at the end of the first year of life (Meltzoff & Moore, 1977, 1983a,b). The data show that there is an innate ability to imitate adult facial displays, with the implication that this is a "psychological primitive," a basic building block in psychosocial development, rather than a product of development.

In the 1977 paper, Meltzoff and Moore reported two studies of neonatal imitation. The first assessed 12- to 17-day-old infants. Four different body actions were tested: lip protrusion, mouth opening, tongue protrusion, and sequential finger movement. The infant's behavior was videotaped and subsequently scored by judges who were blind to the test conditions. The result provided support for the imitation hypothesis; infants differentially copied all four gestures. In this first study, infants were allowed to begin their responses in the presence of the adult's display. The authors considered whether very young infants might be limited to some form of motor resonance, coaction, or mutual imitation, and whether these very early imitative responses might be disrupted if a short temporal delay or any competing motor interference were inserted. A design was needed in which infants were presented with the target gestures, but not allowed to respond until after the experimenter had finished modeling. Experimental control over the infant's behavior was needed. This led to the second study in the 1977 report, in which pacifiers were used. In Study 2 a pacifier was put in the infant's mouth during the demonstration of the gesture so that the infant would engage in another competing motor activity (sucking) rather than imitation. After the experimenter had finished modeling his facial display, he stopped moving, assumed a passive-face pose, and only *then* removed the pacifier from the infant—maintaining his blank face for the entire 2.5-min response period.

Two gestures, mouth opening and tongue protrusion, were tested in a repeated-measures design counterbalanced for order. Analyses showed that the infants did indeed actively suck on the pacifiers during the stimulus-presentation period. The pacifier was thus a good trick for prompting these young infants to delay their facial imitation; the sucking reflex of neonates apparently takes precedence over their tendency to imitate. Even using this pacifier technique, the infants were found to imitate the two displays during the subsequent response periods. Moreover, the infants did not respond with a sudden, reflexive-like mimetic reaction, but studied the adult's now passive face, frowned, and then responded—at first with approximate matches to the now-absent display and then with more accurate matches as they gradually engaged in a self-correction process (Meltzoff & Moore, 1983b).

These experiments showed that young infants could imitate elementary body transformations. The simplest explanation for this precocious imitation behavior might be that infants had learned to copy these displays during earlier mother–infant interaction. Developmentalists have emphasized the rich, nonverbal "dialogues" that occur, often in *en face* position, between mothers and their young infants (Brazelton & Tronick, 1980; Stern, 1985; Trevarthen & Marwick, 1986). Dedicated empiricists might propose that infants had somehow learned to imitate by the time they were tested at 2 to 3 weeks of age.

If postnatal learning is a necessary condition for the emergence of facial imitation, then newborns in the first hours of life should fail on the task. The next study involved 40 infants with a mean age of 32 hours (Meltzoff & Moore, 1983a). No newborn in the sample was older than 72 hours, and the youngest was just 42 minutes old at the time of the test. The infants were tested in a laboratory located within a newborn nursery. Infants acted as their own controls, and each was presented with both mouth-opening and tongue-protrusion gestures in a repeated-measures design, counterbalanced for order of presentation. Again, the experiment was videotaped and subsequently scored by an observer who was blind to the model shown to the infant. The results supported the hypothesis of imitation. There were significantly more infant mouth openings in response to the mouth display, $M = 7.1$, than to the tongue display, $M = 5.4$ ($z = 2.26, p <$ .05, Wilcoxon matched-pairs signed-ranks test). Similarly, the frequency of infant tongue protrusions was greater to the tongue display, $M = 9.9$, than to the mouth display, $M = 6.5$ ($z = 3.31, p < .001$).

We can conclude that infants have the capacity to imitate facial gestures well before the 1-year age period predicted by orthodox theory. Despite the initial surprise engendered by the findings, the phenomenon that young infants can match adult facial displays has now been replicated by researchers in at least seven independent labs since Meltzoff and Moore's 1977 report (Abravanel & Sigafoos, 1984; Field, Woodson, Greenberg; & Cohen, 1982; Fontaine, 1984; Heimann & Schaller, 1985; Jacobson, 1979; Kaitz, Meschulach-Sarfaty, Auerbach, & Eidelman, 1988; Vinter, 1986). Thus, the basic phenomenon—that certain adult gestures will elicit matching responses by neonates—now seems secure and widely elicitable under a range of situations. The key questions now become: What does it imply about the psychology of young infants, and why might it be of interest to those investigating communicative and language development? Although it may be tempting to think that this early behavior can be subsumed under some sort of reflex or releasing mechanism account, such an approach does not seem to provide the most parsimonious explanation, for it ignores several important characteristics of the phenomenon, including the range of different acts imitated (Meltzoff & Moore, 1977), the gradual accommodation of the response (Meltzoff & Moore, 1983b), and the social-emotional nature of these early interchanges (Meltzoff, 1981; Meltzoff & Moore, 1985).

The working hypothesis offered by Meltzoff and Moore has been that early imitation reflects a process of active intermodal mapping (AIM). In this view infants can, at some level, apprehend the equivalences between body transformations they see and body transformations of their own whether they see them or not. The view holds that imitation, even this early imitation, is mediated by an internal representation of the adult's act. What is the nature of this representation?

Meltzoff and Moore's hypothesis is that the newborns are capable of registering *supramodal* information about the adult's movements that is then used directly as the basis for the infant's own motor plans (Meltzoff, 1985b; Meltzoff & Moore, 1977, 1983a,b). Thus conceived, the infant's representation of the adult's act is neither exclusively visual nor exclusively motor, but rather is a modality-free description of the event. In this view, the perception and production of movements are closely linked and mediated by a common representational system right from birth. The existence of this mode of representation might also have interesting implications for other competencies in early infancy (Bower, 1982). Perhaps most relevant to the issue of language learning is recent work connecting early facial imitation to issues of speech perception and production.

Kuhl and Meltzoff (1982, 1988; Meltzoff & Kuhl, 1989) and Studdert-Kennedy (1986) have noted that the early facial imitation involves movements related to the articulatory maneuvers that will be used in speech production (mouth opening, tongue movements). It is possible that the visual-motor mappings involved in oral imitation are useful to infants in their quest to gain voluntary control over articulatory dynamics. In particular, Kuhl and Meltzoff have suggested that one reason (not the sole reason, but one reason) that fronted consonants (/b/ and /d/) emerge relatively early in phonological development is that infants cannot only hear them, but actually can *see* the production of these units as well (as opposed to velar consonants like /g/ that are produced toward the back of the oral cavity). Kuhl and Meltzoff suggest that oral imitation skills may play a role in fostering speech development because infants can imitate the seen articulatory movements of the adult in learning to form certain phonetic units.

This idea ties early visual imitation to aspects of speech and phonological development, not at the expense of vocal imitation, but as a complement to it. The notion is that speech for young infants is a thoroughly intermodal experience — it is seen as well as heard — and that the mastery of elementary speech production skills may capitalize both on gestural as well as vocal imitative skills (Kuhl & Meltzoff, 1984, 1988; Meltzoff & Kuhl, 1989).

Meltzoff and Moore's proposal that early facial imitation reflects a process of active intermodal mapping (rather than simply being a mindless reflex) also has implications for early social development. In particular, it provides leverage for interpreting the fact that infants seem to enjoy it when parents mimic their young infants' motor behaviors. When parents highlight certain infant behaviors by imitating them, this may have significance not only because of the temporal contiguity, but because the infants can recognize some basic similarity between the adult's behavior and their own. In the other forms of early play, there may be a mutual rhythm adopted by the two partners; however, early imitative play goes beyond this and implies a mutuality in the structure of the behavior as well. Imitative play thus offers a unique channel for the very earliest communication. We have observed parents playing imitative exchange games by the hour with their prelinguistic infants, often to peals of laughter. Both partners seem to enjoy the communicative aspects of the "dialogue in gestures" that early motor imitation provides. (For further discussions of this point, see Masur, Chapter 3, this volume; Meltzoff, 1985b; Meltzoff & Moore, 1983b, 1985; Užgiris, 1981, 1984, Chapter 5, this volume.)

Following the argument further, it can be suggested that the representational capacities underlying early imitation allow infants to "run the system in reverse," as it were, and appreciate the adult's imitation of the infant. If true, we have a system that would reach far beyond the confines of simple action imitation proper. For example, this might shed light on the process by which infants first differentiate the animate from the inanimate worlds, and how they become interested in, identify with, and become attached to exemplars from the former and not the latter. In the earliest phases, infants may be especially attracted to other human beings (as opposed to inanimate objects) just because it is other humans who imitate their actions. Because infants can recognize equivalences between the acts they themselves perform and those performed by the adults, they have a mechanism by which to begin to identify with other human beings, to recognize them as "like me."

This recognition of self–other similarity and the fact that adults' imitation of infantile acts seems to be attention-getting and enjoyable to young infants (Meltzoff, 1981; Meltzoff & Moore, 1983b, 1985) may also be picked up and more fully capitalized upon in later verbal imitations. As might be expected, at the older ages when linguistic imitation first takes place, it is not just simple direct mimicry, but duplication coupled with an expansion (Barnes, Gutfreund, Satterly, & Wells, 1983; Cross, 1977; Newport, Gleitman, & Gleitman, 1977; Ryan, 1973; Snow, 1983) and recasting (a change in sentence structure that still picks up on the core meaning of the original sentence [Baker & Nelson, 1984]) that appear to be maximally interesting and useful for the children. Nonetheless, the underlying psychological principle may be quite similar for both motor and linguistic exchanges; children may find the duplication and elaboration of their behavior by adults an attention-getting episode that serves as a frame and motivation for further exchange (cf. Stella-Prorok, 1983). The principal point proffered here is that the development of this format starts quite young – the earliest experiences of reciprocal "imitative dialogues," beginning right from the neonatal period, with the early facial and manual imitation exchanges.

2.6 Connections Among Deferred Imitation, Representation, and Language Learning

The research on nonverbal imitation has implications for early language learning, and we have already suggested some of these. We think the innate ability to imitate facial gestures, for example, plays a role in establishing early communication channels, which some theorists have argued is importantly related to later language development (Bruner, 1975a,b, 1983; Golinkoff, 1983; Masur, Chapter 3, this volume; Trevarthen & Marwick, 1986; and Užgiris, 1981, 1984, Chapter 5, this volume). In this and following sections, we will focus on three particular implications of the findings of early deferred imitation. First, these results suggest that some kind of verbal deferred imitation may take place during early infancy, which could play a role in language learning. Second, this research suggests a reorganization in the classical Piagetian view of the relationship between deferred imitation and language development. Third, the work raises some new possibilities about how the emergence of language, nonverbal imitation, and other cognitive abilities might all be related.

2.6.1 Deferred Imitation as a Mechanism for Language Learning

It has not yet been established that 9-month-old infants are capable of deferred verbal imitation. However, there are at least two pieces of converging evidence that favor this idea: (1) As we have shown, infants are able to delay imitation of other adult behaviors, and (2) experimental work has documented that infants in the first half-year can imitate some elementary aspects of adults' speech productions, including both prosodic characteristics (Kuhl & Meltzoff, 1982; Papousek & Papousek, 1981) and also isolated phonetic units (Kuhl & Meltzoff, 1988; Užgiris, 1972). This certainly provides a foundation for deferred verbal imitation, which is important because a capacity for deferred vocal imitation is a prerequisite for language acquisition. In order for a child to produce a particular word like *book* or *livre* in an appropriate context, the child must be able to remember another speaker's production of this utterance in a particular context and reproduce that behavior in a similar context. In other words, the child must, at the very least, be capable of deferred verbal imitation (Kuczaj, 1987).

In fact, language depends on deferred imitation in a particularly fundamental way, and in this regard speech and language are different from many other types of behavior in infancy. It is possible to imagine how a child might spontaneously generate some of the other motor behaviors we have discussed; but there is little to no likelihood that a child could spontaneously generate the behavior of saying *book* in the presence of books. The only source for this behavior is the behavior of other people, and the only way to produce this behavior in the absence of a model is to produce a deferred imitation.

This is an argument that we owe to Piaget, and we think parts of Piaget's logical analysis were correct, even if his developmental timetable was empirically wrong. If the general ability for deferred imitation first became possible only at 18 months of age (the empirical claim), then indeed productive language use would be difficult if not impossible before that time. On the other hand, if deferred imitation is in place well before that period, it is not only possible but even probable that language learning can also be well underway much earlier.[1]

Some existing capacity for deferred imitation would provide a mechanism that would allow the child to reproduce a behavior in a context. In addition, deferred imitation might allow children to consider, operate on, and reorganize linguistic information. One of the paradoxes of developmental psycholinguistics is that children must use their own grammar to process input and yet must be able to access input that is not generated by their own grammar if they are to make linguistic progress. Understanding an adult utterance involves a kind of "on-line" analysis of the utterance. But it would also be helpful to children if they could store unanalyzed utterances and consider and reflect on those utterances later on, if they could analyze language "off-line" as well as "on-line." Deferred imitation of the utterances of others might help children to store and access linguistic information that they cannot yet analyze (Bloom et al., 1974; Moerk & Moerk,

---

[1]Indeed, a provocative report of the very early production of signs (Bonvillian, Orlansky, & Novack, 1983) is compatible with the new findings of proficient deferred imitation of manual actions as early as 9 months of age.

1979; K. E. Nelson, 1980, 1987, in press; Snow, 1983; Speidel, Chapter 7, this volume).

Some support for this notion comes from studies of crib speech, the private speech some children produce before they go to sleep (Kuczaj, 1983; Weir, 1962). Crib speech often seems to involve a kind of off-line linguistic analysis, and investigators have speculated that children who produce crib speech may simply be overtly producing what other children produce covertly. Kuczaj has claimed that a marked feature of crib speech is the imitation of adult linguistic utterances that occurred during the day. In fact, Kuczaj found more imitation in crib speech than in social speech. In crib speech deferred verbal imitation seems to allow children to process language even when the actual linguistic stimuli are no longer available.

These examples suggest that deferred verbal imitation may play a role in language acquisition, not only because it allows children to reproduce an adult linguistic form, but also because it gives children a way of accessing and operating on linguistic information. The new data show that some aspects of deferred imitation are established at 9 months of age and thus that it could potentially serve this role from the very beginnings of language acquisition. It would now be of interest to investigate whether deferred verbal imitation also occurs this early, and to examine more closely the relationship between these types of imitation and language development. The methodological procedures developed for testing the imitation of actions, and recently adapted for testing the imitation of intonation contours and isolated phonetic units (Kuhl & Meltzoff, 1988), may be useful in organizing such research.

2.6.2 Deferred Imitation and Piagetian Theory

Another set of implications of the new data on deferred imitation concerns Piagetian theory about the emergence of language and its relation to cognitive developments. According to the standard account, there is a global psychological shift at approximately 18 months of age. Infants are supposed to move from a purely enactive or sensorimotor organization to using symbolic representations at this point. According to this account, the mental activity of pre-18-month-old children consists of their immediate perceptions of objects and the schemes they have developed for acting on them. Infants cannot represent an object if they have not acted on it or do not currently perceive it. The shift to a symbolic form of representation is supposed to be reflected in a variety of cognitive abilities emerging at around 18 months of age, including solving complex object-permanence tasks, using insight to solve means–ends tasks, productive language, symbolic play, and deferred imitation.

Deferred imitation is, however, rather different from the other abilities that are supposed to emerge in this period; in particular, it is different from symbolic play and language. For Piaget, symbolic play and especially language are consequences rather than causes of the shift to symbolic representation. The new type of representation allows children to develop these kinds of play and communication. Deferred imitation, however, is not a consequence but rather a contributing case of the shift. For Piaget, deferred imitation is a mechanism by which children could move from a purely sensorimotor intelligence (in which their mental schemes mirror their perceptions and actions) to a more internally driven, symbolic type of representation. In deferred imitation, what begins as a perceptual/action response to a stimulus comes to be under the control of the child. Deferred imitation is a critical transitional step in internalizing the external world.

Piaget's theoretical insight that deferred imitation might be a means for internalizing and acting on information, particularly information about how other humans behave, is a valuable and important one. However, the new findings on deferred imitation alter the implications of this insight. Rather than being a relatively late development, deferred imitation appears to be in place by 9 months of age or earlier. One response to these new data might be to try to reinterpret them to fit traditional theory. We might, for example, want to argue that 9-month-old deferred imitation does not require representation, whereas 18-month-old deferred imitation does.

Another option, and the one we will pursue here, is to liberate oneself from the details of Piaget's stage-developmental timetable, but to adhere to his dual proposals that (1) imitation informs us about the infant's representational abilities, and (2) the initial nonverbal representational system will subsequently interact with language learning. When taken at this abstract level, Piaget's theory might still provide a beacon for understanding aspects of language learning, even if the particulars of his theory need to be revised. In our view, one needs to consider certain unexpectedly powerful representational capacities as already in place in early infancy and now reexamine the question of how this nonverbal representational competence interacts with language learning (cf. K. Nelson, 1985; K. E. Nelson, in press).

In particular, we will argue here that the notion of a global Stage 6 change in all these areas is empirically mistaken. Some key elements of the hypothesized shift, namely, the emergence of deferred imitation and the ability to use words symbolically, emerge at a much earlier age than commonly assumed. Other elements of this shift, however, such as the ability to use deduction and invention to solve object-permanence and means–ends tasks, do emerge at about 18 months; they accompany other changes in language and may also accompany other changes in imitative capacities. This particular psychological mixture is not predicted by any existing theory of development. But, now that the data suggest this state of affairs, it becomes especially important to examine how we got here and what it might mean.

In concordance with the findings of early deferred imitation, there are also studies suggesting that the capacity for productive language use may also be in place at a much earlier age than Piaget supposed. Investigators have reported that children use words (or elements of sign language) well before they show the ability for Stage 6 object-permanence (Bates et al., 1979; Dihoff & Chapman, 1977; Gopnik, 1988; Gopnik & Meltzoff 1985; K. E. Nelson & Bonvillian, 1978;

Tomasello & Farrar, 1984). Similarly, it has been found that children use words productively before they show evidence of Stage 6 means–ends understanding (Gopnik, 1988; Gopnik & Meltzoff, 1987a).

Moreover, our own experiments have established that these early words do not simply include immediate imitations of adult forms, nor are they limited to narrow or event-bound word uses. In recent work (Gopnik, 1988; Gopnik & Meltzoff, 1987a) we analyzed the language of five children before they developed Stage 6 cognitive abilities. These children received object-permanence and means–ends tasks at 3-week intervals, and their parents filled out a questionnaire about their use of early words, which included detailed information about the contexts of use. Children were only counted as having acquired a word if it was used spontaneously in three different appropriate contexts, eliminating immediate imitations and event-bound uses of words. Using this criterion, all five children used words before they showed any signs of the Stage 6 cognitive skills. These words were fully spontaneous, productive, and decontextualized, although as we will see below, they were used in ways that were rather different from later words.

Evidently, some initial ability to use words productively emerges much earlier than Stage 6.[2] In fact, these results fit rather nicely with the recent discoveries concerning deferred imitation, because, as argued previously, Piaget was probably right in thinking that the productive use of a word from a particular language requires some kind of deferred imitation ability. It would have been extremely puzzling if 1-year-olds could spontaneously produce language and yet did not succeed on any laboratory test of deferred imitation.

2.7 On Characterizing the Cognitive-Linguistic Transition at 18 Months of Age: The Shift From *Empirical Representations* to *Hypothetical Representations*

We are still left with something of a paradox. Deferred imitation and aspects of language emerge far earlier than 18 months of age. Yet the supposedly related cognitive activities of complex object-permanence understanding and complex

---

[2]The cognitive abilities we are referring to as "Stage 6" are certain high-level object-permanence and means–ends achievements that seem to be acquired at about 18 months, on average, just as Piaget predicted. The relevant Stage 6 object-permanence task is a "serial invisible displacement." In this task the experimenter hides an object in his or her hand and then moves this hidden object under a series of three cloths, surreptitiously dropping off the object at one of them. Because infants have no perceptual evidence as to where the object is (they never actually saw it dropped off), they must look in the last place they saw the object (the hand) and then deduce that because the object is not there, but continues to exist somewhere, it must be in one of the places the hand traveled along its trajectory. In other words, the object must be under one of the cloths, if it is not in the hand. Children younger than 18 months old typically look in the hand and then are stumped. When they do not find the object where they saw it disappear (the hand), they cannot deduce where it must therefore be. The relevant Stage 6 means–ends task are the tasks described in Piaget (1962) and Užgiris and Hunt (1975) as the "stick," "necklace," and "ring" tasks.

means–ends skills seem to emerge, on average, at the age of 15 to 21 months (Gopnik & Meltzoff, 1984, 1986a; Harris, 1987; Užgiris, 1973; Užgiris & Hunt, 1975). Moreover, other significant cognitive achievements, such as high-level categorization skills, also emerge at about 18 months old (Gopnik & Meltzoff, 1987b; Sugarman, 1983). Thus the paradox: There does seem to be a fundamental reorganization in the psychology of the child at approximately 18 months of age, but at least two of the linchpins of the orthodox Stage 6 — deferred imitation and the ability to use language productively — are possible much earlier than this.

We propose that there is a shift in the relationship between language and cognition in the middle of the second year of life, but this shift does *not* involve the acquisition of the traditional symbolic function in the sense of the global Stage 6 shift. In fact, something like a capacity for symbolic representation must be present far before the child is 18 months old in order to account for the much earlier emergence of deferred imitation and productive word use that has been observed. We believe, however, that there is a developmental change in the *nature of the representations* that children have at approximately 18 months of age.

We think the essence of the new development is the ability to consider a number of hypothetical or possible actions or experiences that have not been directly perceived. For example, in the Stage 6 object-permanence tasks that are first solved at about 18 months of age (serial invisible displacements, see footnote 2), children not only need to figure out that the object continues to exist when it is visually absent (this can be accomplished at earlier ages, when children solve easier hiding tasks); they also need to *hypothesize* the existence of the object at a brand-new location in which they have never before seen it hidden. Given the structure of the "serial invisible" hiding transformation (the Stage 6 task), infants must deduce that an object exists in a novel place even though they have no perceptual evidence to that effect — that is what makes the 18-month-olds' performance different from that of younger children.

Similarly, in the Stage 6 means–ends tasks involving "insight," children must not only be able to represent past actions on an object, but must also be able to hypothesize about the effects of new actions before they are performed — to run through the consequences of their actions before acting, rather than after acting (hence, the use of insight instead of overt trial and error solutions to novel problems).

We suggest that these 18-month-old abilities demand more than the kind of representation that is involved in deferred imitation. Deferred nonverbal imitation involves the retention and re-creation of an empirical reality that was previously perceived. It involves representation and construction (it may not be an entirely faithful reproduction), but relies on what we would call an *empirical representation*, in the sense that the internal description concerns an actual state of affairs that was encountered in the real world. The content of the representations of 18-month-old infants, however, can also be about something else. It involves the ability to construct what we call *hypothetical representations*, the ability to construct novel representations of objects/events that have never before been experienced and for which there is no purely perceptual evidence. By 18 months of age, the average child can represent a possible state of affairs in addition to an empirically experienced one.

2.7.1 Representation and Language at 18 Months

These psychological developments have implications for the child's language. Although children may produce words well before 18 months, there are differences in the kinds of words they begin to produce and the way they use them in the middle of the second year. In the language studies noted earlier, we found that two kinds of words emerged in the pre–Stage 6[3] period, well before 18 months. The first type, "social words," included many words with relational forms such as *no* and *more* as well as forms like *bye-bye* and *hereyare* (Gopnik, 1988; Gopnik & Meltzoff, 1985). These words were used productively and in a decontextualized way, but the important constraint on the usage was that they were always used to influence or to respond to the actions of another person. The second type of word to emerge in this period were a few early names, particularly words for salient or significant objects such as *dog* or *ball*. Again these words were used productively; one child, for example, used *ball* in classical fashion to refer to all round objects (cf. Huttenlocher & Smiley, 1987).

In our research these social words and early names were among the very first words to emerge and often appeared before 15 months of age. Others (Carter, 1975; K. Nelson, 1981, 1985; K. E. Nelson, 1982; K. E. Nelson, Denninger, Bonvillian, Kaplan, & Baker, 1984) have also reported the early emergence of "expressive" or "social-personal" language, particularly in some children. The new information from our work was that such uses of words occurred before Stage 6 object-permanence and means–ends skills were acquired, sometimes as many as 3 months before (Gopnik & Meltzoff, 1985, 1987a). In short, the emergence of these words clearly are not concurrent with or part of a general Stage 6 change at 18 months of age.

These early social words and names require some representational ability. The child must be able to compare the present context or situation to a mentally represented past situation, note the similarity between the two contexts, and access a mentally represented lexical item that applies to both the present and past context. These linguistic abilities require more than a simple "sensorimotor" level of psychological organization. This is compatible with the deferred-imitation studies, which showed that some sort of representational skills that go beyond simple sensorimotor habits are in place at least by 9 months. However, it is striking to us that these early uses of social words and early names do not seem

---

[3]Following the logic in footnote 2, we here mean by "pre–Stage 6" a child who has not yet solved the complex object-permanence tasks (serial invisible displacements) or the complex means–ends tasks (the stick, necklace, rings).

to require the higher-level ability for *hypothetical representations*. Both these types of language simply involve comparisons between present and past experiences — they do not require an ability to consider *possible* new experiences, nor do they require an ability to compare possible and actual experiences.

These early word uses are in contrast to other uses of words that emerge later in the one-word stage, at about 18 months or later. These later words also have relational forms (in fact, rather confusingly they often have the same forms as the early social words). However, after children develop Stage 6 object-permanence and means–ends abilities, these old words (such as *no*, *more*, and *there*) are used in a radically different way (Gopnik & Meltzoff, 1985), and contemporaneously with this shift in use, other new words, such as *gone*, begin to emerge. More specifically, at about 18 months of age and contemporaneously with solving Stage 6 object-permanence and means–ends problems, children now begin to use all these words to encode contrasts between possible and actual events. For example, children begin to use words like *there* and *uh-oh* to encode success and failure (Gopnik & Meltzoff, 1986a), and in doing so the children contrast an intended state, a state they want to bring about, and an actual state. Similarly, words like *gone* begin to encode a contrast between what the child actually perceives and what the child might perceive (e.g., the child might say "gone" when seeing an empty slot in a novel object, indicating that something that has never been seen *should* be in this place [Gopnik & Meltzoff, 1986b]). It can be argued that the concepts that are encoded by these "cognitive-relational" words require an ability to construct and consider hypothetical representations, and that they are similar to the concepts that underlie deduction and invention (Gopnik, 1982, 1984).

In sum, our empirical work has shown that these cognitive-relational words emerge synchronously with the first signs of Stage 6 object-permanence and means–ends abilities (cf. Tomasello & Farrar, 1984, 1986). Moreover, our longitudinal studies showed that these cognitive-relational uses of words emerged after earlier social uses of words and names (Gopnik, 1988; Gopnik & Meltzoff, 1985). Finally, the empirical work has also shown that, although there are individual differences in early cognitive and linguistic development (Gopnik & Meltzoff, 1986a, 1987b; Nelson, 1987, in press), within individual children there is uniformly a close and specific relation between particular Stage 6 cognitive achievements (ones involving hypothetical representations) and particular semantic developments (the new uses of relational words). This is consistent with the proposal made here that a new kind of representation develops in late infancy.

2.7.2 Representation, Imitation, and Symbolic Play at 18 Months

Other changes in imitative behavior also reflect this psychological shift from empirical to hypothetical representation. True symbolic or pretend play, like invention and deduction, seems to emerge at about 18 months of age (Bretherton, 1984; Fenson, 1984; Leslie, 1987, 1988; Lézine, 1973; McCune-Nicolich, 1981; Nicolich, 1977; Sinclair, 1970; Watson & Fischer, 1977). Many instances of symbolic play seem to involve a kind of deferred imitation. In fact, this raises methodological problems because some early instance of purportedly symbolic play may simply be deferred imitations and little more. When, for example, a child "talks" on a toy telephone, or brushes her own hair or a doll's with a toy brush, it is not clear that the child recognizes the inappropriateness of the object and is *pretending*. The child may simply be performing, from his or her own point of view, a faithful deferred imitation with an acceptable object and not be pretending at all. Such activity may simply be a case of deferred imitation, with an ability to categorize the original object and the play one as the same thing; or, even more primitively, perhaps an inability to differentiate the original and play object.

However, in other instances it is clear that the child is both performing a deferred imitation and is also genuinely pretending. Zoe, the 2-year-old daughter of a musician and academic of our acquaintance, used a pencil as a flute, holding it sideways and laughing as she made noise with it; she also was observed to say "mommy computer" as she smiled and tapped out a pattern on the dining room table. There are two relevant points here. First, both these actions (playing the flute and using the computer) are not part of the child's own routine action scripts (in fact, both the flute and computer are forbidden objects), and thus these actions are both good instances of deferred imitation. Second, both the pencil and the table are objects that are very different from the real objects, and the child shows no signs of confusing the two types of objects. Indeed, Zoe laughs, smiles, looks slyly at her parents, and gives all the affective indications that go along with genuinely pretending as she performs these actions.

These imitative behaviors, unlike the earlier deferred imitations, require a capacity for hypothetical representations. Just as deferred imitation requires an ability to represent a past experience and compare it with a present experience, so imitation in these instances of pretend play requires an ability to consider a possible representation of an object that contrasts with the actual present and past experiences of the object itself. In such instances of symbolic play, deferred imitation serves a new function. Not only does it allow the child to access a past representation of an object, it also allows the child to treat that representation as a possibility, even when it contrasts with the child's present experience (see also Leslie, 1987, 1988; Forguson & Gopnik, 1988, for related arguments).

We thus propose, contra the nativists, that there is a significant difference between the 9-month-old's and the 18-month-old's cognitive structures. However, contra Piaget, this difference does not involve the initial emergence of an ability to represent and act on absent objects/events without currently seeing or acting on them. We postulate that this ability is present well within the first year of life, and is reflected both in children's early linguistic behavior and in their ability to produce deferred nonverbal imitation. In our view, the 18-month-old shift in language, thought, and imitation consists of a difference in the type of representation that is available. In the linguistic area, words that encode abstract relationships between the child and the world and that are used in a regulatory problem-solving way systematically begin to emerge after the earlier, more social words (Gopnik & Meltzoff, 1985). Moreover, they emerge in close connection with complex object-permanence and means–ends abilities (Gopnik & Meltzoff, 1987a). Finally, the emergence of deferred imitation in the context of symbolic play may also reflect this deeper underlying psychological shift.

2.8 Summary and Conclusion

We suggested three ways in which the recent investigations of nonverbal deferred imitation are relevant to representational and language development. First, such studies raise important questions about the ontogenesis of deferred verbal imitation, a process that is central to language learning. The studies suggest that some of the cognitive prerequisites for such behavior may be in place as early as 9 months of age. Second, these studies suggest a reworking of the Piagetian notion of a global Stage 6 cognitive shift that encompasses the emergence of object-permanence, means–ends abilities, deferred imitation, and language. Although the hypothesized changes in object-permanence and means–ends behaviors, as well as significant changes in categorization skills, do seem to take place at about 18 months of age, the onset of deferred imitation and productive language use do not seem to be part of this global shift, for they occur earlier. Third, we believe that this work on infants' imitative competence lays the foundation for constructing an alternative to the Piagetian thesis — one that involves a surprisingly rich primary representational system (*empirical representations*) and a later shift to a higher order, secondary representational system (*hypothetical representations*). Although the empirical representations necessary for deferred imitation and the social uses of one-word speech (or signs) are in place by 9 months of age, the content of these representations is rather different from the hypothetical representations that are involved in the linguistic, cognitive, and imitative behavior of the average 18-month-old.

Acknowledgments. We acknowledge the support of grants from the MacArthur Foundation and NICHD (HD-22514) to A.N.M. and the SSHRC (437-82-0054) and NSERC (3-643-757-40) to A.G. We also thank C. Harris and G. Ewing for help on varied aspects of this research.

References

Abravanel, E., Levan-Goldschmidt, E., & Stevenson, M.B. (1976). Action imitation: The early phase of infancy. *Child Development, 47,* 1032–1044.
Abravanel, E., & Sigafoos, A.D. (1984). Exploring the presence of imitation during early infancy. *Child Development, 55,* 381–392.

Anisfeld, M. (1984). *Language development from birth to three*. Hillsdale, NJ: Erlbaum.

Baker, N., & Nelson, K.E. (1984). Recasting and related conversational techniques for triggering syntactic advances by young children. *First Language*, *5*, 3–22.

Barnes, S., Gutfreund, M., Satterly, D., & Wells, G. (1983). Characteristics of adult speech which predict children's language development. *Journal of Child Language*, *10*, 65–84.

Bates, E. (1976). *Language and context: The acquisition of pragmatics*. New York: Academic Press.

Bates, E., Benigni, L., Bretherton, I., Camaioni, L., & Volterra, V. (1979). *The emergence of symbols: Cognition-communication in infancy*. New York: Academic Press.

Bloom, L. (1973). *One word at a time: The use of single word utterances before syntax*. The Hague: Mouton.

Bloom, L., & Capatides, J.B. (1987). Expression of affect and the emergence of language. *Child Development*, *58*, 1513–1522.

Bloom, L., Hood, L., & Lightbown, P. (1974). Imitation in language development: If, when, and why. *Cognitive Psychology*, *6*, 380–420.

Bonvillian, J.D., Orlansky, M.D., & Novack, L.L. (1983). Developmental milestones: Sign language acquisition and motor development. *Child Development*, *54*, 1435–1445.

Bower, T.G.R. (1982). *Development in infancy* (2nd ed.). San Francisco: W.H. Freeman.

Brazelton, T.B., & Tronick, E. (1980). Preverbal communication between mothers and infants. In D.R. Olson (Ed.), *The social foundations of language and thought* (pp. 299–315). New York: Norton.

Bretherton, I. (1984). *Symbolic play*. New York: Academic Press.

Bruner, J.S. (1975a). From communication to language – A psychological perspective. *Cognition*, *3*, 255–287.

Bruner, J.S. (1975b). The ontogenesis of speech acts. *Journal of Child Language*, *2*, 1–19.

Bruner, J.S. (1983). *Child's talk: Learning to use language*. New York: Norton.

Carter, A.L. (1975). The transformation of sensorimotor morphemes into words. *Papers and Reports on Child Language Development*, *11*, 31–48.

Clark, H.H., & Clark, E.V. (1977). *Psychology and language*. New York: Harcourt Brace Jovanovich.

Cross, T.G. (1977). Mothers' speech adjustments: The contribution of selected child listener variables. In C.E. Snow & C.A. Ferguson (Eds.), *Talking to children* (pp. 151–188). Cambridge: Cambridge University Press.

Dihoff, A., & Chapman, R. (1977). First words: Their origins in action. *Papers and Reports on Child Language Development*, *13*, 1–7.

Ervin, S.M. (1964). Imitation and structural change in children's language. In E.H. Lenneberg (Ed.), *New directions in the study of language* (pp. 163–189). Cambridge, MA: MIT Press.

Fenson, L. (1984). Development trends for action and speech in pretend play. In I. Bretherton (Ed.), *Symbolic play* (pp. 249–270). New York: Academic Press.

Field, T.M., Woodson, R., Greenberg, R., & Cohen, D. (1982). Discrimination and imitation of facial expressions by neonates. *Science*, *218*, 179–181.

Flavell, J.H. (1985). *Cognitive development*, (2nd ed.). Englewood Cliffs, NJ: Prentice-Hall.

Folger, J.P., & Chapman, R.S. (1978). A pragmatic analysis of spontaneous imitations. *Journal of Child Language*, *5*, 25–38.

Fontaine, R. (1984). Imitative skills between birth and six months. *Infant Behavior and Development*, *7*, 323–333.

Forguson, L., & Gopnik, A. (1988). The ontogeny of commonsense. In J.W. Astington, P.L. Harris, & D.R. Olson (Eds.), *Developing theories of mind* (pp. 226–243). New York: Cambridge University Press.

Gleitman, H. (1986). *Psychology* (2nd ed.). New York: Norton.

Golinkoff, R.M. (1983). *The transition from prelinguistic to linguistic communication.* Hillsdale, NJ: Erlbaum.

Gopnik, A. (1982). Words and plans: Early language and the development of intelligent action. *Journal of Child Language, 9,* 303–318.

Gopnik, A. (1984). The acquisition of *gone* and the development of the object concept. *Journal of Child Language, 11,* 273–292.

Gopnik, A. (1988). Three types of early words: Social words, names, and cognitive-relational words and their relation to cognitive development. *First Language, 8,* 49–70.

Gopnik, A., & Meltzoff, A.N. (1984). Semantic and cognitive development in 15- to 21-month-old children. *Journal of Child Language, 11,* 495–513.

Gopnik, A., & Meltzoff, A.N. (1985). From people, to plans, to objects: Changes in the meaning of early words and their relation to cognitive development. *Journal of Pragmatics, 9,* 495–512.

Gopnik, A., & Meltzoff, A.N. (1986a). Relations between semantic and cognitive development in the one-word stage: The specificity hypothesis. *Child Development, 57,* 1040–1053.

Gopnik, A., & Meltzoff, A.N. (1986b). Words, plans, things and locations: Interactions between semantic and cognitive development in the one-word stage. In S.A. Kuczaj & M.D. Barrett (Eds.), *The development of word meaning* (pp. 199–223). New York: Springer-Verlag.

Gopnik, A., & Meltzoff, A.N. (1987a). Early semantic developments and their relationship to object permanence, means–ends understanding, and categorization. In K.E. Nelson & A. van Kleeck (Eds.), *Children's language* (Vol. 6, pp. 191–212). Hillsdale, NJ: Erlbaum.

Gopnik, A., & Meltzoff, A.N. (1987b). The development of categorization in the second year and its relation to other cognitive and linguistic developments. *Child Development, 58,* 1523–1531.

Harris, P.L. (1987). The development of search. In P. Salapatek & L. Cohen (Eds.), *Handbook of infant perception* (Vol. 2, pp. 155–207). New York: Academic Press.

Heimann, M., & Schaller, J. (1985). Imitative reactions among 14–21 day old infants. *Infant Mental Health Journal, 6,* 31–39.

Huttenlocher, J., & Smiley, P. (1987). Early word meanings: The case of object names. *Cognitive Psychology, 19,* 63–89.

Jacobson, S.W. (1979). Matching behavior in the young infant. *Child Development, 50,* 425–430.

Kaitz, M., Meschulach-Sarfaty, O., Auerbach, J., & Eidelman, A. (1988). A reexamination of newborn's ability to imitate facial expressions. *Developmental Psychology, 24,* 3–7.

Kuczaj, S.A. (1983). *Crib speech and language play.* New York: Springer-Verlag.

Kuczaj, S.A. (1987). Deferred imitation and the acquisition of novel lexical items. *First Language, 7,* 177–182.

Kuhl, P.K., & Meltzoff, A.N. (1982). The bimodal perception of speech in infancy. *Science, 218,* 1138–1141.

Kuhl, P.K., & Meltzoff, A.N. (1984). The intermodal representation of speech in infants. *Infant Behavior and Development, 7,* 361–381.

Kuhl, P.K., & Meltzoff, A.N. (1988). Speech as an intermodal object of perception. In A. Yonas (Ed.), *Perceptual development in infancy: Minnesota symposia on child psychology* (Vol. 20, pp. 235–266). Hillsdale, NJ: Erlbaum.

Leslie, A.M. (1987). Pretense and representation in infancy: The origins of "theory of mind." *Psychological Review, 94*, 412–426.

Leslie, A.M. (1988). Some implications of pretense for mechanisms underlying the child's theory of mind. In J.W. Astington, P.L. Harris, & D.R. Olson (Eds.), *Developing theories of mind* (pp. 19–46). New York: Cambridge University Press.

Lézine, I. (1973). The transition from sensorimotor to earliest symbolic function in early development. In J.I. Nurnberger (Ed.), *Biological and environmental determinants of early development* (pp. 221–232). Baltimore: Williams & Wilkins.

Masur, E.F., & Ritz, E.G. (1984). Patterns of gestural, vocal, and verbal imitation performance in infancy. *Merrill-Palmer Quarterly, 30*, 369–392.

McCall, R.B., Parke, R.D., & Kavanaugh, R.D. (1977). Imitation of live and televised models by children one to three years of age. *Monographs of the Society for Research in Child Development, 42*(5, Serial No. 173).

McCune-Nicolich, L. (1981). Toward symbolic functioning: Structure of early pretend games and potential parallels with language. *Child Development, 52*, 785–797.

Mehrabian, A., & Williams, M. (1971). Piagetian measures of cognitive development for children up to age two. *Journal of Psycholinguistic Research, 1*, 113–126.

Meltzoff, A.N. (1981). Imitation, intermodal coordination, and representation in early infancy. In G. Butterworth (Ed.), *Infancy and epistemology* (pp. 85–114). Brighton, England: Harvester Press.

Meltzoff, A.N. (1985a). Immediate and deferred imitation in fourteen- and twenty-four-month-old infants. *Child Development, 56*, 62–72.

Meltzoff, A.N. (1985b). The roots of social and cognitive development: Models of man's original nature. In T.M. Field & N.A. Fox (Eds.), *Social perception in infants* (pp. 1–30). Norwood, NJ: Ablex.

Meltzoff, A.N. (1988a). Infant imitation and memory: Nine-month-olds in immediate and deferred tests. *Child Development, 59*, 217–225.

Meltzoff, A.N. (1988b). Infant imitation after a 1-week delay: Long-term memory for novel acts and multiple stimuli. *Developmental Psychology, 24*, 470–476.

Meltzoff, A.N. (1988c). Imitation of televised models by infants. *Child Development, 59*, 1221–1229.

Meltzoff, A.N., & Kuhl, P.K. (1989). Infants' perception of faces and speech sounds: Challenges to developmental theory. In P. Zelazo & R. Barr (Eds.), *Challenges to developmental paradigms*. Hillsdale, NJ: Erlbaum.

Meltzoff, A.N., & Moore, M.K. (1977). Imitation of facial and manual gestures by human neonates. *Science, 198*, 75–78.

Meltzoff, A.N., & Moore, M.K. (1983a). Newborn infants imitate adult facial gestures. *Child Development, 54*, 702–709.

Meltzoff, A.N., & Moore, M.K. (1983b). The origins of imitation in infancy: Paradigm, phenomena, and theories. In L.P. Lipsitt (Ed.), *Advances in infancy research* (Vol. 2, pp. 265–301). Norwood, NJ: Ablex.

Meltzoff, A.N., & Moore, M.K. (1985). Cognitive foundations and social functions of imitation and intermodal representation in infancy. In J. Mehler & R. Fox (Eds.), *Neonate cognition: Beyond the blooming, buzzing confusion* (pp. 139–156). Hillsdale, NJ: Erlbaum.

Moerk, E.L. (1977). Processes and products of imitation: Additional evidence that imitation is progressive. *Journal of Psycholinguistic Research, 6,* 187–202.

Moerk, E.L., & Moerk, C. (1979). Quotations, imitations, and generalizations: Factual and methodological analyses. *International Journal of Behavioral Development, 2,* 43–72.

Moore, M.K., & Meltzoff, A.N. (1978). Object permanence, imitation, and language development in infancy: Toward a neo-Piagetian perspective on communicative and cognitive development. In F.D. Minifie & L.L. Lloyd (Eds.), *Communicative and cognitive abilities – Early behavioral assessment* (pp. 151–184). Baltimore, MD: University Park Press.

Nelson, K. (1981). Individual differences in language development: Implications for development and language. *Developmental Psychology, 17,* 170–187.

Nelson, K. (1985). *Making sense: The acquisition of shared meaning.* New York: Academic Press.

Nelson, K.E. (1980). Theories of the child's acquisition of syntax: A look at rare events and at necessary, catalytic, and irrelevant components of mother–child conversation. *Annuals of the New York Academy of Sciences, 345,* 45–67.

Nelson, K.E. (1982). Experimental gambits in the service of language acquisition theory: From the Fiffin Project to operation input swap. In S.A. Kuczaj (Ed.), *Language development: Syntax and semantics* (pp. 159–199). Hillsdale, NJ: Erlbaum.

Nelson, K.E. (1987). Some observations from the perspective of the rare event cognitive comparison theory of language acquisition. In K.E. Nelson & A. van Kleeck (Eds.), *Children's language* (Vol. 6, pp. 289–331). Hillsdale, NJ: Erlbaum.

Nelson, K.E. (in press). Strategies for first language teaching. In R. Schiefelbusch & M. Rice (Eds.), *The teachability of language.* Baltimore, MD: Paul H. Brookes.

Nelson, K.E., & Bonvillian, J.D. (1978). Early language development: Conceptual growth and related processes between 2 and 4½ years of age. In K.E. Nelson (Ed.), *Children's language* (Vol. 1, pp. 467–556). New York: Gardner Press.

Nelson, K.E., Denninger, M.S., Bonvillian, J.D., Kaplan, B.J., & Baker, N.D. (1984). Maternal input adjustments and non-adjustments as related to children's linguistic advances and to language acquisition theories. In A.D. Pellegrini & T.D. Yawkey (Eds.), *The development of oral and written languages in social contexts* (pp. 31–56). Norwood, NJ: Ablex.

Newport, E.L., Gleitman, H., & Gleitman, L.R. (1977). Mother, I'd rather do it myself: Some effects and non-effects of maternal speech style. In C.E. Snow & C.A. Ferguson (Eds.), *Talking to children* (pp. 109–149). New York: Cambridge University Press.

Nicolich, L.M. (1977). Beyond sensorimotor intelligence: Assessment of symbolic maturity through analysis of pretend play. *Merrill-Palmer Quarterly, 23,* 89–99.

Papousek, M., & Papousek, H. (1981). Musical elements in infants' vocalization: Their significance for communication, cognition, and creativity. In L.P. Lipsitt & C.K. Rovee-Collier (Eds.), *Advances in infancy research* (Vol. 1, pp. 163–224). Norwood, NJ: Ablex.

Piaget, J. (1952). *The origins of intelligence in children.* New York: Norton.

Piaget, J. (1962). *Play, dreams and imitation in childhood.* New York: Norton.

Piattelli-Palmarini, M. (1980). *Language and learning: The debate between Jean Piaget and Noam Chomsky.* Cambridge, MA: Harvard University Press.

Ramer, A. (1976). The function of imitation in child language. *Journal of Speech and Hearing Research, 19,* 700–717.

Rodgon, M.M., & Kurdek, L.A. (1977). Vocal and gestural imitation in 8-, 14-, and 20-month-old children. *Journal of Genetic Psychology, 131*, 115–123.

Ryan, J. (1973). Interpretation and imitation in early language development. In R.A. Hinde & J. Stevenson-Hinde (Eds.), *Constraints on learning* (pp. 427–443). London: Academic Press.

Sinclair, H. (1970). The transition from sensory-motor behaviour to symbolic activity. *Interchange, 1*, 119–126.

Smolak, L. (1986). *Infancy*. Englewood Cliffs, NJ: Prentice-Hall.

Snow, C.E. (1981). The uses of imitation. *Journal of Child Langauge, 8*, 205–212.

Snow, C.E. (1983). Saying it again: The role of expanded and deferred imitations in language acquisition. In K.E. Nelson (Ed.), *Children's language* (Vol. 4, pp. 29–58). New York: Gardner Press.

Stella-Prorok, E.M. (1983). Mother–child language in the natural environment. In K.E. Nelson (Ed.), *Children's language* (Vol. 4, pp. 187–230). Hillsdale, NJ: Erlbaum.

Stern, D.N. (1985). *The interpersonal world of the infant*. New York: Basic Books.

Studdert-Kennedy, M. (1986). Development of the speech perceptuomotor system. In B. Lindblom & R. Zetterström (Eds.), *Precursors of early speech* (pp. 205–217). New York: Stockton.

Sugarman, S. (1983). *Children's early thought: Development in classification*. Cambridge: Cambridge University Press.

Tomasello, M., & Farrar, M.J. (1984). Cognitive bases of lexical development: Object permanence and relational words. *Journal of Child Language, 11*, 477–493.

Tomasello, M., & Farrar, M.J. (1986). Object permanence and relational words: A lexical training study. *Journal of Child Language, 13*, 495–505.

Trevarthen, C., & Marwick, H. (1986). Signs of motivation for speech in infants, and the nature of mother's support for development of language. In B. Lindblom & R. Zetterström (Eds.), *Precursors of early speech* (pp. 279–308). New York: Stockton.

Užgiris, I.Č. (1972). Patterns of vocal and gestural imitation in infants. In F.J. Mönks, W.W. Hartup, & J. deWit (Eds.), *Determinants of behavioral development* (pp. 467–471). New York: Academic Press.

Užgiris, I.Č. (1973). Patterns of cognitive development in infancy. *Merrill-Palmer Quarterly, 19*, 181–204.

Užgiris, I.Č. (1981). Two functions of imitation during infancy. *International Journal of Behavioral Development, 4*, 1–12.

Užgiris, I.Č. (1984). Imitation in infancy: Its interpersonal aspects. In M. Perlmutter (Ed.), *Minnesota symposia on child psychology* (Vol. 17, pp. 1–32). Hillsdale, NJ: Erlbaum.

Užgiris, I.Č., & Hunt, J.McV. (1975). *Assessment in infancy: Ordinal scales of psychological development*. Urbana: University of Illinois Press.

Vinter, A. (1986). The role of movement in eliciting early imitations. *Child Development, 57*, 66–71.

Watson, M.W., & Fischer, K.W. (1977). A developmental sequence of agent use in late infancy. *Child Development, 48*, 828–836.

Weir, R.H. (1962). *Language in the crib*. The Hague: Mouton.

CHAPTER 3

Individual and Dyadic Patterns of Imitation: Cognitive and Social Aspects

Elise Frank Masur

3.1 Introduction

Infants' imitation has been an important focus not only of language developmentalists, but also of researchers concerned with infants' cognitive (e.g., McCall, 1979; Piaget, 1962; Užgiris, 1981) and social (Baldwin, 1895; Pawlby, 1977; Užgiris, 1981, 1984) development. In fact, two competing views of the function of imitation in language development are derived from the contrasting cognitive and social approaches to imitation.

3.1.1 Nonverbal Imitation

From a cognitive perspective, Piaget (1962) regarded infants' imitation as one aspect of their overall intellectual development during the first 2 years of life. He charted qualitative changes in infants' imitative ability through his stages of sensorimotor thought from immediate matching of simple, familiar, visible or audible acts to deferred reproduction of complex and novel behaviors, including nonvisible ones they cannot see themselves perform, such as eye blinking (see Masur, 1988, for a detailed summary). A number of researchers following Piaget in considering imitation a reflection of cognitive functioning have employed infants' imitation performance on fixed batteries of items under controlled conditions to measure their cognitive developmental levels (e.g., Užgiris & Hunt, 1975). Experimental studies have reported a change in imitation performance that parallels a transition in cognitive development (McCall, 1979; Piaget, 1962). Around the beginning of the second year of life, children begin to repeat not only simple, familiar, visible behaviors, but also some novel and nonvisible actions. In a study that Elsbeth Ritz and I conducted (Masur & Ritz, 1984), 42 first-born infants, ranging in age from 10 to 16 months, were presented by their mothers with a variety of familiar and novel communicative gestures, other actions with and without objects, vocalizations, and words for imitation. Our analyses revealed a major contrast between those children who repeated only familiar behaviors and those who reproduced novel behaviors, especially vocal or verbal ones, as well as many familiar acts.

Alternatively, rather than viewing imitation as an index of cognitive development, other researchers, including Užgiris (1981), have seen imitation as a process of behavioral acquisition. Imitation can function as a cognitive strategy for mastering novel or complex behaviors. As a mechanism for learning new behaviors, imitation serves as a means both for representing information and for re-presenting behaviors for further analysis.

Besides its cognitive functions, imitation has also been considered from a social perspective. Behavioral matching has been found to be a component of mother–infant social interactions, even from the first few months of life (Papousek & Papousek, 1977; Trevarthen, 1977; Užgiris, 1984). As an aspect of interpersonal interaction, imitation can express mutual understanding and shared involvement (Užgiris, 1981, 1984). Repeating the partner's action fills a turn in the interchange and is responsive to the other's contribution.

Whereas cognitive developmentalists emphasize children's ability to reproduce novel behaviors, researchers with a social focus concentrate on the achievement of a match between the partners regardless of the novelty or familiarity of the behaviors replicated. Infants' reproduction of familiar behaviors as well as their involvement in familiar routines and games further illustrate the social function of imitation performance. Moreover, researchers with such an interactional focus have examined mothers' as well as children's imitative behaviors, and in situations more naturalistic than those employed to assess infants' imitation from a cognitive perspective (Pawlby, 1977; Užgiris, 1984). However, most studies of mothers' and infants' matching in a social context so far have concentrated on behavior during the first year of life (Pawlby, 1977; Užgiris, 1984). Even during this early age period, substantial individual differences have been reported among dyads in their imitative tendencies and in the frequencies with which they engage in imitation during social interactions. The imitative interchanges of mothers and infants during the second year remain to be examined. Furthermore, the relationship between individual differences in mothers' and infants' frequencies of matching behavior in a social context and infants' cognitive abilities to imitate familiar and novel behaviors in an experimental situation has yet to be explored.

3.1.2 Language Imitation

Although the role of imitation in language acquisition has long been controversial (e.g., Clark, 1977; Ervin, 1964; Snow, 1981), imitation has aroused interest because it may answer investigators' search for an active process that is both responsive to the social environment and linked to cognitive development (see Bates, Bretherton, Beeghly-Smith, & McNew, 1982; Bloom, Hood, & Lightbown, 1974; Gelman, 1983; Shatz, 1984). In fact, the views of language researchers who grant imitation some role in communicative and language development can be considered within either the cognitive or social perspectives delineated above.

Paralleling cognitive approaches to imitation in general, language researchers with a cognitive perspective have focused on imitation alternately as a manifestation of a child's underlying development prerequisite to language acquisition or as a strategy for mastering new linguistic items or structures. The first point of view is represented by studies showing significant correlations between experimental imitative performance and early communicative production, including gestures and first words (Bates, Benigni, Bretherton, Camaioni, & Volterra, 1979; Bates, Bretherton, Snyder, Shore, & Volterra, 1980). For example, Bates et al. (1979) reported significant correlations between 11-month-olds' combined gestural and vocal experimental imitation scores on the Uzgiris–Hunt Scales and their production of communicative pointing gestures and referential words.

The strategic orientation is evident both in experimental studies of elicited verbal imitation (e.g., Corrigan & diPaul, 1982; Masur & Ritz, 1984) and in observational studies of children at the end of their second or beginning of their third years who are developing rudimentary syntax. They demonstrate that some children produce verbal imitations that are "progressive"; that is, their imitations contain lexical items or semantic, syntactic, or morphological constructions initially absent from, or more complex than, their spontaneous utterances, but subsequently incorporated into spontaneous productions (Bloom et al., 1974; Clark, 1977; Moerk & Moerk, 1979; Ramer, 1976; Snow, 1981).

These studies have also discovered marked differences between children in the proportions of their utterances that are imitations (e.g., Bloom et al., 1974; Ramer, 1976). However, the origins of these individual differences in strategic use of verbal imitation have not been systematically investigated. In addition, although these studies focus on the role of imitation in assisting young children's acquisition of new words and language structures, substantial proportions of children's reproductions contain familiar items and constructions (see Bloom et al., 1974). The function of such familiar imitation has not been considered by these cognitively oriented language developmentalists.

From a social standpoint, language imitation has been considered in terms of its roles in the conversational interaction (Kuczaj, 1982; Rees, 1975; Shatz, 1983; Stine & Bohannon, 1983). Imitation allows children with minimal linguistic skills to take a conversational turn and sustain the social exchange (Leonard, Schwartz, Folger, Newhoff, & Wilcox, 1979). Children may be most likely to repeat their partners' speech when they have no other adequate response available (Boskey & Nelson, cited in Shatz, 1983; Mayer & Valian, cited in Stine & Bohannon, 1983; Shipley, Smith, & Gleitman, 1969). Within a conversation, replication can serve as a means for acknowledging the speaker's utterance and/or continuing the discourse topic (Keenan, 1974; Rees, 1975; Shatz, 1983). Imitation also permits even young infants to participate in familiar routines and games,

(Masur, 1980, 1982). By imitating, says Rees (1975), children learn to "establish and maintain communication" (p. 347).

Language imitation studies with such a social orientation have frequently been interactional, examining maternal as well as child imitation within natural conversations. Like their general social-imitation counterparts, these studies have focused on the existence of a match without regard to the novelty or familiarity of verbalizations reproduced. Unlike the studies of general social imitation, however, they have investigated children at the end of the second year or older. Several researchers (Broome & Užgiris, 1985; Folger & Chapman, 1978; Kuczaj, 1983; Nelson, Baker, Denninger, Bonvillian, & Kaplan, 1985; Seitz & Stewart, 1975) have reported dramatic individual differences in imitation behavior and also significant positive correlations between maternal and child verbal imitation rates. In fact, Folger and Chapman (1978) attributed 2-year-olds' imitative tendencies to the influence of their mothers' speech styles, concluding that "an imitative child may be one whose parents imitate her" (p. 37). Because these studies investigated children at the end of the second and into the third year of life, it would be valuable to explore the origins of such dyadic associations. What are the characteristics of imitative interactions between mothers and their infants at the beginning of the second year when they are just beginning to communicate with conventional gestures and sounds?

In addition, although these imitation studies have concentrated exclusively on verbal imitation, it would be worthwhile to consider language imitation within a broader context and investigate whether the verbal imitation behavior of children and mothers is representative of their other imitation performance—gestural, vocal, and motoric: Do individuals demonstrate a general imitative or nonimitative pattern of performance across behavioral categories, or is imitation domain specific? The few studies that have investigated vocal/verbal and gestural/motoric imitation performance simultaneously have examined experimental rather than spontaneous matching (see Masur, 1988, and Masur & Ritz, 1984, for reviews). Although a number of researchers (e.g., McCall, Parke, & Kavanaugh, 1977; Rodgon & Kurdek, 1977) had failed to find significant correlations between vocal/verbal and gestural/motoric imitation in children younger than 20 months and Užgiris and Hunt (1975) reported no relationship ($r = .07$) between infants' performance on their gestural and vocal imitation scales, Masur and Ritz (1984) revealed relationships across these diverse behavioral domains when elicited imitation of familiar and novel items was analyzed separately. Whether similar cross-category consistency exists in spontaneous matching of motor, vocal, and verbal behaviors during natural mother–infant interactions remains to be determined (see also Snow, Chapter 4, this volume.)

Finally, another unanswered question involves the relationship between the cognitive and social aspects of imitation. Studies of verbal imitation from both the cognitive and social perspectives have found striking differences between children or dyads in imitativeness. Are children who participate frequently with their mothers in conversational imitative interchanges more likely to employ imitation as a language acquisition strategy? Are there correlations between mothers' and children's spontaneous verbal matching and children's elicited verbal imitation performance?

The cross-sectional analyses reported in this chapter were designed to address these questions by examining the vocal and motoric imitations of 10- to 16-month-old infants and their mothers during natural routine and play interactions. The patterns of communicative imitation uncovered in the children's and mothers' social interactions were then compared to the children's performance of vocal and verbal items in an elicited imitation task.

3.2 Method

3.2.1 Participants and Procedure

The analyses reported here are for 30 first-born infants and their mothers. The children were selected from a larger sample of 42 who had participated in a structured imitation task (Masur & Ritz, 1984) and in natural interactions with their mothers. The original sample consisted of equal numbers of girls and boys in five age groups: 10 to 11, 12, 13, 14, and 15 to 16 months old. The age range from 10 to 16 months was chosen to span the normative period from the emergence of communicative gestures to the acquisition of first words (Masur, 1983) and to bridge the cognitive transition from imitation of familiar behaviors only to reproduction of both familiar and novel acts (Masur & Ritz, 1984). The families, recruited for a study of infants' interactions with people and objects in their environment, were white, English speaking, and lower-middle to middle class.

Each dyad was videotaped in the home in two counterbalanced natural situations each lasting about 13 minutes, as the mother bathed the infant and during free play with the infant's own toys. No mention was made of imitation at the time of this session.

About a week later, the infants were visited again, and the mothers were instructed to present a fixed set of 21 behaviors for the children to imitate. The items included vocalizations (*ma-ma-ma*, *ba-ba-ba*, *eeee*, *zzzz*), words (*car*, *book*, *chalk*, *gnome*), conventional communicative gestures, comparable but arbitrary visible hand and arm actions, and some other actions. The novelty or familiarity of particular items for individual children was assessed by maternal reports.

For the present analyses, three girls and three boys were selected from each age group. The children were randomly chosen from those for whom complete videotapes of the natural interactions were available and whose experimental imitation performance could be classified into one of the three major patterns: imitation of familiar, but not novel, behaviors; reproduction of familiar acts and at least one novel vocalization or word; or replication of familiar acts, novel vocalizations and/or words, plus at least one novel visible action (Masur & Ritz,

1984). Masur & Ritz (1984) provide a complete description of the elicited vocal and motoric imitation performance of the original sample of 42 children. In this report, only the relation between the 30 infants' patterns of elicited imitation and their own and their mothers' spontaneous communicative matching is examined.

3.2.2 Transcription and Coding

Three research assistants identified and transcribed from the videotapes of the natural interactions all interactive episodes that included imitation by either the mother or the infant of the partner's discrete behaviors. The transcribers based their judgments of imitation on three criteria:

(1) *Attention*: The transcribers looked for evidence that the imitator saw or heard the model, including examining the imitator's direction of regard.
(2) *Contingency*: The imitator's behavior must have been evoked by the model's act rather than occurring spontaneously. Only those matching behaviors that occurred within 15 seconds of the model's performance were considered contingent; any multiround imitative interchange interrupted by a change of activity or by 15 seconds without matching was considered two separate episodes. The clearest cases of contingency involve instances where the imitator stops one activity to repeat a different action performed by the partner.
(3) *Quality of the imitation*: Only exact copies or close approximations of sounds and actions, but not smiling or other subtle facial expressions, were counted as imitation. For actions involving objects, the similarity of the behaviors (e.g., pushing a car and pushing a truck) rather than that of the objects (e.g., pushing a car and throwing a car) was considered.

Interobserver agreement in identifying imitation episodes was computed for six videotapes independently transcribed by two assistants working as a pair and a third assistant. Agreement, calculated as the number of episodes identified on both transcripts divided by the total number of different episodes identified, averaged 0.90. All disagreements were resolved through discussion.

For coding these data, only the first imitation in each episode was examined, and the imitator, infant or mother, was identified. The imitated behavior was then coded as belonging to one of the following five categories:

(1) *Vocalizations*: nonverbal sounds and laughter. The vocalizations were subsequently further divided into the following three categories, ranging from least to most language related:
    (a) *Miscellaneous vocalizations*: laughter and sounds not employed in speech, such as fake coughs and "the raspberries."
    (b) *Discrete vocalizations*: vowel sounds and consonant-vowel (CV) babbles.
    (c) *Conventional vocalizations*: conventional communicative sound patterns, including engine and animal noises and expressions such as *uh-oh* and *ka-boom*.

(2) *Words*: conventional words and phrases. Those word imitations that were exact and immediate were also tallied. Exact imitations excluded any matches that changed the order of the words in the modeled utterance or added any words other than exclamations or acknowledgments. Immediate imitations were matches of the partner's immediately preceding words with at most one word intervening.

(3) *Gestures*: conventional communicative hand, arm, or head motions, such as waving or nodding.

(4) *Actions without objects*: nongestural motor behaviors not involving an object, such as clapping or tongue protrusion.

(5) *Object-related actions*: nongestural motor behaviors involving an object, such as stacking blocks.

In rare cases when the imitator reproduced two different behaviors performed by the partner (e.g., pointing at a picture and labeling it), both imitations were coded. When the modeled act was of one category (e.g., clapping blocks together, an object-related action), but the matching behavior was approximate and would be classified into a different category (e.g., clapping hands, an action without an object), the imitation was coded according to the modeled behavior.

Agreement in coding the imitations between the pair of research assistants and the third assistant averaged 93%, with disagreements resolved through discussion. (More details of the procedures, transcription, and coding of the natural mother–infant interactions are provided in Masur's 1987 report of the imitative interchanges of 18 of these dyads.)

Each individual's number of first imitations of each kind during bath and play situations was adjusted to compensate for differences among dyads in the lengths of situation times and then summed across situations to yield an imitation score for each category of behavior during the entire observation session.

In the experimental imitation task, infants' best responses were coded from transcripts as exact or approximate imitation (combined for these analyses) or no imitation and later compared to the experimenter's notes of infants' performance made during the experimental session. Interobserver agreement equaled or exceeded 95% (see Masur & Ritz, 1984, for details.)

3.3 Results and Discussion

3.3.1 Mothers' and Infants' Spontaneous Imitation

Since the first goal was to characterize the naturally occurring imitative interchanges of these infants and their mothers, their imitation scores were analyzed by a 5 (Age Group) $\times$ 2 (Sex) $\times$ 2 (Partner, Infant vs. Mother) $\times$ 5 (Behavior Category) mixed analysis of variance with repeated measures on the last two factors. This analysis yielded a significant Age $\times$ Partner $\times$ Behavior Category interaction, $F(16, 80) = 1.80$, $p < .05$. However, inspection of the means

Table 3-1. Infants' and Mothers' Mean Spontaneous Imitative Interchanges

Participants	Behavior categories[a]					
	V	W	G	A	O	Total
Infants						
Younger	0.74	1.91	0.75	0.49	4.25	8.14
Older	1.40	2.75	1.18	0.44	3.26	9.03
M	1.07	2.33	0.96	0.46	3.76	8.58
Mothers						
Of younger	10.21	1.78	0.13	0.40	2.12	14.64
Of older	4.36	3.96	0.69	0.52	1.35	10.88
M	7.28	2.87	0.41	0.46	1.74	12.76

[a] V = vocalizations, W = words, G = gestures, A = actions without objects, and O = object-related actions.

revealed no easily interpretable pattern of infants' or mothers' repetitions of different kinds of behaviors across the age groups. Therefore, to attempt to provide a clearer picture of developmental trends, the analysis was redone with the two younger age groups, (infants < 13 months), combined and compared to the three combined older age groups (infants ≥ 13 months).

Table 3-1 shows that imitative interchanges were a frequent occurrence during these mother–infant interactions. Overall, mothers matched an average of 12.76 infant behaviors, and infants repeated their mothers' acts 8.58 times during the approximately 26-min sessions. However, there were marked individual differences in both partners' imitation: Mothers' scores ranged from 0 to 27.07, and infants' from 0 to 27.63. Despite the large amount of variation, the difference between mothers' and infants' matching behavior was statistically significant, $F(1, 26) = 7.30, p = .01$. In addition, a sex difference in performance favoring the girls (which had been found in other analyses involving participants contained in or by this sample [see Masur, 1987; Masur & Ritz, 1984]) approached significance, $F(1, 26) = 3.03, p = .09$.

The analysis also revealed a main effect of behavior category, $F(4, 104) = 12.76, p < .001$, and a Partner × Behavior Category interaction, $F(4, 104) = 26.18, p < .001$. As Table 3-1 demonstrates, infants most often imitated their mothers' object-related actions and words, whereas mothers frequently matched their children's vocalizations and words.

Furthermore, there was a significant three-way interaction of Age × Partner × Behavior Category, $F(4, 104) = 7.62, p < .001$, as well as the two-way interaction of Age × Behavior Category, $F(4, 104) = 3.43, p = .01$. Inspection of the means in Table 3-1 indicates that both infants' and mothers' reproductions of words and gestures increased with age while their repetitions of object-related actions declined. In addition, although infants' vocal matching rose somewhat across the two age groups, their mothers' imitation of vocalizations dropped sharply.

Table 3-2. Pearson Product-Moment (and Partial, Controlling for Age Group) Intercorrelations Among Categories of Imitation for Infants and Mothers

Participants	Behavior categories[a]			Age group
	W	G	O	
Infants				
V	$.34^b$ $(.32^b)$	.04 (.00)	.09 (.16)	$.28^d$
W		$.28^d$ $(.27^d)$	.16 (.19)	.10
G			−.15 (−.12)	.13
O				−.23
Mothers				
V	−.03 (.11)	−.23 (−.06)	$.26^d$ (.17)	$−.49^c$
W		$.42^c$ $(.36^b)$	−.16 (−.11)	$.24^d$
G			.10 (.21)	$.37^b$
O				$−.24^b$

[a] V = vocalizations, W = words, G = gestures, and O = object-related actions.
[b] $p < .05$.
[c] $p < .01$.
[d] $p \leq .10$.

Follow-up t-tests comparing the children's mean scores for each category by age revealed no significant differences. Thus, the variation among individual children in their spontaneous imitation of different kinds of behaviors was not systematically related to age. Similar follow-up t-tests for mothers' matching behavior showed that the decrease in the mothers' vocalizations and the increase in their gestures across age groups were significant, ts (28) = −2.99 and 2.08, ps < .01 and .05, respectively. However, the doubling with age in mothers' mean replication of their infants' words did not reach the .05 level of significance, t (28) = 1.34, p < .10, one-tailed, because of the considerable variability among mothers in their spontaneous verbal imitation during these natural routine and play interactions.

To investigate the question of consistency between infants' and mothers' verbal imitations and their other imitation performance, separate correlation matrices were computed for infants' and mothers' scores, with the exception of actions without objects, which were so infrequent (see Table 3-2). The only correlation to reach the 0.5 level of significance in this sample of infants was that between vocalizations and words, $r = .34$, $p < .04$, although the correlation between words and gestures approached significance, $r = .28$, $p < .07$. For mothers, because reproduction of some kinds of behaviors was age related, partial correlations, controlling for age group, were calculated. The only significant relation was between words and gestures, $r = .36$, $p < .03$. These findings suggest relationships only among communicative behaviors for both infants and mothers, rather than general imitative tendencies across unrelated vocal and motoric behavioral domains.

Table 3-3. Infants' and Mothers' Mean Vocal and Verbal Imitation Scores

Participants	Behavior categories[a]				
	MV	DV	CV	Words	Total
Infants					
Younger	0.28	0.19	0.27	1.91	2.65
Older	0.33	0.17	0.90	2.75	4.15
M	0.30	0.18	0.58	2.33	3.40
Mothers					
Of younger	2.18	7.45	0.58	1.78	11.99
Of older	0.97	1.90	1.49	3.96	8.32
M	1.58	4.68	1.04	2.87	10.16

[a] MV = miscellaneous vocalizations, DV = discrete vocalizations, and CV = conventional vocalizations.

3.3.2 Vocal and Verbal Imitation

Because the infants' and mothers' language-related imitation was of particular interest, their vocal and verbal reproductions were examined more closely. As mentioned previously, vocal reproductions were further categorized from least to most language related as miscellaneous nonlanguage vocalizations, discrete babbling vocalizations, and conventional vocalizations. Infants' and mothers' imitation scores for vocal and verbal behaviors were analyzed by a 2 (Age Group) × 2 (Sex) × 2 (Partner) × 4 (Behavior Category) mixed analysis of variance with repeated measures on the last two factors.

The analysis yielded a significant three-way interaction of Age × Partner × Vocal Behavior Category, $F(3,78) = 6.06$, $p = .001$, and all three component two-way interactions Age × Partner, $F(1, 26) = 4.95$, $p < .05$, Age × Behavior Category, $F(3, 78) = 4.60$, $p < .01$, and Partner × Behavior Category, $F(3, 78) = 7.21$, $p < .001$. Main effects for partner, $F(1, 26) = 30.14$, $p < .001$, and behavior category, $F(3, 78) = 4.74$, $p < .01$, were also significant.

Table 3-3 displays infants' and mothers' vocal and verbal imitation by age group and category. The classification of vocalizations further clarifies the general trends for infants' and mothers' vocal imitation presented in Table 3-1. It is apparent that any increase with age in infants' mean overall vocal imitation scores is entirely attributable to the older infants' greater reproduction of the communicative conventional vocalizations because infants of both ages rarely imitated miscellaneous or discrete vocalizations, behaviors unlikely to be frequently modeled. Because of the high variability in individual production, follow-up t-tests between younger and older infants' mean scores revealed no significant differences, although the increase with age in children's repetition of conventional vocalizations did approach significance, $t(28) = 1.48$, $p < .08$, one-tailed. Infants' scores for matching conventional vocalizations ranged from 0 to 1.58 in the younger group and from 0 to 5.29 in the older, whereas their scores for verbal imitation varied from 0 to 9.45 and from 0 to 18.84 in the two age groups, respectively.

Furthermore, the mothers' decrease in overall vocal replication across the age groups (see Table 3-1) actually represents a decline with age only in their repetition of the less language-related vocal behaviors, miscellaneous and discrete vocalizations, ts (28) $= -1.73$ and $-3.17, ps = .09$ and .004, respectively. The mothers' mean imitation of conventional vocalizations, as well as words, increased across the age groups, although the differences did not reach the .05 level of significance because of high variability, ts (28) $= 1.30$ and $1.34, ps \leq .10$, one-tailed, respectively. Mothers' scores for reproducing conventional vocalizations ranged from 0 to 2.28 to the younger infants and from 0 to 8.58 to the older infants, whereas their scores for matching infants' verbalizations varied from 0 to 7.83 and from 0 to 17.67 to the two age groups, respectively.

A qualitative examination of the verbal imitative episodes disclosed that virtually all ($M = 96\%$) of the children's imitations of their mothers' words were exact immediate reproductions, according to the criteria defined above. Of these, an average of 75% involved a reduction of the mothers' utterances, as in the following example:

(1) MOTHER.   Can you spin that ball?
    CHILD.   Ball.

The other 25% were exact copies without reduction, as in the following two examples:

(2) MOTHER.   Who's that? Blotch *(a cat)*.
    CHILD.   Otch?
(3) MOTHER.   All gone. All gone. All gone *(as water goes down the drain)*.
    CHILD.   Ah gah.

The few children's verbal imitations not classified as exact immediate had too many words intervening to meet the criterion of immediate. None failed because it involved the addition of words not contained in the model. An example follows:

(4) MOTHER.   Look at this ugly baby. Uh! Scare ya. Ah.
    CHILD.   Bay-bay.

On the other hand, only an average of 59% of the mothers' verbal repetitions were exact and immediate, as in the following:

(5) CHILD.   *(Picks up a small doll.)* Hi, baby!
    MOTHER.   Well, hi, baby!

Fully 41% involved maternal expansion of their children's productions:

(6) CHILD.   *(Looks at and splashes the water.)* Wa-a?
    MOTHER.   Yeah, that's water.

Notice the increasing expansions in the following example:

Table 3-4. Pearson Product-Moment (and Partial, Controlling for Age Group) Intercorrelations Among Infants' and Mothers' Vocal and Verbal Imitation Scores

| Group | Behavior categories[a] | | | |
	DV	CV	Words	Age
Infants				
Miscellaneous Vocalizations	−.13 (−.13)	−.14 (−.16)	−.04 (−.04)	.05
Discrete Vocalizations		−.17 (−.17)	−.16 (−.16)	−.02
Conventional Vocalizations			.43^c (.42^c)	.27^d
Words				.10
Mothers				
Miscellaneous Vocalizations	.11 (−.06)	−.15 (−.08)	−.16 (−.09)	−.31^b
Discrete Vocalizations		−.12 (.01)	−.10 (.03)	−.51^c
Conventional Vocalizations			.38^b (.34^b)	.24^d
Words				.24^d

[a] DV = discrete vocalizations, and CV = conventional vocalizations.
[b] $p < .05$.
[c] $p < .01$.
[d] $p \leq .10$.

(7) CHILD.   Dada. Dada.
    MOTHER.   Daddy bye-bye. Daddy go bye-bye, huh? Did daddy go bye-bye?

Five of the 21 mothers who replicated their children's words first produced exact immediate imitations and then followed those with expanded imitations. This combination characterized 60% of those 5 mothers' imitative episodes, as in the following example:

(8) CHILD.   Ball.
    MOTHER.   Ball. Ball's in the other room.

3.3.3 Individual and Dyadic Patterns of Vocal and Verbal Imitation

These findings indicate considerable diversity, not always age related, among children and their mothers in reproduction of communicative and other vocal behaviors. However, these results do not reveal whether infants or mothers who repeat more of the most languagelike vocalizations also reproduce more words. Nor do they indicate whether highly imitative children have highly imitative mothers.

To address the first question, intercorrelations were computed separately for infants' and mothers' vocal and verbal behaviors. Table 3-4 presents both the

Pearson and partial, controlling for age group, intercorrelations. Regardless of the significance of the correlation between imitation of total vocalizations and words reported above, for both infants and mothers only replications of conventional vocalizations and words were significantly related, partial $rs = .42$ and $.34$, $ps = .01$ and $.04$, respectively.

Thus, regardless of age, those infants and their mothers who matched more of their partners' conventional communicative sounds, but not other vocalizations, also imitated more words. This again indicates a communicative imitation pattern characterizing the natural social interactions of some infants and mothers. Such a relationship between conventional sounds and words might be expected for infants of this age because some have viewed conventional vocalizations as early nonreferential words (Bates et al., 1979). For succeeding analyses, then, these conventional sounds and words were combined.

The question of correspondence between infants' and mothers' communicative imitation behavior was considered next by examining the relation between infants' and mothers' production of conventional vocalizations plus words. The association was significant, $rs = .64$ and $.63$ for Pearson and partial correlations, respectively, $ps < .001$, demonstrating a relationship between partners' matching of conventional sounds and words even for mothers and young infants who are just beginning to communicate vocally.

3.3.4 Social and Cognitive Functions of Vocal and Verbal Imitation

Thus far these analyses have uncovered marked individual differences among mothers and infants, even infants of the same age, in their imitation of communicative vocal and verbal behaviors. There are also strong dyadic correspondences in imitation of communicative sounds and words; highly imitative mothers have highly imitative children during natural social interactions even at this age. But what, if any, relationship holds between infants' or mothers' social uses of communicative matching and children's employment of imitation as a cognitive strategy to acquire new language forms? We can approach an answer to this question by comparing the infants' and mothers' spontaneous vocal and verbal matching behavior with the infants' performance of familiar or novel behaviors in the elicited imitation session.

Examination of the children's experimental imitation (see Masur & Ritz, 1984) had revealed three distinct patterns of infants' performance across diverse behavior categories when the familiarity or novelty of particular items for individual children was taken into account. Some children repeated only familiar, but no novel, behaviors—gestures, actions, vocalizations, or words. Others reproduced at least one novel behavior as well as familiar ones. The infants who imitated novel behaviors could be further divided into those who matched novel vocalizations and/or words and those who replicated novel vocalizations and/or words plus at least one novel visible action. Children in the most advanced pattern group also imitated more familiar behaviors than those in either of the other two groups and more novel sounds and words than children in the second pattern group.

Table 3-5. Spontaneous Vocal Imitation by Three Groups of Infants and Their Mothers

	Behavior categories[a]			
Participants	MV	DV	CV plus words	Total
Pattern 1: No novel imitation				
Infants	0.30	0.27	1.43	2.00
Mothers	1.63	6.26	2.80	10.69
M	0.96	3.26	2.12	6.34
Pattern 2: Imitation of novel vocalizations and/or words				
Infants	0.31	0.21	1.90	2.43
Mothers	1.36	3.37	3.56	8.29
M	0.84	1.79	2.74	5.36
Pattern 3: Imitation of novel vocalizations and/or words and novel actions				
Infants	0.32	0.00	6.89	7.21
Mothers	1.35	2.20	7.06	10.61
M	0.84	1.10	6.98	8.91

[a] MV = miscellaneous vocalizations, DV = discrete vocalizations, and CV = conventional vocalizations.

Thus, the following three groups were obtained: (1) Eleven of the 30 infants considered here displayed the first pattern of performance and matched familiar but no novel behaviors. (Actually, one child failed to match any familiar behaviors either.) Eight of the 11 children were 12 months old or younger while 3 were older than 13 months of age. (2) Another 11 children, 3 of whom were less than 13 months old and 8 of whom were 13 months of age or older, repeated familiar behaviors and at least one novel sound or word. (3) The 8 remaining children, classified as belonging to the third, most advanced, pattern group, included one 10-month-old and 7 children 13 months of age or older.

To see whether infants who produced more novel experimental vocalizations and words came from dyadic interactions with more matching of communicative sounds and words during the natural social interactions, infants' and mothers' spontaneous vocal and verbal imitation scores were subjected to a 3 (Pattern Group) × 2 (Partner) × 3 (Behavior Category: miscellaneous vocalizations, discrete babbling vocalizations, and conventional vocalizations plus words) mixed analysis of variance with repeated measures on the last two factors. Besides effects for partner and behavior category and the partner by behavior category interaction, all of which replicate analyses reported above, there was a significant Pattern × Behavior Category interaction, $F(4, 54) = 3.63$, $p = .01$, which is illustrated in Table 3-5.

Dyads in all three pattern groups produced miscellaneous vocalizations infrequently, whereas repetition of discrete vocalizations by both infants and mothers declined across pattern groups. In contrast, imitation of conventional vocalizations and words increased across dyads in the three pattern groups, with both mothers and infants classified in Pattern 3 matching considerable more of these communicative behaviors. Newman-Keuls follow-up tests confirmed that individuals in Pattern 3 replicated more communicative sounds and words than those in either Pattern 1 ($p < .01$) or Pattern 2 ($p < .05$). Thus, infants who imitated more novel experimental sounds and words and also more kinds of novel behaviors had participated in more spontaneous communicative imitative interchanges with their mothers.

To corroborate this finding, partial correlations, controlling for age, were computed between mothers' and infants' matching of conventional vocalizations plus words during the natural interactions and infants' experimental imitation of familiar and of novel sounds plus words. Infants' imitative production of conventional sounds and words were related to their experimental replication of both familiar sounds and words, $r = .66, p < .001$, and novel sounds plus words $r = .35, p = .03$. Similarly, mothers' matching of conventional sounds and words was associated with their infants' experimental performance of both familiar vocalizations plus words, $r = .45, p < .01$, and novel vocalizations plus words $r = .27$, $p = .08$. These results demonstrate correspondences between infants' experimental vocal and verbal imitation and both their own and their mothers' spontaneous language-relevant matching behavior.

3.4 Conclusion

This study has described the naturally occurring imitative interchanges of mothers and their 10- to 16-month-old infants. Although spontaneous matching behavior was a frequent occurrence, on the whole, during their familiar routine and play interactions, the variation in amount of imitation among individuals and dyads was striking. Total imitation scores for dyads ranged from a low of 1.98 to a high of 52.59 during the approximately 26 min of interaction time.

Yet, despite the heterogeneity of performance, some general conclusions can be drawn. One concerns consistency in individuals' imitation of a variety of kinds of behaviors. The pattern of cross-category correlations for both infants and mothers indicates relationships only among spontaneous matching of communicative behaviors, rather than general imitative tendencies across unrelated vocal/verbal and motor action behavioral domains (see also Snow, Chapter 4, this volume.)

In addition, some general developmental trends were discernible, although mean differences between age groups were not always statistically significant. On the average, infants 13 months or older imitated relatively more conventional vocalizations and words and relatively fewer object-related actions than did those under 13 months of age. The developmental trend in their mothers' vocal matching was comparable. Mothers of younger children replicated more miscellaneous nonlanguage sounds and considerably more discrete babbling vocalizations, whereas mothers of older infants more frequently repeated their children's conventional vocalizations and words. From these data we cannot determine whether the children's nonimitative rates of various kinds of vocalizations changed as well, but it is reasonable to assume that the mothers were mirroring their children's most linguistically advanced productions at each age. If so, maternal imitation may serve to emphasize and reinforce children's emerging communicatively meaningful vocal behaviors (see also Masur, 1987). The examples of mothers' exact immediate verbal imitation seem particularly to support such a conclusion. For instance, in example (8), the mother first echoes her child's labeling word and then continues the topic of conversation by providing further specifying information about the object.

We can hypothesize two consequences of the mother's vocal matching behavior, one social and the other cognitive. First, mothers' modeling of imitation as an aspect of social interactions may teach or encourage their children to follow suit (Folger & Chapman, 1978; Pawlby, 1977). Although we cannot determine the origins of social matching from a cross-sectional study, findings by others (e.g., Užgiris, 1984) as well as some evidence reported here support the influence of maternal matching on infant matching. Mothers reproduced more behaviors overall than did children, and mothers of younger children in particular repeated more vocal behaviors than did their infants. Even without regard to the question of direction of influence, however, it is clear that some dyads have developed a pattern of mutual imitative interaction. The positive relation between partners' language imitation behavior, which has been identified among mothers and more linguistically advanced infants at the end of the second or beginning of the third year (e.g., Folger & Chapman, 1978), was present in the communicative imitations of these dyads while the children were in the early period of 10 to 16 months of age. Those mothers who matched more of their infants' language-relevant behaviors had infants who replicated more of their conventional vocalizations plus words.

Furthermore, the cognitive implications of these differential dyadic social patterns are suggested by the correspondence between infants' natural and experimental matching behavior. Infants, and their mothers, who had participated in more spontaneous communicative imitative interactions reproduced not only more familiar sounds and words, but also more novel vocalizations and words when these were modeled by their mothers under controlled conditions. These infants also exhibited the qualitatively most advanced pattern of elicited imitation performance, replicating novel visible actions as well. Thus, these results suggest a possible link between the social and cognitive functions of language imitation: Those infants more practiced in social vocal and verbal matching during familiar interactions may be the ones most likely to adopt imitations as a strategy for acquiring new language forms and structures. The origins of individual differences in children's utilization of imitation as a language acquisition mechanism should then be sought in their early social interactions with their mothers. Longitudinal investigations are needed to test this hypothesis.

Acknowledgments. I thank the people involved during the course of this research project, especially Dayle Ashley, Elsbeth Ritz, and the participating mothers and children.

References

Baldwin, J.M. (1895). *Social and ethical interpretations in mental development.* New York: Macmillan.

Bates, E., Benigni, L., Bretherton, I., Camaioni, L., & Volterra, V. (1979). *The emergence of symbols: Cognition and communication in infancy.* New York: Academic Press.

Bates, E., Bretherton, I., Beeghly-Smith, M., & McNew, S., (1982). Social bases of language development: A reassessment. In H. W. Reese and L. P. Lipsitt (Eds.), *Advances in child development and behavior* (Vol. 16, pp. 7–75). New York: Academic Press.

Bates, E., Bretherton, I., Snyder, L., Shore, C., & Volterra, V. (1980). Vocal and gestural symbols at 13 months. *Merrill-Palmer Quarterly, 26,* 407–423.

Bloom, L., Hood, L., & Lightbown, P. (1974). Imitation in language development: If, when, and why. *Cognitive Psychology, 76,* 380–420.

Broome, S., & Užgiris, I.Č. (1985, April). *Imitation in mother–child conversations.* Paper presented at the Biennial Meeting of the Society for Research in Child Development, Toronto, Canada.

Clark, R. (1977). What's the use of imitation? *Journal of Child Language, 4,* 341–359.

Corrigan, R., & diPaul, L. (1982). Measurement of language production in two-year-olds: A structured laboratory technique. *Applied Psycholinguistics, 3,* 223–242.

Ervin, S. (1964). Imitation and structural change in children's language. In E. Lenneberg (Ed.), *New directions in the study of language* (pp. 163–189). Cambridge, MA: MIT Press.

Folger, J.P., & Chapman, R.S. (1978). A pragmatic analysis of spontaneous imitation. *Journal of Child Language, 5,* 25–38.

Gelman, R. (1983). Reconsidering the transition form prelinguistic to linguistic communication. In R.M. Golinkoff (Ed.), *The transition from prelinguistic to linguistic communication* (pp. 275–279). Hillsdale, NJ: Erlbaum.

Keenan, E.O. (1974). Conversational competence in children. *Journal of Child Language, 1,* 163–183.

Kuczaj, S.A., II. (1982). Language play and language acquisition. In H.W. Reese (Ed.), *Advances in child development and behavior* (Vol. 17, pp. 197–232). New York: Academic Press.

Kuczaj, S.A., II. (1983). *Crib speech and language play.* New York: Springer-Verlag.

Leonard, L., Schwartz, R., Folger, M., Newhoff, M., & Wilcox, M. (1979). Children's imitations of lexical items. *Child Development, 59,* 19–27.

Masur, E.F. (1980). The development of communicative gestures in mother–infant interactions. *Papers and Reports on Child Language Development,* No. 19, 121–128.

Masur, E.F. (1982). Mothers' responses to infants' object-related gestures: Influences on lexical development. *Journal of Child Language, 9,* 23–30.

Masur, E.F. (1983). Gestural development, dual-directional signaling, and the transition to words. *Journal of Psycholinguistic Research, 12,* 93–109.

Masur, E.F. (1987). Imitative interchanges in a social context: Mother–infant matching behavior at the beginning of the second year. *Merrill-Palmer Quarterly, 33,* 453–472.

Masur, E.F. (1988). Infants' imitation of novel and familiar behaviors. In T.R. Zentall and B.G. Galef, Jr. (Eds.), *Social learning: Psychological and biological perspectives* (pp. 301–318). Hillsdale, NJ: Erlbaum.

Masur, E.F., & Ritz, E.G. (1984). Patterns of gestural, vocal, and verbal imitation performance in infancy. *Merrill-Palmer Quarterly, 30*, 369–392.

McCall, R.B. (1979). Qualitative transitions in behavioral development in the first two years of life. In M.H. Bornstein & W. Kessen (Eds.), *Psychological development from infancy: Image to intention* (pp. 183–224). Hillsdale, NJ: Erlbaum.

McCall, R.B., Parke, R.D., & Kavanaugh, R.D. (1977). Imitation of live and televised models by children one to three years of age. *Monographs of the Society for Research in Child Development, 42*(5, Serial No. 173).

Moerk, E., & Moerk, C. (1979). Quotations, imitations, and generalizations: Factual and methodological analyses. *International Journal of Behavioral Development, 2*, 43–72.

Nelson, K.E., Baker, N.D., Denninger, M., Bonvillian, J.D., & Kaplan, B.J. (1985). *Cookie* versus *Do-it again*: Imitative-referential and personal-social-syntactic-initiating styles in young children. *Linguistics, 23*, 433–454.

Papousek, H., & Papousek, M. (1977). Mothering and the cognitive head-start. In H.R. Schaffer (Ed.), *Studies in mother–infant interaction* (pp. 63–85). New York: Academic Press.

Pawlby, S.J. (1977). Imitative interaction. In H.R. Schaffer (Ed.), *Studies in mother–infant interaction* (pp. 203–224). New York: Academic Press.

Piaget, J. (1962). *Play, dreams and imitation in childhood.* New York: Norton.

Ramer, A. (1976). The function of imitation in child language. *Journal of Speech and Hearing Research, 19*, 700–717.

Rees, N.S. (1975). Imitation and language development: Issues and clinical implications. *Journal of Speech and Hearing Disorders, 40*, 339–350.

Rodgon, M.M., & Kurdek, L.A. (1977). Vocal and gestural imitation in 8-, 14-, and 20-month-old children. *Journal of Genetic Psychology, 131*, 115–123.

Seitz, S., & Stewart, C. (1975). Imitations and expansions: Some developmental aspects of mother–child communication. *Developmental Psychology, 11*, 763–768.

Shatz, M. (1983). Communication. In J. Flavell and E. Markman (Eds.), *Cognitive Development.* P. Mussen (Gen. Ed.), *Handbook of Child Psychology* (4th ed., pp. 841–889). New York: Wiley.

Shatz, M. (1984). Contributions of mother and mind to the development of communicative competence: A status report. In M. Perlmutter (Ed.), *Minnesota Symposium on Child Psychology* (Vol. 17, pp. 33–59). Hillsdale, NJ: Erlbaum.

Shipley, E.F., Smith, C.S., & Gleitman, L.R. (1969). A study in the acquisition of language: Free responses to commands. *Language, 45*, 322–342.

Snow, C.E. (1981). The uses of imitation. *Journal of Child Language, 8*, 205–212.

Stine, E.L., & Bohannon, J.N., III. (1983). Imitations, interactions, and language acquisition. *Journal of Child Language, 10*, 589–603.

Trevarthen, C. (1977). Descriptive analyses of infant communicative behavior. In H.R. Schaffer (Ed.), *Studies in mother–infant interaction* (pp. 227–289). New York: Academic Press.

Užgiris, I.Č. (1981). Two functions of imitation during infancy. *International Journal of Behavioral Development, 4*, 1–12.

Užgiris, I.Č. (1984). Imitation in infancy: Its interpersonal aspects. In M. Perlmutter (Ed.), *Minnesota Symposium on Child Psychology* (Vol. 17, pp. 1–32). Hillsdale, NJ: Erlbaum.
Užgiris, I.Č., & Hunt, J.McV. (1975). *Assessment in infancy.* Urbana: University of Illinois Press.

CHAPTER 4

Imitativeness: A Trait or a Skill?

Catherine E. Snow

Imitation has been dealt with in so many different ways by different subfields of psychology that it, in fact, may constitute a number of quite different conceptual phenomena, related only in that they all have the same name and somewhat similar external forms. Researchers on infant development, starting with Piaget himself, considered imitation an accomplishment, a developmental milestone to be achieved, a position that is, of course, supported by the findings that children's ability to imitate increasingly complex and novel models improves with age (e.g., Masur & Ritz, 1984; McCall, Parke, & Kavanaugh, 1977; Piaget, 1962). Many researchers in child language have viewed verbal imitation as exactly the opposite — the fallback strategy of the child whose language competence is unequal to the comprehension of incoming material (e.g., Leonard, Schwartz, Folger, Newhoff, & Wilcox, 1979). Thus, whereas imitating a maternal gesture was seen by Piaget as a reflection of the child's competence, imitation of a maternal utterance is seen by many in child language as an indication of failure to process or understand. Indeed, parents evidently share this view and often respond to child imitations of adult utterances with repetitions in somewhat simplified forms (Stine & Bohannon, 1983). Many child-language researchers have also noted the wide individual differences in tendency to imitate among children (see, e.g., Dunkeld, 1978; Field, 1982; Hayes & Watson, 1981; Heimann & Schaller, 1985; Masur, 1984), and have assumed furthermore that imitation is a behavior related to "imitativeness," which is seen as something very like a personality trait, a characteristic of the child resulting in certain kinds of behavior under certain conditions. Thus, it has been hypothesized that imitativeness should relate to other relatively stable characteristics of the child, such as willingness to take risks, preference for holistic rather than analytic strategies, and a social/expressive style of language development (see, e.g., Bates, Bretherton, & Snyder, 1988; K. Nelson, 1981).

A few researchers have transcended the simplistic interpretation of imitation as solely an achievement, a sign of incompetence, or a trait. Uzgiris (1981, 1984), for example, points out the double function of imitation – a marker of cognitive achievement, but also a socially effective way for the child to stay engaged in the ongoing interaction and to elicit responses from the other participants. Keenan (1974), Bruner (1983), Rees (1975), Shatz (1983), and others have likewise pointed out the social function of imitations, especially for children so young that they have few other effective social responses available. In the domain of social interaction, then, imitations have been seen as skillful strategies.

Some basis can also be found for the claim that imitation is an effective strategy for learning at least some things about language. Bloom, Hood, and Lightbown (1974) found that some children use imitations as a way of introducing new words into their output, whereas others introduce new syntactic structures in imitations of utterances with familiar vocabulary. Clark (1977) and Snow (1981) both give case-study data suggesting that imitation was a major mechanism by which the children they were studying first produced various sorts of complex constructions. Thus, for some children at least, imitation must be seen as a useful strategy in language acquisition as well as in social interaction (see Bohannon & Stanowicz, Chapter 6, this volume, for a model of imitation's contribution to language development).

Quite a different angle on imitation is provided by the studies suggesting that imitation is a technique learned by children whose mothers model it frequently, but not learned by children whose mothers rarely model it (Folger & Chapman, 1978; Kuczaj, 1983; Masur, 1984; Nelson, Baker, Denninger, Bonvillian, & Kaplan, 1985; Seitz & Stewart, 1975). These observations link most closely to the conceptualization of imitation presented in this chapter – that imitation is a skill. I believe the evidence supports the following position:

(1) Imitating is a skill that some children have more opportunity to learn than others;
(2) once learned, it tends to be relied on, thus accounting for the phenomenon of highly imitative children;
(3) acquiring the skill of imitation allows the development of certain procedures for processing language that those not skilled at imitation may not have; and
(4) finally, both the process of acquisition and the nature of what is acquired may be different for the skilled imitator temporarily, but given the availability of many additional procedures for acquiring information about language, such differences would be likely to disappear ultimately.

One source of evidence that imitation can better be viewed as a skill than as a trait is provided by reports of how elicited imitation is used as a language-teaching strategy in some cultures. Among both the Kwara'ae (Watson-Gegeo & Gegeo, 1986) and the Kaluli (Schieffelin, 1986), children are often told what to say in social settings and are instructed to repeat the modeled utterance. The utterances presented for imitation in these cases are often quite complex, both semantically and syntactically; it is not expected that the child understand exactly what the utterance means, only that he or she repeat it accurately. Somewhat surprisingly to those of us who have studied American children, the accuracy of whose imitations is limited by their comprehension, Kaluli and Kwara'ae children at very young ages evidently can repeat quite long and complex utterances, suggesting that they have become relatively skilled in imitating. If imitativeness were a relatively fixed trait, children who did not possess the trait would be very badly adapted to language learning in a Kaluli or Kwara'ae family; needless to say though, children are as universally successful in learning Kaluli or Kwara'ae as they are in learning English or French. It is also tempting to hypothesize that children whose mothers give them many models for elicited imitation have become relatively skilled at using their own imitative output as a source of information about the structure of the adult language — a processing skill that nonimitative children may never acquire.

The analyses I will describe in this chapter form part of a much larger study of individual differences, undertaken collaboratively with Steven Reznick, Edward Mueller, Malcolm Watson, and Dennis Wolf. The plan was to collect data at several points from a sample of 100 children, in order to assess individual differences in a number of domains (language, play, temperament, sociability, activity level, etc.) and ultimately to see if these domain-specific dimensions of individual difference related across domains in any comprehensible way. The study thus provides the potential to relate imitativeness to temperamental factors (degree of inhibition), a relationship we might expect if imitativeness is, indeed, a tendency associated with the willingness to take risks. The study also provides the potential to assess imitativeness in a number of different domains — social imitation with mother and with peers, spontaneous verbal imitation, elicited verbal imitation, spontaneous and elicited imitation of fantasy play acts, and so forth. If imitativeness is a trait rather than the reflection of a differentially developed skill, we might expect to see rather high correlations on imitativeness across domains (gesture, language, and play); if, on the other hand, imitativeness derives from a skill that children have acquired, it might be expected to be much more specific to the domains in which children have had imitation modeled, and to show low cross-domain correlations. Masur (Chapter 3, this volume) finds that mothers imitate children's vocalizations and words most frequently, not their gestures or their object-mediated actions. We would expect, then, that the correlation between maternal and child imitation holds only for vocal/verbal imitation, not for other types of child imitations. Užgiris, Broome, and Kruper (Chapter 5, this volume) report precisely this — that mothers' and children's imitations correlate within but not across behavioral categories. If, furthermore, verbal imitativeness reflects a skill that is acquired in interaction with adults who do a lot of verbal imitating, one might expect that children who are highly verbally imitative and who have highly imitative mothers perform better on elicited verbal imitation tasks. Finally, one might expect to find some differences in the language of the verbally highly imitative and the verbally less imitative children;

previous research suggests that highly imitative children might produce more unanalyzed chunks (Nelson, 1981), show more variation in phonological systems as a function of recency of model (Ferguson, 1979; Macken, 1979), have generally less easily describable systems in both syntax and in phonology, but be better than nonimitative children in both short- and long-term auditory memory (Speidel, Chapter 9, this volume).

It will not be possible to present the analyses that relate to all the above hypotheses in this chapter. In fact, the data that one would like to have to test some of them optimally are not even available. However, data relevant to the following predictions will be presented:

(1) A trait view of imitativeness predicts that children who are highly vocally imitative will also be highly imitative in other domains (gesture, object, unelicited actions), whereas a skill view predicts that frequency of spontaneous imitation will not correlate highly across domains.
(2) A skill view of imitativeness predicts that children whose mothers are highly vocally or verbally imitative will show high levels of imitation only in the verbal/vocal domain.
(3) A skill view of imitativeness predicts that children who take more opportunity to imitate verbally at younger ages will become better at it and thus will perform better on elicited verbal imitation tasks later.
(4) A skill view of imitativeness predicts that children who are highly verbally imitative will develop a different set of language processing and language-acquisition procedures from children who do not engage in verbal imitation, which will be revealed in various aspects of their developing language systems (e.g., sloppy articulation, absence of clear phonological or syntactic rules, and extensive use of unanalyzed chunks and social routines interspersed with rule-generated utterances).

As we shall see, the analyses that have been finished accord with the predictions from the skill view better than those for the trait view of imitativeness; they also open up many new questions that can be tackled from further analyses of the available data on these 100 children.

4.1 The Study

4.1.1 Data Collection

One hundred children whose mothers were contacted by letter were tested in two 1- to 1½- hour sessions in the laboratory at 14 months, and again at 20 months. Interaction during videotapes of the first 20 min of the first laboratory session was coded for spontaneous imitations by the child. These 20-min sessions started with a 5-min warm-up, during which the mother and child were asked to wait but were told they could play with any of the available toys. A standard set of toys was present, including a book, a small car, a rubber duck, a jack-in-the-box, and a few others. After 5 min, the experimenter entered, placed the child in a sassy seat at a low table, and deposited a variety of small toys on the table. The mother was asked to fill out a questionnaire at another table in the room, not to initiate interaction with her child, but to respond normally to the child. The small-scale toy-activity segment ended with the presentation of a forbidden object for 30 sec; this interval was not coded. Subsequently, the mother and child were asked to play successively with the contents of four boxes. The mother was told the whole play session would be 10 min and that she should get through all four boxes. The boxes contained a ball, a cloth for peekaboo, a set of crayons with paper, and a book.

Two formal test procedures were used at 20 months to elicit information about the child's phonological system and skill at elicited imitation. Using a high-quality tape recorder and microphone, the child was asked to name the pictures from the Expressive One-Word Vocabulary Test (EOWVT; Gardner, 1979); if the child could not name the picture spontaneously, then a model was provided, and imitation of the model encouraged. This test provides the data that can be analyzed to understand the child's phonological system and to assess phonological strategies. Elicited sentence-imitation data were collected during a home session at 20 months, using a set of sentences that increased in length and syntactic complexity, and that included novel as well as familiar words. The experimenter asked the child to repeat each sentence, giving a second chance if the first produced no attempt. The test was abandoned if no attempts at imitation were made to five successive sentences. Unfortunately, some subject attrition and technical difficulties reduced the number of subjects available for each of these two tests below the 100 who were coded for spontaneous imitation. Only 82 subjects attempted the EOWVT, of whom only 36 named enough items to yield usable data, and only 61 subjects completed enough items to be scored on the elicited sentence-imitation test. The primary reason for failure to complete the formal tests was that the children were very young; the mean vocabulary size of the 36 children completing the articulation test was only marginally higher than that of the larger sample, and there was no difference between the 61 who completed the sentence imitation test and the larger sample.

Table 4-1 gives an overview of the data collected. For purposes of clarity of presentation and brevity, full-scale analyses of only two sources of data will be presented here: the 14-month mother–child play session, and the 20-month elicited sentence-imitation task. We will also rely on data available on about 62 of the children at both 14 and at 20 months from the administration of the age-appropriate versions of the Communicative Development Lexical Inventory (Bates et al., 1988; Snyder, Bates, & Bretherton, 1981) to their mothers. The Lexical Inventory consists of a list of words compiled from the early vocabularies of many children, which is administered in a questionnaire format to mothers, who are given examples of what it means to "say" a word, and are asked to check off words their children say. The words are organized semantically (animals, vehicles, food and drink, etc.) and can be analyzed in various categories (nouns, verbs, etc.). Data on articulation from the EOWVT will be presented for a few

Table 4-1. Data Collection and Analysis

Age	14 months	20 months
Observations	20-min mother–child interaction: Coded for frequency of child imitations	20-min mother–child interaction: Coded for frequency of child imitations
Tests administered		Elicited sentence imitation: Coded for percentage of models imitated and for accuracy of imitations
		EOWVT: Coded for percentage of words not known spontaneously that were imitated, and results assessed for articulatory accuracy
Interview data	Lexical inventory (maternal report)	Lexical inventory (maternal report)

children who represent extremes on imitativeness, to give a flavor of how future analyses will proceed.

4.1.2 Coding

Separate coding procedures had to be developed for each of the types of data collected. Given the sample size, there were also constraints on the exhaustiveness of the possible coding systems; for example, we could not transcribe all of the 100 14-month mother–child sessions prior to coding them, but had to develop a method for coding directly off the videotapes.

The mother–child sessions were coded for the occurrence of full or partial child imitations in any of three domains: vocal, gestural, or object mediated. Gestures were defined as movement of the limbs, adoption of whole-body posture, head nods or shakes, or marked shifts of facial expression (e.g., wide smile, pout, laugh). Object-mediated actions were any actions on or with an object, for example, shaking a rattle, rolling a ball, turning a crank. A full imitation was scored if it was judged that the child was attempting to repeat the entire utterance, gesture, or object-mediated action of the adult. Failure to replicate the adult's behavior due to inability (e.g., imitation of the adult's "Wanna play?" as "Enne pay?", or making the motion of cranking the jack-in-the-box after the adult but failing to make a full turn because of insufficient strength) was counted as full imitation. A partial imitation was scored if the child imitated only part of the adult's utterance or gesture, imitated the intonation of the adult utterance but not the segments or vice versa, imitated an adult action on one object using a different object, or produced a complete action (e.g., opening a box) after only a partial demonstration (e.g., the adult jiggling but not removing the lid of the box). Imitations were scored only if they occurred immediately after the model (i.e., with no intervening child behavior) and within 3 sec. Interjudge agreement calculated on eight tapes coded independently by both judges was 84% for category of imitations identified by both (vocal, gestural, or object mediated) and 92% for full or partial. One coder identified an average of .5 more instances of imitation than the other, but the rank order of the subjects on frequency of imitation was identical according to both coders.

Coders were trained to observe instances of imitation on the tape, to transcribe the relevant adult and child utterances and behaviors on the score sheet, and then to code each instance as vocal, gestural, or object mediated, and as full or partial. Subsequent imitations within imitative episodes (e.g., rolling a ball back and forth several times, or a lengthy exchange of imitated babble sounds) were described but not coded as separate imitations. Because the tapes were not fully transcribed, there was no basis for comparing children in terms of their opportunities to imitate, that is, there were no data on number of maternal vocalizations, gestures, or object-mediated actions. Obviously, some mothers were much more active and/or vocal than others, and some engaged their children more effectively in interactive play than others, thus providing many more opportunities for child imitations to occur. Some mothers, however, are so active that they reduce opportunities for child imitations by leaving few pauses in the interaction. To be able to assess at least roughly such maternal effects, coders were also trained to rate each mother globally using a 4-point scale on the following dimensions: level of physical activity, degree of interactivity, talkativeness, directiveness, and tendency to imitate child. (In our observations, as in those reported by Masur in Chapter 3, maternal imitations were almost exclusively of words and vocalizations.) In addition, to get a rough estimate of the children's level of development, each child was globally rated on a 4-point scale on use of clear conventional words, use of semiconventional vocalizations (protowords), use of conventional communicative gestures (points, waves, etc.), and sophistication of object play. The 14-month sessions were coded by one of two research assistants (BK or CB); eight mother–child dyads were coded by both to establish comparability of judgment. The elicited sentence-imitation task was coded from transcriptions of the children's imitative attempts. Each attempt was compared to the model, to determine whether the modeled syllables were reproduced correctly or partially. For example, the model "I live in Boulder" could be reproduced as "live duh boduh." The syllables *live* and *bo* were reproduced correctly, the syllables *in* and *der* were attempted in the imitation but not reproduced correctly, and the syllable *I* was deleted. The child would receive a syllable score of 2 points for a correctly reproduced syllable, 1 point for a "mushily" imitated syllable, and 0 points for any omitted syllable. The child's syllable score per modeled utterance was then calculated as a percentage of maximum possible score (i.e., number of syllables in model times 2).

In addition to the syllable score that reflected accuracy of imitations, we calculated a score to reflect willingness to imitate, by taking the number of utterances the child attempted to imitate as a percentage of total number offered for imitation. Furthermore, each child's imitations were globally rated on a 5-point scale on articulation (1 = very mushy, hard to understand; 5 = exceptionally clear and precise) and on intonation (1 = limited intonational range, monotonic; 5 = perfect mimicking of adult intonation patterns).

4.2 Results

4.2.1 Frequency of Imitations

The first point to note about our findings is that, in a session of only 15 min of mother–child interaction, the number of child imitations could be as high as 40. All the children produced at least a few partial imitations. Gestural imitations were much less frequent than object-mediated imitations, a finding that replicates Abravanel, Levan-Goldschmidt, and Stevenson (1976) and Masur (1984), and reflects perhaps the greater ease of object-mediated imitation for children in this age range (Masur & Ritz, 1984).

4.2.2 Interrelations Among Types of Imitations

The first question that arises in attempting to determine whether imitation operates more like a trait or a skill is whether children who produce many of one kind of imitation also produce many of the other kinds. The pattern here is quite clear (see Table 4-2; Snow & Reznick, in preparation, give more detail on statistical analyses): Frequency of spontaneous gestural full or partial imitation relates to no other imitative frequency, but there is a slight tendency for children who produce many vocal imitations to also produce many object-mediated imitations ($r = .30$). Furthermore, it is interesting to note that the frequency of full and partial imitations does not correlate within category of imitation except for vocal imitations. For example, whereas frequency of full and partial object-mediated imitations correlates only .04, the frequency of full and partial vocal imitations correlates .37. It would seem, then, that it does make sense to identify vocal imitativeness as a salient dimension of individual difference at 14 months, but that vocal imitativeness relates not at all to gestural imitativeness and only weakly to object-mediated imitation. These findings extend and confirm others' results on interrelationships among imitation types. Masur (1984) reported a stronger relationship ($r = .47$) than we found between vocal and object-mediated imitation, in 18 children aged 10 to 14 months (see also Masur, Chapter 3, this volume). Uzgiris and Hunt's (1975) vocal and gestural imitation scales correlate at a level as low as we found, and Hardy-Brown (personal communication, 1983) found a correlation of .01 between gestural and vocal imitation in 100 12-month-olds. It seems clear, then, that vocal and gestural imitativeness are not related — a surprising finding given that in children in the age range under study vocal and gestural behaviors are both components of the communication system and are often used together for communication, and that spontaneous exploitation

Table 4-2. Correlations Among Child Imitation Frequencies at 14 Months[a]

Object-mediated imitation	1	2	3	4	5	6	7	8	9
(1) Full	—	−.05	.85^c	.02	−.17	−.03	.10	.25	.19
(2) Partial		—	.48^c	.03	.03	.03	.24	.15	.24
(3) Total			—	.03	−.13	−.01	.21	.30^b	.30^b
Gestural imitation									
(4) Full				—	.04	.95^c	.13	−.01	.09
(5) Partial					—	.33^c	.08	−.04	.04
(6) Total						—	.14	−.02	.09
Vocal imitation									
(7) Full							—	.37^c	.90^c
(8) Partial								—	.74^c
(9) Total									—

[a] Because approximately 100 correlations were calculated on this data set, coefficients significant only at the .05 level are neither specially noted nor considered further. All correlations reported in this table were based on an n of 100.

[b] $p < .01$.

[c] $p < .001$.

of gestural and vocal resources for communication are highly related (Bates, Benigni, Bretherton, Camaioni, & Volterra, 1979).

Since the tendency to imitate any particular modeled act or utterance is known to be influenced by the novelty and difficulty of the model compared to the child's own ability level (Masur & Ritz, 1984), it might be hypothesized that large differences among the children in their verbal skills would affect the pattern of relationships among kinds of imitation found. Hardy-Brown (1981), for example, found that frequency of vocal imitations was a component of the single communicative competence factor she found for 100 12-month-olds, although Scarborough and Davidson (1985) found no relation between proportion of child utterances that were imitations and any measure of language proficiency in 24- and 30-month-olds. A verbally precocious 14-month-old might imitate many more maternal utterances than an age-mate whose verbal skills were somewhat below average, whereas the second child might show considerable gestural or object-mediated imitation. To assess this possibility, partial correlations among the various types of imitation were calculated, partialing out in separate analyses the effects of total vocabulary size and of number of verbs produced (based on the Communicative Development Lexical Inventory administered at 14 months to the mothers). The pattern of relationships found remained essentially unchanged: Correlations between gestural and vocal or object-mediated imitations remained close to zero, and the correlation between vocal and object-mediated imitations remained significant but low. The correlations between partial and complete vocal imitations were increased considerably by partialing out the effect of total vocabulary, however.

Table 4-3. Correlations Between Maternal Measures and Child Imitation at 14 Months[a]

	Maternal measures				
Child imitations	Activity	Interactivity	Verbosity	Imitativeness	Directiveness
Object mediated					
Full	.10	.17	.10	.33[c]	.28[b]
Partial	.12	−.01	−.17	.09	.07
Total	.16	.15	.01	.34[c]	.28[b]
Gestural					
Full	.07	.07	−.01	.14	.03
Partial	−.03	.13	−.07	.10	−.10
Total	.06	.10	−.03	.16	.00
Vocal					
Full	−.02	.01	.04	.45[c]	.15
Partial	.21	.19	.12	.35[c]	.20
Total	.08	.10	.08	.49[c]	.20

[a] Because approximately 100 correlations were calculated on this data set, coefficients significant only at the .05 level are neither specially noted nor considered further. All correlations reported in this table were based on an n of 100.

[b] $p < .01$.

[c] $p < .001$.

The correlations between the rating scales of maternal behavior and children's imitation revealed the predicted strong relation between maternal imitativeness and child vocal imitations (see Table 4-3). Maternal imitativeness also related significantly, but more weakly, to child object-mediated imitations, as did maternal directiveness. It was not the case that those mothers who talked more, were more active, or were more interactive had children who produced more vocal imitations.

4.2.3 Imitations at 14 and 20 Months

The next question of interest is whether tendency to imitate at 14 months relates at all to performance on the elicited imitation task at 20 months. The pattern of findings here was quite clear (see Table 4-4): Correlations between object-mediated and gestural imitation at 14 months and elicited verbal imitation at 20 months were low and mostly negative, but the 14-month vocal-imitation scores showed moderate positive correlations with elicited verbal imitation at 20 months. In short, we have yet another support for the notion that imitation is a rather domain-specific phenomenon. The elicited sentence-imitation task generated two kinds of scores: the number of models that the child attempted to imitate, and the accuracy of the imitation attempts. Although these two scores correlated highly (.78) with one another, it was consistently the case that the first

Table 4-4. Spontaneous Imitation at 14 Months Related to Elicited Imitation at 20 Months

| | 20-month scores | | | |
| | Raw correlations | | With total vocabulary at 20 months partialed out | |
14-month scores	Percentage of models imitated	Accuracy	Percentage of models imitated	Accuracy
Object mediated				
Full	−.04	−.01	−.06	−.01
Partial	−.22	−.19	−.18	−.16
Total	−.15	−.11	−.14	−.09
Gestural				
Full	−.05	−.16	−.02	−.14
Partial	.14	.18	.08	.16
Total	−.02	−.11	−.00	−.10
Vocal				
Full	.31[a]	.18	.13	.01
Partial	.15	.17	.04	.05
Total	.29[a]	.19	.12	.02

[a] $p < .05$; N for these analyses is 42.

related more strongly to vocal imitation at 14 months. Because verbally precocious children might have produced more vocal imitations at 14 months and be more likely to score high on the elicited imitation task 6 months later, we redid these correlations, partialing out the total productive vocabulary derived from the Communicative Development Lexical Inventory at 20 months. This eliminated the correlation between vocal imitativeness at 14 months and the accuracy score at 20 months, suggesting that this relationship was an artifact of verbal skill (see Table 4-4). It substantially reduced but did not entirely eliminate the correlation between tendency to produce vocal imitations spontaneously and in eliciting settings.

4.2.4 Imitativeness and Language Development

These various findings all seem to confirm the hypothesis that imitativeness is a highly domain-specific characteristic, not a general response strategy that a child uses across a variety of domains. We know from previous work (see Masur, Chapter 3, this volume; Užgiris, Broome, & Kruper, Chapter 5, this volume) that mothers primarily imitate children's vocalizations and words and that the frequency of children's verbal imitations relates to the frequency with which their utterances are repeated by their mothers. We replicated this latter finding using our very rough index of maternal imitativeness, a 3-point scale. Despite the minimization of correlations associated with such a truncated scale, our measure of maternal imitativeness correlated .49 ($p < .0001$) with children's vocal imitations. Some children evidently have considerable opportunity to learn from their mothers that imitation is an appropriate verbal strategy, and they seem to adopt it for their own use. Indeed, Masur (1984) describes interactions that suggest some mothers are instructing their children to imitate novel actions and utterances. Other children's mothers do not reveal to them the appropriateness or usefulness of imitation as an interactive device or processing strategy, so those children presumably adopt other procedures for processing novel information.

It is clear that imitation is a useful strategy for some interactive problems — taking a turn when one has nothing to say, keeping up one's end of the conversation despite not having fully understood the previous talk, signaling miscomprehension, and so forth. It is less clear (and, indeed, rather controversial) whether the verbal imitations of vocally highly imitative children contribute to their language development. We cannot offer any clear-cut answer to this question with the data available to us (see Bohannon & Stanowicz, Chapter 6, this volume; Speidel & Herreshoff, Chapter 8, this volume), but we do have correlations between imitativeness at 14 months and scores reflecting language sophistication from the Communicative Development Lexical Inventory both contemporaneously and 6 months later. Vocal imitativeness at 14 months correlates significantly with a number of measures of language skill at 14 months: number of nouns produced ($r = .41$), number of verbs produced ($r = .39$), total productive vocabulary ($r = .41$), and the production/comprehension ratio ($r = .39$). Interestingly, gestural imitativeness also showed significant (though smaller) correlations with language measures, including number of verbs produced ($r = .23$), total productive vocabulary ($r = .21$), and the production/comprehension ratio ($r = .23$), whereas object-mediated imitations showed generally negative (though nonsignificant) correlations with language measures. These findings recall those of Heimann and Nelson (1986), who found a negative correlation between object-mediated imitation at 15 months and communication skill at 12 months, but a positive correlation between gestural imitation and communication skill. They also replicate Hardy-Brown's (1981) positive correlations between vocal imitation and productive vocabulary and Bayley Language items at 12 months.

Vocal imitativeness at 14 months also showed significant correlations with several language measures at 20 months, suggesting at the very least that imitative children were not handicapped in their acquisition of total vocabulary ($r = .50$ for total vocal imitations at 14 months and total productive vocabulary at 20 months), nor in their acquisition of verbs, which reflects greater syntactic and semantic complexity in 20-month-olds' speech ($r = .50$ between total vocal imitations at 14 months and number of verbs used in production at 20 months). This pattern of correlations is absolutely specific to vocal imitations at 14 months; no correlation between gestural or object-mediated imitations and any of the language measures at 20 months reached even marginal significance.

Conversely, total productive vocabulary and number of verbs produced at 14 months showed significant but only moderate correlations to number of models imitated in the elicited imitation task at 20 months, and no correlations at all to the accuracy score. Not surprisingly, language measures at 20 months related to performance on the elicited imitation task at 20 months, but here again stronger relationships were found with number of models imitated than with accuracy of imitation. It might have been expected that the large amounts of practice at imitating amassed by the vocally imitative children between 14 and 20 months would have made them more accurate imitators, but such seems not to be the case, at least as measured by our task.

4.2.5 Performance on Articulation Task

One of the directions for future research with this data set includes looking at the children's strategies for pronunciation as related to their imitativeness. There has been considerable speculation that children who refuse to imitate have more orderly phonological systems than children who willingly imitate (Ferguson, 1979; Macken, 1979). It would ultimately be desirable to assess the children's phonological systems by looking at their spontaneous, conversational speech at both 14 and 20 months, but at the moment we have not even finally solved the problem of how to judge their phonological strategies by looking at their performance on a relatively standardized confrontation naming task, the EOWVT. The difficulties inherent in scoring data of this sort will be familiar to all who have tried to test 20-month-olds. Presented with a picture of a dog, one child says quite clearly "dog," another says "goggie," and another says "woof-woof." We have no evidence about production of initial stops from the third; although we know that the first child shows no consonant assimilation in monosyllabic words, we know nothing about his strategies in producing multisyllabic words such as the second child chooses to produce. Such problems recur with every test item. Some children respond to a picture of a telephone with "phone," others with something like "wawafo," clearly modeled on a different adult version of the word, whereas still others respond "hello." Given these difficulties with quantification, we resort here to an older procedure in child language research: a case-study presentation.

Table 4-5 presents data on 5 children in the study—the 3 most vocally imitative children for whom all relevant data sets were available, and 2 randomly selected from among the 37 children who produced no vocal imitations, limiting the group further to those for whom all information was available. All these children except Thomas showed comparable and relatively high frequencies of object-mediated imitation. It can be seen that, for this small subsample as for the entire sample, the children who were less imitative at 14 months had smaller vocabularies at 20 months, and showed less tendency to imitate on the sentence-imitation task.

Let us now consider how these children functioned in the articulation task. Carla, a low vocal imitator, produced 12 of the 22 target words spontaneously, but

Table 4-5. Imitation and Language Data from Five Children

| | Frequencies of spontaneous imitations at 14 months | | Percent elicited imitations at 20 months | | Language measures from Communicative Development Lexical Inventory at 20 months | | |
	Object-mediated	Vocal	Utterance score	Syllable score	Referential words	Action words	Total vocabulary
Carla	7	0	0	0	132	22	181
Evan	11	0	13	20	112	18	146
Mark	8	12	58	28	193	47	283
Thomas	1	14	43	26	273	102	486
Alex	14	25	38	48	232	96	406

refused to imitate 9 of the other 10 even after several elicitations. She did produce /bək/ for *book*, but refused to imitate *phone, plane, swing, boy, bus, tree, truck*, or *pumpkin*. Her spontaneous productions were all consonant/vowel (CV) or consonant/vowel/consonant (CVC) forms in which the final *C* was /t/, except for *apple*, which she produced as /æbə́/. She did not attempt any target words with consonant clusters in them (she responded to the train with /bot/), and her mother interrupted the test session to report, "She doesn't say anything with a blend." Carla clearly has a rather conservative approach in her phonological development, as evidenced by her restricted set of productive word forms and her refusal to misrepresent more complex target words by reproducing them within her own phonological formats.

Evan, who also failed to produce spontaneous vocal imitations at 14 months, produced 3 elicited imitations of model words: /ai/ for *eyes*, /kə/ for *truck*, and /pəfə/ for *pumpkin*, though he also refused to imitate 4 other unknown words despite repeated attempts at elicitation. His spontaneously produced words were all CV or CVCV (consonant/vowel/consonant/vowel) forms, and included /hɛwo/ for *phone*, /kiyə/ for *key*, /pɛpɛ/ for *plane*, and /kɪʔi/ for *cat*. Like Carla, Evan utilized a rather limited set of word formats, and refused even to attempt imitations of words that violated his productive format, such as ones with initial consonant clusters.

Mark, a more spontaneously vocally imitative child, refused to imitate only 2 of the 6 words he did not know, though his imitations were not very close to the target, for example, /dẽi/ for *train*, /bæp/ for *apple*, and /di/ for *tree*. His spontaneous responses were often equally far from the target: /bəi/ for both *boy* and *bus*, and /bei/ for both *bird* and *plane*. His 15 spontaneously produced responses included several types: CV (the most common by far), CCV (consonant/consonant/vowel), CVC, CVCV, and V (vowel). Based on the rather small amount of data available, it seemed his system was characterized by considerable variability; for example, a final consonant produced in one word was omitted in a different word of no greater complexity, and /b/ was produced correctly at the beginning of *book*, *bird*, *boat*, and several other words, but reduced to /h/ in *ball*. This accords well with Macken's findings that imitative children have "messier" phonological systems.

Neither Alex nor Thomas fits the picture one would like to base on the above three cases, however. Alex would only sit still for 13 words, of which he produced 7 spontaneously, imitated 3 quite well, and refused to imitate 3. His phonological system is fairly sophisticated (several final consonants, initial consonant clusters), but also somewhat variable (e.g., /meko/ and /šeko/ were alternating attempts at *bicycle*), though the variability was not increased by the imitations he was willing to produce. Thomas was even more unwilling than Alex to imitate (2 words imitated of 7 he did not know), and particularly refused to attempt the more difficult words like *pumpkin* and words with initial clusters. Clearly, he, like Carla the nonimitator, was unwilling to stretch his system (which included no spontaneously produced initial clusters) to incorporate new forms by using imitation.

This small group of case studies suggests some strategies for looking further for differences between vocally highly imitative and vocally nonimitative children, but also serves to warn us that clear-cut distinctions cannot be expected. It seems, based on these five children, that nonimitators may have more restricted phonological systems, and may be disinclined to imitate words that fall outside the word formats they have already mastered. Imitative children seem to have somewhat more options for word shapes, but note that they also have larger vocabularies; their phonological sophistication may reflect the larger number of words available—or conversely may have enabled the child to learn more words! Imitative children also seem to have somewhat more variability in their phonological production systems, though it is not inevitably the case that they will expand this variability indefinitely by imitating novel or difficult words.

4.3 Conclusion

Many fascinating claims have been made about the sources of children's tendencies to imitate, and about the consequences of imitation for development, and in particular for language learning. We feel our data are consistent with the view that imitativeness is not a general tendency on the part of the child, but a strategy learned for a particular domain. Verbally imitative children have been shown to have verbally highly imitative mothers—presumably their mothers have created interactive situations that enable the children to learn the value of verbal imitations, and to develop skill with imitation as a technique for interaction. The skill thus developed evidently carries over to a task in which imitations are elicited, and may be one of the factors determining how children choose to expand their phonological systems. It does not, however, carry over very strongly to other domains within which imitation might also be a useful strategy—gesturing, or operating on objects—nor does it predict very exactly what the course of a child's phonological development will be.

Many questions remain to be addressed using the data set available from these 100 children. A first question is the degree of stability in spontaneous imitativeness from 14 to 20 months. A second question is whether the relation between spontaneous and elicited imitation reported here for the verbal domain can be replicated in the domain of object-mediated imitation. At both 14 and 20 months, the children engaged in a play interaction with an experimenter who modeled increasingly abstract fantasy actions (e.g., taking a mock bite out of a real apple, taking a mock bite out of a red wooden ball, taking a mock bite out of a blue block). We will analyze the children's imitations of the adult object-mediated actions for relationships with spontaneous object-mediated imitation at both 14 and 20 months. High correlations will strengthen our conclusion that imitativeness is not a general trait that some children possess, but the result of domain-specific skills that different children have differential opportunities to acquire.

Acknowledgments. I would like to express my appreciation to the John D. and Catherine T. MacArthur Foundation Network on the Transition from Infancy to Childhood, which funded the collection of the data presented here and portions of the analysis, and to the Spencer Foundation, which funded a part of the analysis. Elise Masur was very helpful in developing the coding system for spontaneous imitations. Jane Gibbons collected the data, Becky Kennedy, Cornelia Baigorria, and Laura Bodin coded them, and Steven Reznick supervised the entire project and aided immeasurably in data analysis. I am grateful to Mick Watson and to the editors for helpful comments on an earlier version of the manuscript. The collaborative efforts of Steven Reznick, Dennis Wolf, Malcolm Watson, and Edward Mueller were indispensable to the success of the project.

References

Abravanel, E., Levan-Goldschmidt, E., & Stevenson, M.B. (1976). Action imitation: The early phase of infancy. *Child Development, 47*, 1032–1044.

Bates, E., Benigni, L., Bretherton, I., Camaioni, L., & Volterra, V. (1979). *The emergence of symbols: Cognition and communication in infancy.* New York: Academic Press.

Bates, E., Bretherton, I., & Snyder, L. (1988). *From first words to grammar: Individual differences and dissociable mechanisms.* New York: Cambridge University Press.

Bloom, L., Hood, L., & Lightbown, P. (1974). Imitation in language development: If, when, and why. *Cognitive Psychology, 76*, 380–420.

Bruner, J. (1983). *Child's talk.* New York: Norton.

Clark, R. (1977). What's the use of imitation? *Journal of Child Language, 4*, 341–359.

Dunkeld, J. (1978). *The function of imitation in infancy.* Unpublished doctoral dissertation. University of Edinburgh.

Ferguson, C.A. (1979). Phonology as an individual access system: Some data from language acquisition. In C.S. Fillmore, D. Kempler, & W.S.Y. Wang (Eds.), *Individual differences in language ability and language behavior.* New York: Academic Press.

Field, T.M. (1982). Individual differences in the expressivity of neonates and young infants. In R.S. Feldman (Ed.), *Development of nonverbal behavior in children*. New York: Springer-Verlag.

Folger, J.P., & Chapman, R.S. (1978). A pragmatic analysis of spontaneous imitation. *Journal of Child Language*, *5*, 25–38.

Gardner, G. (1979). *Expressive one-word vocabulary test*. Novato, CA: Academic Therapy Publications.

Hardy-Brown, K. (1981). Individual differences in development. *Developmental Psychology*, *17*, 704–717.

Hayes, L.A., & Watson, J.G. (1981). Neonatal imitation: Fact or artifact? *Developmental Psychology*, *17*, 5, 655–660.

Heimann, M., & Nelson, K.E. (1986). The relationship between nonverbal imitation and gestural communication in 12 to 15 month old infants. *Goteborg Psychological Reports*, *16*, 2.

Heimann, M., & Schaller, J. (1985). Imitative reactions among 14-21 days old infants. *Infant Mental Health Journal*, *6*, 31–39.

Keenan, E.O. (1974). Conversational competence in children. *Journal of Child Language*, *1*, 163–183.

Kuczaj, S.A., II. (1983). *Crib speech and language play*. New York: Springer-Verlag.

Leonard, L., Schwartz, R., Folger, M., Newhoff, M., & Wilcox, M. (1979). Children's imitations of lexical items. *Child Development*, *59*, 19–27.

Macken, M.A. (1979). Developmental reorganization of phonology: A hierarchy of basic units of acquisition. *Lingua*, *49*, 11–19.

Masur, E.F. (1984). *Imitation in a social context: Mother–infant interactions at the beginning of the second year*. (Unpublished manuscript.)

Masur, E.F., & Ritz, E.G. (1984). Patterns of gestural, vocal, and verbal imitation performance in infancy. *Merrill-Palmer Quarterly*, *30*, 369–392.

McCall, R.B., Parke, R.D., & Kavanaugh, R.D. (1977). Imitation of live and televised models by children one to three years of age. *Monographs of the Society for Research in Child Development*, *42*(5, Serial No. 173).

Nelson, K. (1981). Individual differences in language development. *Developmental Psychology*, *17*, 170–187.

Nelson, K.E., Baker, N.D., Denninger, M., Bonvillian, J.D., & Kaplan, B.J. (1985). Cookie versus do-it-again: Imitative-referential and personal-social-syntactic-initiating language styles in young children. *Linguistics*, *23*, 433–454.

Piaget, J. (1962). *Play, dreams, and imitation in childhood*. New York: Norton.

Rees, N.S. (1975). Imitation and language development: Issues and clinical implications. *Journal of Speech and Hearing Disorders*, *40*, 339–350.

Scarborough, H., & Davidson, R. (1985). *Style and skill in language development*. Unpublished manuscript, Psychology Department, Rutgers University, New Brunswick, NJ.

Schieffelin, B. (1986). *How Kaluli children learn what to say, what to do, and how to feel*. New York: Cambridge University Press.

Seitz, S., & Stewart, C. (1975). Imitations and expansions: Some developmental aspects of mother–child communication. *Developmental Psychology*, *11*, 763–768.

Shatz, M. (1983). Communication. In J. Flavell & E. Markman (Eds.), *Cognitive Development*. P. Mussen (Gen. Ed.), *Handbook of Child Psychology* (4th ed.). New York: Wiley.

Snow, C.E. (1981). The uses of imitation. *Journal of Child Language*, *8*, 205–212.

Snow, C.E., & Reznick, S. (in preparation). Imitativeness of verbal, gestural, and object-mediated models in 14 to 20 month old children.

Snyder, L.S., Bates, E., & Bretherton, I. (1981). Content and context in early lexical development. *Journal of Child Language, 8*, 565–582.

Stine, E.L., & Bohannon III, J.N. (1983). Imitations, interactions, and language acquisition. *Journal of Child Language, 10*, 589–603.

Užgiris, I.Č. (1981). Two functions of imitation during infancy. *International Journal of Behavioral Development, 4*, 1–12.

Užgiris, I.Č. (1984). Imitation in infancy: Its interpersonal aspects. In M. Perlmutter (Ed.), *Minnesota Symposium on Child Psychology, 17*. Hillsdale, NJ: Erlbaum.

Užgiris, I.Č., & Hunt, J.McV. (1975). *Assessment in infancy*. Urbana: University of Illinois Press.

Watson-Gegeo, K., & Gegeo, D. (1986). Calling out and repeating routines in Kwara'ae children's language socialization. In B. Schieffelin & E. Ochs (Eds.), *Language socialization across cultures*. New York: Cambridge University Press.

CHAPTER 5

Imitation in Mother–Child Conversations: A Focus on the Mother

Ina Č. Užgiris, Susan Broome, and Jan C. Kruper

Studies of children's first language acquisition conducted during the past 2 decades have revealed the great complexity of this process, even though it takes place successfully and seemingly effortlessly in quite varied social environments. The proposition that linguistic input is important in nontrivial ways has come to be accepted, although its precise role during the acquisition process remains to be clarified. Finer-grained analyses have indicated the need to consider the role of language directed to the child during each of the phases of the acquisition process and in relation to each of the different aspects (phonemic, semantic, syntactic, pragmatic) constituting language. Moreover, language has come to be viewed within the broader framework of communication, which, in turn, has encouraged a more interactive approach to the study of the role of input in language acquisition. The assumptions that communication provides a framework for early language development and that an interactive approach is appropriate to the analysis of early language behaviors have guided our research on mother–child conversations.

The mother is the primary source of linguistic experience for a young child in most societies. A number of studies have convincingly demonstrated that maternal speech addressed to young children is distinct from that used with adults (e.g., Phillips, 1973; Remick, 1976; Snow, 1972, 1977); the utterances are simple, grammatical, repetitive, and concerned with the here and now of the situation. Chapman (1981) has provided a thorough review of the specific features characterizing maternal speech addressed to children in the second year of life. The relationship between the characteristics of maternal speech and child language acquisition, however, continues to be debated. Brown (1977) has proposed that the nature of maternal speech may reflect attempts to be understood by a partner having limited cognitive and verbal skills as well as to teach the child linguistic skills through appropriate demonstration and responsiveness. These ideas underlie much of the research on the role of maternal input in language acquisition.

Several studies have shown that maternal speech changes in keeping with the level of children's language ability (e.g., Cross, 1977; Moerk, 1974; Newport, Gleitman, & Gleitman, 1977; Smolak & Weinraub, 1983). It has been more difficult to demonstrate that specific characteristics of maternal speech influence children's progress in language skills. Some relationships between maternal speech characteristics and children's progress in language have been found (e.g., Furrow, Nelson, & Benedict, 1979; Gleitman, Newport, & Gleitman, 1984; Newport et al., 1977), but it remains unclear whether the obtained relations are due to the input provided by the speech addressed to the child or to the kinds of verbal interactions that certain features of maternal speech encourage. Recent studies have begun to examine the functions that particular features of maternal speech serve during conversations with children at different levels of linguistic skill (e.g., Harris, Jones, Brookes, & Grant, 1986; Howe, 1980; Lieven, 1978; Stella-Prorok, 1983). This more interactive approach to the role of maternal input in child language acquisition helps bring together the research on the importance of children's practice with that on maternal speech characteristics.

5.1 Imitation in Early Interactions

One form of interaction between mothers and young children consists of imitation. The role of imitation in early language acquisition has been debated for a number of years (e.g., Clark, 1977; Ramer, 1976; Snow, 1981, 1983). One source of confusion has been the varied definition of imitation (e.g., Kuczaj, 1982; Snow, 1981). More importantly, the role of imitation was obscured because it was studied as a characteristic of one of the participants and not as a form of interaction. Most frequently, imitation has been conceived as a learning strategy used by the child and sometimes as a form of input provided by the mother; rarely has it been examined as a form of exchange having several potential communication functions (McTear, 1978). We think that an understanding of the role of imitation in language acquisition as much as an understanding of its role in early social interaction requires a recognition of the interpersonal nature of imitative activity (Užgiris, 1984).

Currently, imitation is no longer viewed as a process of mechanically repeating motoric, expressive, or verbal actions demonstrated by others. It is recognized that cognitive understanding of the observed actions is important and influences the occurrence as well as the specific form of imitations. This recognition has led some to view imitation as an index of the child's cognitive understanding of various models. However, in the context of interpersonal interaction, imitation is not restricted to the repetition of novel or incompletely understood acts; highly familiar and mutually known acts are often matched. Such observations (e.g., Killen & Užgiris, 1981; Nadel-Brulfert & Baudonniere, 1982; Pawlby, 1977) have suggested that imitation also has a social function, facilitating mutual understanding and promoting further interaction (Užgiris, 1981). It seems likely that imitations occurring during verbal exchanges between mothers and children reflect the social as well as the cognitive function of imitation.

It has been shown that children tend to imitate those phonological forms that they are just learning (Scollon, 1979) or those lexical items that are relatively new to them (Moerk, 1977; Ramer, 1976; Rodgon & Kurdek, 1977; Stine & Bohannon, 1983). In addition, imitation has been found to contribute to the acquisition of new syntactic-semantic relations (Corrigan, 1980), at least for some children (Bloom, Hood, & Lightbown, 1974). Broader definitions of imitation in children's speech have indicated that it may be more prevalent and more significant than previously thought (e.g., Moerk & Moerk, 1979; Snow, 1981). After reviewing available studies, Snow (1983) concluded that, because of definitional and methodological difficulties, the importance of children's imitation for their progress in language acquisition has been underestimated.

In contrast, maternal imitation of children's utterances has been more often related to the ongoing interaction with the child. However, the kinds of maternal imitation distinguished by different investigators and the terms applied to them have varied, making comparison between studies rather difficult. For example, Schachter (1979) referred to maternal imitations as repetitions-of-child and distinguished between exact complete repetitions, exact partial repetitions (in which a part of the child's utterance is left out), and expansions, defined as utterances that add words or morphemes missing from the child's grammatically incomplete utterance, while preserving its meaning. In Schachter's study, expansions were substantially more frequent in the speech of advantaged than disadvantaged mothers. Cross (1977), on the other hand, used the term *repetition* for self-repetitions in maternal speech and also differentiated *imitations* (exact or partial), *expansions* (additions to the child's utterance to form a grammatically complete sentence), and *extensions* (additions that incorporate a part of the child's utterance and elaborate on some other part). She found that the percentage of expansions as well as the percentage of expansions plus extensions was higher in the speech of mothers whose children were accelerated in language skills (Cross, 1978), but the percentage of self-repetitions did not differ significantly in the two groups. We think it might be useful to reserve the term *repetition* for the duplication of a speaker's own utterances and to agree on another broad term, such as *imitation*, to refer to the duplication of a partner's utterances.

Probably the greatest variation in usage and in the types of distinctions made is found with respect to the category of expansions. It has been broadly defined as a type of maternal response that adds to the child's preceding utterance to make it more comprehensible or more grammatical (Brown, 1973; Slobin, 1968); also, it has been used narrowly to refer to a specific reformulation of the child's preceding utterance (Cross, 1977; Nelson, Bonvillian, Denninger, Kaplan, & Baker,

1984; Wells, 1980). For example, Nelson (Nelson et al., 1984) considered expansions to be a subset of simple recasts, defined as contingent maternal responses that continue reference to the central meaning of the child's preceding utterance, while changing one of its structural components (the subject, the verb, or the object). Although there has been some disagreement concerning the effect of expansions on language acquisition (cf. Brown, Cazden, & Bellugi-Klima, 1969; Nelson, Carskaddon, & Bonvillian, 1973), many recent studies indicate that maternal expansions and recasts facilitate linguistic progress (e.g., Barnes, Gutfreund, Satterly, & Wells, 1983; Nelson, 1977, 1981; Nelson et al., 1984; Stella-Prorok, 1983; Wells, 1980). The obtained effect has been attributed to several features of the interactions that may be tapped by this measure of maternal imitation.

Because maternal imitations are frequent during the very early phases of language acquisition, it has been suggested that they may function as a confirmation of the child's previous utterance or may serve as a request for confirmation that the mother's understanding of the child's utterance is in fact correct (Brown, 1977). By being closely linked to the child's existing interest, maternal expansions and recasts may also be optimal models of appropriate expressions for the child's intended communications (Chapman, 1981). Moreover, by accepting the child's interest, such maternal utterances may ensure a joint focus of interest (Cross, 1978; Nelson et al., 1984; Slobin, 1968) and help maintain the child's involvement in the conversation (Bohannon & Hirsh-Pasek, 1984; Stella-Prorok, 1983). It is interesting to note that imitation by mothers has been found to be highly correlated with imitation by children (Folger & Chapman, 1978; Masur, Chapter 3, this volume; Seitz & Stewart, 1975), which indicates that imitation is reciprocal during mother–child conversations.

The suggested functions of imitation observed during mother–child verbal interactions fit well with the functions evident in early interpersonal interactions. Once imitation is conceptualized as an interpersonal exchange in which both partners attend to each other's actions, it becomes clear that mutual effects must be considered, whatever the functional format of the interaction (Užgiris, Benson, Kruper, & Vasek, 1989). In a teaching format, the partner serving as the model attends to the approximation achieved by the learner and adjusts subsequent modelings appropriately, while the learner is aware of the responsivity of the partner serving as the model. In a sharing format, the similarity that is mutually constructed by the two partners is of main concern, and it matters less which partner's matching creates the similarity. However, the achievement of similarity promotes continuing interaction through convergence of feelings or interests. In a structural format, imitation by either partner can be used to maintain the turn-taking, reciprocal structure of the interaction and thereby support its continuation.

An approach to imitation as an interpersonal activity suggests a number of different emphases (Užgiris, 1989). First, it highlights the reciprocal nature of imitation. In an episode of imitation, the roles of model and imitator can shift several times, making it difficult to connect imitation with the turns of only one of the participants. Moreover, in the course of an interaction, the imitator can become the model at a different time and establish symmetry with the partner over longer stretches of interaction. Second, it points out that the meaning of an imitative exchange must be considered from the perspective of both participants. The response of each participant is influenced by the interpretation given to the other's act. Thus, the term *matching activity* may be preferable to *imitation* when its interactive aspect is being emphasized, because the attainment of congruence is the central feature for both participants. Not only understanding of or agreement with the other, but also sharing of interest and of perspective is indicated by engagement in the same act. Finally, this approach suggests that a unit of analysis such as a *round* (composed of at least one turn by each partner) might be more appropriate for studying matching activity than an individual imitative turn.

Our study of imitation during mother–child conversations grew out of our more general interest in matching activity during early interpersonal interactions. We thought it important to study spontaneously occurring conversations in the child's usual environment. We also thought it important to apply the same set of categories to the contributions made to those conversations by children and by mothers. In research on children's language acquisition, although utterances attempting to match those of the partner have been examined for both children and mothers, this has been rarely done within the same study. Moreover, different categories have been usually applied to their replications. Children's replications of adult utterances have been usually categorized as partial or complete and considered to be imitations, but adults' replications have been typically distinguished by the types of additions or modifications made and have been viewed in different terms. We thought that a similar category system applied to the utterances of both partners would facilitate the comparison of their respective contributions to the conversation. In addition, by studying the same mother–child pairs over a 6-month interval, we hoped to be able to relate interactional characteristics to children's language skills.

In our study, imitative utterances of both mothers and children were identified and coded in terms of the same four categories in order to better specify the role of imitation during the early phases of language acquisition. This report will focus on a description of the occurrence of the various types of imitative utterances in the speech of mothers and on a presentation of the relation between their frequency and the language skills of the children. At this point, our goal is to describe the links between the occurrence of various types of imitative interactions and the language skills of the participants, but not to demonstrate a causal connection between any particular type of interaction and children's linguistic progress. In addition, a pragmatic analysis of maternal imitative utterances was carried out to help clarify the function of such utterances during mother–child conversations.

5.2 Method

5.2.1 Subjects

The mother–child pairs in this sample were participants in a previous study of mother–child interaction during the child's first year of life. For the present study, they were asked to be observed in their homes twice, when the child was around 18 months and around 24 months of age. Of the 17 families who completed the 1-year observation session, 14 agreed to the two additional observations. The observations took place when the children were on the average 18 months, 2 days (SD = 25 days) and 24 months, 12 days (SD = 23 days) old.

The educational and social status of these families was above average. Of the 14 children, 7 were girls. Seven of the children were firstborn, another 4 had one older sibling, and 3 had more than one older sibling.

5.2.2 Procedure

The families were aware that we were interested in their interactions now that the children were beginning to use language. The visits to a family's home were arranged for a time when the mother and child were together free of pressing tasks or distractions by other family members. During each of the visits, the mother was asked to interact with her child as she usually did while they ate a snack, read a picture book, and played with some toys provided by the investigator. The visits were around 1 hour in length. All the visits were conducted by the same investigator. The conversations between the mothers and children were audiotaped using an external omnidirectional microphone. The investigator also made a written record of the conversations and included notes about their context. The recording activity of the investigator discouraged extensive discussions between her and the mother or the child.

The audiotapes of these conversations were transcribed by one listener and checked by the investigator. The notes made during the visits were used to clarify the transcripts. Utterances that included any unintelligible words were coded as unintelligible and omitted from further analysis. Those maternal utterances that constituted straight reading from a book and were not in a conversational mode were also excluded from further analysis. Comments made to the investigator by either mother or child were not coded.

5.2.3 Coding

The transcripts of mother–child conversations in both visits were divided into utterances on the basis of intonational contours and pauses and coded for the following: (1) mean length of utterance (MLU) for both mother and child, (2) vocabulary size for the child, (3) imitation of the partner by both mother and child, (4) self-repetition by both mother and child, and (5) pragmatic function of all utterances for both mother and child.

Calculation of MLU was based on all intelligible utterances and followed the procedure of using words rather than morphemes (e.g., Fraser & Roberts, 1975; Nelson, 1977; Seitz & Stewart, 1975). Utterances that resulted from book reading, recitation of nursery rhymes, or songs were not included in the calculations. Agreement in calculating MLU was 96.1%.

An estimate of the child's vocabulary was derived from the same transcripts by counting the number of different words used nonimitatively by the child. Singular and plural forms of a word, different tenses of a verb, and words used in stock phrases were counted as separate words. Agreement in counting vocabulary size was 97.5%.

Both maternal and child utterances were coded for imitation. An utterance that replicated the partner's utterance was regarded as an imitation. In judging imitation, the procedure of considering the five preceding utterances used by Bloom et al. (1974) was adopted. On the basis of imitation categories found in the literature, especially on the work of Snow (1981), four categories for coding imitation were defined. These four categories were as follows:

(1) *Exact imitation* is reproduction of all the words in the partner's utterance in their modeled order, with no changes or additions. Some examples follow:

   (1) MOTHER.   Not like that.
       CHILD.   Not like that.
   (2) CHILD.   Have it.
       MOTHER.   Have it.

(2) *Reduced imitation* is less than full reproduction of the partner's utterance with inclusion of at least one content word from the partner's utterance and no addition of words not present in the partner's utterance.

   (1) MOTHER.   No, Michael is in school.
       CHILD.   Michael.
   (2) CHILD.   What is that right there?
       MOTHER.   What is that?

(3) *Expanded imitation* is reproduction of the complete modeled utterance in its modeled order plus at least one word, but not more than three words not in the modeled utterance. This definition corresponds to the category of expansions as used in some previous studies, but does not require that the imitation constitute a syntactically complete utterance. In contrast to Snow's (1981) system, no distinction was made with respect to whether the expansion preceded or followed the imitated segment.

   (1) MOTHER.   Duck.
       CHILD.   This duck.
   (2) CHILD.   Baby kitties.
       MOTHER.   Look at the baby kitties.

    (3) MOTHER. My spoon.
          CHILD. My spoon too.
    (4) CHILD. Gramma gave.
          MOTHER. Grandma gave it to you.

(4) *Modified imitation* is reproduction of at least one content word from the partner's utterance plus at least one word, but not more than three words not in
the modeled utterance. The main difference from the category of expanded
imitations is that full reproduction of the modeled utterance is not required.
This definition corresponds to a broad use of the category of expansions in
previous studies and to some forms of recasts studied by Nelson (1981), and
overlaps in part the category of topic continuation suggested by Bloom,
Rocissano, and Hood (1976).

    (1) MOTHER. We're gonna go swimming.
          CHILD. Go swimming in shirt.
    (2) CHILD. Me make a lot of noises.
          MOTHER. You make a lot of noises?
    (3) MOTHER. Yeah, she has arms.
          CHILD. Her have some arms.
    (4) CHILD. Put that in there.
          MOTHER. Put it in where, Bridg?

In coding imitations, only spontaneous imitations were included. Those utterances that were elicited by the mother's request that the child say a particular
word or phrase were not counted. Very few such elicited imitations occurred in
the transcripts. Moreover, although the procedure of referring back to the preceding five utterances in judging imitations was adopted, most imitations were
immediate. Over 90% of maternal imitations replicated the child's immediately
preceding utterance; the same was true of about 70% of children's imitations.
Agreement in coding imitations was 86.4%.

5.2.3.1 Self-Repetition

Because repetitiveness has been described as one characteristic of maternal
speech to young children (for review, see Chapman, 1981), maternal self-
repetitions as well as child self-repetitions were coded. A system of categories
parallel to the imitation categories was applied (Kuczaj, 1982). These repetitions
were also judged in relation to the previous five utterances; however, about 64%
of maternal self-repetitions and 50% of child self-repetitions were replications of
the speaker's immediately preceding utterance. Agreement in coding repetitions
was 84.7%.

5.2.3.2 Pragmatic Functions

All maternal and child utterances were also coded for their pragmatic function,
using a system of categories derived from those proposed by Dore (1975), Folger

and Chapman (1978), and Dale (1980). In keeping with their procedures, exact and reduced imitations were assigned only the specific function of imitation. Because the pragmatic function of expanded and modified imitations could be determined independently of the utterance that they replicated, each of these imitations was double-coded in the imitation category, and in one other pragmatic category. The following 12 categories were used for coding pragmatic function:

(1) NAME—verbal identification of observable or abstract objects;
(2) DESCRIBE—description of perceivable information;
(3) COMMENT—verbalization that goes beyond the immediately perceivable information;
(4) REQUEST INFORMATION—verbalization seeking an informational response;
(5) REQUEST ACTION—verbal request for behavioral action taking the form of a command, question, and so forth; requests for permission to do or say something were rare and were collapsed into this category;
(6) REJECT—verbal rejection of an object or action when there is a choice;
(7) DENY—verbal denial of a proposition;
(8) AFFIRM—verbalization affirming a statement or proposition;
(9) CONVERSATIONAL DEVICE—verbalization used to establish, maintain, or terminate interpersonal contact;
(10) IMITATION—exact or reduced imitation of a partner's utterance;
(11) SELF-REPETITION—immediate self-repetition; and
(12) OTHER—utterances that are not conventional words.

Agreement between four judges in coding the pragmatic function of maternal and child utterances averaged 88.6%.

5.3 Results

The findings presented in this chapter are organized around four topics: (1) prevalence of the specific categories or imitation, (2) correlation between maternal imitation prevalence and measures of children's language skills, (3) relation between maternal and child imitations, and (4) the pragmatic functions of maternal imitations and their role in conversation.

The basic characteristics of the language of mothers and children in this sample are shown in Table 5-1. The sessions were long enough to yield a sufficient number of utterances for analysis, but as is clear from the children's MLU, all the children were at Brown's (1973) Stage 1 during both observation sessions. At the 18-month session, the children's longest utterances ranged between 1 and 3 words, with a mean of 2.0 words. Six months later, their longest utterances had a mean of 5.1 words, with a range from 1 to 7 words. Preliminary analyses indicated that there were no notable differences between the conversations obtained

Table 5-1. Characteristics of Mothers' and Children's Language at the Two Observation Sessions

Observation session	Mean (and range)		
	Total utterances	MLU	Vocabulary
18 months			
Mother	546.5	3.6	–
	(182–901)	(3.1–5.5)	
Child	163.4	1.2^a	33.7
	(19–303)	(1.0–1.9)	(0–98)
24 months			
Mother	590.5	4.3	–
	(217–939)	(3.4–5.6)	
Child	293.2	2.1	129.6
	(56–468)	(1.0–2.9)	(12–199)

[a] Two children did not have any conventional words during this visit, and the mean MLU was calculated for $N = 12$.

in the three contexts sampled (snack, book reading, and play). Therefore, all subsequent calculations were carried out on each session's record as a whole.

5.3.1 Prevalence of Specific Imitation Categories

There are several ways in which imitative utterances can be examined. Analysis of the frequency of such utterances in a transcript may be the most straightforward approach, but it is very vulnerable to variations in transcript length and the length of observation sessions. If the length of sessions is constant across participants, the frequency measure becomes equivalent to a rate measure for any category of interest. A second approach is to express the frequency of different categories of utterances as a percentage of the total number of utterances for each speaker. A still different approach is to express the prevalence of different categories of utterances as a percentage of the partner's, not the speaker's, total number of utterances.

In a preliminary way, we examined our data on imitative utterances using all three approaches. Results on data expressed in frequencies and as percentages of the speaker's own utterances were quite similar. Results on data expressed as percentages of the partner's utterances gave a different and not very coherent picture. We opted for the second approach in our main data analyses because, as is clear from Table 5-1, the number of utterances obtained for both mothers and children varied greatly across the dyads. We converted the frequency of utterances in different imitation categories into percentages of the total number of utterances for each speaker. The results for the mothers are shown in Table 5-2.

Although the mean percentage of imitative utterances almost doubled from the first to the second session, mothers varied considerably in the percentage of imitative utterances in their speech. Because of the relatively small size of the

Table 5-2. Prevalence of Different Types of Utterances in Maternal Speech

	Observation session	
Types of utterances	18 months	24 months
Imitations of child		
Mean percentage	6.9	12.8
Range	0–19.6	3.1–21.5
Mean percentage of different imitation categories		
Exact	3.2	4.7
Reduced	0.1	0.9
Expanded	3.5	4.7
Modified	0.1	2.5
Self-repetitions		
Mean percentage	12.0	7.0
Range	4.5–23.7	1.6–14.0

sample and constricted variability, we utilized mainly nonparametric statistics in our analyses. By Sign test, the increase in maternal imitative utterances between the two sessions was significant ($p < .05$). This increase was very likely a result of the greater number of utterances contributed by the child during the second session. In contrast, the percentage of self-repetitions declined between the two sessions, from an average of 11.9% to 7.0%. This decline was also statistically significant ($p < .01$). These opposite trends suggest that the functions of maternal self-repetition and imitation differ and they should not be treated as a single category of redundancy in maternal language.

The different categories of imitations were not equally prevalent in maternal speech. At the 18-month session, maternal imitations were almost totally composed of exact imitations (52.7%) and expanded imitations (44.4%). This was probably because the children's single-word utterances do not allow reduced imitation or modified imitation. At the 24-month session, with an increase in children's language skills, reduced imitations and especially modified imitations became more prominent among maternal imitations. Nevertheless, exact and expanded imitations still were the most frequent categories of maternal imitations.

In contrast to maternal speech, the mean percentage of imitative utterances in the speech of children changed little between the two observation sessions; imitative utterances constituted around 16% of children's speech at both ages (see Table 5-3). At the 18-month observation, reduced and exact imitations accounted for almost all imitations in children's speech, but at the 24-month observation, modified imitations became more prominent, while reduced and exact imitations declined. Self-repetitions, on the other hand, increased, possibly reflecting the children's tendency to practice newly acquired words and grammatical forms.

Table 5-3. Prevalence of Different Types of Utterances in Child Speech

Types of utterances	Observation session	
	18 months	24 months
Imitations of mother		
Mean percentage	16.7	15.0
Range	0–42.8	4.4–31.1
Mean percentage of different imitation categories		
Exact	5.2	3.9
Reduced	11.2	8.4
Expanded	0.2	0.8
Modified	0.1	1.9
Self-repetitions		
Mean percentage	10.8	13.4
Range	0–25.7	3.6–24.8

More complete analyses of children's imitations are presented elsewhere (Broome & Užgiris, in preparation). The results shown in Tables 5-2 and 5-3 suggest that an overall imitation percentage may not adequately reflect the kinds of imitative interactions taking place at different ages in the conversations of mothers and children.

To facilitate comparison between studies presented in this volume, we also calculated the prevalence of exact immediate imitations for mothers and children as a percentage of their own utterances as well as a percentage of their partners' utterances. As shown in Table 5-4, exact immediate imitations increased for mothers, but declined for children when viewed as a percentage of their own utterances. This result is largely a function of the greater increase in the total number of utterances for children than for mothers across the 6-month period (see Table 5-1). In terms of absolute frequency of utterances in this category, both mothers and children increased in the second session (for mothers, $M = 18.14$ and $M = 31.85$ for the two observations, and for children, $M = 21.64$ and $M = 24.07$, respectively). In contrast, when viewed as a percentage of their partners' utterances, the category of exact immediate imitations was more prevalent for mothers than children and remained unchanged across the two observation sessions. Mothers responded to almost 11% of their children's utterances with exact immediate imitations.

We found that the category of exact immediate imitations is very closely approximated by adding our categories of exact and reduced imitations; Spearman rank-order correlations between these two ways of coding ranged between $r = .97$ and $r = .99$ for mothers and children at the two observation sessions. In view of this result, all subsequent analyses were based on our previously given coding categories.

Table 5-4. Mean Percentage of Exact Immediate Imitations at Two Ages

	Percentage of own utterances		Percentage of partner's utterances	
	18 months	24 months	18 months	24 months
Mother				
Mean	3.11	5.13	10.83	10.71
Range	0–9.83	1.16–8.38	0–26.67	3.04–23.45
Child				
Mean	12.31	9.11	4.43	4.12
Range	0–31.44	1.81–23.63	0–9.90	0.80–8.73

For analyzing the 18-month session, because mothers had few reduced imitations and children had very few modified imitations, the categories of exact and reduced imitation were combined into one category, while the categories of expanded and modified imitation were combined into another category. The percentages of imitation in these combined categories were analyzed by a 2 (Partner) $\times$ 2 (Observation) $\times$ 2 (Category) analysis of variance and yielded a significant Partner effect, $F(1, 26) = 4.10, p < .05$, a significant Category effect, $F(1, 26) = 17.00, p < .01$, but no overall Observation effect. Also, the Category by Partner interaction, $F(1, 26) = 21.71, p < .01$, the Category by Observation Interaction, $F(1.26) = 5.49, p < .05$, and the Partner by Observation interaction, $F(1, 26) = 4.38, p < .05$, were significant. Comparison of cell means by Tukey's test showed that a higher overall percentage of mothers' imitative utterances were in the expanded plus modified category and a higher overall percentage of children's utterances were in the exact plus reduced category. For children, the percentage of utterances in the expanded plus modified category was significantly higher at 24 months than at 18 months, but the smaller increase for mothers did not reach statistical significance. These results suggest that the prevalence of different types of imitative interactions changes in the course of language acquisition.

One striking aspect of the data already presented is that mother–child dyads vary greatly in the frequency of imitative utterances during their verbal interactions. Our sample did not split easily into two subgroups, one of imitators and another of nonimitators as indicated by Bloom et al. (1974). It formed a continuum in terms of the prevalence of imitation, supporting in this respect the findings of Folger and Chapman (1978). To illustrate some of the characteristics of the speech of dyads falling at the extremes of this continuum, we present in Table 5-5 individual data for six dyads. They were selected on the basis of the total proportion of imitative utterances in the speech of both children and mothers at the 18-month observation. To further illustrate the type of conversation taking place, excerpts from the transcripts of two of these mother–child dyads are given in the Appendix. These excerpts exemplify the tenor of interaction in the two

Table 5-5. Language Characteristics of Dyads at the Extremes of the Imitation Continuum

	High imitation dyads			Low imitation dyads		
	B	T	A	C	F	G
Percent imitation in mother's speech						
18 months	19.5	12.4	7.6	1.8	3.1	5.1
24 months	19.4	12.4	12.9	5.8	13.1	19.5
Percent imitation in child's speech						
18 months	27.4	42.8	34.7	8.1	5.2	6.0
24 months	8.7	10.7	31.1	15.5	17.1	14.2
Percent self-repetition in mother's speech						
18 months	6.7	21.1	1.9	9.2	12.8	10.0
24 months	5.4	14.0	4.8	4.4	9.2	3.6
Percent self-repetition in child's speech						
18 months	12.8	18.0	4.0	3.1	0.7	11.3
24 months	6.7	11.1	15.6	13.5	10.0	24.8
Number of mother's utterances						
18 months	539	662	901	426	556	475
24 months	462	585	939	382	796	704
Number of child's utterances						
18 months	303	194	150	98	135	150
24 months	468	280	347	230	366	499
Mother's MLU						
18 months	3.82	3.67	3.40	4.44	3.82	3.42
24 months	4.41	3.36	4.75	4.01	3.68	3.97
Child's MLU						
18 months	1.20	1.15	1.11	1.00	1.11	1.23
24 months	2.80	1.85	1.72	1.98	1.59	1.93
Child's vocabulary						
18 months	98	36	41	10	6	24
24 months	176	107	147	155	74	136

Table 5-6. Correlations Between Different Categories of Maternal Imitation and Measures of Child Language at 18 Months

	Child's		
	Number of utterances	MLU	Vocabulary
Maternal imitations			
Overall	.82[b]	.62[b]	.81[b]
Exact	.72[b]	.72[b]	.75[b]
Expanded	.83[b]	.55[a]	.77[b]
Modified	.45[a]	.48[a]	.36

[a] $p < .05$.
[b] $p < .01$.

mother–child dyads, but are not a random sampling from their conversations. The individual data illustrate that average trends are not an exact reflection of patterns characterizing specific dyads. The individual patterns suggest that children's language skills as well as mothers' interaction strategies influence the prevalence of imitation during mother–child conversations.

5.3.2 Correlation Between Maternal Imitation and Child Language

To examine the connection between maternal imitation and children's language skill in the sample as a whole, we related the prevalence of different types of maternal utterances to children's language at each of the two observation sessions. Spearman rank order correlations were calculated between the percentage of different categories of imitation in mothers' speech and several measures of children's linguistic skill. As shown in Table 5-6, the overall frequency of maternal imitation and the frequency of the different categories of maternal imitation were significantly correlated with the children's MLU and vocabulary size at 18 months as well as with their number of intelligible utterances. At this period in development, various measures of children's language skill appear to be closely related to the sheer frequency of their participation in verbal interaction (e.g., number of utterances to MLU, $r = .38$, to vocabulary size, $r = .94$). The correlation for reduced imitation is not presented, because mothers in several of the dyads did not have any reduced imitations, leaving a constricted sample.

Similar correlations were calculated for the data from the 24-month observation. The results were rather different. Overall maternal imitation was significantly correlated with the children's vocabulary size, but not with their MLU. Maternal exact imitations did not correlate with either measure of children's linguistic skill. As shown in Table 5-7, only the category of modified imitation correlated significantly with children's MLU as well as vocabulary size. Once the children became more capable speakers, imitations in the form of modifications of children's utterances appeared to be associated with higher levels of language

Table 5-7. Correlations Between Different Categories of Maternal Imitation and Measures of Child Language at 24 Months

	Child's		
	Number of utterances	MLU	Vocabulary
Maternal imitations			
Overall	.88[b]	.42	.50[a]
Exact	.47[a]	.02	−.11
Expanded	.74[b]	.26	.47[a]
Modified	.64[b]	.69[b]	.59[a]

[a] $p < .05$.
[b] $p < .01$.

skill. However, overall maternal imitation and all separate categories of maternal imitation continued to be highly correlated with the number of children's utterances. Children's imitation of maternal utterances, on the other hand, was less consistently correlated with their language skill, particularly at 24 months (Broome & Užgiris, in preparation). These data suggest that maternal imitation may promote children's attempts to accomplish their goals verbally, but further research is definitely needed to explicate the path of influence.

5.3.3 Relationship Between Mother and Child Imitation

Although it is important to determine whether maternal imitation contributes to children's long-term linguistic progress, it is no less important to understand its role in contemporaneous verbal interactions with young children. On the basis of positive concurrent correlations between maternal and child imitations, a number of researchers have speculated that imitation by the mother teaches the child to imitate his or her partner (e.g., Folger & Chapman, 1978; Kuczaj, 1983; Seitz & Stewart, 1975), but longitudinal data have been largely lacking. We examined the relations between different categories of maternal and child imitation both concurrently and across time.

Because we had observed the dyads in our sample throughout the children's first year of life, we also included a measure of vocal matching obtained during face-to-face interaction at 12 months. Vocal matching was defined as an immediate replication of the partner's vocal sounds (discrete sounds, babbles, and conventional verbalizations), but not necessarily their intonation or number. The different categories of imitation for mothers and children were intercorrelated at 12, 18, and 24 months. At each of these ages, significant correlations were obtained between maternal and child imitations for some imitation categories, but the specific categories differed at each age. As shown in Table 5-8, mothers and children had commensurate levels of vocal matching at one year, exact imitation at 18 months, and modified imitation at 24 months. Correlations across time and across categories were minimal. These results do not support the proposal

Table 5-8. Reciprocity of Imitation Between Mothers and Children[a]

Maternal imitation categories	Child imitation categories		
	Vocal matching (12 months)	Exact imitation (18 months)	Modified imitation (24 months)
Vocal matching (12 months)	.82[c]	−.18	.37
Exact imitation (18 months)	.37	.50[b]	.18
Modified imitation (24 months)	.51[b]	.09	.69[c]

[a] Spearman Rank Order Correlations.

[b] $p < .05$.

[c] $p < .01$.

that individual differences in children's tendency to imitate their mothers is a function of maternal imitation at an earlier age. They do indicate that imitation by one partner is reciprocated by the other in terms of the category that is developmentally progressive and focal at that time.

Moreover, to examine the stability of the tendency to imitate during verbal interactions, we correlated the prevalence of different types of imitations at the 18-month observation with their prevalence at the 24-month observation for mothers and children separately. Over the 6-month interval, little stability was found for either mothers or children (see Table 5-9). This suggests that imitation is not a global characteristic of the individual, but is a mode of interaction relied upon by mothers and children to varying degrees in different contexts and at different developmental periods.

5.3.4 Pragmatic Function of Maternal Imitation

The role of imitation in mother–child conversations may be also clarified by an examination of the pragmatic functions that imitative utterances serve. For this analysis, all children's utterances were coded for pragmatic function. All exact and reduced imitations were assigned the function of IMITATION, as had been

Table 5-9. Stability of Imitation Between 18 and 24 Months[a]

Imitation categories	Mother	Child
Overall	.25	.36
Exact	−.08	.13
Reduced	−.13	.22
Expanded	.11	−.38
Modified	.44	.17

[a] Spearman Rank Order Correlations.

Table 5-10. Proportions of Various Pragmatic Function Categories in Children's Speech and Proportions of Speech in Each Category Imitated by Mothers

	18-month observation		24-month observation	
Pragmatic function category[a]	In children's total utterances	Imitated by mother	In children's total utterances	Imitated by mother
NAME	.18	.46	.15	.44
DESCRIBE	.03	.33	.12	.44
COMMENT	.01	.52	.10	.28
REQUEST INFORMATION	.02	.34	.09	.18
REQUEST ACTION	.02	.48	.08	.30
REJECT	.02	.30	.01	.29
DENY	.02	.43	.02	.29
AFFIRM	.01	.25	.05	.16
CONVERSATIONAL DEVICE	.04	.14	.05	.17
IMITATION	.17	.40	.12	.21
SELF-REPETITION	.07	.21	.07	.22
OTHER	.41	.06	.14	.03

[a] The category of IMITATION includes only exact and reduced imitations; expanded and modified imitations were categorized according to their pragmatic function.

done by Folger and Chapman (1978), but expanded and modified imitations were categorized according to their other pragmatic function coding. At the 18-month observation, many of the children's utterances could not be assigned a pragmatic function because they consisted of unconventional vocalizations. As shown in Table 5-10, NAME and IMITATION were the most frequent functions of children's speech; they accounted for over a third of children's utterances. Maternal imitation of any type of their children's utterances in various function categories is also shown in Table 5-10. The mothers imitated a relatively high proportion of their children's utterances, except for the category containing unconventional vocalizations.

At the 24-month observation, the functions of children's utterances were more varied and unconventional vocalizations were substantially less frequent, but the four categories of NAME and IMITATE, together with DESCRIBE and COMMENT, accounted for almost half of children's utterances. Maternal imitations were somewhat more selective at this age, but mothers still imitated around a third of their children's utterances in many function categories.

Three functional groups of children's utterances tended to be more highly imitated by mothers. As shown in Table 5-10, close to half of children's NAME utterances were imitated by their mothers at both observation sessions. Similarly, a high proportion of children's DESCRIBE and COMMENT utterances were imitated. It seems likely that these maternal imitations addressed and expanded upon the topics introduced by the children and functioned to establish consensus regarding the object of their conversation.

A different type of interaction may be represented by mothers' imitation of the categories REJECT, DENY, and AFFIRM. Although these categories occurred very infrequently in children's utterances, mothers imitated utterances from these categories close to a third of the time. It is possible to think of these maternal imitations as functioning to establish consensus with the child regarding their positions in relation to the topic of conversation.

Maternal imitations of children's REQUEST utterances seemed to aim to clarify their children's requests. This interpretation is supported by a decline in maternal imitation of REQUEST utterances with an increase in children's verbal skills at the 24-month observation. Maternal imitation of IMITATION utterances was also much higher during the 18-month observation, supporting previous findings that imitative sequences are more frequent during the early phases of language acquisition.

In summary, the results of our study show that maternal imitations do not represent a uniform set of utterances either in terms of their form or their function. Because they correlate with measures of children's linguistic skills, maternal imitations cannot be dismissed as irrelevant to children's acquisition of such skills. However, the differential distribution of maternal imitations in relation to the functional categories of children's utterances imply that they need to be considered not only as models of linguistic forms, but also as acts in communicative exchanges, and need to be studied as part of verbal interaction sequences.

5.4 Discussion

The results of the present study speak to several issues that have been extensively discussed in the literature on children's language acquisition. They indicate that maternal imitation of children's utterances is a prominent aspect of mother–child conversations and merits further study. Furthermore, they support previous findings that maternal imitations correlate with children's language skills, indicating that the ways through which such imitations influence language acquisition merit attention. They also suggest that imitation is part of the broader system of communicative exchanges between mothers and children and needs to be examined within that broader context.

One difficulty in comparing studies dealing with imitation during early language acquisition is the diversity of terms applied to imitative utterances as well as the varying definitions of categories designated by the same term. In agreement with Kuczaj (1982), we think it is valuable to differentiate self-repetitions from imitations and to reserve the term *imitation* for replications of a partner's acts. In certain cases, imitations and self-repetitions may serve similar functions, for example, as turn-filling acts or as means for linguistic assimilation (Bohannon & Stanowicz, Chapter 6, this volume). Nevertheless, our results suggest that imitations and self-repetitions follow different trajectories during the period of language acquisition (cf. Kuczaj, 1983) and need to be investigated separately.

In the early phases of language acquisition (MLU 1.0–2.6), we found maternal imitations to be a prominent and increasing part of mother–child conversations. They may become less frequent once the child's linguistic skills reach a higher level. In this regard, our results do not contradict previous studies (e.g., Moerk, 1974; Nelson, Baker, Denninger, Bonvillian, & Kaplan, 1985; Kuczaj, 1982) showing that children's imitations decline in the 3rd year of life or that maternal imitations are negatively related to children's later linguistic accomplishment (e.g., Cross, 1977).

However, our results also suggest that it is important to differentiate between various categories of maternal imitation. The pattern of change for exact, expanded, and modified imitations obtained in our study parallels the pattern for exact repetitions, reductions, and modifications reported by Stella-Prorok (1983) for a similar age group. We found that exact imitations are most prevalent in the earliest phases of language acquisition. Their subsequent decline may indicate the mothers' sensitivity to the greater attentional and comprehension abilities of their children as well as to the use of imitation in more varied formats of interaction. The prominence of exact imitations at the 18-month observation is of interest in itself, because exact imitation of the child certainly cannot be seen as modeling of input to teach the child language. Yet, exact imitations are highly related to the child's level of language skill at this observation. It is possible that the mother's immediate reflection of the child's attempts at verbal communication helps the child to consolidate those achievements (Bohannon & Stanowicz, Chapter 6, this volume; Masur, Chapter 3, this volume). However, it seems more likely that the importance of exact imitations rests on the responsivity and interest that they communicate to the child. They establish similarity between the mother and the child in the realm of verbal interaction and thereby support the child's involvement in conversational interactions.

Our category of expanded imitations overlaps with the category of expansions used in some previous studies, but is not identical to it. We suspect that our differing results with respect to the categories of expanded and modified imitations parallel the inconsistent results in the literature regarding expansions. The type of utterance included in our category of expanded imitations may be prominent during the early phases of language acquisition and hold importance then more as a communication strategy for clarifying children's utterances than as a modeling technique. By remaining close to the child's focus of interest, expanded imitations may hold the child's involvement in verbal interaction and function to help clarify the topic of the conversation.

In contrast, modified imitations became more frequent during the 24-month observation. They may play a somewhat different role in early verbal interaction. The category of modified imitation appears to be comparable to transformed expansions considered by Cross (1977), recasts studied by Nelson et al. (1973; Nelson, 1977, 1981; Nelson et al., 1984), and contingent speech analyzed by

Bloom et al. (1976). Because we allowed the addition of only three new words, our category of modified imitation is probably closer to Nelson's simple than complex recasts, and he found simple recasts to be related to children's growth in language skill between 22 and 27 months (Nelson et al., 1984).

By introducing moderate change into the child's utterance, the category of modified imitation may contribute to the acquisition of new ways for expressing the child's realized and related meanings as well as to the clarification of the conversational positions held by mother and child. The significant correlation between maternal modified imitations and measures of children's language skill at the 24-month observation indicates that modified imitations continue to be important at later phases of language acquisition. It can be argued that modified imitations require more complex productions on the part of the child and therefore gain significance later. Although this may be true, modified imitations may also have continued importance because they convey critical linguistic information to the child as discussed by Nelson (1981; Nelson et al., 1985) with respect to the impact of rare events. Moreover, modified imitations may have a more complex discourse function, which comes into play once the child becomes a more sophisticated conversational partner.

The significant correlations obtained in our study between the various categories of maternal imitation and measures of children's language skill are in agreement with several other studies reporting significant correlations between maternal expansions or extensions and children's MLU (Wells, 1980) or extensions and gain in MLU (Barnes et al., 1983). But the differential pattern of correlation between the specific categories of maternal imitation and the two measures of children's language skill used in our study shows that it is important to distinguish between types of imitation when investigating their role in language acquisition. Our results also indicate that it is valuable to include measures of different aspects of children's linguistic accomplishment in studies on the effects of maternal input (cf. Nelson et al., 1984).

The finding of a significant association between the frequency of maternal imitation and children's imitation at different observation times during the 2nd year of life supports the interpretation of imitation as a reciprocal activity, fostering mutuality in the relationship. Our results are in agreement with previous findings of high correlations between mothers' and children's rates of imitation (e.g., Folger & Chapman, 1978; Masur, Chapter 3, this volume; Seitz & Stewart, 1975; Snow, Chapter 4, this volume), but they do not support the conclusion that imitativeness is a personal characteristic, possibly acquired during preverbal interactions. We found that mothers and children are concordant with respect to different types of imitation at different periods of development, but that there is little continuity across time. This suggests that imitation is not a characteristic learned by one partner from the other, but an expression of reciprocity in a particular context of interaction (cf. Snow, Chapter 4, this volume).

Our results on the distribution of expanded and modified imitations across the different pragmatic-function categories indicate that imitations do not simply reflect the proportions of these categories in children's speech, but rather are clustered within several pragmatic categories. Imitations serve to confirm children's verbal indications of their current interest and to clarify expressions of their goals. However, they also serve to pick up on children's emerging abilities to verbally express attitudes and judgments and to support their attempts to learn those modes of interpersonal interaction that language makes possible. The use of imitation by mothers to highlight and encourage developing language functions merits further investigation.

The interactive aspect of imitations has been recognized by other investigators. Cross (1977) has noted the possible significance of interchanges combining maternal self-repetition and expansion, which she called synergistic sequences. Others have commented on the likelihood of sequences in which a maternal imitation of a child's utterance, possibly an expansion, is followed by the child's imitation of the mother's utterance, creating an opportunity for the construction of mutually shared meaning (Bohannon & Stanowicz, Chapter 6, this volume; Slobin, 1968). The learning that meaning is mutually constructed may be no less important than the learning of the forms of verbal expression (Barnes et al., 1983). The part that children's failure to respond to maternal utterances plays in provoking maternal self-repetition has also been noted (Stella-Prorok, 1983). These kinds of observations emphasize the desirability of analyzing longer sequences of interaction for their functional significance rather than focusing on the contribution of one or the other of the participants.

Moreover, our results are in agreement with the suggestion that maternal speech serves various functions during mother–child conversations. Maternal imitations may contribute particularly to the maintenance of the child's involvement in verbal interaction. In analyzing maternal speech, McDonald and Pien (1982) isolated two clusters of utterances, one oriented toward controlling the child's actions, the other toward eliciting the child's participation in conversation. Maternal imitations seem to be particularly relevant to the second cluster. In addition, maternal imitations may exert an effect not only by affecting the child when they do occur, but also by their failure to occur. The selectivity characterizing maternal imitations may shape the flow of mother–child conversations. Stella-Prorok (1983) has found that children's primitive utterances receive more nonreplies from the mothers than more comprehensible utterances. In turn, children reply more often to simple than to complex maternal utterances. The use of imitation to fill in turns in the conversation has been noted in studies focused on children's speech (e.g., Keenan, 1977; McTear, 1978; Stine & Bohannon, 1983). These kinds of observations suggest that the responsivity of one partner to the other is a dimension of mother–child conversations that needs to be taken into account when analyzing the impact of specific types of exchanges such as imitations (cf. Nelson et al., 1985).

5.5 Interaction and Conversation

In studies of parent–child interaction, the characteristic of responsivity has been singled out as the principal component of development-fostering relationships. Responsivity may be thought of simply as attentiveness and timely reaction to the needs and efforts of the young child. In the context of interaction, however, it takes various forms. It may be useful to elaborate several aspects of responsivity evident in interactions with young children.

One important aspect of responsivity is *sharing*. It is manifest in the reciprocity of interactions, that is, in doing the same things, pursuing the same goals, and focusing on the same features of the situation as the other. Sharing is exemplified by matching exchanges, where the actions of one person are repeated by the other, but also by other types of symmetrical exchanges carried out over a period of time. But there is another aspect to sharing that is important in relation to interactions between children and caregivers. This has to do with sensitivity to a child's changing competencies and skills. Sharing requires changing with the child, adjusting the shared interests and actions to the child's changing level of functioning. This implies that in responsive interactions the nature of the exchanges will vary with development and track the child's level of competence.

Responsivity entails another aspect, that of *tutoring* the child in the skills and knowledge that are needed in order to pursue interests and sustain actions important to the child. It involves demonstrating how to act in specific situations as well as evaluating what has been learned, what needs to be redemonstrated, and what can be acknowledged as achieved. A sensitivity to the child's level of functioning is required, but not so much in order to meet the child at that level, as in order to take the child further. Exchanges during tutoring interactions appear nonsymmetrical, but have sharing as a goal to be eventually achieved.

A third aspect of responsivity refers to the arrangement of opportunities for the child to engage in actions that would permit a realization of relations between objects or among people that might not be otherwise evident. It requires understanding of the means through which different insights can be gained by a child. These *enabling* interactions help the child to acquire specific knowledge and skills, but more importantly, they lead toward a grasp of the structure and organization of means for gaining knowledge.

Within the larger framework of parent–child interactions, verbal interchanges take on an increasing importance after the first year of life. In the conversations between mothers and children, imitative utterances play an important part in conveying the mother's responsivity to the child. They are involved in sharing experiences, teaching forms of linguistic expression, and enabling children to participate in conversations so that they may become competent at "doing things with words" (Bruner, 1978). We think that the study of imitations from an interactional perspective illuminates not only the functions of imitation, but also the nature of early mother–child conversations.

Acknowledgments. Research reported in this chapter was supported by a grant from the Spencer Foundation to Ina Č. Užgiris. We thank Dorothy Campaniello, Wendy Praisner, Ora Jezer, Stephanie Pollak, and Sherry Smerigan for help in transcription and coding. We also thank the children and their families for letting us share their conversations. We are especially grateful for Kathy Sutton's expertise and patience during the preparation of this chapter.

References

Barnes, S., Gutfreund, M., Satterly, D., & Wells, G. (1983). Characteristics of adult speech which predict children's language development. *Journal of Child Language, 10,* 65–84.

Bloom, L., Hood, L., & Lightbown, P. (1974). Imitation in language development: If, when, and why. *Cognitive Psychology, 6,* 380–420.

Bloom, L., Rocissano, L., & Hood, L. (1976). Adult–child discourse: Developmental interaction between information processing and linguistic knowledge. *Cognitive Psychology, 8,* 521–552.

Bohannon III, J.N., & Hirsh-Pasek, K. (1984). Do children say as they are told? A new perspective on motherese. In L. Feagans, C. Garvey, & R. Golinkoff (Eds.), *The origins and growth of communication* (pp. 176–195). Norwood, NJ: Ablex.

Broome, S., & Užgiris, I.Č. (in preparation). The role of imitation in mother–child conversations.

Brown, R. (1973). *A first language.* Cambridge, MA: Harvard University Press.

Brown, R. (1977). Introduction. In C.E. Snow & C.A. Ferguson (Eds.), *Talking to children* (pp. 1–27). Cambridge: Cambridge University Press.

Brown, R., Cazden, C., & Bellugi-Klima, U. (1969). The child's grammar from I to III. In J.P. Hill (Ed.), *Minnesota Symposia on Child Psychology* (Vol. 2, pp. 28–73). Minneapolis: University of Minnesota Press.

Bruner, J.S. (1978). Learning how to do things with words. In J.S. Bruner & A. Garton (Eds.), *Human growth and development* (pp. 62–84). Oxford: Clarendon Press.

Chapman, R.S. (1981). Mother–child interaction in the second year of life. In R.L. Schiefelbusch & D.D. Bricker (Eds.), *Early language: Acquisition and intervention* (pp. 201–250). Baltimore: University Park Press.

Clark, R. (1977). What's the use of imitation? *Journal of Child Language, 4,* 341–358.

Corrigan, R. (1980). Use of repetition to facilitate spontaneous language acquisition. *Journal of Psycholinguistic Research, 9,* 231–241.

Cross, T.G. (1977). Mothers' speech adjustments: The contribution of selected child listener variables. In C.E. Snow & C.A. Ferguson (Eds.), *Talking to children* (pp. 151–188). Cambridge: Cambridge University Press.

Cross, T.G. (1978). Mothers' speech and its association with rate of linguistic development in young children. In N. Waterson & C. Snow (Eds.), *The development of communication* (pp. 199–216). New York: Wiley.

Dale, P.S. (1980). Is early pragmatic development measurable? *Journal of Child Language, 7,* 1–12.

Dore, J. (1975). Holophrases, speech acts and language universals. *Journal of Child Language, 2,* 21–40.

Folger, J.P., & Chapman, R.S. (1978). A pragmatic analysis of spontaneous imitations. *Journal of Child Language, 5,* 25–38.

Fraser, C., & Roberts, N. (1975). Mothers' speech to children of four different ages. *Journal of Psycholinguistic Research, 4*, 9–16.

Furrow, D., Nelson, K., & Benedict, H. (1979). Mothers' speech to children and syntactic development: Some simple relationships. *Journal of Child Language, 6*, 423–442.

Gleitman, L.R., Newport, E.L., & Gleitman, H. (1984). The current status of the motherese hypothesis. *Journal of Child Language, 11*, 43–79.

Harris, M., Jones, D., Brookes, S., & Grant, J. (1986). Relations between the non-verbal context of maternal speech and rate of language development. *British Journal of Developmental Psychology, 4*, 261–268.

Howe, C.J. (1980). Mother–child conversation and semantic development. In H. Giles, W.P. Robinson, & P.M. Smith (Eds.), *Language: Some psychological perspectives* (pp. 35–40). Oxford: Pergamon Press.

Keenan, E.O. (1977). Making it last: Repetition in children's discourse. In S. Ervin-Tripp & C. Mitchell-Kernan (Eds.), *Child Discourse* (pp. 125–138). New York: Academic Press.

Killen, M., & Užgiris, I.Č. (1981). Imitation of actions with objects: The role of social meaning. *Journal of Genetic Psychology, 138*, 219–229.

Kuczaj II, S.A. (1982). Language play and language acquisition. In H.W. Reese (Ed.), *Advances in child development and behavior* (Vol. 17, pp. 197–232). New York: Academic Press.

Kuczaj II, S.A. (1983). *Crib speech and language play.* New York: Springer-Verlag.

Lieven, E.V.M. (1978). Turn-taking and pragmatics: Two issues in early child language. In R.N. Campbell & P.T. Smith (Eds.), *Recent advances in the psychology of language* (pp. 215–236). New York: Plenum.

McDonald, L., & Pien, D. (1982). Mother conversational behaviour as a function of interactional intent. *Journal of Child Language, 9*, 337–358.

McTear, M.F. (1978). Repetition in child language: Imitation or creation? In R.N. Campbell & R.T. Smith (Eds.), *Recent advances in the psychology of language* (pp. 293–311). New York: Plenum.

Moerk, E.L. (1974). Changes in verbal child–mother interactions with increasing language skills of the child. *Journal of Psycholinguistic Research, 3*, 101–116.

Moerk, E.L. (1977). Processes and products of imitation: Additional evidence that imitation is progressive. *Journal of Psycholinguistic Research, 6*, 187–202.

Moerk, E.L., & Moerk, C. (1979). Quotations, imitations and generalizations. Factual and methodological analyses. *International Journal of Behavioral Development, 2*, 43–72.

Nadel-Brulfert, J., & Baudonniere, P.M. (1982). The social function of reciprocal imitation in 2-year-old peers. *International Journal of Behavioral Development, 5*, 95–109.

Nelson, K.E. (1977). Facilitating children's syntax acquisition. *Developmental Psychology, 13*, 101–107.

Nelson, K.E. (1981). Toward a rare-event cognitive comparison theory of syntax acquisition. In P.S. Dale & D. Ingram (Eds.), *Child language—An international perspective* (pp. 229–240). Baltimore, MD: University Park Press.

Nelson, K.E., Baker, N.D., Denninger, M., Bonvillian, J.D., & Kaplan, B.J. (1985). *Cookie* versus *do-it-again*: Imitative-referential and personal-social-syntactic-initiating language styles in young children. *Linguistics, 23*, 433–454.

Nelson, K.E., Bonvillian, J.D., Denninger, M.S., Kaplan, B.J., & Baker, N.D. (1984). Maternal input adjustments and non-adjustments as related to children's linguistic advances and to language acquisition theories. In A.D. Pellegrini & T.D. Yawkey

(Eds.), *The development of oral and written language in social contexts* (pp. 31–56). Norwood, NJ: Ablex.

Nelson, K.E., Carskaddon, G., & Bonvillian, J.D. (1973). Syntax acquisition: Impact of experimental variation in adult verbal interaction with the child. *Child Development, 44*, 497–504.

Newport, E.L., Gleitman, H., & Gleitman, L.R. (1977). Mother, I'd rather do it myself: Some effects and non-effects of maternal speech style. In C.E. Snow & C.A. Ferguson (Eds.), *Talking to children* (pp. 109–149). Cambridge: Cambridge University Press.

Pawlby, S.J. (1977). Imitative interaction. In H.R. Schaffer (Ed.), *Studies in mother–infant interaction* (pp. 203–224). New York: Academic Press.

Phillips, J.R. (1973). Syntax and vocabulary of mothers' speech to young children: Age and sex comparisons. *Child Development, 44*, 182–185.

Ramer, A.L.H. (1976). The function of imitation in child language. *Journal of Speech and Hearing Research, 19*, 700–717.

Remick, H. (1976). Maternal speech to children during language acquisition. In W. von Raffler-Engel & Y. Lebrun (Eds.), *Baby talk and infant speech* (pp. 223–233). Amsterdam: Swets & Zeitlinger.

Rodgon, M.M., & Kurdek, L.A. (1977). Vocal and gestural imitation in 8-, 14-, and 20-month-old children. *Journal of Genetic Psychology, 131*, 115–123.

Schachter, F.F. (1979). *Everyday mother talk to toddlers*. New York: Academic Press.

Scollon, R. (1979). A real early stage: An unzippered condensation of a dissertation on child language. In E. Ochs & B. Schieffelin (Eds.), *Developmental pragmatics* (pp. 215–227). New York: Academic Press.

Seitz, S., & Stewart, C. (1975). Imitations and expansions: Some developmental aspects of mother–child communications. *Developmental Psychology, 11*, 763–768.

Slobin, D.I. (1968). Imitation and grammatical development in children. In N.S. Endler, L.R. Boulter, & H. Osser (Eds.), *Contemporary issues in developmental psychology* (pp. 437–443). New York: Holt, Rinehart & Winston.

Smolak, L., & Weinraub, M. (1983). Maternal speech: Strategy or response? *Journal of Child Language, 10*, 369–380.

Snow, C.E. (1972). Mothers' speech to children learning language. *Child Development, 43*, 549–565.

Snow, C.E. (1977). Mothers' speech research – From input to interaction. In C.E. Snow & C.A. Ferguson (Eds.), *Talking to children* (pp. 31–49). Cambridge: Cambridge University Press.

Snow, C.E. (1981). The uses of imitation. *Journal of Child Language, 8*, 205–212.

Snow, C.E. (1983). Saying it again: The role of expanded and deferred imitations in language acquisition. In K.E. Nelson (Ed.), *Children's language* (Vol. 4, pp. 29–58). Hillsdale, NJ: Erlbaum.

Stella-Prorok, E.M. (1983). Mother–child language in the natural environment. In K.E. Nelson (Ed.), *Children's language* (Vol. 4, pp. 187–230). Hillsdale, NJ: Erlbaum.

Stine, E.L., & Bohannon III, J.N. (1983). Imitations, interactions, and language acquisition. *Journal of Child Language, 10*, 589–603.

Užgiris, I.Č. (1981). Two functions of imitation during infancy. *International Journal of Behavioral Development, 4*, 1–12.

Užgiris, I.Č. (1984). Imitation in infancy: Its interpersonal aspects. In M. Perlmutter (Ed.), *The Minnesota Symposia on Child Psychology, Vol. 17: Parent–child interactions and parent–child relations in child development* (pp. 1–32). Hillsdale, NJ: Erlbaum.

Užgiris, I.Č. (1989). Infants in relation: Performers, pupils, and partners. In W. Damon (Ed.), *Child development today and tomorrow*. San Francisco: Jossey-Bass.

Užgiris, I.Č., Benson, J.B., Kruper, J.C., & Vasek, M.E. (1989). Contextual influences on imitative interactions between mothers and infants. In J.J. Lockman & N.L. Hazen (Eds.), *Action in social context: Perspectives on early development*. New York: Plenum.

Wells, G. (1980). Adjustments in adult–child conversation: Some effects of interaction. In H. Giles, W.P. Robinson, & P.M. Smith (Eds.), *Language: Some psychological perspectives* (pp. 41–48). Oxford: Pergamon Press.

Appendix

Excerpts from mother–child conversations of dyads at the two extremes of the imitation continuum during both the 18-month and the 24-month observations. Dyad T was at the high end of the imitation continuum (Hi Im), and dyad C was at the low end (Low Im).

18-Month Observation

Dyad T/Hi Im (Play with Doll)

MOTHER.   Okay. What happened? What happened to that baby?

CHILD.   Baby.

MOTHER.   Pick up the head. T., T., what happened to that baby? Here, put the baby down. Go pick up the head. Fix the baby.

CHILD.   Baby.

MOTHER.   Fix the baby's head?

CHILD.   Baby.

MOTHER.   Yeah. Put the baby's head on. Can you put that on there?

CHILD.   Baby.

MOTHER.   Right here. Put the baby's head on here. See? There. Look. There.

CHILD.   Baby.

MOTHER.   Uh huh, that's the baby. Can you cover the baby up?

CHILD.   Up.

MOTHER.   Cover him up; he's cold.

CHILD.   Baby.

MOTHER.   Baby cold.

CHILD.   Baby.

MOTHER.   T., do you want to take the baby for a ride on the school bus? Where's your school bus? Hm? T., where's your school bus?

CHILD.   Eye.

MOTHER.   Eye. Where's the baby's eye? Where's the baby's eye? Right there.

CHILD.   Eye.

MOTHER.   Eye. Where's the baby's nose? Where's the baby's nose? Right there. No, that's the mouth. The baby's nose is right there. The baby's nose. Uh-huh. Baby's sleeping.

CHILD.   Baby.

MOTHER.   Baby's sleeping? He's sleeping. Baby's going night-night. Cover him up. Cover him up. There. Baby go night-night.

CHILD.   G'night, g'night.

MOTHER.   Give him a hug?

CHILD.   Hi-ee.

MOTHER.   Gonna give him a hug?

CHILD.   Baby.

MOTHER.   Here. Okay. Let's cover up the baby. There. Lookit. There.

CHILD.   Baby.

Dyad C/Lo Im (Play with Dump Truck)

MOTHER.   Ooh.

CHILD.   Ooh. Tra.

MOTHER.   Trucks, yes. Put the truck down, and we will put the blocks in it. Here, here. Oh, that is fun. Vroom, vroom. Watchout, C., watch out. Here they go! Whoosh. Vroom, vroom. Fill it up. Vroom, vroom, see. Vroom. Vroom, vroom. Oh, where is the man? No man in there.

CHILD.   Man.

MOTHER.   Where is he?

CHILD.   Ahh, ahh.

MOTHER.   He is not there. Let's put the blocks in these, put the blocks in. Dump them out. Vroom, vroom.

CHILD.   Pa.

MOTHER.   Pat, yah.

CHILD.   Pa.

MOTHER.   Say Pat, I have a nice truck with blocks in it. Huh?

CHILD.   Yah.

MOTHER.   Are you going to dump it out?

24-Month Observation

Dyad T/Hi Im (Play with Tea Set)

MOTHER.   T., why don't you pull up your sock.

CHILD.   Okay.

MOTHER.   You're losing it. Okay. Pull up your sock.

CHILD.   Pull up.

MOTHER.   Pull 'em up. There, that's a girl.

CHILD.   Pull up.

MOTHER.   Yep. There.

CHILD.   One more.

MOTHER.   One more. There.

CHILD.   There.

MOTHER.   Put your pants' leg down now.

CHILD.   Um.

MOTHER.   T. was making coffee for us.
CHILD.   Here you go. In here.
MOTHER.   Okay. Hmm, good.
CHILD.   Uh-hm.
MOTHER.   There. Drink your coffee. It's good.
CHILD.   Mama. Mama, drink coke.
MOTHER.   Drink coke? Isn't that Daddy's coke?
CHILD.   Daddy coke. I found a pop-up.
MOTHER.   Gonna cover up your sheep? Hm?
CHILD.   Baby blanket. Baby blanket.
MOTHER.   Okay.
CHILD.   Drink coffee.
MOTHER.   Okay.
CHILD.   Coke. Drink coffee. Coke.
MOTHER.   Yeah it is coffee, or coke. Whatever you want.
CHILD.   Milk?

Dyad C/Lo Im (Play with Telephone)

MOTHER.   Did she hang up?
CHILD.   She hang up. Who is it?
MOTHER.   Who is this? Did you tell her it was C.? Say, this is C.
CHILD.   C.
MOTHER.   This is C.
CHILD.   This is C.
MOTHER.   There.
CHILD.   You call Mrs. X.
MOTHER.   Who else, who else are you going to call? You going to call somebody
   else?
CHILD.   Hello. Tommy. (*Whispers.*)
MOTHER.   Tommy. (*Whispers.*) All right. I'll ring the number. Say hello.
CHILD.   Hello.
MOTHER.   Is Tommy there?
CHILD.   Tommy there? No.
MOTHER.   Where did he go?
CHILD.   Don't know. Where'd Tommy go? Call Michael.
MOTHER.   Call Michael? OK. I think he is in school. I'll call his school. OK?
CHILD.   You come.
MOTHER.   Hello. F. School? May I speak to Michael?
CHILD.   Hello. Hello. Hello.
MOTHER.   Say goodbye, Michael. Go back to school.
CHILD.   Goodbye. Go. Goodbye. He go?!
MOTHER.   He went back to school.
CHILD.   You talk again.
MOTHER.   Who do you want to talk to now?
CHILD.   Don't know. To Bobby.

MOTHER.   How about Dad?
CHILD.   How about Daddy?
MOTHER.   Want to call his office?
CHILD.   I call his office.
MOTHER.   All right. You make the numbers.

CHAPTER 6

Bidirectional Effects of Imitation and Repetition in Conversation: A Synthesis Within a Cognitive Model

John Neil Bohannon III and Laura Stanowicz

6.1 Introduction

Despite a colorful and controversial history, imitation has been prematurely rejected as an explanatory mechanism in language acquisition. During the 1950s, behaviorists asserted that simple or exact imitation was the primary means of language learning (e.g., Skinner, 1957). Critics later argued that imitation could not logically account for the rich, generative language behavior of children (see Chomsky, 1959, 1979, 1980). For example, Brown and Bellugi (1964) argued that, because children's overregularizations (*taked, swimmed*) were not and could not be imitative in nature, then neither could other acquisition phenomena be imitative. What seemed particularly damaging was the observation that children's imitative speech was no more sophisticated than their spontaneous utterances (Ervin, 1964; Slobin, 1967). What followed in the 1970s was a bifurcation of the field; researchers with more applied interests continued to work in imitation, while a few mainstream developmental psycholinguists relegated imitation to debates over appropriate definitions (e.g., McTear, 1978; Moerk, 1977; Snow, 1979, 1981b; Whitehurst & Vasta, 1975). Unfortunately, this division has widened the conceptual distance between current theory and applications such that modern thinkers (e.g., Pinker, 1984; Wexler & Cullicover, 1980) virtually ignore imitation data from clinical or applied sources. In fact, neither Pinker's (1984) nor Wexler and Cullicover's (1980) books on language learnability theory mention the term *imitation* at all, nor do they cite data on imitation or other phenomena reported in the applied journals of the American Speech and Hearing Association. Not surprisingly, clinicians may well despair of using modern theories in practice, as they appear to be too abstract for application or simply irrelevant for clinical populations. Thus, each "camp" proceeds for the most part, independently, focusing on different facets of the problem of language acquisition, with neither trying to account for the other's data. The aim of this chapter is to bridge this crevasse and reintegrate imitation into explanatory models of language acquisition.

If any reconciliation is to be achieved concerning the concept of imitation, then some basic, mutually acceptable points must be acknowledged. Once agreed, the logical and empirical consequences of that common ground may be explored. Fortunately, despite the seemingly cavernous gulf between current language development theorists and those researching imitative behavior and its applications, there are a few basic facts or postulates that all concerned should find acceptable.

Postulate 1. Imitation is a pervasive behavior in conversations.

The first point is that *imitation* (the phenomenon of words and structures from prior utterances appearing in following sentences) is pervasive in language behavior. Adults often repeat themselves and their conversational partners. Maintaining a common conversational topic (e.g., a football game) often requires using identical lexical items by both speakers in adjoining turns. Moreover, simple declarative sentences or prepositional phrases are so common that such structures may appear in conversational proximity by chance alone. But imitation specifically serves functions over and beyond mere topic maintenance and common structure usage in conversation. It may be employed to convey many distinct intentions, such as requests for clarification, affirming prior information, or providing a bridge to new information (Keenan, 1977; McTear, 1978). As the basic language skill of one's listener decreases, as in addressing younger and younger children, the rate of imitation increases. Brown & Bellugi (1964) noted that adults find it almost impossible not to imitate children. Others have reported that adults also find it equally difficult not to repeat themselves when talking to children (e.g., Bohannon & Marquis, 1977; Cross, 1977; Snow, 1972). Although self- and child-repetition probably serve different communicative functions (see Užgiris & Broome, Chapter 5, this volume), frequent repetitive and imitative sequences are one of the distinguishing characteristics of child-directed speech (for a review of CDS features see Bohannon & Warren-Leubecker, 1988; Cross, 1977; DePaulo & Coleman, 1986). Although estimates vary, repetitions compose a large part of conversations with children. Depending on the specific definition of imitation employed, imitative sequences compose 10% to 40% of the speech directed to children (Stine & Bohannon, 1983), and 5% to 40% of children's speech is imitative (Bloom, Hood, & Lightbown, 1974; Leonard, Chapman, Rowan, & Weiss, 1983; Nelson, Denninger, Bonvillian, Kaplan, & Baker, 1983). Whatever one's theoretical tilt, accounting for the frequency of imitation in conversation should be a significant issue.

Postulate 2. Children learn language within the context of conversation.

The second basic point that should be accepted is that children do *not* acquire a first or second language from mere exposure to language evidence. Some current nativistic theorists continue to insist that the language addressed to children

Table 6-1. A Microcosm of Conversational Interaction

Adult Turn A	Child Turn	Adult Turn B
Utterance A_1	Utterance 1	Utterance B_1
Utterance A_2	Utterance 2	Utterance B_2
.	.	.
.	.	.
.	.	.
Utterance A_n	Utterance n	Utterance B_n

merely triggers children's innate language biases. All children are supposed to need are regularities and connections between the sounds of language and meanings (Gleitman & Landau, 1985). Despite the impression that televised material would seem sufficient for that purpose in normal children, there exist no reports of its success in the absence of true interactive conversation. Several unfortunate quasi-experiments with children of deaf parents prove that children exclusively exposed to spoken language through the medium of television do not learn to speak (Bonvillian, Nelson, & Charrow, 1976; Sachs & Johnson, 1972). Nor do European children acquire a second language from exposure to foreign language television programming (Snow, 1981a). Therefore, some aspects of the interactional nature of conversation are responsible for children coming to speak and understand their mother tongue, although exactly which features of conversation hold the key for children is not yet known. Clearly, one possibility is the bidirectional nature of imitation and repetition. That is, no matter how much children may echo what they might hear from television, the TV will rarely repeat the child, nor will it repeat itself at the child's request.

6.1.1 Repetitive Sequences in Conversation

It is possible that some confusion over the definition and characterization of imitative behavior in language interactions is responsible for the concept's exclusion from current theory. Thus, a brief delineation of repetitive sequences in conversation may prove helpful as a focus for the current contribution (for similar analyses, see Moerk, 1983, 1985). We may characterize conversation between any two speakers (or as in this example between an adult and child) as interlocking blocks of a basic, three-behavior sequence (see Table 6-1). The leading turn consists of adults producing a single utterance or series of uninterrupted utterances. This initial adult offering has been characterized as *language modeling* by behaviorists (e.g., Whitehurst & Vasta, 1975), or as provision of *positive exemplars* by some psycholinguists (e.g., Pinker, 1984). The children's task is to comprehend and respond to the form and content of the utterances contained in their partners' prior turn. If some or all of a child's utterance contains structural or lexical elements of their partner's immediately preceding speech, it is said to be an imitation. In one sense, this is a rather narrow definition, as Snow (1981b) found imitations may be delayed over several turns or even days. Following the child's turn, the partner again responds, possibly modeling new exemplars, or repetitiously incorporating elements of the child's immediately prior speech in any of several ways. Depending on the form of the final repetition, the amount of child material incorporated, the extent of new material introduced, and the intention of the child's partner, these utterances have been variously known as repetitions (Hirsh-Pasek, Treiman, & Schneiderman, 1984), imitations and expansions (Brown & Bellugi, 1964), corrections (Bohannon & Stanowicz, 1988; Moerk, 1985), synergistic sequences (Cross, 1977) or recasts (Nelson, 1977, 1987; Nelson et al., 1983).

The above three-term interaction is a deliberate reduction and simplification, although we recognize that imitative sequences often extend over many alternating turns. We concentrate on this basic three-term relationship for two reasons: First, the most obvious and easily assessed form of imitation is a set of successive, contiguous utterances. As we shall see later, there is considerable support for the cognitive saliency of adjoining utterances that makes immediate self-repetitions and imitation of others within such sequences particularly meaningful (K. E. Nelson, et al., 1983). Second, the above sequence is the minimal unit of conversation that captures most of the basic bidirectional relations of immediate repetition: the child repeating the adult and the adult repeating the child.

Using this simple, three-behavior construct (see Moerk, 1983, 1985), parallels may be drawn between a number of important concepts across areas. All agree that children must obtain language data from others. In a simplified manner, this is captured in the first adult turn, as the first turn supplies a referential topic or context, and structural and semantic exemplars to the child for processing. The utterances in the child's turn are a microcosm of the child's linguistic response to the data initially provided by the adult. Children may, in their turn, imitate all or part of the adults' prior statements, display different degrees of comprehension mastery, productive skill (errorless or flawed speech), and their own pragmatic intentions. Finally, the adult has an opportunity to respond to the content, forms, and intentions contained in the child's turn: to affirm, reinforce, question, correct, ignore, or move on to new information and forms. In miniature and compressed time, the above model reflects the larger transactional model of language development that we have outlined elsewhere (see Bohannon & Hirsh-Pasek, 1984; Bohannon & Warren-Leubecker, 1988), in which the process of acquisition results from conversational interaction between mature and immature language users.

The purpose of the present chapter is not to recapitulate the old arguments, nor is it to present the historical trends. Nor shall we simply rehash the debates over definitions of imitation. Our contribution to this book attempts to place self-repetition and imitation in a more general model of conversation and information processing as it pertains to issues of language acquisition. In pursuit of these ends, we shall outline a cognitive model of both receptive and productive language processing and its developmental implications. Using this model, we shall examine the reported evidence of repetitive and imitative sequences by both adults and children within the conversational microcosm (Table 6-1) and relate it to its functions in conversation and acquisition. This will also allow us to address issues of child-directed speech and the comprehension-imitation-production (CIP) hypothesis. Finally, we will discuss the phenomenon of adults imitating prior child utterances. This includes the work of Keith Nelson and his associates on recasts, and new data from our lab indicating that forms of such imitations serve as error correction or negative evidence. Throughout our discussion we will attempt to support our hypothesis that these disparate phenomena are simply different facets of the same primary cognitive procedures used in language.

6.2 Language as a Cognitive Process

There are two reasons why developmental psycholinguists should seriously consider cognitive models of language processing. First, mature language behavior borrows heavily from a general social and cognitive system (see Bates & MacWhinney, 1982). Adults' language behavior serves to regulate social interaction and often mediates other cognitive activities including reasoning and problem solving. The various components of the linguistic system are also affected to differing degrees by social, memory, and other cognitive demands of conversational contexts. Thus, children are not acquiring an abstract and completely isolable algebra of grammar, but a set of cognitive procedures that allow more mature linguistic processing in a number of different contexts serving a myriad of different pragmatic goals (Bates, Beeghly-Smith, Bretherton, & McNew, 1982). The more those contexts and uses of language place additional demands on the general cognitive system, the more the supposedly "independent" language system is affected both in form and content (for evidence in children, see Carr & Evans, 1984; for adults, see Bock, 1982; Grossberg & Stone, 1986). A few obvious examples should suffice to illustrate this point. Children's general auditory memory capacity will affect their ability to process lengthy word strings; the longer the sentence, the poorer the recall (Bohannon, 1975, 1976). The effect of contextual factors is easily observed when children's primitive speech on the telephone is compared to their relatively sophisticated speech with the same person "in person" (Warren-Leubecker & Tate, 1986). Although such performance considerations have often been assumed to be trivial in comparison to idealized speaker–hearer competence or linguistic intuitions and knowledge (Chomsky, 1972), such performance limitations continually affect children's linguistic productions and comprehension. Therefore, accurate plotting of developmental language functions is virtually impossible without consideration of the processing demands of the language behavior involved, or of the context in which the developmental changes are observed.

Working Memory

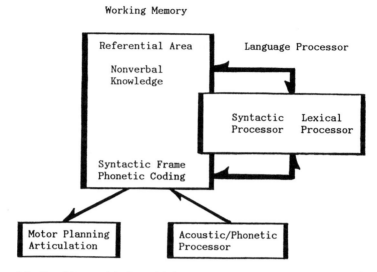

Figure 6-1. Cognitive model of an adult language processor. (Adapted from Bock, 1982.)

The second reason for employing a cognitive model of language processing concerns a strategy or heuristic of developmental investigation. Gleitman and Wanner (1984) have argued that the course or trajectory of development may be more easily investigated if the target or *end state* of that trajectory is known. Thus, if we know that adults process language in certain ways, then we might examine elements of that processing in children, while ignoring possible blind-alley explanations that point to different end states. For example, Brown (1973) criticized Braine's (1963) Open-Pivot grammar because it did not logically lead to, nor empirically predict more mature forms of, grammatical use in children. In the context of the current thesis, we argue that the end state for mature adult language behavior is a cognitive process that allows accurate deciphering of linguistic information as well as its rapid and efficient encoding into motor plans for speech.

One such model of speech production has been proposed by Bock (1982; see also Grossberg & Stone, 1986; Rumelhart & McClelland, 1986). To simplify for the purposes of the current chapter, Bock's model identifies a language-production system that incorporates features of both a syntactic parser (e.g., Anderson, 1980), and a word-retrieval system (e.g., Grossberg & Stone, 1986). She reviews a considerable body of evidence supporting the parallel processing of lexical-phonological information and syntactic information, both of which interact to construct language representations of clauses within working memory (for a more complete model of the characteristics of parallel distributed process-ing, see McClelland & Rumelhart, 1981; Rumelhart & McClelland, 1987). Briefly, the language production system functions in the following fashion (see Figure 6-1): Utterances start in working memory as interlocking chunks of nonverbal knowledge representing communicative intentions (see Chafe, 1977). For example, suppose an adult sees a red ball and wishes to comment on it. The concepts of *redness* and *ball* initially exist in working memory as nonverbal concepts or perceptual events. Information that defines relations between elements of these chunks (e.g., X [red] is a defining feature of Y [ball]) as well as semantic information about the elements themselves (e.g., X is a color, Y is a sphere) is simultaneously passed in parallel to a syntactic processor and a lexical processor, respectively. Each parallel processor then interactively borrows information from each other to specify a *syntactic frame* in working memory that contains multiply coded elements (words). These codes specify the serial position in the utterance (first, second, etc.), syntactic roles (determiner−adjective−noun), and phonetic codes (*the, red, ball*). As each phrase in a clause is completed, the ordered phrases of ordered elements (words) are then passed to a motor-planning system for articulation.

Although she did not describe a system of comprehension in her model, Bock's (1982) system may be adapted to a receptive language processor. Bloom (Bloom, 1974; Bloom, Rocissano & Hood, 1976) has argued that a language-comprehension system should be separate but interactive with the production system. A similar proposal was made by Pinker (1984), who suggested that the language system should be considered as a processing unit of both receptive and productive capacities, unless contrary evidence is provided of procedures unique to each subsystem. The minimum unique requirements for such a dual system are a motor planning system for articulation (as specified by Bock), and a processor that extracts relevant phonetic information from the acoustic environment and arrives at a phonological representation of speech in echoic memory (Grossberg & Stone, 1986). The receptive system may be adapted to our model in any of several ways. We will tentatively propose that phonetic information may be fed into Bock's system at the phonetic coding level in working memory, reversing the path of production to generate a matching syntactic frame and a corresponding set of meanings.

6.2.1 Development of Automatic Processing Procedures

There are several important aspects of the above system relevant to the present problem. First, the system uses *procedures* at all levels of analysis within the language processor: To define the syntactic relations, isolate the semantic-lexical items, determine the appropriate phonetic codes for those items, and place each within a correct syntactic frame. To understand the concept of *procedures*, one can borrow the notion of procedures from structured computer programming. In a Pascal program, all operations on the flow of data in a program are accomplished within separate procedures. Different procedures are called from the main program as needed. Data are passed to them for processing, and the results are passed back to the main program. Similarly, within natural language processing, procedures are *activated* by conditions of information passed from other processing stages. For example, the conditional information marking a concept for animacy, agency, and topicality might be sufficient to activate or *gate* the syntactic procedure identifying a concept as *subject of sentence*. Inadequately specified referential information might hinder the activation of the lexical procedure to the point where no phonetic code is found, as in the tip-of-the-tongue phenomenon (Brown & McNeill, 1966).

The activation of procedures is specifically said to subsequently lower the threshold of those procedures and make them more sensitive to the presence of the conditions for their use. In short, using specific words, sounds, and syntactic structures carries a sort of transitory cognitive momentum, *priming* the system, and making their use more likely in immediately subsequent constructions of *syntactic frames*. For example, exposure to passive constructions makes it more likely that a speaker will subsequently produce passives, or will comprehend them more rapidly than is normally the case (Bock, in press). A common example of phonetic priming involves repeating the word *silk* several times and then asking the question "What do cows drink?", which primed subjects almost unanimously to answer "Milk," despite their knowledge that cows rarely consume what they themselves produce. Almost all levels of language may be primed in this fashion: word retrieval is facilitated by either semantic (Collins & Loftus, 1975) or phonetic (Rubin, 1975) priming (see Grossberg & Stone, 1986; Meyer & Schwaneveldt, 1971). Syntactic structures may also be activated via prior use (Bock, in press). Thus, some self-repetition and imitation in conversation may be seen as a natural, and possibly unavoidable, result of the manner in which speech itself is generated and understood. It may also be viewed as a tactic that eases the processing load in both directions: either in generating syntactic frames from referential meanings or in generating referential meanings from heard phonetic information. The unused cognitive capacity may then be devoted to other tasks, such as metacognition, or the acquisition of new lexical items and syntactic procedures.

A second important feature of Bock's model is that language processing occurs in two modes: automatic and controlled. As procedures are used more frequently (practiced), their function becomes more automatic and requires less and less of the basic resource of working memory for their success (see Shiffrin & Schneider, 1977). In adults, most of the procedures used in the syntactic and lexical processors are automated and function more or less independently, once receiving their conditional information from working memory. The construction of the referential, nonverbal information chunks prior to sentence formulation and, to a lesser extent, the penultimate step where the completed syntactic clauses are held in memory before articulation involve the controlled mode of processing. Additional controlled processing is required for self-monitoring of the speech actually produced.

Children's language processing abilities may differ from adults' in many ways. First, they may simply have less resources for such processing (Ornstein, 1978). Within this *space* metaphor, children simply have smaller working memories than adults and cannot handle all the required elements needed to generate

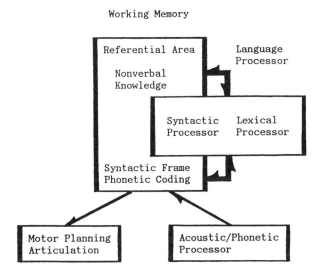

Figure 6-2. Cognitive model of a child's language processor. (Adapted from Bock, 1982.)

sophisticated speech. Second, these processes may be more controlled or *effort-ful* for children, as they are not well practiced, and thus the same processes could use more active memory space than for adults (Carr & Evans, 1984). A third possibility may be that children are less likely to muster an adequate amount of information for the activation of processing procedures that do exist. In any event, children may be characterized as having less available processing capacity during language activity than adults (see Figure 6-2).

The model requires that both nonverbal meanings and the syntactic frame are held in memory at the same time. This allows some direct association between the two cognitive events, such that highly practiced, unanalyzed word strings may bypass the generative system altogether. Both adults and children use such formulaic utterances by rote or as unanalyzed block productions (e.g., "How do you do?" "Whazzat?"). It is possible that this is also the first form of language production. Unanalyzed blocks of speech are reproduced to specific cues, such as "bye-bye." But, by the very nature of the system, the nonverbal cues, such as Grandma walking out the door, are concurrently held in working memory along with the articulatory codes for the string-to-be-uttered ("bye-bye"). Thus, the learning of new language procedures may take place within working memory where the relations between the child's coextant nonverbal knowledge and the phonetic string are available for discovery.

This process of procedure extraction may proceed through notation of privileged co-occurrences (e.g., Maratsos & Chalkey, 1980). For example, *das* and *die* denote the gender and case markings of words in German and typically co-occur with nouns. These articles may come to cue both grammatical status and word gender to children. In general, children learn language-processing procedures through detection of competing functional cues that exist in the language addressed to the child (Bates & MacWhinney, 1982). How rapidly these cue conditions become associated with the activation or *priming* of specific words or syntactic procedures is due to their frequency and reliability in signaling meaning relations (Bates & MacWhinney, 1982; MacWhinney, 1987). These theories use the notions of priming and self-organizing networks to account for automatic recoding that is the essence of language acquisition (Grossberg & Stone, 1986; Rumelhart & McClelland, 1987). Further, once children extract language-processing procedures of several types, they must repeatedly use them to the point where the procedures are automated and less demanding of precious cognitive capacity in working memory (note difference in overlap between the adult and child models in Figures 6-1 and 6-2). To be a true language user, it is not enough to know the correct processing procedures if those procedures require so much memory resources that their use is prohibitive of other aspects of language, such as pragmatic appropriateness (Warren-Leubecker & Bohannon, 1985).

In summary, the general implications for imitation within the proposed system are numerous. The two basic features of imitation in the cognitive model are the use of *priming* and the capacity for rote repetition. Priming predicts that processing known components of a particular language sample facilitates the processing of subsequent strings (either in reception or production) containing the same structures, words, or sounds. Therefore, it is assumed that imitative and repetitious sequences ease the general processing burden, resulting in faster automatic processing in adults and more accurate controlled processing in children. Further, differences in the procedures, either syntactic, lexical, or phonological, between closely related and temporally sequential utterances, *afford* comparison and analysis of the differences (Baker & Nelson, 1984; Bohannon & Stanowicz, 1988; Nelson, 1981, 1987). Lastly, rote imitation is also symptomatic of the capacity of the cognitive system. One version of rote imitation (unanalyzed mimicry) in conversation results from the *looping* of ordered phonetic codes arriving from the receptive acoustic processor straight off to the articulator, bypassing the bulk of the language processor altogether (see Figures 6-1 and 6-2). Rough and primitive links may be formed between the concurrent perceptual events and the unanalyzed syntactic frame resulting from conversational mimicry. These crude associations may be used later in a second type of rote imitation that involve self-generated, but unanalyzed, productions (e.g., "bye-bye" as discussed above). Indeed, as some (e.g., Moerk, 1975, 1983) suggest, these forms of primitive imitation by children may be reflective of the initial state of the general acquisition process itself.

6.3 Imitation and Repetition in Conversation

The various forms of imitation in conversation may now be examined within the cognitive model. A considerable amount of descriptive and experimental research has already been reported in the area of imitation. Unfortunately, few have attempted to construct a unifying theoretical framework within which all of the myriad definitions of and empirical results on imitation can peacefully coexist. The theory presented in the current chapter is just such an attempt. We argue below that the variously described examples of imitation from the literature are better understood within a single framework, rather than isolated instances of different behaviors.

6.3.1 Sources of Imitation and Repetition: Priming and Rote

Basically, the cognitive model predicts that imitative and repetitive sequences arise from two different sources in the linguistic processing system: The first source, *priming*, is the activation of existing processing procedures making their employment in subsequent operations of production or comprehension more likely. The second source, *rote* reproduction, is the imitation of ordered, but unanalyzed, phonetic codes from working memory. These two imitative sources jointly determine the various types or forms of imitative and repetitive sequences reported in the literature. The further removed the imitated form is spatially and temporally from its model, the less likely the cognitive advantages of priming or rote repetition from working memory are responsible for its use. Therefore, our current focus is the cognitive benefits that imitation or repetition bestows upon speakers and listeners during language processing within conversation. With this perspective, we shall now examine the probability of occurrence of the various types of imitation in adult and child speech.

6.3.2 Adult Self-Repetition

The first type of repetition within the conversational microcosm (see Figure 6-1) would consist of adults repeating themselves either within a turn or across turns. Uninterrupted self-repetition (within a turn) is characteristic of child-directed speech (CDS) and is negatively correlated with the language level of the child listener (Cross, 1977; Newport, Gleitman, & Gleitman, 1977). Within the present model, such self-generated sequences would tend to assist in processing the elements of the repeated string. That is, previously activated receptive procedures would be more easily employed in subsequent processing efforts, allowing devotion of more working memory to processing difficult or unfamiliar elements of the string (similar to self-recasts; see Nelson, et al., 1983).

Exactly how adults know which strings to repeat, lacking obvious and immediate cues from the child (i.e., an interruptive signal of comprehension difficulty), is unknown. One explanation is that adults may attend to subtle nonverbal cues of listener noncomprehension (e.g., facial expression, head nods, or body movement; see Patterson, Cosgrove, & O'Brien, 1980). It is also likely that unfilled pauses, in which the adult is expecting a relevant response, serve as feedback that the child is experiencing processing difficulty (Garvey, 1977, 1978). Mature speakers may generate general expectations concerning the language skill of their listeners and simply tend to repeat themselves more often when addressing linguistically primitive listeners. Several studies support this hypothesis. In the absence of an immediate noncomprehension cue, speakers who expect language difficulties in their listeners will also repeat themselves (Bohannon, Stine, & Ritzenberg, 1982; DePaulo & Coleman, 1986; Warren-Leubecker & Bohannon, 1982). When listeners do signal comprehension difficulty, adult speakers tend to repeat themselves more often across adult turns (Bohannon & Marquis, 1977; Stine & Bohannon, 1983), as in the following example:

ADULT. See the rabbit?
CHILD. What?
ADULT. See the rabbit?

6.3.3 Children's Imitations

The second type of imitation to be addressed occurs when children imitate material from the prior adult turn. An examination of such sequences in a single child (Stine & Bohannon, 1983) revealed that, in over 80% of all such sequences, the child repeated some elements of the last utterance in the adult's preceding turn, within the first utterance of the child's turn (see Table 6-1). Similarly, Bloom, Hood, and Lightbown (1974) observed that, when child imitations occurred, they tended to be immediate, "with no utterances intervening between an imitative utterance and its model" (p. 388). Because the cognitive model predicts that the facilitation afforded by repetition is brief, we should expect that exact pattern. Interpolated adult utterances should interfere with the process of priming and make extended imitation of any type much less likely.

The different types of child imitations that have been identified may also yield clues concerning the cognitive sources of imitation. Exact and partial imitation tend to be the most frequently reported imitation types in young children (e.g., Whitehurst, 1977), and they become less frequent as children grow older (Bloom et al., 1976; Snow, 1981a,b). It is possible that a good deal of these primitive imitations are of the unanalyzed, *rote* variety. Within the cognitive model, the acoustic processor feeds ordered phonetic codes into working memory, and some or all of these codes may be redirected straight to the articulator, resulting in fairly simple mimicry or parroting. Exact rote repetition only requires enough space in working memory to briefly hold the elements before articulation. New incoming material or an interpolated delay of any kind prior to articulation should reduce the probability of successful parroting. McDade, Simpson, and Lamb (1982) showed that repetition of poorly comprehended linguistic forms was disrupted following a 3-second delay between model sentence presentation and the child's response in an elicited imitation task. Moreover, increasing the processing load by increasing utterance length should also inhibit imitation. Stine and Bohannon (1983) reported that one child's repetitions in conversation occurred after adult utterances that were only slightly longer than the adult average, whereas a cue of total comprehension failure ("What?") was observed more often after very long adult utterances.

Slobin (1967) found that, when children are asked to imitate sentence structures not yet mastered, the major elements of the sentence are retained in simpler syntactic frames already mastered. Elements such as pronouns, prepositions, and articles were dropped from the imitation. This phenomenon is the likely result of processing incoming sentences by employing existing syntactic procedures. Difficult syntactic structures may result in only a partial parse, whereupon the child might elect to reformulate and generate a string for the conversational partner to assess rather than the more primitive, rote mimicry (Moerk, 1983).

Shipley, Smith, and Gleitman (1969) also observed that 2- and 3-year-old children will repeat nonsense words placed in short simple sentences, for example:

ADULT. Show me the *gup*.
CHILD. *Gup?*

At first glance, this might seem to counter the contention that imitation results exclusively from either rote parroting or the employment of existing processing procedures. Why would children imitate the only element from a sequence that could not be processed? The answer may reside in working memory where meanings and phonetic codes co-occur. As the child attempts to process the string, the phonetic codes for nonsense words yield little semantic information (reverse tip-of-tongue phenomenon). The easiest (and perhaps most efficient and informative) type of query or response would be a rote imitation of the semantically null phonetic element. But, for more sophisticated children and adults, a syntactic structure exists that performs the exact same function, the *occasional question*. The response "You went sledding where?" to the statement "I went sledding in Florida" cues the speaker about the exact elements of the prior utterance that caused problems.

Snow (1981b) recorded the incidence of exact imitations, partial imitations, and expanded imitations (the child expands, or elaborates another's utterance while retaining some of the elements) in children's speech, and found that the number of expanded imitations increased with age. Thus, expanded imitations seemed to reflect the child's growing competence with syntactic and semantic forms, and with complex discourse sequences. These expanded imitations incorporate both increasingly sophisticated constructive language skills and more mature forms of the priming function of repetition. As children make some highly practiced procedures more automatic, formulation of utterances containing those structures should be less effortful and demanding of cognitive resources (see Speidel & Herreshoff, Chapter 8, this volume). Moreover, once automated, they may be activated by prior use as in comprehending a string from a previous adult turn. Children may then incorporate some of the primed, automated elements in their response and still have enough processing capacity to add new structures and elements to their response (i.e., expanded imitations).

Another form of child repetition, *selective imitation*, has generally been overlooked in the literature. Whitehurst (1977) defined selective imitation as a repetition of syntactic form that incorporates new lexical items. Bock (in press) has shown that this repetition effect occurs in adults through the process of priming. Using previously activated syntactic procedures would permit the child's limited processing resources to be allocated to other aspects of production, such as greater fluency or diversity of meaning. Several studies have examined selective imitation either directly or indirectly by exposing children to grammatical constructions through modeling and observing the extent to which the children's subsequent speech incorporated the modeled forms. Depending on the specific methods employed, these studies have demonstrated facilitation of the use of complex sentences (Harris & Hassemer, 1972) and the passive voice (de Villiers, 1980; de Villiers & de Villiers, 1972; Lempert, 1984; Whitehurst, Ironsmith, & Goldfein, 1974) in young children. Therefore, selective imitation of already available syntactic forms is common to both adult and child speech and may arise from the same cognitive source—to wit, syntactic priming.

We now turn our attention to developmental data in order to illuminate the functions of priming and rote repetition in language learning.

6.4 The Developmental Nature of Children's Imitation

The developmental or progressive function of imitation refers to its putative role in facilitating semantic and/or syntactic learning in children's language development. An imitated form could be said to be progressive if it is more complex than the child's spontaneous speech. Such complexity may be estimated by longer mean length of utterance (MLU), the appearance of new grammatical forms, or new vocabulary items in imitations when compared to spontaneous speech. Whitehurst and Vasta (1975) argued that children first comprehend the element, that is, children react appropriately to some target linguistic element used by adults in conversation. Children then begin to repeat this structure when they hear it, and, finally, produce it spontaneously in the absence of any discernible imitative component. Stine and Bohannon (1983) found that all three stages (C, I, P) overlapped, with adequate performance in one stage increasing the probability of adequate performance in the other. Thus, according to the CIP hypothesis, imitations serve a progressive function in language acquisition; that is, comprehended (C) grammatical forms appear in imitated (I) speech prior to their appearance in spontaneous productive (P) speech. Further, once these forms appear in spontaneous speech, they will tend to disappear from imitated speech.

Despite the intuitive appeal of the CIP hypothesis, research aimed at clarifying this relationship has yielded a wide range of contradictory findings. One research strategy has involved a comparison of samples of children's imitative and nonimitative speech (Ervin, 1964; Rodd & Braine, 1970) in terms of MLU and the appearance of new grammatical forms or vocabulary items. With few exceptions (e.g., Moerk, 1977), these studies have failed to support the progressive nature of imitation in children's speech.

There are several plausible explanations for the absence of differences in complexity between imitative and spontaneous speech (see also Speidel & Herreshoff, Chapter 8, this volume). First, as Ryan (1973) and others have noted, operational definitions of imitation were generally restricted to exact or partial imitations in these studies. In light of the observation that children only imitate within the span of their working memory and are often unable to imitate sentences they themselves had previously produced (Bloom, Hood, & Lightbown, 1974), it is not surprising that repetitive speech should appear shorter or less complex than spontaneous speech under certain circumstances. Second, research has demonstrated that children tend to imitate relatively unfamiliar, as opposed to well-learned, linguistic forms. Thus, it is likely that children's imitations may appear more errorful or degenerate than some spontaneous speech that often has the advantage of contextual support and communicative intent (Bloom, 1974). For example, a child might spontaneously describe a picture that she is examining, "Mommy, look at the mother duck and all the little ducks." If asked to imitate that sentence without the contextual support of the picture book, the child may well do poorly. Finally, two studies (Leonard et al., 1983; Stine & Bohannon, 1983) have shown that linguistic forms do not immediately disappear from repetitive sequences after their appearance in spontaneous speech. The probability of imitation of a form slowly declines as the appearance of that form becomes more likely in spontaneous speech. In fact, as has been shown above, imitated forms never totally disappear from speech due to priming effects. This temporal overlap between the gradually decreasing probability of imitation and the gradually increasing probability of spontaneous production tends to make both look similar depending on the point of measurement during the acquisition process.

The second research strategy for showing the progressive function of imitation compares children's performance on tasks assessing comprehension, imitation, and production of a variety of linguistic forms. The typical comprehension task requires the child to listen to a stimulus sentence before selecting the corresponding picture from an array (George & Tomasello, 1984). Alternatively, children have been asked to act out a sentence with puppets or props. Production tasks generally require a child to describe a picture or event aloud, whereas imitation tasks simply ask children to repeat a stimulus sentence verbatim. Using these methods, researchers have reported a wide range of contradictory findings. Imitation has been observed both to precede (Fraser, Bellugi, & Brown, 1973; Lovell & Dixon, 1967) and to follow comprehension (Ruder, Hermann, & Schiefelbusch, 1977; Stine & Bohannon, 1983) and production. To further complicate matters, a number of investigators (Chapman & Miller, 1975; Keeney & Wolfe, 1972; McClelland, Yerchuk, & Holdgrafer, 1986) have shown that, under some conditions, production precedes both comprehension and imitation. In spite of this apparent confusion, the methods employed by the various studies suggest a possible resolution. Bloom (1974) and Clark (Clark, Hutcheson, & Van Buren, 1974) have both argued that children's linguistic performance (comprehension and production) may be facilitated by nonlinguistic cues commonly available from the environment. Adults tend to talk about concrete objects and events immediately perceivable to the child (Tomasello, 1988), and consequently, children may rely on such contextual cues rather than the linguistic form of the adult's spoken message. Similarly, children may provide simultaneous descriptions of ongoing environmental events (e.g., child describing elements of a picture), thereby reducing the load of syntactic and lexical processing. To the extent that language development involves decontextualization of the linguistic code from external supports, tasks that supply such support will overestimate children's true linguistic abilities.

Clearly, comprehension, imitation, and production tasks differ in the amount of contextual support provided to the child during responding across the different reported studies. For example, Chapman and Miller (1975) found that children performed better on a production task than on a comprehension task. The comprehension task required the children to select two named toys from an array (of six toys) and demonstrate the sentence using the toys as props. The production task involved watching an adult perform an action with the toys and, immediately after, describing that action. Clearly, the comprehension task had a greater load in terms of delay to responding and memory than the production task. In defense of the prior research, equating task and processing demands is actually rather difficult. For example, designing an adequate production task that does not rely on contextual cues or delayed imitation (e.g., Fernald, 1972) is next to impossible. At present, we agree with Chapman and Miller (1975), who suggest that the developmental order of tested comprehension, imitation, and production depends entirely on both the specific linguistic form and the cognitive demands of the task.

The current cognitive model predicts different developmental sequences of comprehension, imitation, and production depending on the employment of the linguistic processor. Clark (1977) has argued that children do not always comprehend what they imitate. This is certainly true in terms of the imitation and comprehension of novel words. Clark also provides evidence that children do not fully comprehend the syntactic structure of some of their imitations ($I > C$). Further, some research has noted that children frequently fail to repeat sentences verbatim, but imitate in terms of existing productive procedures ($I = P$) (Slobin, 1967; Speidel, Chapter 7, this volume). Within the cognitive model, the presence of contextual support and priming from previously processed material eases the load of processing sentences. Imitation tasks without such benefits, such as that employed by Bloom et al. (1974), can easily demonstrate the limitation of imitation (i.e., $P > I$ or $C > I$). The progressive nature of imitative sequences is due to the appearance of novel unanalyzed lexical or syntactic forms, reproduced from working memory. Given that familiar words and structures have been activated, appropriate nonverbal concepts are already present in working memory, and a to-be-processed sentence composed of to-be-learned (i.e., novel) elements is presented to the child, then the to-be-learned element may be imitated. The fact that children may imitate new semantic items in familiar syntactic frames (Chapman, Leonard, & Mervis, 1986; Shipley et al., 1969) or repeat new syntactic structures using familiar words (Whitehurst & Vasta, 1975) supports this interpretation. What remains to be explained is how mistaken associations between nonverbal conceptual chunks and linguistic procedures are winnowed out over the course of development. In short, how do children correct their errors over the course of development?

6.5 The Issue of Negative Evidence

The last application of the model is concerned with adult imitations of children's prior utterances (see Table 6-1). Within this repetitious sequence lies a candidate for the elusive *negative evidence* long declared nonexistent (Brown & Hanlon, 1970; Ervin-Tripp, 1971; MacWhinney, 1987; Pinker, 1984, 1987). Negative evidence, briefly defined, is any information from the environment concerning correct and errorful language forms. This can occur as either adults explicitly demonstrating both correct and incorrect forms (e.g., "This is the right way to say this . . ." and "This is the wrong way to say this . . .") or correcting the child's own productive speech errors. Because few believe in the first possibility, we will focus on the second form of negative evidence: adults correcting the child's language mistakes.

Information theorists (e.g., Pinker, 1979, 1984, 1987; Wexler, 1982; Wexler & Cullicover, 1981) have tried to ascertain how much information is provided to the language learner during the learning process, either from the structure of language itself or from the environment. This method of computing information availability has come to be known as *learnability theory* (Gleitman & Wanner, 1984). These theorists suggest that mere exposure to the simple language exemplars of CDS would be ineffective in teaching syntax. If all that children heard were simple, active, declarative sentences, then how could they learn the full range of language expression? Learnability theory also assumes that mothers do not provide corrections for children's grammatical mistakes (e.g., Brown & Hanlon, 1970). If this is so, then children will learn language rules outside their native grammar, such as past-tense overgeneralizations (e.g., *taked*, *swimmed*). An absence of knowledge of results within language learning should lead to relatively random grammars. These authors argue that CDS does not provide enough language information to correct hypotheses, to narrow down hypotheses about the candidate grammars, or to permit generation of the more complex constructs in the grammar. In short, how could the child, exposed only to the simple positive evidence of CDS, learn to speak the complex language evidenced in his or her speech by 5 years of age? They conclude that children do, indeed, learn their native language, and if no reliable feedback mechanism is available, then most of the relevant information about the nature of language must come from the structure of the grammar itself (i.e., be innate to the child).

To account for the course of acquisition, learnability theorists (e.g., Pinker, 1984) propose the following learning algorithm: When each new input sentence is provided, children attempt to apply all their existing grammatical rules to the exemplar (Gold, 1967). Exemplars counter to current grammars then weaken the various rules invalidated by the new model. Although there are some serious logical problems with the omnibus algorithm itself (see MacWhinney, 1987; Valian, 1986), we suggest that empirically such comparisons rarely occur (for a similar argument, see K. E. Nelson, 1981, 1987, 1988). In contrast, the cognitive model predicts that comparison of processing procedures in closely contiguous sentences serves that function. When children produce a sentence, thereby activating procedures in linguistic processing, those procedures (and only those procedures) may then be compared with immediately subsequent processing. Thus, we propose that as children learn new grammatical procedures (the exact method is unimportant to the negative evidence issue), some of them are correct and some incorrect.. When children produce errorful utterances, the most beneficial type of correction in the cognitive model would be to immediately imitate the child, using as many of the child's elements as possible while correcting the faulty procedure, as in the following example:

CHILD.   I *swimmed* all the way across the pool!
ADULT.   You *swam* all the way across the pool?

In this fashion, the procedures (some faulty, some not) used to generate an ill-formed utterance are self-primed for the child through his or her own use. The immediately following adult imitation is processed using many of the same procedures. The contrasting procedures may then be weakened or changed depending on the degree of similarity of the rest of the string.

Obviously, such a position stands in stark contradiction to the learnability and strict nativistic approaches, and this contrast has led to a critical and pivotal role for the negative evidence issue in current explanations of language development (see Bohannon & Warren-Leubecker, 1985, 1988; Pinker, 1979, 1984). Initial data bearing on this issue were reported by Brown and Hanlon (1970), who found that their three children received no explicit, verbal corrections (e.g., "No, you said that wrong!") during an intermediate stage of syntactic development where the children were producing both correct and incorrect forms of the same construction. New studies have begun to question the Brown and Hanlon (1970) conclusion. Hirsh-Pasek et al. (1984) found that parents tend to repeat their young child's utterances containing language errors significantly more often than the child's well-formed sentences. Demetras, Post, and Snow (1986) also observed that parents tend to break their conversational flow of information with more questions and imitations following a syntactic error than following an errorless utterance. Penner (1987) found that such responses were not the sole domain of mothers. She reported that both mothers and fathers tend to imitate or recast children's language errors about twice as often as well-formed children's utterances. Unfortunately, most of the above studies had differing definitions of imitations, and children's error types. For example, Hirsh-Pasek et al. (1984) lumped parental exact, contracted, and recasted imitations into a single category of adult imitation. Penner (1987) lumped pragmatic, syntactic, phonological, and semantic errors into a single category of children's language errors.

Recently, another research group (Bohannon & Stanowicz, 1988) closely examined adult responses to children's well- and ill-formed speech. The data came from two sources. One set (Bohannon & Marquis, 1977) consisted of naturalistic conversations between 13 adults and a single child (aged 2:8). This set of transcripts allowed the comparison of one child's differential error rates and adult responses across a variety of listeners. The second data set consisted of transcribed conversations between 8 children (aged 1:8 to 3:1) and both their parents (Warren-Leubecker & Bohannon, 1984b). These data provided confirmation of some of the basic relations found with the single child, and a broader developmental scope (some of the children were still holophrastic). Both sets of transcripts (about 4,000 adult and 3,000 child utterances) were coded for language errors in the child.

Three types of children's language errors were independently coded: semantic, syntactic, and phonological. Semantic errors consisted of children's inaccurate use of particular words (calling a dog a "horse"). Syntactic errors consisted of, but were not limited to, (1) mistakes in word order (e.g., "What that is?"); (2) mismatching number, gender, or tense between the sentential subject and the verb (e.g., "They is getting mad"); or (3) errors involving missing obligatory articles (e.g., "That is horse"). Any string judged ungrammatical by all raters (e.g., "That give") was also scored as a syntax error. Phonological errors were specifically errors of pronunciation (e.g., "Those are lellow bawoons"). All errors were independently coded for each of the children's utterances and in general may be considered conservative in that we coded some of the children's utterances as errors that the parents may have considered permissible. In addition, the number of errors in each sentence of each type was coded as either a single error of that type (e.g., "Is that horse?") or multiple errors of that type (e.g., "Is that is horse?"). The different error types were treated separately to test the adults' sensitivity to each type.

Adult responses to well- or ill-formed child utterances were examined in two ways. The first centered on the probability of adult imitation following both well- and ill-formed utterances (following Hirsh-Pasek et al., 1984). Although almost any differential response would serve the informational requirements of negative evidence (Demetras et al., 1986), adult imitation served as the focus of the current analysis. Within the cognitive model, the time-dependent, sequential processing of similar strings is the primary candidate for providing information on the correct form of language.

Three types of adult repetition were coded. Exact repetitions consisted of verbatim reproduction of the child's entire preceding utterance. Recasts were scored if the adult preserved the child's meaning but replaced elements of the child's utterance, as in the following example:

CHILD.   That be monkey.
ADULT.   That is a monkey.

Expanded repetitions were coded if the adult reproduced major elements of the child's utterance and added new information, as in the following example:

CHILD.   Monkey climbing.
ADULT.   The monkey is climbing to the top of the tree.

The number of imitations of each type were then divided by the total number of opportunities to respond to either well- or ill-formed children's speech.

Data from the first set of transcripts revealed that adult imitations (exact + recasts + expansions) were dependent on the length of the child's utterance, with little differential adult responding (and also fewer child errors) in sentences less than four words in length (17% to 22% imitated). In contrast, when the child's sentences were five or more words in length (and containing 65% errors), the rate of adult imitation of ill-formed child utterances grew to over 40%, while the rate of imitation of well-formed utterances shrank to 10% ($p < .01$). This effect disappeared when the various types of adult imitations were considered separately. When adults used exact imitation responses, they almost exclusively followed well-formed child utterances (78 of 81 cases), which tended to be less than five words in length. Modified imitations (recasts + expansions) tended to follow children's language errors, regardless of the length of the child's previous utterance. Adults differentially used modified imitation after a syntax (well = 18%, ill = 27%) or phonology (well = 13%, ill = 29%) error. It seemed that adults were both reinforcing well-formed child utterances with confirming exact imitations, and correcting the child's ill-formed productions with modified imitations (see Bohannon & Stanowicz, 1988).

In the second data set of mothers and fathers with their children, each of the children's utterances were coded for the total number of syntax, semantic, and phonological errors that occurred within it. Moreover, the adult responses were examined for corrections of the exact error that occurred in the preceding child utterance, as in the following example:

CHILD.   I *goed* there.
ADULT.   You *went* where?

The results indicated that the adults were differentially sensitive to errors of different types. They almost always corrected semantic errors (88%) with obvious interruptions (e.g., CHILD. "Nana." ADULT. "No, that's an orange."), while providing negative evidence about syntactic (32%) and phonological (34%) errors much less often and with a form of modified imitation.

Adult corrective imitations typically occurred more often after single errors (37%) than after multiple errors (20%). At first glance, this may seem counterintuitive. Why not correct the more flawed (multiple-error) sentences rather than those that are "close" to being correct (single-error sentences). From a learnability theory point of view, more information should logically lead to more acquisition. However, both adults and children have information-processing limitations. Adults may not know how to correct an utterance with multiple errors, and children might not know what to correct if they did. In other words, if only a single error is made and corrected, the child should be less confused over what went wrong. Thus, the parents in this study appeared to provide a corrective repetition primarily when the relation between the surface error and the child's underlying intention should be most clear. Coincidentally, the child's comparison processing seems eased considerably; only a single contrast between an incorrect procedure and a correct procedure need be made. The literature on recasts (K. E. Nelson, 1987, 1988; K. E. Nelson et al., 1983) reveals the benefits of this phenomenon. When young children are repeated by adults with only a single modification of the child's prior utterance (simple recasts), they acquire the new procedure more quickly than when they are confronted with complex recasts that change two or more features of the child's prior utterance (for a more complete discussion, see Bohannon & Stanowicz, 1988).

As intriguing as these results may be, there is as yet little data to suggest that differential adult responses have any effect on the children's speech. That is, no matter how differently adults treat children's language errors, it would go for naught if children did not gain something in terms of stored information and/or analysis. One strong clue to the adult's impact would be differential responding by the children in their turn.

A recent study (Farrar, 1987) suggests that children may be more likely to imitate adults following specific types of adult imitations, such as recasted imitations. Therefore, children's tendency to imitate their parents following different types of parental utterances was examined. The data set consisted of transcribed conversations between eight children (aged 1:8 to 3:1) and their parents, for 16 separate interactions (Warren-Leubecker & Bohannon, 1984b). Both sets of transcripts, one from the mothers and one from the fathers (about 900 adult and 800 child utterances), were coded for types of imitations in all participants. The children's imitation was coded if it (1) occurred in the exactly following turn from its model and (2) if the majority of the constituents of the child's utterance were contained in the preceding adult model. Adult utterances were coded for two basic types of imitation: exact and recast elaborations. Exact adult imitations were word-for-word reproductions of the immediately preceding child utterance, whereas recast and elaborated adult imitations contained major sentential elements from the child's preceding utterance with either changes in form and/or the addition of new information. The number of children's imitations that followed the adult imitations of the different types were divided by the total number of all of the children's imitations.

The data were analyzed by a 2 (gender of parent) × 3 (imitative probabilities: total, exact, and recast), split-plot, factorial ANOVA. Gender of parent was a between-subject variable and the type of imitative probability served as the within-subject variable. The analysis revealed no significant effect of parental gender; children responded similarly to both their mothers and fathers. The type of preceding adult utterance was the single significant effect, $F(2, 13) = 12.23$, $p < .001$. This resulted from children being twice as likely to imitate a parental utterance that was recast ($[p] = .256$, $SD = .15$) than just any immediately preceding adult utterance ($[p] = .126$, $SD = .076$). Children were least likely to imitate a parental repetition that was an exact copy of the child's own prior utterance ($[p] = .036$, $SD = .125$). All the means were significantly different from each other.

In summary, the above analysis revealed that the nature of the preceding adult utterance is a significant predictor of children's tendency to imitate. Prior work (Stine & Bohannon, 1983) has shown that children's probability of imitation also depends on their acquisition state for the imitated material. Grammatical structures that are "in transition" tend to be imitated over structures that are either well mastered or totally unfamiliar (Bloom et al., 1974; Stine & Bohannon, 1983). Taken together with the present findings, a pattern emerges. Children in the process of acquiring elements of language (phonology, semantics, syntax) probably use those elements in a faulty fashion. Utterances containing such errors are likely to be imitated with correction by the parents in recast and elaborated imitations. Finally, children tend to imitate those imitations (recasts) that differ from their own initial errors. Within the cognitive model proposed herein, the functions of priming primitive, errorful structures may be a two-stage process: First the child must use the error in his or her speech. Then the adult must recast the child's utterance possibly correcting the error (modified imitation). Only then, with the dual prime of self and other, will the child imitate the other, incorporating the new structure in an imitation. Initially, it is possible that the new structure will be simply parroted. It is also probable that children are influenced by the adult's recasts of their errors in the absence of subsequent child imitation. The differential child imitation rate following corrective recasts is merely a symptom of the more general process.

The results of the above reported studies indicate three problems for learnability theories of language acquisition. First, the assumption that adults ignore grammatical errors is clearly false. Although it is still unknown exactly how children might make use of this information, a comparison process involving some minimal contrast between procedures that generate ill-formed utterances and receptive processing of well-formed adult versions of the same utterance is a promising candidate mechanism. Second, the results indicate that the provision of negative evidence may be partially based on processing considerations, such as working memory limitations (affected by sentence length and complexity). Bohannon, Stanowicz, Ness, and Warren-Leubecker (1986) reported that when children's sentences follow demanding adult responses, more pragmatic and syntactic errors tend to occur. Thus, children must be careful of willy-nilly accepting evidence about their errors to avoid making a syntactic correction following a mere processing problem (Nakayama & Crain, 1985). Fortunately, adults seem to provide such negative evidence primarily in restricted contexts: namely, when the child makes only a single error. Third, there is new evidence, reported above and by others (Farrar, 1987), that adult's recasts of children's initial utterances set the stage for children's differential imitation of the adult recast. Thus, the children's attention to the negative evidence available in corrective recasts is also indicated.

The above results might also help to explain the moderate rates of repetition and correction. Not only are adults interested in developing mature language in children, but conversation also serves a myriad of other purposes such as socialization, broadly construed, and the simple maintenance of information flow between the participants (Bates et al., 1982; Ginsburg & Shatz, 1982). If children's conversational partners were constantly and overtly correcting the form of the child's speech (especially the child's attempts at complex and unfamiliar sentences), the resulting conversations might then be severely limited. In fact, K. Nelson (1973) found that mothers who systematically, overtly corrected their children's pronunciations had children who developed new vocabulary items at a slower rate. The currently proposed system that bases language correction on the selective provision of contrasting correct forms avoids such complications. We suggest the relatively low rates of adult-modified imitations of children is due to the limited number of times that children make exactly a single error of a particular type. Further, as adults reflect the child's structure in recasts and elaborative imitations, correcting the child's solitary error, the child then imitates the recast. Thus, the overall pattern seems to be that, as children incorporate faulty grammatical rules into their speech, adults recast the portions of the children's utterances that contain but a single error. The minimal contrasts between the child's utterance and the adult model are the conditions under which children are most likely to imitate the correct parental form. Regardless of whether or not the child does imitate the corrected form, it is also likely that such sequences make relatively permanent changes in the children's processing procedures (cf. K .E. Nelson, 1987, 1988).

6.6 Summary

As we stated in Postulate 2, language acquisition occurs within and during conversation. One of the more common features of conversation with children is exact and modified imitations (Postulate 1). Why are these imitative sequences so naturally abundant in conversations with children? We have argued that replication of prior linguistic material is in many ways easier than starting from scratch. Bock's (1982) model of a cognitive language processor was described that predicts performance benefits from employing imitation during language use. Although the cognitive model is still only tentative in its particulars (Figures 6-1 and 6-2), there is considerable support for such a system in adults. We proposed a scaled-down and primitive version of the adult system to account for children's limited capacity to process and coordinate information of various types (Figure 6-2).

The cognitive model we present allows imitations from two different processing sources: rote repetition and primed procedures. Rote repetition allows children to draw simple associations between the linguistic and contextual contents of working memory. If the ordered phonetic codes in working memory are not too numerous, they may be fed straight to the articulator for "parroted" pronunciation, without additional processing. Further, as children continue to use such associations, specific processing procedures are constructed and become automated and somewhat independent of the other processing resources in working memory. The other type of imitation involves priming of existing procedures. The use of procedures specifically makes them more sensitive for a brief period of time, with several related consequences. Not only are they more likely to be employed in further processing, but their use is also faster and less demanding of the cognitive system as a whole, freeing cognitive resources for devotion to other tasks.

We argued that much of the conversational use of imitation arises from simple processing demands. Simple imitation of unknown elements and the occasional question are both efficient means of repairing communicative breakdowns. Further, the controversy over the developmental sequence of comprehension, imitation, and production of any form is rendered mute. The answer lies in the varied demands particular tasks place on the limited extent of the child's working memory capacity. Children imitate only certain elements and only when other demands do not preclude the relatively difficult coordination of processing unknown elements.

With respect to adult-modified and exact imitation of children, we may have an excellent candidate for negative evidence (Bohannon & Stanowicz, 1988). Clearly, adults do not repeat with correction (i.e., provide negative evidence for) every errorful sentence that children utter. The reason may lie within the cognitive model. When children make multiple errors and adult processing cannot ascertain the intentions of the child, then the likelihood of adult imitation is halved. Only when single errors occur do adults have enough information to contrast imitatively what the child intended to say in a correct form. Given that such negative evidence or competing procedures are available to children when they make linguistic errors, the requirement of extensive innate linguistic universals is considerably reduced (Pinker, 1984, 1987). Further evidence suggests that such sequences of [child error] → [adult recast] has further consequences within conversation. Children are about twice as likely to imitate adult utterances that are recasts of the child's own utterance. Intuitively, this pattern suggests that children may be especially sensitive to recast corrections and use the opportunity to imitate the correct form. Thus, both recent evidence and the power of the cognitive model lead us to conclude that imitation has been prematurely rejected as a candidate mechanism in the acquisition of language.

Acknowledgments. The authors would like to thank Keith Nelson, Brian Mac-Whinney and especially Gisela Speidel for their helpful suggestions on earlier versions of this chapter. We also acknowledge that, despite their assistance, we are still culpable for any remaining errors.

References

Anderson, J. (1980). *Cognitive psychology and its implications.* San Francisco: Freeman Press.

Baker, N., & Nelson, K. (1984). Recasting and related conversational techniques for triggering syntactic advances by young children. *First Language, 5,* 3–22.

Bates, E., Beeghly-Smith, M., Bretherton, I., & McNew, S. (1982). Social basis of language development: A reassessment. In H. Reese & L. Lipsett (Eds.), *Advances in child development and behavior* (Vol. 16, pp. 8–75). New York: Academic Press.

Bates, E., & MacWhinney, B. (1982). Functionalist approaches to grammar. In E. Wanner & L. Gleitman (Eds.), *Language acquisition: The state of the art* (pp. 173–218). Cambridge, MA: Cambridge University Press.

Bloom, L. (1974). Talking, understanding and thinking. In R. Schiefelbusch & R. Lloyd (Eds.), *Language perspective: Acquisition, retardation, and intervention* (pp. 285–312). Baltimore, MD: University Park Press.

Bloom, L., Hood, P., & Lightbown, P. (1974). Imitation in language development: If when and why? *Cognitive Psychology, 6,* 380–420.

Bloom, L., Rocissano, L., & Hood, L. (1976). Adult–child discourse: Developmental interaction between information processing and linguistic knowledge. *Cognitive Psychology, 8,* 521–552.

Bock, K. (1982). Toward a cognitive psychology of syntax: Information processing contributions to sentence formulation. *Psychological Review, 89,* 1–47.

Bock, K. (in press). Syntactic persistence in language production. *Cognitive Psychology.*

Bohannon, J. (1975). The relationship between syntax discrimination and sentence imitation in children. *Child Development, 46,* 444–451.

Bohannon, J. (1976). Normal and scrambled grammar in discrimination, imitation, and comprehension. *Child Development, 47,* 669–681.

Bohannon, J., & Hirsh-Pasek, K. (1984). Do children say as they are told? A new perspective on motherese. In Feagans, L., Garvey, C., & Golinkoff, R. (Eds.), *The origins and growth of communication* (pp. 176–195). Norwood, NJ: Ablex.

Bohannon, J., & Marquis, A.L. (1977). Children's control of adult speech. *Child Development, 48,* 1002–1008.

Bohannon, J., & Stanowicz, L. (1988). Adult response to children's language errors: The issue of negative evidence. *Developmental Psychology, 24,* 684–689.

Bohannon, J., Stanowicz, L., Ness, J., & Warren-Leubecker, A. (1986, April). *Errors in sentence production: Evidence from a limited information processor.* Paper presented at the Conference on Human Development, Nashville, TN.

Bohannon, J., Stine, E.L., & Ritzenberg, D. (1982). Motherese: The effects of feedback and experience. *The Bulletin of the Psychonomic Society, 19,* 201–204.

Bohannon, J., & Warren-Leubecker, A. (1985). Theoretical approaches to language acquisition. In J.B. Gleason (Ed.), *The development of language* (pp. 173–226). Columbus, OH: Merrill.

Bohannon, J., & Warren-Leubecker, A. (1988). Recent developments in child directed speech: You've come a long way, baby-talk. *Language Science 10*(1), in press.

Bonvillian, J., Nelson, K.E., & Charrow, V. (1976). Languages and language-related skills in deaf and hearing children. *Sign Language Studies, 12,* 211–250.

Braine, M. (1963). The ontogeny of English phrase structure: The first phase. *Language*, *39*, 1–14.

Brown, R. (1973). *A first language: The early stages.* Cambridge, MA: Harvard University Press.

Brown, R., & Bellugi, U. (1964). Three processes in the child's acquisition of syntax. *Harvard Education Review, 34*, 133–151.

Brown, R., & Hanlon, C. (1970). Derivational complexity and the order of acquisition in child speech. In J.R. Hayes (Ed.), *Cognition and the development of language.* New York: Wiley.

Brown, R., & McNeill, D. (1966). The "tip of the tongue" phenomenon. *Journal of Verbal Learning and Verbal Behavior, 5*, 454–462.

Carr, T., & Evans, M. (1984). The ontogeny of description. In L. Feagans, C. Garvey, & R. Golinkoff (Eds.), *The origins and growth of communication* (pp. 297–316). Norwood, NJ: Ablex.

Chafe, W. (1977). Creativity in verbalizations and its implications for the nature of stored knowledge. In R. Freedle (Ed.), *Discourse production and comprehension* (Vol. 1). Norwood, NJ: Ablex.

Chapman, K., Leonard, L., & Mervis, C. (1986). The effects of feedback on young children's inappropriate word usage. *Journal of Child Languages, 13*, 101–117.

Chapman, R., & Miller, J. (1975). Word order in early two and three word utterances: Does production precede comprehension? *Journal of Speech and Hearing Research, 18*, 355–371.

Chomsky, N. (1959). Review of *Verbal Behavior* by B.F. Skinner. *Language, 35*, 26–58.

Chomsky, N. (1972). *Language and mind.* New York: Harcourt, Brace, Jovanovich.

Chomsky, N. (1979). Human language and other semiotic systems. *Semiotica, 25*, 31–44.

Chomsky, N. (1980). On binding. *Linguistic Inquiry, 11*, 1–46.

Clark, E. (1977). What's the use of imitation? *Journal of Child Language, 4*, 341–358.

Clark, R., Hutcheson, S., & Van Buren, P. (1974). Comprehension and production in language acquisition. *Journal of Linguistics, 10*, 39–54.

Collins, A., & Loftus, E. (1975). A spreading activation theory of semantic processing. *Psychological Review, 82*, 407–428.

Cross, T.G. (1977). Mother's speech adjustments: Contributions of selected child listener variables. In C. Snow & C. Ferguson (Eds.), *Talking to children: Language input and acquisition* (pp. 151–188). Cambridge, MA: Cambridge University Press.

Demetras, M., Post, K., & Snow, C. (1986). Feedback to first language learners: The role of repetitions and clarification questions. *Journal of Child Language, 13*, 275–292.

DePaulo, B., & Coleman, L. (1986). Talking to children, foreigners, and retarded adults. *Journal of Personality and Social Psychology, 51*, 945–959.

de Villiers, J. (1980). The processing of rule learning in child speech: A new look. In K. Nelson (Ed.), *Children's Language* (Vol. 2, pp. 1–44). New York: Gardner Press.

de Villiers, P., & de Villiers, J. (1972). Early judgements of semantic and syntactic acceptability by children. *Journal of Psycholinguistic Research, 1*, 299–310.

Ervin, S. (1964). Imitation and structural change in children's language. In E. Lenneberg (Ed.), *New directions in the study of language* (pp. 163–189). Cambridge, MA: MIT Press.

Ervin-Tripp, S. (1971). An overview of theories of grammatical development. In D. Slobin (Ed.), *The ontogenesis of grammar.* New York: Academic Press.

Farrar, M. (1987, April). Adult recasts as conditions for imitation in children. Paper presented at the meeting of the Society for Research in Child Development, Baltimore, MD.

Fernald, C. (1972). Control of grammar in imitation, comprehension, and production. *Journal of Verbal Learning and Verbal Behavior, 11*, 606-613.

Fraser, C., Bellugi, U., & Brown, R. (1973). Control of grammar in imitation, comprehension, and production. In C. Ferguson & D. Slobin (Eds.), *Studies in child language development* (pp. 465-485). New York: Holt, Rinehart & Winston.

Garvey, C. (1977). The contingent query: A dependent act in conversation. In M. Lewis & L. Rosenblum (Eds.), *Interaction, conversation, and the development of language.* New York: Wiley.

Garvey, C. (1978). Contingent queries and their relations in discourse. In E.O. Keenan (Ed.), *Studies in linguistic pragmatics.* NY: Academic Press.

George, B., & Tomasello, M. (1984). The effect of variation in sentence length on young children's attention and comprehension. *First Language, 5*, 115-128.

Gleitman, L., & Landau, B. (1985). *Language and experience: Evidence from the blind child.* Cambridge, MA: Harvard University Press.

Gleitman, L., Newport, E., & Gleitman, H. (1984). The current status of the motherese hypothesis. *Journal of Child Language, 11*, 43-80.

Gleitman, L., & Wanner, E. (1984). Current issues in language learning. In M. Bornstein & M. Lamb (Eds.), *Developmental psychology: An advanced textbook.* Hillsdale, NJ: Erlbaum.

Gold, E. (1967). Language identification in the limit. *Information and Control, 10*, 447-474.

Grossberg, S., & Stone, G. (1986). Neural dynamics of word recognition and recall: Attentional priming, learning, and resonance. *Psychological Review, 93*, 46-74.

Hamburger, H., & Crain, S. (1984). Acquisition of cognitive compiling. *Cognition, 17*, 85-136.

Harris, M., & Hassemer, W. (1972). Some factors affecting the complexity of children's sentences: The effects of modeling, age, sex, and bilingualism. *Journal of Experimental Child Psychology, 13*, 447-455.

Hirsh-Pasek, K., Treiman, R., & Schneiderman, M. (1984). Brown and Hanlon revisited: Mother's sensitivity to ungrammatical forms. *Journal of Child Language, 11*, 81-88.

Hoff-Ginsburg, E., & Shatz, M. (1982). Linguistic input and the child's acquisition of language. *Psychological Bulletin, 92*, 3-26.

Keenan, E. (1977). Making it last: repetition in children's discourse. In S. Ervin-Tripp & C. Mitchell-Kernan (Eds.), *Child discourse* (pp. 125-138). New York: Academic Press.

Keeney, T., & Wolfe, J. (1972). The acquisition of agreement in English. *Journal of Verbal Learning and Verbal Behavior, 11*, 698-705.

Lempert, H. (1984). Topic as a starting point for syntax. *Monographs of the Society for Research in Child Development, 49*(Serial No. 5).

Leonard, L., Chapman, K., Rowan, L., & Weiss, A. (1983). Three hypotheses concerning young children's imitation of lexical items. *Developmental Psychology, 19*, 591-601.

Lovell, K., & Dixon, E. (1967). The growth of the control of grammar in imitation, comprehension and production. *The Journal of Child Psychology and Psychiatry, 8*, 31-39.

MacWhinney, B. (1987). The competition model of language acquisition. In B. MacWhinney (Ed.), *Mechanisms of language acquisition* (pp. 249-308). Hillsdale, NJ: Erlbaum.

Maratsos, M., & Chalkey, M. (1980). The internal language of children's syntax: The ontogenesis and representation of syntactic categories. In K.E. Nelson (Ed.), *Children's language* (Vol. 2, pp. 127-214). New York: Gardner Press.

Mayer, J., & Valian, V. (1977, October). When do children imitate? When imitate? When necessary. Paper presented at the annual Boston University Conference on Language Acquisition, Boston, MA.

McClelland, J., & Rumelhart, D. (1981). An interactive activation model of context effects in letter perception: An account of the basic findings. *Psychological Review, 88,* 375–402.

McClelland, J., & Rumelhart, D., & the PDP Research Group. (1986). *Parallel distributed processing: Explorations in the microstructure of cognition* (Vol. 2). Cambridge, MA: Bradford Books.

McClelland, J., Yerchuk, C., & Holdgrafer, G. (1986). Comprehension and production of word order by two year old children. *Journal of Psycholinguistic Research, 15,* 97–116.

McDade, H., Simpson, M., & Lamb, D. (1982). The use of elicited imitation as a measure of expressive grammar: A question of validity. *Journal of Speech and Hearing Disorders, 47,* 19–24.

McTear, M.F. (1978). Repetition in child language: Imitation or creation. In R. Campbell & P. Smith (Eds.), *Recent advances in the psychology of language* (pp. 293–312). New York: Plenum.

Meyer, D., & Schwaneveldt, R. (1971). Facilitation in recognizing pairs of words: Evidence of a dependence between retrieval operations. *Psychological Review, 90,* 227–234.

Moerk, E. (1975). Verbal interactions between children and their mothers during the preschool years. *Developmental Psychology, 11,* 788–794.

Moerk, E. (1977). Processes and products of imitation: Additional evidence that imitation is progressive. *Journal of Psycholinguistic Research, 6,* 187–202.

Moerk, E. (1983). *The mother of Eve as a first language teacher.* Norwood, NJ: Ablex.

Moerk, E. (1985). A differential interactive analysis of language teaching and learning. *Discourse Processes, 8,* 113–142.

Nakayama, M., & Crain, S. (1985, October). Performance factors in children's spontaneous sentence production. Paper presented at the Boston University Conference on Language Development, Boston, MA.

Nelson, K. (1973). Structure and strategy in learning to talk. *Monographs of the Society for Research in Child Development, 38*(Serial No. 1–2).

Nelson, K.E. (1977). Facilitating children's syntax acquisition. *Developmental Psychology, 13,* 101–107.

Nelson, K.E. (1981). Toward a rare-event cognitive comparison theory of syntax acquisition. In P. Dale & D. Ingram (Eds.), *Child language: An international perspective.* Baltimore, MD: University Park Press.

Nelson, K.E. (1987). Some observations from the perspective of the rare event cognitive comparison theory of language acquisition. In K.E. Nelson & A. van Kleeck (Eds.), *Children's Language.* Hillsdale, NJ: Erlbaum.

Nelson, K.E. (1988). Strategies for first language teaching. In R. Schiefelbusch & M. Rice (Eds.), *Teachability of language.* Hillsdale, NJ: Erlbaum.

Nelson, K.E., Denninger, M., Bonvillian, J., Kaplan, B., & Baker, N. (1983). Maternal input adjustments and non-adjustments as related to children's linguistic advances and the language acquisition theories. In A. Pelligrini & T. Yawkey (Eds.), *The development of oral and written languages: Readings in developmental and applied linguistics.* Norwood, NJ: Ablex.

Newport, E., Gleitman, L., & Gleitman, H. (1977). Mother I'd rather do it myself: Some effects and non-effects of motherese. In C. Snow & C. Ferguson (Eds.), *Talking to children: Language input and acquisition.* Cambridge, MA: Cambridge University Press.

Ornstein, P. (Ed.), (1978). *Memory development in children*. Hillsdale, NJ: Erlbaum.

Patterson, C., Cosgrove, J., & O'Brien, R. (1980). Nonverbal indicants of comprehension and noncomprehension in children. *Developmental Psychology, 16*, 38–48.

Penner, S. (1987). Parental responses to grammatical and ungrammatical child utterances. *Child Development, 58*, 376–384.

Pinker, S. (1979). Formal models of language learning. *Cognition, 7*, 217–283.

Pinker, S. (1984). *Language learnability and language development*. Cambridge, MA: Harvard University Press.

Pinker, S. (1987). The bootstrapping problem in language acquisition. In B. Mac-Whinney (Ed.), *Mechanisms of language acquisition* (pp. 399–442). Hillsdale, NJ: Erlbaum.

Rodd, L., & Braine, M. (1970). Children's imitations of syntactic construction as a measure of linguistic competence. *Journal of Verbal Learning and Verbal Behavior, 10*, 430–441.

Rubin, D. (1975). Within word structure in the tip-of-the-tongue phenomenon. *Journal of Verbal Learning and Verbal Behavior, 13*, 392–397.

Ruder, K., Hermann, P., & Schiefelbusch, R. (1977). Effects of verbal imitation and comprehension training on verbal production. *Journal of Psycholinguistic Research, 6*, 59–72.

Ryan, J. (1973). Interpretation and imitation in early language development. In R. Hinde & J. Stevenson-Hinde (Eds.), *Constraints on learning*. New York: Academic Press.

Sachs, J., & Johnson, M. (1972, July). Language development in a hearing child of deaf parents. Paper presented at the International Symposium on First Language Acquisition, Florence, Italy.

Shiffrin, R., & Schneider, W. (1977). Controlled and automatic human information processing: II. Perceptual learning, automatic attending, and a general theory. *Psychological Review, 84*, 127–190.

Shipley, E., Smith, C., & Gleitman, L. (1969). A study of the acquisition of language: Free responses to commands. *Language, 8*, 322–342.

Skinner, B.F. (1957). *Verbal behavior*. New York: Appleton-Century-Crofts.

Slobin, D.I. (1967). Imitation and grammatical development in children. In N. Endler, S. Boulter, & H. Osser (Eds.), *Contemporary issues in developmental psychology*. New York: Holt, Rinehart & Winston.

Snow, C.E. (1972). Mothers' speech to language learning children. *Child Development, 43*, 549–569.

Snow, C.E. (1979). The role of social interaction in language acquisition. In A. Collins (Ed.), *Children's language and communication: 12th Minnesota Symposium on Child Psychology*. Hillsdale, NJ: Erlbaum.

Snow, C.E. (1981a). Social interaction and language acquisition. In P. Dale and D. Ingram (Eds.), *Child language: An international perspective*. Baltimore, MD: University Park Press.

Snow, C.E. (1981b). The uses of imitation. *Journal of Child Language, 8*, 205–208.

Snow, C.E., & Ferguson, C.A. (Eds.), (1977). *Talking to children: Language input and acquisition*. Cambridge, MA: Cambridge University Press.

Stine, E.L., & Bohannon, J. (1983). Imitations, interactions and language acquisition. *Journal of Child Language, 10*, 589–604.

Tomasello, M. (1988). The role of joint attentional processes in early language development. *Language Sciences, 7*, in press.

Valian, V. (1986, October). A problem about positive and negative evidence. Paper presented at the meeting of the Boston University Conference on Language Development, Boston, MA.

Warren-Leubecker, A., & Bohannon, J. (1982). The effects of expectation and feedback on speech to foreigners. *Journal of Psycholinguistic Research*, *11*, 207–215.

Warren-Leubecker, A., & Bohannon, J. (1983). The effects of verbal feedback and listener type on the speech of preschool children. *Journal of Experimental Child Psychology*, *35*, 540–548.

Warren-Leubecker, A., & Bohannon, J. (1984). Intonation patterns in child-directed speech: Mother–father differences. *Child Development*, *55*, 1541–1548.

Warren-Leubecker, A., & Bohannon, J. (1985). Language in society: Variation and adaptation. In J. Berko-Gleason (Ed.), *The development of language* (pp. 331–367). Columbus, OH: Merrill.

Warren-Leubecker, A., & Tate, C. (1986, October). Is preschoolers' speech egocentric? Evidence of pragmatic errors and routines in telephone conversations. Paper presented at the Boston University Conference on Language Development, Boston, MA.

Wexler, K. (1982). A principle theory for language acquisition. In E. Wanner & L. Gleitman (Eds.), *Language acquisition: The state of the art* (pp. 288–318). Cambridge, MA: Cambridge University Press.

Wexler, K., & Cullicover, P. (1980). *Formal principles of language acquisition*. Cambridge, MA: MIT Press.

Whitehurst, G. (1977). Imitation, response novelty, and language acquisition. In B.C. Etzel, J.M. LeBlanc, & D.M. Baer (Eds.), *New developments in behavioral research: Theory, method and application*. Hillsdale, NJ: Erlbaum.

Whitehurst, G., Ironsmith, M., & Goldfein, M. (1974). Selective imitation of the passive construction through modeling. *Journal of Experimental Child Psychology*, *17*, 288–302.

Whitehurst, G., & Vasta, R. (1975). Is language acquired through imitation? *Journal of Psycholinguistic Research*, *9*, 1–22.

CHAPTER 7

Imitation: A Bootstrap for Learning to Speak?

Gisela E. Speidel

> Our minds seem especially tuned to pick out corre-
> lations of features in the environment and to
> develop categories around these correlations.
>
> J. R. Anderson

The literature on imitation in language learning has been fraught not only with problems of what should be considered an imitation, but also with vague views of how imitation can help (for a discussion, see Oksaar, 1982; Snow, 1983). We must construct models of language learning in order to advance our understanding of that learning process. Predictions and hypotheses of how imitation can help should then be made from such models. These models should also be the basis for (1) definitions of subcategories of imitation and (2) the aspects of language chosen in order to study the effects of imitation.

Two distinct positions regarding the effects of imitation can be discerned in the past literature. (The authors of these positions, however, may have very different notions of imitation today.) The one position is stated very clearly by Whitehurst and Vasta (1975) in their *Comprehension-Imitation-Production* hypothesis: Speaking, in general, and imitation, in particular, are not necessary for learning the use of linguistic rules in *comprehension*. They propose a three-stage process in the acquisition of grammar: "Comprehension of a grammatical form sets the stage for selective imitation of that structure, which leads in turn to spontaneous production. Thus imitation is a process by which new syntactic structures can be first introduced into the *productive* mode" (italics added; p. 37).

Contrasting with this position is the view that imitation plays a direct role in the learning of grammar. Snow (1981), for instance, suggested that expanded and deferred imitation might "provide the learner with linguistic material which is susceptible to segmentation and further analysis" (p. 211). Clark (1977) argued this point even more strongly:

The important question is no longer whether children retain and use structures that they do not fully understand, since it is clear that they do. The questions are, rather, by what variety of means do they gradually come to release the information about syntactic structure which is trapped in the utterances they regularly use, and by what processes do they gradually correct errors that arise through the operation of the simple [imitation] strategies I have been discussing? This could be regarded as a return to the view, originally advocated in Brown & Fraser (1963), that remembered reduced imitations of adult utterances form a storehouse of information from which children gradually induce the rules of their language. (p. 355)

Bloom, Hood, and Lightbown's (1974) conception of the function of imitation falls somewhere in between these two views:

It appears that when and why the imitating child would imitate depended upon what he already knew about the behavior presented to him. . . . The results confirmed the observations of Preyer (1882), Guillaume (1926), and Valentine (1930), that the child imitates only what he is already able to understand to some extent. . . . One might explain imitation as a form of encoding that continues the processing of information that is necessary for the representation of linguistic schemas (both semantic and syntactic) in cognitive memory. (p. 418)

Bloom's position is similar to that of Whitehurst and Vasta's (1975) in that children are thought to imitate selectively, when they have comprehended. Yet, the statement that imitation is a form of encoding that continues the processing of information necessary for the representation of linguistic schemata suggests that imitation may also be of assistance in the induction of linguistic patterns.

The differing views seem to result from diverging opinions of what language learning entails: comprehension or production. Whitehurst and Vasta draw a clear distinction between understanding language and speaking. They claim that imitation is useful only for learning to speak — language comprehension precedes production and guides imitation. Clark and Snow do not explicitly state how understanding and speaking interact and how imitation functions with respect to these two components of language learning. Implicit in their writings, though, is that imitation can help the induction of linguistic patterns for speaking as well as for comprehension.

How learning to understand language and learning to speak are thought to relate to each other has implications for the role assigned to imitation. Such views must be plainly stated. Much of the controversy over imitation would become clearer if one knew whether the authors referred to comprehension or production when discussing the effects of imitation on grammatical progressivity. This chapter presents a model of language learning and describes how the use of imitation may help that learning. Recent developments in cognitive psychology as well as recent findings from research on articulation and speech pathology have shaped the present model.

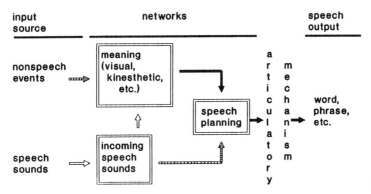

Figure 7-1. The structure of the language-processing model. Activation among networks during comprehension is shown by white arrows and during speaking by black arrows. Dotted arrows show activation sources that may be operating in the adult, but are crucial during development.

7.1 The Model

Language learning, it is suggested, consists of the development of three separate types of neural networks and their progressive integration with each other (see Figure 7-1). The three types of networks are as follows:

(1) *Incoming speech-sound* network or acoustic speech-sound network. This network records and integrates the sounds of speech.
(2) *Meaning* networks. These networks consist of the representations of the many nonspeech-sound events—visual, kinesthetic, tactile, or olfactory, as well as auditory.
(3) *Speech-planning* network for the movements required in speech. The planning network organizes the sequence and temporal spacing of activation of the neurons innervating the many muscles in the vocal tract active during speaking.

The notion underlying the term *network* is that simpler processing units of information become connected with each other and come to have some organization. The term *network* was chosen to indicate the fluidity and patterning of information processing and storage characterized by *parallel distributed processing* (e.g., Rumelhart & McClelland, 1987).

According to this model, *comprehension* of speech results from activation of units in the incoming speech-sound network together with units in the meaning network, as shown by the open arrows in Figure 7-1. In short, the understanding of words or sentences occurs when units in the incoming speech-sound and in the meaning network are active in a manner that leads to behaviors considered appropriate by the speech community. The nature of activation will be somewhat different if the activation of the meaning networks is solely through the incoming speech-sound network or also through nonspeech events. *Speaking* is thought to result mainly from activation of the meaning and the speech-planning networks, as shown by the filled arrow in Figure 7-1. The dotted arrows show activation sources that may or may not be operating in the adult, but are most important during the development of comprehension and speaking.

Obviously this is an abbreviated model: There are many more neural networks active when understanding language and when speaking (e.g., Bock, 1982; Edwards, 1984; Laver, 1980). The aim here is to show how imitation can be an integral part of language learning, and the present simplicity was chosen to achieve this aim. I will first briefly describe two general implications of the model and then talk about how, given this model, imitation can help in the learning of various aspects of speech.

7.1.1 Language Has a Significant Motor Component

One implication is that language has an important motor component. Although most of us recognize this fact, it has been given minimal attention in language-development theories. The view proposed here is that this motor component is an integral part of learning to speak. Differences in the rate or the manner in which it develops play a central part in speech development. Indeed, if there are serious problems in the motor component, a child may never acquire normal syntax in speaking (cf. Grimm, 1986; Netsell, 1986; Speidel, Chapter 9, this volume).

Researchers in the field of articulation have come to recognize the importance of this motor aspect in language development. Kent (1983) claims, "Speech is a complex recoding of a linguistic message into movements of the speech organs and the acoustic signal of speech.... Speech has to be recognized as a motor skill but also as a mode of language expression" (p. 86). Oller and MacNeilage (1983) state this view even more strongly: "Of the three factors that appear to be involved in the development of speech patterns of children—perceptual, cognitive, and motor factors—motor factors may, in spite of Jakobson's objections, be the dominant ones" (p. 96). The significance of the motor component in verbal learning was already recognized during the 1950s by researchers of paired associate learning. Reviewing the literature, Underwood and Shulz (1960) concluded that, in learning to associate two nonsense syllables, the *frequency with which a response was practiced* was very important for its retrieval, but even more important was its *pronunciability*.

As with other motor skills, it is becoming increasingly clear that for speech there are central neural networks that guide the sequencing and temporal organization of the muscle movements for target speech sounds (e.g., Kelso, Tuller, & Harris, 1983). Skilled sequences of movements are thought to be not the result of fixed, finite patterns of motor activity for making particular speech sounds, but rather the result of temporal space-coordinate systems, or plans, which include specification of the target, the behavioral goal. This allows targeted speech sounds to be obtained even when there are large variations in the initial position of the speech musculature (MacNeilage, 1970; Oller & MacNeilage, 1983). These space-coordinate systems, therefore, not only permit very rapid execution of the behavior, but also the adjustment of the speech muscles depending on their position at any given moment. Therefore, in the mature speaker a relatively small number of higher-order systems must be intentionally activated in order to trigger automatically lengthy and complex sequences of motor activity.

It is uncertain what the linguistic units of these central plans are, whether phonemes (Liberman & Mattingly, 1985), syllables (Fromkin, 1968), words (Netsell, 1986), phrases, or perhaps even sentences, or whether all levels coexist. Whatever the nature of these central plans for producing speech sounds is in the adult, they take time and practice to develop and to become integrated with each other. The speech-planning network in the present language-processing model is viewed as having a similar function as these space-coordinate systems.

7.1.2 Comprehension and Speaking: Related but Separate Processes

That comprehension and speaking are not identical is something with which most language researchers would agree. Yet many reports read as if language development were a unitary phenomenon and there were no distinction. Take, for example, the fascinating book by Peters (1983) on the units of language acquisition, in which she suggests that the units may not only be words, but also whole phrases and sometimes even sentences. She does not say whether these units are units of production or comprehension, or whether the units are identical in comprehension and production.

Different distinctions between comprehension and production have been made. For instance, Huttenlocher (1974) saw comprehension and production as requiring different memory processes. Anderson focused on different representational systems (1983, pp. 268–269) with different syntactical rule access. Whitehurst and DeBaryshe (Chapter 11, this volume) suggest that the distinction might be between associative (comprehension) and operative (speaking) learning.

The distinction drawn in our network model is compatible with all three of the above views. The relationship between comprehension and speaking in this model may become clearer with the following example from bilingual language development: The hypothesis is that in bilinguals two different sets of incoming speech-sound networks and two different sets of speech-planning networks develop. The meaning representations will be the same to the extent to which the environments in which the languages are learned are the same. In Figure 7-2 there is a unitary meaning network shown with separate incoming-sound and separate speech-planning networks for the two languages. (It is clearly possible, that the two speech-planning systems are overlapping and not entirely separate.)

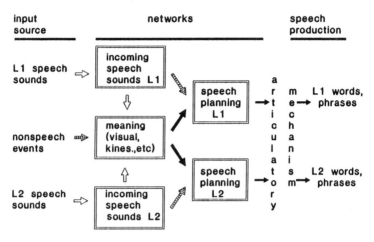

Figure 7-2. The structure of the model for language processing in bilinguals. Activation among networks during comprehension is shown by white arrows and during speaking by black arrows. Dotted arrows show activation sources that may be operating in the adult, but are crucial during development.

A 3-year-old German-English bilingual boy was told to say to his auntie, "I love you." He said "Ich love Du." *Ich* is the German equivalent of *I*, and *Du* is the German equivalent of *you* in the nominative case. He clearly understood the message. Why did he then "translate"? Why was it not simpler for him just to imitate? The different activation patterns that are possible among the networks can readily explain what may have happened. Let us say that English in this case is *L*1 and German is *L*2. Since the boy understood the message, the English speech stream must have activated the appropriate units in the *L*1 incoming speech-sound network, which in turn activated corresponding units in the meaning network. However, the connections between the meaning unit *I* and units in the speech-planning networks were stronger for *L*2, the German *ich*, than for *L*1, the English *I*. The same happened for the meaning *you* where he used *Du* to express this thought (in German it should have been *Dich* rather than *Du*). Only with *love* was the unit in the meaning network sufficiently strongly connected with the corresponding *L*1 speech-planning unit.

A very similar kind of behavior has been noted in Hawaiian-English/English bidialectal children (Day, Boggs, Tharp, Gallimore, & Speidel, 1974). When 5- or 6-year-olds were given such sentences to imitate as "Michael didn't come to school yesterday," they would repeat back the Hawaiian-English equivalent, "Michael, him neva come school yesterday." In other words, they also did the seemingly more difficult thing—translate rather than imitate exactly what they heard. Again units in the incoming speech-sound network activated the appropriate units in the meaning network. These, however, were probably more strongly connected with the Hawaiian-English speech-planning network, yielding the Hawaiian-English repetition.

7.1.3 Development of Comprehension and Speaking

Activation patterns within each network and across networks are gradually built up from experiences into organized units (i.e., knowledge). The manner in which the units within and across networks become organized and integrated with one another is thought to happen in the way described by Stern (1985), Mandler (1985), Bjorklund (1985, 1987), or Rumelhart and McClelland (1987). These views of representational development stress that events have multiple features, and that knowledge representation is distributed, making a parallel processing system necessary. It is argued that *similarity* between two events in time Y and time Z, and *co-occurrence* (or contiguity) of two events, A and B, are basic processes in the development of mental representations and their integration with each other. They all propose that the frequency with which similarities and co-occurrences within and between events are registered shapes the development of representations and their organization and affects the ease with which mental representations are accessible and retrievable. Emotional/arousal factors such as the value of an object or event will also affect to what degree something becomes represented (cf. Whitehurst & DeBaryshe, Chapter 11, this volume).

The three sets of mental networks in our language model—the incoming speech-sound, the meaning, and the speech-planning networks—are thought to develop and become integrated with each other as the result of the processes described above: similarity of an event Y to an event Z (even when they are separated by time), co-occurrence of event A and B, and the frequency with which these two processes happen. Important here is that frequency is not identical to environmental frequency. The distinction here is between input (environmental frequency) and uptake (activation frequency), or that which the learner selects. (See K. E. Nelson, 1987.)

With some exceptions (see Bohannon & Stanowicz, Chapter 6, this volume; K. E. Nelson & Bonvillian, 1978), language comprehension is thought to be a few steps ahead of speaking. For instance, young children find it easier to locate an object whose name they hear than to recall the word upon being shown the object (Huttonlocher, 1974). The studies by Sinclair (Sinclair-de Zwart, 1967; Sinclair, Sinclair, & de Marcellus, 1971) and replications (Speidel, 1984) show that grammar in comprehension is much further developed than in speech. The same advance of comprehension over speaking occurs for speech sounds (Bernthal, Greenlee, Eblen, & Marking, 1987; Oller & MacNeilage, 1983). It is also a common experience of second-language learners who can understand their new language fairly well, but find it extremely difficult to speak.

The usual developmental differences between comprehension and speaking suggest that the networks involved in comprehension are, on the whole, more readily developed, integrated, and accessed, than those involved in speaking.

This difference may be due to any or all of the following reasons: (1) the incredible complexity of the motor systems involved in speaking, (2) the manner in which the speech-planning units are developed and activated, and (3) sheer differences in frequency of activation. In the first stages of language learning, the networks active in comprehension—the incoming-sound and the meaning networks—will be much more often activated than the networks involved in speaking—the meaning and the speech-planning networks.

7.1.3.1 Development of Comprehension

What happens in the development of comprehension? An infant typically hears speech in some form of nonverbal context—diapering, eating, and so forth. The speech sounds of the care giver will activate units in the infant's incoming-speech-sound network. At the same time, the nonverbal context in which the speech sounds are heard will activate certain visual, kinesthetic units in the meaning networks. Such co-occurrence of activation of units in the two networks should strengthen their connection and foster their integration: The activation of the particular units in the incoming speech-sound network should increasingly bring about the activation of the corresponding units in the meaning network without the actual occurrence of the nonspeech event. For example, if a child has often heard the sound "milk" in a variety of speech-sound contexts such as "Here's your milk," "Do you want some milk?" together with seeing and experiencing milk in a variety of ways, then, when the child hears "milk" in the absence of milk, some units in the meaning network that had been previously activated by the presence of milk should become activated by the incoming speech-sound units. In plain words, the speech of the care giver will gradually come to be understood, even in the absence of the nonverbal context.

7.1.3.2 Development of Speaking

Much more difficult to explain is the development of speaking. Let us first look at what is thought to happen when a skilled person speaks. When such a person speaks, particular units in the meaning network are thought to activate units in the speech-planning network. For this to come about, the units in the meaning network must be highly integrated with the appropriate units in the speech-planning network. How do the necessary activation patterns get established?

In order that units of these two sets of networks can become connected, they must be active together close in time. Under what conditions does this happen? One way in which the meaning and the speech-planning networks could be activated close together in time is when the incoming speech-sound network activates both the meaning and the speech-planning networks almost simultaneously, that is, during meaningful (as opposed to rote) imitation. The manner in which imitation can help in this integration will be the focus of the next sections.

7.2 Patterns of Activation During Verbal Imitation

Imitation is defined here as the reproduction, or attempted reproduction, of a behavior observed in someone else: whether that reproduction be immediate or deferred, whether it be the repetition of a single phoneme or a whole sentence, whether it is reduced or expanded, whether the model has been observed once or many times, and whether the model has been imitated once or many times.

Within the network language model, different patterns of activation are possible during verbal imitation. Some of these possibilities will be discussed below.

7.2.1 Pattern 0: Partial Activation of the Speech-Planning Network

It is evident that there must be close links between the incoming speech-sound and the speech-planning networks. The activity in the incoming speech-sound network must somehow guide the development of the speech-planning network, for how else could children learn so quickly to make the sounds of their speech community. This means that *activation of the incoming speech-sound network must result at least in partial activation of the speech-planning network*. Liberman and his colleagues (e.g., Liberman, 1982; Liberman & Mattingly, 1985) have suggested that there is "a biologically based link between perception and production" of speech (see also Menyuk, 1971). They hold that the human brain has evolved a specialized phonetic module (similar to special neural modules for songs in birds) in which *speech perception is actually a neuromuscular process*. Their evidence and rationale for the existence of a special link, tightly bonding perception and production, are quite convincing.

In the same way that the incoming speech-sound and the meaning networks develop gradually through repeated activation, the activation of the incoming speech-sound network does not result initially in complete activation of the speech-planning network so that not everything that can be understood can also be repeated accurately. Rather, when an infant or toddler first hears a word, the resulting incoming speech-sound activation may first only partially activate the relevant units in the speech-planning network, and only after several experiences with the same word (or phrase) may the speech-planning networks become more fully activated so that an overt imitation can be performed. Since the meaning networks are often active together with the incoming speech-sound network, in the manner described above for the development of comprehension (i.e., hearing speech in context), the meaning networks would also frequently be active during such partial activation of the speech-planning network. In this way the crucial activation conditions for the development of speech would be met without *overt* imitation.

It is suggested that this pattern of neural activity, in which the incoming speech-sound network partially activates the speech-planning network while the meaning networks are active, is a major avenue for the integration of the meaning and the speech-planning networks, or in simple words, for learning to speak. The pattern is probably the unobserved precursor to immediate, self-selected, meaningful imitation and also to deferred imitation, described in the sections below. The only difference between this activation pattern and activation in overt self-selected imitation (i.e., spontaneous imitation [Oksaar, 1982]) is in terms of strength or degree of elaboration of the neural activity. In overt imitation the activation of units in the speech-planning network is sufficiently strong and elaborate to produce a response.

7.2.2 Pattern 1: Immediate Self-Selected Imitation

In this activation pattern, the incoming speech-sound and the meaning networks are active and play a part in the activation of the speech-planning network to produce overt repetition: Since all three networks are active close in time, such imitation should, according to such theories as Bjorklund's (1987), Mandler's (1985), and Rumelhart and McClelland's (1987), lead to their further integration, particularly the integration between the meaning and the speech-planning networks.

Adam's imitation of his mother while doing a puzzle (cf. Slobin, 1968; Speidel & Nelson, Chapter 1, this volume) is a good example of such *self-selected imitation* and the activation pattern thought to underlie it. As Adam is repeating some of his mother's words, he probably has some degree of understanding of these words. Moreover, his repetition of the words would seem to yield a further round of activation of the particular incoming speech-sound units and corresponding units in the meaning networks, while there are still traces of activity in the speech-planning network.

In fluent speakers, thought and speech are usually so closely integrated as the result of frequent joint activation of the meaning and the speech-planning networks that they give the speaker the sensation they are inseparable. Only when occasionally we cannot think of the desired word, and a meaning unit does not automatically activate its corresponding speech-planning unit, do we realize their distinctiveness.

With toddlers, however, the units in the networks are still in the process of being formed, as well as the connections between units in the different networks. The way in which immediate imitation can help in the development and integration of the meaning and the speech-planning networks is thought to happen as follows: If a child is just beginning to use a word, it will be easier for the child to say the word if he has just heard it, namely, in immediate imitation (cf. Bohannon & Stanowicz, Chapter 6, this volume; Speidel & Herreshoff, Chapter 8, this volume), because the activity in the incoming speech-sound network partially activates units in the speech-planning network automatically, as described above, and thereby *primes* them.

Once the child has used the word, it should be more readily retrievable the next time—that is, immediate imitation is a form of *rehearsal*. Rehearsal, or the immediate "verbal repetition of to-be-remembered material" (Ornstein & Naus, 1978), has been found to be an effective strategy for remembering items. Although the frequency with which an item is repeated is directly related to recall (e.g., Rundus, 1971; Rundus & Atkinson, 1970), the type of rehearsal is also important (Craik & Watkins, 1973; Woodward, Bjork, & Jongeward, 1974). Cuvo (1975), Naus, Ornstein, and Aivano (1977), and Ornstein, Naus, and Stone (1977) have shown that items *rehearsed together* will more likely be *retrieved together* from long-term memory.

This finding is congruent with the arguments made by Bjorklund, Mandler, Rumelhart, and McClelland summarized above, namely, that co-occurrence of events is a most significant variable in knowledge representation and retrieval. The finding also has significant implications for what kind of imitation would be helpful in integrating the meaning with the speech-planning networks: The meaning networks must be active during imitation. This kind of activation pattern is more likely to occur during self-selected imitation, as in the example with Adam, than during the rote imitation described below.

To summarize, it is thought that immediate imitation has a priming (cf. Chapter 6, this volume; Moerk, Chapter 12, this volume) as well as a rehearsal or memory function. In these ways overt imitation can be a major vehicle for developing the speech-planning network and for integrating the speech-planning with the meaning networks. Some evidence that imitation facilitates the use of words and grammatical forms in speech exists (Moerk, 1977; Ramer, 1976; Reger, 1986; Whitehurst, Ironsmith, & Goldfein, 1974). The manner in which these immediate imitations may help in articulation, word, and syntactic learning will be described in more detail in later sections.

7.2.2.1 Pattern 1a: Immediate Reduced Imitation

It has long been known that we are limited in how much we can hold in short-term memory, or working memory (e.g., Baddeley, 1976; Baddeley & Hitch, 1974; Case, 1985; Dempster, 1981; Mandler 1985; Miller, 1956). It is therefore not surprising that language-learning toddlers can repeat only pieces of the longer sentences they have just heard. Limitations on uptake mean that the child must select certain speech sounds from the speech stream. What determines the child's selection of speech sounds has been the focus of many studies and hypotheses (e.g., Braine, 1974; Brown, 1973; Nelson, 1973; K. E. Nelson, 1987; Reger, 1986; Schieffelin, 1981; Sinclair, 1975). The selection process yields two kinds of *reduced imitations*:

(1) The exact repetition of a sequence of words comprising a portion of the partner's speech. For example, Adam's mother, when talking about a puzzle piece in Adam's hand, said, "No, the other way," and Adam asked, "Other way?"

(2) The repetition of two or more words that are *not adjacent* in the utterance that served as the model. For example, Adam's mother said, "I guess you have to turn it around," and Adam repeated, "Guess turn round."

Given that these reduced imitations are self-selected imitations, the reasoning for how they could help in the integration of the meaning and the speech-planning networks is the same as described for Pattern 1.

7.2.3 Pattern 2: Immediate Rote Imitation

In immediate *rote imitation*, units in the incoming speech-sound network activate units in the speech-planning network, without activation of the corresponding units in the meaning network. The result is parroting. This form of imitation occurs when a child is asked to repeat something and does so without understanding or reflection.

From repetitive use of this form of imitation with the same words or sentences, such as chanting nursery rhymes or the Pledge of Allegiance, rote memorization of verbal strings occurs. Some language-development programs for little children foster this kind of imitation when they demand frequent rehearsal of words and sentence patterns without letting the children put their own thoughts into words. For example, some activities from the Peabody Kit (Dunn, Horton, Smith, 1968) or Bereiter and Engelman's (1966) language program, which is part of DISTAR, encourage rote imitation. Although such rote imitation can result in the learning of word strings and may even yield a sense of syntactic structures (Braine, 1971), it has not been found useful in developing children's ability to express their own thoughts in speech (Speidel, 1987a).

A situation that seems to fall in between Pattern 1 and Pattern 2 occurs when a child is asked to repeat specific phrases within a very well-defined social context. An example of this is the "Say 'bye-bye'" routine during leave-taking. This seems to be a favorite strategy for language interaction with toddlers in some cultures such as the Kaluli (Ochs & Schieffelin, 1982), the Kwara'ae described by Watson-Gegeo and Gegeo (1986), and working-class families in the United States (Miller, 1982). The care giver tries to ensure the child's attention to the context by pointing or the context is so obvious that the care giver believes the child is paying attention to the situation, thereby making it very likely that the relevant meaning units are activated together with the speech-planning units. However, it is possible that the child is paying attention to something very different while repeating the words.

7.2.4 Pattern 3: Deferred Imitation and the Road to Spontaneous Speech

Another possible activation pattern is the one in which the meaning and speech-planning networks are active, something that happens during spontaneous speech. But this same activation pattern also happens by definition during *deferred imitation*, a form of imitation in which the model has not occurred recently (Snow, 1983).

The following is an example of deferred imitation presented by Snow. *N* told his father to do something and then added, "That's a good idea," an expression he frequently heard his mother use (Snow, 1983). In line with our reasoning above, hearing the phrase on previous occasions should have activated the incoming speech-sound and the meaning networks and at least partially the speech-planning network. With repeated exposure to the phrase, the speech-planning network should have become more fully and more readily activated until it was possible for N to say the phrase without having just heard it. In other words, this kind of deferred imitation can be viewed as the result of previous activation in the form of either Pattern 0 or 1.

We can distinguish, somewhat artificially, between productive spontaneous speech and deferred imitation in terms of the size and flexibility of the mappings of units between the meaning and the speech-planning networks: In adult spontaneous, "productive" speech, the mapping is (or appears to be) at the word level, whereas in deferred imitation it is a phrase, or even a whole sentence. An adult can use each word in N's "That's a good idea," separately in a different context, whereas for N the whole sentence has more the status of a single word (see Peters, 1983; Snow, 1983).

The overlap between spontaneous speech and deferred imitation is reflected in Snow's (1983) definition of deferred imitations along the following criteria: "1) similarity . . . in words used and in order of stressed items; 2) prosodic identity; 3) . . . similarity between the situation in which the model utterance was heard and the situation in which it was produced" (p. 43). These criteria seem to distinguish deferred imitation from spontaneous speech only in degree and not qualitatively. Every word that a child retrieves from long-term memory is in some sense a deferred imitation: The word must sound similar to one already heard, the stress must be similar to how it has been stressed in utterances heard before, and the situation must have some similarity to ones in which the word was heard before.

The concept of deferred imitation illustrates the continuum between imitated language and spontaneous speech and suggests that no clear distinction is possible. What we label spontaneous speech may be seen as speech in which meaning units and matching units in the speech-planning network, stored in long-term memory by either covert (Pattern 0) or overt (Pattern 1) imitation, are arranged in novel ways. Thus, in the present model, deferred imitations are viewed as essential building blocks for spontaneous speech. How productive and flexible use could grow out of these imitations will be shown in the next section and in the section on imitation and the acquisition of syntactic speech.

7.2.5 Pattern 4: Expanded Immediate Imitation

Expanded imitation, in which one part of an utterance is imitated and another part is constructed without an immediately preceding model, can be seen as the result of a combination of Patterns 1 and 3: Some units of the speech-planning network are activated solely through activity in units of the meaning network (i.e., deferred imitation), whereas others are activated by simultaneous activity in the incoming speech-sound and corresponding units in the meaning networks (i.e., immediate imitation). In other words, expanded imitations may be viewed as a form of speech in which one part is the result of immediate imitation and another part is viewed as the result of deferred imitation, that is, retrieval of speech sounds from long-term memory. The child uses these two forms together creatively to serve his or her communication needs.

Snow (1983) provides us with some excellent examples of expanded imitations as follows:

MOTHER.   What did we crash into last night?
NATHANIAL.   Crash into living room.

Crash into is produced as an immediate imitation (Pattern 1), whereas *living room*, according to the present reasoning, is produced from long-term memory as a deferred imitation (Pattern 3), in that Nathanial has probably heard and said *living room* a number of times before, perhaps initially in immediate imitation, but now clearly without the need for an immediate model.

Expanded imitations show the interweaving of the diverse sources of information and processing modes from which speech develops. The task for language learners is to activate appropriate speech sounds for expressing their thoughts. Some of the words and phrases from the speech partner can be used (i.e., immediate imitation); other parts must be retrieved from memory as deferred imitations from earlier instances in which the meanings were paired with speech sounds. This combinatory work calls for the creativity described by Jakobson (Section 1.6).

7.2.6 First Word Combinations

Many of the first word combinations of children could, without much stretch of the imagination, be called *reduced deferred* imitations. (However, see Slobin, 1971, for a different view.) For example, most of the first word combinations Bowerman (1973) listed, such as "Kendall read," "Daddy here," and "Find Mommy," could be reduced deferred imitations of utterances that Kendall heard very often: "Kendall read" may have had as its models "Does Kendall want to read?" "Kendall, let's read," and "Kendall, go and read." "Daddy here" can be derived from "Daddy's here," "Wait until Daddy's here," or "Let's see if Daddy's here." "Find Mommy" could be modeled after "Let's find Mommy," "Go find Mommy," and "Where can we find Mommy?" In short *no single utterance* needs to be the model for these first word combinations. Rather, the *regularities and co-occurrences* of the words in the input are reflected in these first word combinations (cf. Braine, 1987; Rumelhart & McClelland, 1987).

Thus, the following kinds of utterances seem to be the basis of first word combinations: (1) They are frequently addressed to the child, (2) they are salient to the child, and (3) although not necessarily identical, *the utterances contain in close temporal contiguity the words used by the child*. Braine (1976) has collected early language corpora from 16 children learning to speak various languages.

Most of the early word combinations contained in these corpora appear to be consistent with these three criteria.

This account of activation patterns among the networks is by no means complete, having only briefly touched upon the development within each network and the integration across networks. The intent was merely to show how the present processing model could help us understand the different forms of imitation, and what roles these forms could play in speech development. In the following sections, we explore how imitation may help in learning to speak:

(1) How imitation and articulation are interdependent processes that affect the development of the speech-planning networks will be briefly discussed.
(2) How imitation might help in making longer utterances will only be introduced in this chapter because Chapter 8 deals with this topic in detail.
(3) How imitated units of speech can become the building blocks to spontaneous speech will be discussed at some length because the function of imitation has been most seriously questioned in this development.

7.3 Imitation and Articulation

Articulation, and therefore speaking, is an extremely complex motor skill. Learning to make the movements required by speech takes much practice: Adult-like articulation emerges only around the age of 5 or 6 (Oller & MacNeilage, 1983). As the production of any single sound may involve upwards of 35 muscles (Hardcastle, 1976), recent theories of articulation (e.g., Edwards, 1984; Kent, 1983; Laver, 1980; MacNeilage, 1970), as mentioned above, hold that spatiotemporal coordinate systems develop for efficient, automatic production of speech sounds—systems in which the goal of the action guides the movement. These systems are similar to those proposed early on by Hebb (1949) for the production of very fast and highly skilled movements and their ability to adjust to situational variation. The speech-planning network of our language-processing model is seen as functioning in a manner similar to these central coordinate systems for articulation.

What is the size of the articulatory speech-planning units that develop? Netsell (1986) wrote,

> Some theorists argue it is the syllable that is the basic programming unit of the speech motor command structure, others maintain these units are smaller than the syllable, whereas some imagine command structures as large as the phrase or sentence. Regardless of the size of the programming unit the child eventually uses . . ., the basic units of practice (especially in the second year of life) appear to be words of rather motorically simple syllabic structure. (pp. 17–18)

How might imitation help in the development of such spatiotemporal coordinate systems required for articulation? Netsell (1986) described a model for such development: "The normal child learns to talk by listening, watching, and *imitating* [italics added] an external model.... The model provides both auditory and visual afferent cues ... which the child attempts to *imitate* with his or her own movements and vocalizations" (p. 8). The previous discussion on patterns of activation suggests that the attempt to imitate the model just after it has been heard (Pattern 1) would appear to be most effective in developing the speech-planning networks. There is some supportive evidence. For instance, some children in immediate imitation are able to produce speech sounds they do not yet produce in their natural speech (Leonard, Schwartz, Folger, & Wilcox, 1978). Articulation therapies typically use one form of immediate imitation or another to overcome difficulty with articulation (Winitz, 1984).

The manner in which articulation develops as children attempt to repeat new words can be seen in the two examples described by Moerk (Chapter 12, this volume): Eve attempts to say *Fraser* just after she heard her mother say it. Her mother corrects her. Eve within a very short time makes several attempts at *Fraser*, each time becoming better, until she is able to pronounce the name correctly. Similarly, Adam has difficulty repeating *locomotive* and also makes several attempts at repeating it. Although his attempted imitations improve with repetition, he does not acquire the correct pronunciation of *locomotive* during the session analyzed.

This brings us to a discussion of individual differences in ability to imitate speech sounds and to articulate. Snow (Chapter 4, this volume), recognizing the difficulty some children have in articulating words correctly, even during immediate imitation, has distinguished between attempted and correctly realized imitations. Articulatory difficulties in children have been associated with poor auditory short-term memory (e.g., Grimm, 1986; Menyuk & Looney, 1976; Smith, 1967; Speidel, Chapter 9, this volume). Short-term auditory memory in these studies was measured by some form of elicited verbal imitation, such as the repetition of digits, unrelated or related words, or sentences. In other words, children with articulation problems also appear to have difficulty with elicited verbal imitation tasks. There seems to be an interdependence here: Children who articulate poorly will have trouble with imitation, but because imitation is the vehicle for the development of articulation, such children do not have readily available the process by which articulation develops.

An example of this relationship between articulation, imitation, and language development is the case history reported in Chapter 9: The child with the better articulation was the better imitator on elicited imitation tasks and was more advanced in her speaking. The examples of Eve and Adam just described may also reflect these differences: Eve was able to use imitation successfully to articulate *Friday*, whereas Adam, using the same strategy, was not totally successful with *locomotive*. Eve learned to speak much more quickly than Adam (Brown, 1973).

Earlier we had cited the work of Liberman and Mattingly (1985), who argued for a special biological module for the perception and production of speech sounds. It is, therefore, not unlikely that some individual differences in articulation skill reflect constitutional differences in the development of such a specialized module like the speech-planning network. If there are individual differences in ability to plan or make speech sounds, these differences would have implications for the quality of articulation as well as the amount of imitation observed in children.

In sum, it seems that during early stages of speech development, immediate imitation is a *product* of ability to articulate, as well as a *process* in the further development of articulation. Differences in the neurological substrate from which the spatiotemporal coordinate systems for planning speech sounds are developed may be one reason for different rates of development of articulation and the skills that build upon these speech-planning systems (e.g., Netsell, 1986; Speidel, Chapter 9, this volume). The relationship between articulation, imitation, and learning to speak will be discussed further in the section on short-term memory, imitation, and syntactic development.

7.4 Imitation and the Production of Longer Utterances

Only a few events or things can be consciously apprehended by the mind at any particular moment in time (e.g., Baddeley, 1976, 1986; Baddeley & Hitch, 1974; Case, 1985; Dempster, 1981; Mandler, 1985; Miller, 1956). This limited information-processing capacity of the mind suggests another way in which imitation can help the language learner. The learner must exert much mental effort in activating and organizing the relevant speech-planning units (Bock, 1982; Bohannon & Stanowicz, Chapter 6; Speidel & Herreshoff, Chapter 8). If able to incorporate a part of someone else's words or phrases, the learner will use up less processing space because he will be using words or phrases that are already in working memory and do not have to be retrieved from long-term memory. This should free mental processing capacity so that further meaning and speech-planning units can be activated. In plain words, imitating portions of another's speech should allow the language learner to make longer utterances.

The idea that imitation should help to make longer utterances has been studied several times. No supporting evidence has been found: Imitated sentences were no longer than those the child made by himself (Brown & Fraser, 1963; Ervin, 1964; Moerk, 1977; Snow, 1983). Speidel and Herreshoff, in Chapter 8, used a methodology derived from the present language-processing model and from a limited-capacity, working-memory model and found that imitation does help in making longer utterances.

7.5 Imitation and the Acquisition of Syntactic Speech

7.5.1 Bootstrapping Operations

Different approaches to the bootstrapping problem in language acquisition have been taken (Pinker, 1987; Shatz, 1987). In this section we look at the question of how imitated, that is, remembered units of language can provide the raw material for the creative way in which language becomes used by the proficient speaker. However, first it must be made clear again that, in the present language-processing model, language comprehension and speaking are the product of different patterns of activation among the various networks. The conditions of learning syntax may not be identical for comprehension and for speaking, and the role that imitation plays may be quite different for the two processes. Of the two components of imitation—observation and production—the observational component would appear to be most relevant to the development of comprehension (cf. Whitehurst & DeBaryshe, Chapter 11, this volume). How comprehension and speech development influence and support each other are central issues, but the discussion here will be restricted to how imitated units of speech, which have been stored in long-term memory, can become the building blocks for syntactic speech.

The section on activation patterns showed how the various kinds of imitation could promote the development of connections between the meaning and speech-planning networks. In this section a number of processes will be described that could operate on these imitated phrases and thereby lead to the use of the productive syntactic skill we have as adults. We will restrict ourselves here to the processes that can operate on deferred imitations (Pattern 3). Specifically, we will talk about how a child can produce novel and longer utterances from those first word combinations already available as organized units of activity in the speech-planning network.

There are at least four cognitive operations that could expand children's ability to create utterances they have not heard before from such deferred imitations.

7.5.1.1 Chaining

First there is the discredited process of chaining. For example, from *Kendall sit* and *Daddy sit* and from *sit lap*, *sit pool*, and *sit there*, Kendall could create through chaining six novel three-word utterances, namely, *Kendall sit lap*, *Daddy sit lap*, *Kendall sit pool*, *Daddy sit pool*, *Kendall sit there*, and *Daddy sit there*. From *pillow fell* and *fell off*, he could create the novel utterance *pillow fell off*.

7.5.1.2 Insertion

Utterances can be expanded on the basis of insertion. *Kendall bed* and *play bed* provide the foundation for *Kendall play bed*, which Kendall actually says. From *Mommy bathroom* and *Mommy in*, he can create *Mommy in bathroom*. Learning one further word combination such as *big bed*, Kendall could create variations of all his other existing two-word combinations with bed, for instance, *Kendall big bed* and *Kendall play big bed*.

7.5.1.3 Replacement/Equivalence

A third process is replacement/equivalence. Suppose that Kendall has mastered the following:

Kendall sit	*Kendall read*	*Kendall fix it*
Daddy sit	*Daddy read*	*Daddy fix it*
Mommy sit	*Mommy read*	*Mommy fix it*

The process of co-occurrence and similarity can combine to produce a replacement/equivalence operation that results in generalization: Wherever there is *Kendall*, one can put *Mommy*, or *Daddy*, and vice versa. In short, learning any new two-word combination with one of the three names means that the new word can be used syntactically in the same way with the other two words: If *Kendall swim* is learned, then one could also say *Mommy* (or *Daddy*) *swim*. A moment's reflection shows that the development of equivalence of words in similar positions is a powerful way of building syntax. The complex equivalences/replacements that could develop out of this seemingly simple process has been shown in the work by Braine (1987), Maratsos (1982), and Maratsos and Chalkley (1980) in their theoretical analysis of the development of grammatical word classes.

7.5.1.4 Sense of Temporal Position

When similar sequences of words are heard, a sense of temporal position for the words develops (Braine, 1963; see also research on serial learning, e.g., Kausler, 1966). For instance, when a child can produce a number of copula sentences, such as "The house is big; the girl is small," a sense of position for the word *is* develops: *The* is never placed immediately before *is*; *is* is never at the end of an utterance. This does not mean that an absolute position sense develops. Rather, a relational position sense develops out of experiences with how words occur together, with word sequences, with the meaning they convey in different situational contexts, and with the grammatical roles of words and their position in the sentences. It is co-occurring words, their relative position in an utterance, and the meaning derived from context that promote, for instance, the functional difference between grammatical subject and object (see Braine, 1987; Braine & Hardy, 1982; Schieffelin, 1981). That the position of a word in a sentence becomes a part of its meaning in that sentence is consonant with arguments that lexicon and syntax overlap (e.g., Peters, 1983; Bolinger & Sears, 1981; Speidel, 1987b).

Such a sense of position should allow two separate deferred imitations to be strung together without a common link having ever been heard, that is, without chaining. For example, David (Braine, 1976) had a clear sense that *want* goes early in an utterance. He also had used "more balloon," "sit down," and "gimme." Thus, it would not be surprising to hear him say "Want more balloon," "Want sit down," "Want gimme," without his ever having heard these combinations. The role of meaning attributes, such as actor, object, or instrument in this development of position sense is seen in the imitation given by the bilingual child described earlier. He must have had a position sense based at least partly on a sense for sequencing the meaning units (who does what to whom) and not purely based on speech sounds, because he sequenced the meaning units correctly, even though he translated some of the words in the original model.

Utterances initially created by using any one of these operations could, in turn, become stepping stones for more complete syntactical utterances by having a further round of operation of chaining, insertion, replacement/equivalence, or position sense applied to them.

7.5.2 Implications and Evidence

When all these operating strategies are added together, one can see a very powerful sentence-generating system emerging that is founded initially on separately imitated units, then combinations of two units, and so on to ever-increasing complexity, flexibility, and creativity. The operation may work on immediate or deferred imitations, or their combination, as in expanded imitation. The critical part is that the child has heard the words used together at least once. The words in the model utterances do not need to be adjacent, but merely need to occur together in the utterances. Thus, "Mommy shoe" can be the cumulative result of such diverse models as, "Mommy puts on shoe," "Mommy gets shoe," or "Mommy ties shoe." From such bootstrap imitations, children could accumulate sufficient examples to begin to apply chaining, insertion, equivalence/replacement, and the sense of position. From these operations, it is suggested, our sense of word classes develops (e.g., Maratsos & Chalkley, 1980). In short, observed correlations between words in speech and between these words and situational contexts could result in the grammatical classes and syntactic regularities to which we, as adults, intuitively and automatically adhere when speaking.

What is imitated, and *which* combination processes are applied to the remembered imitations are guided by the meaning networks. Moreover, there is no one-to-one relationship between units in the meaning and the speech-planning networks. The same meaning units can be communicated by different speech-planning units, and the same speech-planning units can be used to communicate different meanings. Which combination of units across the networks becomes activated at any one point in time is a function of other concurrent mental activities. It is beyond the scope of this chapter to discuss in more detail than in the section on patterns of imitation how units in the meaning networks activate and become related to units in the speech-planning network for the production of syntactic speech. It would seem, however, that integrating the present network model with semantic and pragmatic approaches to syntax (e.g., Braine & Hardy, 1982; Schieffelin, 1981) would be fruitful.

Although the present model is far from capturing the total picture of learning to speak, some of its critical features receive support in others' writing. Anderson (1983) has developed a computer model of language learning that simulates his son's learning to speak. Relevant to the present arguments is that he built a rule into his program so that it does not allow the use of two words in sequence *unless the sequence has been encountered at least five times*:

The program's initial utterances are repeats of sequences in the adult model; only later does it come up with novel utterances. The same was observed of J.J. His first uses of *more* were utterances like *more gish* (*I want more cheese*) and *more nana* (*I want more banana*), and only later did he produce novel generations that had not been modeled. (p. 294)

In another program into which Anderson had not built this developmental rule for permissible sequences between two words, transition errors occurred such as "The tall lawyer *has is* jumping."

Similarly, Rumelhart and McClelland (1987), in their study of learning past tenses, found that after 10 exposures to each of the 18 patterns from which generalization was to occur, their computer model had learned a set of connection strengths that captured the regularities in the patterns. These two studies suggest that the learner must have available in memory a certain number and a certain representativeness of instances of the pattern so that pattern generalization can take place. The actual frequency of required positive instances would in part depend on the difficulty of the pattern to be learned (Braine, 1987; K. E. Nelson, 1987).

The present position is also consistent with Braine's (1971) description of his model of language learning: "In the initial stages of learning it may well be that only a small fraction of the input, e.g., single lexical items and short phrases, contributes materially to grammar acquisition. In effect, the learner is protected from being confused by the variety of the long utterances that occur in his environs because he has not learned enough for his scanning mechanism to register the structure they contain" (p. 170). The scanning mechanism, according to Braine, must be able to detect *temporal position and co-occurring events*.

Further support for the notion that there is an initially small set of word combinations to which the operations described above are applied comes from Braine's (1976) careful analysis of the early word combinations of 16 toddlers. Braine concluded that these combinations are based on a "limited scope formula." He writes, "The literature as a whole contains an analytic bias toward attributing considerably more grammatical structure to young children than is warranted by the corpora" (p. 93).

Observations of natural language learning are also consonant with the present model. First, there is the finding of changes in the kinds of imitation accompanying increased skill in speaking. The four children studied by Bloom, Rocissano, and Hood (1976) all show a relative decrease in exact imitations and a relative increase in expanded imitations with development. Similar trends were found by K. E. Nelson, Baker, Denninger, Bonvillian, and Kaplan (1985) for a sample of 24 children and by Kuczaj (1982) for his son. Snow (1983) showed, in a microanalysis of her son's language development, how deferred and expanded imitations can become building blocks to more independent speech.

Further evidence that imitated units of language provide the raw material for learning to speak syntactically correctly comes from studies of children who have trouble with both imitation and syntax (Grimm, 1986; Menyuk & Looney, 1976; Speidel, Chapter 9, this volume). We will now briefly turn to some of this evidence.

7.6 Articulation, Imitation Span, and Syntactic Development

In order that chaining, insertion, replacement/equivalence, and position sense can be brought into operation, the child must have some memory trace of the meaning and speech-planning units to be used in these operations. The units activated within the speech-planning network must be of sufficient length; that is, they must consist of at least two words in their appropriate sequence (though not necessarily adjacent) in order that the work of building longer sentences from chunks in memory can begin. In other words, the child must at least be able to hold in short-term memory, that is, must be able to imitate, two words in their appropriate sequence (more, probably, for making longer and more complex utterances).

Baddeley (1986), upon reviewing a large number of studies, concludes that the development of verbal memory span—in other words, verbal imitation span—is based on the improvement of articulatory skill. He proposes that as "children become older articulatory skills improve, either as a result of practice, maturation of the nervous system or both. This allows them to rehearse subvocally at a faster rate, and hence maintain more items in the phonological store" (p. 201).

In Section 7.3 it was already pointed out that there seems to be a reciprocal relationship between imitation skill and articulatory skill. By referring to our model of language processing, the relationship between articulation, imitation span, and learning of syntax will become clearer. Short-term verbal memory can be viewed as a function of neural traces in the incoming speech-sound network as well as a function of the development of the speech-planning network. More specifically, if activity in the incoming speech-sound network in response to verbal input is limited in time, its activation of the speech-planning network will also be limited in time. If in younger children and in children with articulation problems the activation of the speech-planning network by the incoming speech-sound network is less efficient, or if these children need more time to make the speech sounds, the guiding trace of activity from the incoming speech-sound network will have faded before they have been able to repeat much, and their immediate imitations will therefore be shorter.

Support for this idea that children must be able to imitate a minimum length of modeled utterances in order that syntactic speech can develop properly comes from studies by Grimm (1983, 1986), who compared normal and dysphasic children's language development. Dysphasic children have trouble with expressive language, particularly with syntax, although they have no known other cognitive deficit and no reported trauma to the brain. Grimm writes that normal "children imitate the complete maternal utterance. Except for one single case, this imitation strategy is completely lacking by the D-children [dysphasic children]. . . . The elementaristic strategy of repeating single words is still predominant in these children" (Grimm, 1986, p. 10). The difficulty dysphasic children have with verbal imitation was also noted by Menyuk (Menyuk, 1969; Menyuk & Looney, 1976). These children typically have also pronounced difficulty with articulation.

Even in children without severe language delay, the ability to imitate longer phrases appears to be related to rate of learning to speak. In the longitudinal case study on two bilingual children's language development in Chapter 9, the child who learned to speak faster in both languages and has less problems with syntax was also better on elicited sentence imitation in both languages and had better articulation. Another study that bears on these issues is the longitudinal study of imitation development in two children by Reger (1986). The children first tended to imitate more words in the final sentence positions. In short, the traces of the incoming speech sounds most recently activated were those with greater strength for activating the corresponding units in the speech-planning network. With further development, words earlier in the modeled utterances were imitated more frequently. The child whose speech was more mature began to imitate words in the middle earlier than the child with slower speech development.

However, immediate self-selected imitation (and its variations) acts like rehearsal and helps to move into long-term memory the words that are imitated. If children are able to imitate immediately only one or two words, they cannot store in long-term memory imitations of sufficient length upon which to apply the operations for induction of syntax discussed above, that is, chaining, insertion, replacement/equivalence, and sense of position.

7.7 Conclusion

The purpose of this chapter is to show how imitation might help in learning to speak. A language-processing model consisting of three types of networks was described. In this model the development of comprehension of language is seen as the development of an incoming speech-sound network and its integration with meaning networks active at the same time. Speech development, on the other hand, is seen as the development of a speech-planning network and its integration with the meaning networks. The development of the speech-planning network is thought to be guided by activity in the incoming speech-sound network.

It is shown how the various patterns of activation that are possible among the networks could be the basis for the different kinds of imitation, such as precursors to overt imitation, self-selected and elicited immediate imitation, and deferred, reduced, and expanded imitation. The way these different forms of imitation might play a role in the development of articulation, in making longer utterances, and in learning to use syntactic conventions when speaking is explored. The purposefully imitated units of speech sounds (overt or covert) are viewed as the child's building blocks for putting thoughts into speech. Operations upon these remembered units of imitated speech from which creative and spontaneous speech could emerge are chaining, insertion, sense of temporal position for words, and replacement/equivalence of words. However, unless word strings of sufficient length can be retained in short-term memory, that is, can co-occur during activity in the speech-planning network, the remembered imitations may be too short and cannot provide the adequate raw material for the operations to yield elaborate and flexible, syntactically correct speech.

The imitations are themselves not ready-made. They themselves are both processes (patterns of neural activity) as well as products (more permanent changes in neural activity, i.e., long-term memory stores). As products they are the result of a history of hearing, remembering, and practicing speech. As processes they provide the bootstrap by which thoughts become capable of being transmitted using the speech conventions of the community. Longitudinal, microanalytical studies of language development (cf. Speidel & Herreshoff, 1985) are now required to provide further evidence on how these processes work.

There is one further critical assumption about imitation in this chapter – the partial activation of the speech-planning network by the incoming speech-sound network. This partial activation can be a *covert* precursor to deferred imitation as defined here. Such a process could account for the lack of overt imitation noted in some children (Bloom et al., 1974; K. E. Nelson et al., 1985; in this volume, Chapters 3 to 5). Since this activity is unobservable to our ears and tape recorders, it is a weak part of the present model. It is, however, a plausible one. Perhaps new techniques in the study of electrical brain activity can provide support for this covert form of imitation.

In the next two chapters, the language-processing model is applied to observations in language development. In Chapter 8 the model is used to predict and explain the finding that immediate self-selected imitation is associated with the generation of longer utterances. In Chapter 9 differences in the language development of two bilingual children are described. The delayed and syntactically anomalous speech in both languages of one of the children is thought to be due to greater difficulties with the development of the speech-planning networks.

Acknowledgments. I wish to thank Madeleen Herreshoff, Keith Nelson, and Janet Cooke for their insightful comments and suggestions on earlier versions of this chapter.

References

Anderson, J.R. (1980). *Cognitive psychology and its implications.* San Francisco: Freeman.

Anderson, J.R. (1983). *The architecture of cognition.* Cambridge, MA: Harvard University Press.

Baddeley, A.D. (1976). *The psychology of memory.* New York: Basic Books.

Baddeley, A. (1986). *Working memory.* Oxford: Clarendon Press.

Baddeley, A.D., & Hitch, G.J. (1974). Working memory. In G.H. Bower (Ed.), *The psychology of learning and motivation, 8* (pp. 47–90). New York: Academic Press.

Bereiter, C., & Engelmann, S. (1966). *Teaching disadvantaged children in the preschool.* Englewood Cliffs, NJ: Prentice-Hall.

Bernthal, J.E., Greenlee, M., Eblen, R., & Marking, K. (1987). Detection of mispronunciations: A comparison of adults, normal-speaking children, and children with articulation errors. *Applied Psycholinguistics, 8,* 209–222.

Bjorklund, D.F. (1985). The role of conceptual knowledge in the development of organization in children's memory. In C.J. Brainerd & M. Pressley (Eds.), *Basic processes in memory development: Progress in cognitive development research.* New York: Springer-Verlag.

Bjorklund, D.F. (1987). How age changes in knowledge base contribute to the development of children's memory: An interpretive review. *Developmental Review, 7,* 93–130.

Bloom, L., Hood, L., & Lightbown (1974). Imitation in language development: If, when and why. *Cognitive Psychology, 6,* 380–420.

Bloom, L., Rocissano, L., & Hood, L. (1976). Adult–child discourse: Developmental interaction between information processing and linguistic knowledge. *Cognitive Psychology, 8,* 521–552.

Bock, J.K. (1982). Toward a cognitive psychology of syntax: Information processing contributions to sentence formulation. *Psychological Review, 89,* 1–47.

Bolinger, D., & Sears, D. (1981). *Aspects of language* (3rd ed.). New York: Harcourt Brace Jovanovich.

Bowerman, M. (1973). *Early syntactic development: A cross-linguistic study with special reference to Finnish.* London: Cambridge University Press.

Braine, M.D.S. (1963). On learning the grammatical order of words. *Psychological Review, 70,* 323–348.

Braine, M.D.S. (1971). On two types of models of the internalization of grammars. In D.I. Slobin (Ed.), *The ontogenesis of grammar: A theoretical symposium* (pp. 153–186). New York: Academic Press.

Braine, M.D.S. (1974). Length constraints, reduction rules, and holophrastic processes in children's word combinations. *Journal of Verbal Learning and Verbal Behavior, 13,* 448–461.

Braine, M.D.S. (1976). Children's first word combinations. *Monographs of the Society for Research in Child Development* (1, Serial No. 164).

Braine, M.D.S. (1987). What is learned in acquiring word classes—A step toward an acquisition theory. In B. MacWhinney (Ed.), *Mechanisms of language acquisition* (pp. 65–87). Hillsdale, NJ: Erlbaum.

Braine, M.D.S., & Hardy, J.A. (1982). On what case categories there are, why they are, and how they develop: An amalgam of *a priori* considerations, speculations, and evidence from children. In E. Wanner & L.R. Gleitman (Eds.), *Language acquisition: State of the art* (pp. 219–239). Cambridge, MA: Cambridge University Press.

Brown, R. (1973). *A first language.* Cambridge, MA: Harvard University Press.

Brown, R., & Fraser, C. (1963). The acquisition of syntax. In C.N. Cofer & B. Musgrave (Eds.), *Verbal behavior and learning: Problems and processes* (pp. 158–201). New York: McGraw-Hill.

Case, R. (1985). *Intellectual development: Birth to adulthood.* New York: Academic Press.

Clark, R. (1977). What's the use of imitation? *Journal of Child Language, 4*, 341–358.

Craik, F.I.M., & Watkins, M.J. (1973). The role of rehearsal in short-term memory. *Journal of Verbal Learning and Verbal Behavior, 12*, 599–607.

Cuvo, A.J. (1975). Developmental differences in rehearsal and free recall. *Journal of Experimental Child Psychology, 19*, 265–278.

Day, R.R., Boggs, S.T., Tharp, R.G., Gallimore, R., & Speidel, G.E. (1974). A standard English performance measure for young children: The Standard English Repetition Test (SERT). *Working Papers in Linguistics, 6*, 73–85. Honolulu, HI: University of Hawaii.

Dempster, F.N. (1981). Memory span: Sources of individual and developmental differences. *Psychological Bulletin, 89*, 63–100.

Dunn, L.M., Horton, K.B., & Smith, J.O. (1968). *Peabody language development kits: Manual for level # P.* Circle Pines, MN: American Guidance Service.

Edwards, M. (1984). *Disorders of articulation: Aspects of dysarthria and verbal dyspraxia.* New York: Springer-Verlag.

Ervin, S. (1964). Imitation and structural change in children's language. In E.H. Lenneberg (Ed.), *New directions in the study of language* (pp. 163–189). Cambridge, MA: MIT Press.

Fromkin, V.A. (1968). Speculations of performance models. *Journal of Linguistics, 4*, 47–68.

Grimm, H. (1983). *On the interrelation of internal and external factors in the development of language structures in normal and dysphasic preschoolers: A longitudinal study* (Occasional Paper No. 5). Honolulu, HI: The Kamehameha Schools.

Grimm, H. (1986). Developmental dysphasia: New theoretical perspectives and empirical results. *The German Journal of Psychology, 11*, 8–22.

Hardcastle, W.J. (1976). *Physiology of speech.* New York: Academic Press.

Hebb, D.O. (1949). *The organization of behavior.* New York: Wiley.

Huttenlocher, J. (1974). The origins of language comprehensions. In E.R. Solso (Ed.), *Theories in cognitive psychology* (pp. 331–368). Hillsdale, NJ: Erlbaum.

Kelso, J.A., Tuller, B., & Harris, K.S. (1983). A "dynamic pattern" perspective on the control and coordination of movement. In P.F. MacNeilage (Ed.), *The production of speech* (pp. 137–173). New York: Springer-Verlag.

Kent, R.D. (1983). The segmental organization of speech. In P.F. MacNeilage (Ed.), *The production of speech* (pp. 57–89). New York: Springer-Verlag.

Kuczaj, S.A. (1982). Language play and language acquisition. *Advances in Child Development and Behavior, 17*, 197–132.

Laver, J. (1980). Neurolinguistic control of speech production. In V.A. Fromkin (Ed.), *Errors in linguistic performance.* New York: Academic Press.

Leonard, L.B., Schwartz, R.G., Folger, M.K., & Wilcox, M.J. (1978). *Journal of Child Language, 5*, 403–415.

Liberman, A.V. (1982). On finding that speech is special. *American Psychologist, 37*, 148–167.

Liberman, A.V., & Mattingly, I.G. (1985). The motor theory of speech perception revised. *Cognition, 21*, 1–36.

MacNeilage, P.F. (1970). Motor control of serial ordering of speech. *Psychological Review, 77*, 182–196.

Mandler, G. (1985). *Cognitive psychology: An essay in cognitive science.* Hillsdale, NJ: Erlbaum.

Maratsos, M.P. (1982). The child's construction of grammatical categories. In E. Wanner & L.R. Gleitman (Eds.), *Language acquisition: The state of the art* (pp. 240–266). Cambridge, MA: Cambridge University Press.

Maratsos, M.P., & Chalkley, M.A. (1980). The internal language of children's syntax: The ontogenesis and representation of syntactic categories. In K.E. Nelson (Ed.), *Children's language* (Vol.2, pp. 127–214). New York: Gardner Press.

Menyuk, P. (1969). *Sentences children use.* Cambridge, MA: MIT Press.

Menyuk, P. (1971). *The acquisition and development of language.* Englewood Cliffs, NJ: Prentice-Hall.

Menyuk, P., & Looney, P.L. (1976). A problem of language disorder: Length versus structure. In D.M. Morehead and A.E. Morehead (Eds.), *Normal and deficient child language* (pp. 259–279). Baltimore, MD: University Park Press.

Miller, G.A. (1956). The magical number seven, plus or minus two: Some limits on our capacity for processing information. *Psychological Review, 63,* 81–97.

Miller, P.J. (1982). *Amy, Wendy, and Beth: Learning language in South Baltimore.* Austin, TX: University of Texas Press.

Moerk, E.L. (1977). Processes and products of imitation: Additional evidence that imitation is progressive. *Journal of Psycholinguistic Research, 6,* 187–202.

Moerk, E.L. (1983). *The mother of Eve—As a first language teacher.* Norwood, NJ: Ablex.

Naus, M.J., Ornstein, P.A., & Aivano, S. (1977). Developmental changes in memory: The relationship between rehearsal and memory as test expectations change. *Journal of Experimental Child Psychology, 23,* 237–251.

Nelson, K. (1973). Structure and strategy in learning to talk. *Monographs of the Society for Research in Child Development, 48*(Serial No. 149).

Nelson, K.E. (1987). Some observations from the perspective of the rare event cognitive comparison theory of language acquisition. In K.E. Nelson & A. van Kleeck (Eds.), *Children's language* (Vol. 6, pp. 289–331). Hillsdale, NJ: Erlbaum.

Nelson, K.E., Baker, N.D., Denninger, M., Bonvillian, J.D., & Kaplan, B.J. (1985). Cookie versus do-it-again: Imitative-referential and personal-social-syntactic-initiating language styles in young children. *Linguistics, 23,* 433–454.

Nelson, K.E., & Bonvillian, J.D. (1978). Early semantic development: Conceptual growth and related processes between 2 and 4½ years of age. In K.E. Nelson (Ed.), *Children's language* (Vol. 1, pp. 467–556). New York: Gardner Press.

Netsell, R. (1986). *A neurobiologic view of speech production and the dysarthrias.* San Diego, CA: College-Hill Press.

Ochs, E., & Schieffelin, B.B. (1982). Language acquisition and socialization: Three developmental stories and their implications. *Sociolinguistic Working Paper* (No. 105). Austin, TX: Southwest Educational Development Laboratory.

Oksaar, E. (1982). *Language acquisition in the early years.* New York: St. Martin's Press. Translated from German. *Spracherwerb im Vorschulalter* (1977). Stuttgart: Kohlhammer.

Oller, D.K., & MacNeilage, P.F. (1983). Development of speech production: Perspectives from natural and perturbed speech. In P.F. MacNeilage (Ed.), *The production of speech* (pp. 91–108). New York: Springer-Verlag.

Ornstein, P.A., & Naus, M.J. (1978). Rehearsal processes in children's memory. In P.A. Ornstein (Ed.), *Memory development in children* (pp. 69–99). Hillsdale, NJ: Erlbaum.

Ornstein, P.A., Naus, M.J., & Stone, B.P. (1977). Rehearsal training and developmental differences in memory. *Developmental Psychology, 13*, 15–24.

Peters, A.M. (1983). *The units of language acquisition.* Cambridge, UK: Cambridge University Press.

Pinker, S. (1987). The bootstrapping problem in language acquisition. In B. MacWhinney (Ed.), *Mechanisms of language acquisition* (pp. 399–441). Hillsdale, NJ: Erlbaum.

Ramer, A.L.H. (1976). The function of imitation in child language. *Journal of Speech and Hearing Research, 19*, 700–717.

Reger, Z. (1986). The functions of imitation in child language. *Applied Psycholinguistics, 7*, 323–352.

Rumelhart, D.E., & McClelland, J.L. (1987). Learning the past tenses of English verbs: Implicit rules or parallel distributed processing. In B. MacWhinney (Ed.), *Mechanisms of language acquisition* (pp. 195–248). Hillsdale, NJ: Erlbaum.

Rundus, D. (1971). Analysis of rehearsal processes in free recall. *Journal of Experimental Psychology, 89*, 63–77.

Rundus, D., & Atkinson, R.C. (1970). Rehearsal processes in free recall: A procedure for direct observation. *Journal of Verbal Learning and Verbal Behavior, 9*, 99–105.

Schieffelin, B.B. (1981). A developmental study of pragmatic appropriateness of word order and casemarking in Kaluli. In W. Deutsch (Ed.), *The child's construction of language* (pp. 105–120). New York: Academic Press.

Shatz, M. (1987). Bootstrapping operations in child language. In K.E. Nelson & A. van Kleek (Eds.), *Children's language* (Vol. 6, pp. 1–22). Hillsdale, NJ: Erlbaum.

Sinclair, A., Sinclair, H., & de Marcellus, O. (1971). Young children's comprehension and production of passive sentences. *Archives de Psychologie, 41*, 1–22.

Sinclair, H. (1975). The role of cognitive structures in language acquisition. In E.H. Lenneberg & E. Lenneberg (Eds.), *Foundations of language development* (pp. 223–238). New York: Academic Press.

Sinclair-de Zwart, H. (1967). *Acquisition du langage et développement de la pensée.* Paris: Dunod.

Slobin, D.I. (1971). Data for the symposium. In D.I. Slobin (Ed.), *The ontogenesis of grammar* (pp. 3–14). New York: Academic Press.

Smith, C.B. (1967). Articulation problems and abilities to store and process stimuli. *Journal of Speech and Hearing, 10*, 348–355.

Snow, C.E. (1981). The uses of imitation. *Journal of Child Language, 8*, 205–212.

Snow, C.E. (1983). Saying it again: The role of expanded and deferred imitations in language acquisition. In K. Nelson (Ed.), *Children's language* (Vol. 4, pp. 29–58). Hillsdale, NJ: Erlbaum.

Speidel, G.E. (1984). The acquisition of linguistic structures and cognitive development. In C.L. Thew & C.E. Johnson (Eds.), *Proceedings of the Second International Congress for the Study of Child Language* (Vol. 2, pp. 283–296). Lanham, MD: University Press of America.

Speidel, G.E. (1987a). Language differences in the classroom: Two approaches to language development. In E. Oksaar (Ed.), *Sociocultural perspectives of multilingualism and language acquisition* (pp. 239–259). Tübingen: Gunter Narr Verlag.

Speidel, G.E. (1987b). Conversation and language learning in the classroom. In K.E. Nelson & A. van Kleek (Eds.), *Children's language* (Vol. 6, pp. 99–135). Hillsdale, NJ: Erlbaum.

Speidel, G.E., & Herreshoff, M. (1985). Learning to speak standard English as a second dialect. In G.E. Speidel (Chair), *The many faces of imitation*. Symposium conducted at the Biennial Meeting of the Society for Research in Child Development, Toronto, Canada.

Stern, L. (1985). *The structures and strategies of human memory.* Homewood, IL: Dorsey Press.

Underwood, B.J., & Schulz, R.W. (1960). *Meaningfulness and verbal learning.* Philadelphia: Lippincott.

Watson-Gegeo, K.A., & Gegeo, D.W. (1986). Some aspects of calling out and repeating routines in Kwara'ae children's language acquisition. In B.B. Schieffelin & E. Ochs (Eds.), *Language socialization across cultures.* New York: Cambridge University Press.

Whitehurst, G.J., Ironsmith, E.M., & Goldfein, M. (1974). Selective imitation of the passive construction through modeling. *Journal of Experimental Child Psychology, 17,* 288–302.

Whitehurst, G.J., & Vasta, R. (1975). Is language acquired through imitation? *Journal of Psycholinguistic Research, 4,* 37–59.

Winitz, H. (1984). Auditory considerations in articulation training. In H. Winitz (Ed.), *Treating articulation disorders: For clinicians by clinicians* (pp. 21–49). Baltimore, MD: University Park Press.

Woodward, A.E., Bjork, R.A., & Jongeward, R.H. (1974). Recall and recognition as a function of primary rehearsal. *Journal of Verbal Learning and Verbal Behavior, 12,* 608–617.

CHAPTER 8

Imitation and the Construction of Long Utterances

Gisela E. Speidel and Madeleen J. Herreshoff

There are, indeed, many faces to verbal imitation. In this book we get a glimpse of how many: Imitation can be used to show agreement, to encourage speaking, to taunt, to question, to show the speech partner one hasn't understood, to promote emotional bonds between toddler and mother, to retain topic cohesiveness, and more. One cannot but wonder why so many different possible functions should be expressed through one type of behavioral act. Given this myriad of functions, we must be as clear and precise as possible about the functions) of imitation we are studying and the processes by which imitation is thought to bring about its effects. At the same time, we must be aware that the specific imitative acts we are studying for one function may have other, equally valid functions.

8.1 A Model of Language Comprehension and Production

The view one has of language processes and how language is learned specifies the role given to imitation in language learning. The language-learning and processing model that provides the framework for the present study is based on the view that language comprehension and speaking are two rather different mental activities that use only partially overlapping neural systems. Although much has been written about the separateness of these systems (e.g., Anderson, 1983; Bock, 1982; Huttenlocher, 1974), studies in language development often neglect to say whether the arguments, conclusions, or hypotheses are relevant to production or comprehension or both. This neglect is also true of most studies of imitation. (An exception is Whitehurst and Vasta's, 1975, *Comprehension-Imitation-Production* hypothesis.)

The language-processing model we apply here is described in detail in Chapter 7. To recapitulate briefly, in this model three sets of mental representations are thought to develop as part of language learning: (1) the *incoming speech-sound* network registers and integrates speech sounds picked up from the environment, (2) the *meaning* networks register and integrate the nonspeech sound events, and (3) the *speech-planning* network consists of the motor plans that guide and activate the neural systems involved in the articulatory movements required to produce the desired speech sounds. This is clearly a very simplified model of reality. As discussions and theories of semantic processes (e.g., Bowerman, 1977; Carey, 1982; Fodor, 1977; Johnson-Laird, 1987) and of speech production (Bock, 1982; Edwards, 1984) show, each of these networks consists of many components.

Comprehension in the accomplished language user is thought to occur when the incoming speech-sound and corresponding meaning networks are active. The meaning networks may be activated either by the incoming speech-sound network alone, or by a combination of activation from the incoming speech-sound network and the environment. *Spontaneous speech* is thought to be the result of activation of corresponding units of the meaning and the speech-planning networks.

8.2 Implications of the Network Model for Imitation

This three-network language model has implications for the roles imitation could play in the establishment of connections among the networks. The process of learning to understand verbal messages requires that appropriate, nonlinguistic meaning information accompany the verbal message. Of the two components of imitation described in Chapter 1, only observation would be needed in providing this nonlinguistic information (cf. Whitehurst & DeBaryshe, Chapter 11, this volume). The repetition component of imitation could help comprehension in a secondary way: By imitating, or repeating, learners can give themselves another input opportunity, which will allow them to process the input better.

The repetition component of imitation is thought, however, to play an important role in learning to speak. The child must learn to make the speech sounds of his language community; that is, the speech-planning network must come to mediate the reproduction of sounds registered in the incoming speech-sound network. If the speech-sound is heard just before the attempt to reproduce it is made—that is, corresponding units in the incoming speech-sound and the speech-planning networks are active almost simultaneously—the ability to reproduce the sound is facilitated somehow and thereby also the development of the speech-planning network. The exact process or manner is still not clear, but there is evidence that new sounds are easier to produce when they have just been heard. Thus, Leonard, Schwartz, Folger, and Wilcox (1978) found that children were able to make sounds in immediate imitation that were not yet in their spontaneous speech. In diverse kinds of speech therapy (e.g., Winitz, 1984), the immediate repetition of sounds to be learned or to be improved is a central feature. There appear to be very close neural linkages between speech-sound perception and the neural representations of speech production. Some researchers even believe that they are identical (Liberman & Mattingly, 1985; Menyuk, 1971).

The network model distinguishes between rote and meaningful imitation depending on whether the meaning networks are activated or not: During rote imitation they are not active, whereas during meaningful imitation they are. Meaningful and selective imitation occurs when the child uses some of the words he just heard someone else use in order to express his thoughts. As described in Chapter 7, it is meaningful imitation that helps to establish the connections between the meaning and the speech-planning networks and guides the development of the speech-planning network in reproducing the sounds of language. Rote imitation, on the other hand, may only serve to develop the speech-planning network. Obviously the distinction between rote and meaningful imitation is one of degree.

This distinction between rote and meaningful imitation is relevant to *elicited* versus *self-selected* or spontaneous (cf. Oksaar, 1982) imitation. In elicited imitation an utterance is presented and the listener is told to repeat it exactly. In self-selected imitation the individual selects and incorporates all or part of another's utterance into his own message. The language-processing model suggests that the neural activation patterns among the three networks can be different in the two kinds of imitation.

In elicited imitation, where exact copy of the input is requested, the speech-planning network, which activates the articulatory neuromuscular system, may receive signals from two sources. One source of activation comes from the incoming speech-sound network, which has registered the utterance to be imitated. This may be the only source if the child imitates the utterance by rote. However, the units in the incoming speech-sound network may also activate corresponding units in the meaning networks. The meaning networks, in turn, may activate the speech-planning network, but not necessarily the same words and grammatical constructions as those activated by the incoming speech-sound network. Instead, the meaning networks may activate units in the speech-planning network that have in the past been the ones most often activated for particular units of meaning. The two activation signals, one from the incoming speech-sound and one from the meaning networks, may actually conflict. In such a conflict situation, elicited imitation may be more difficult than spontaneously produced speech (see Fig. 7.1).

Such conflict, arising during elicited imitation, is readily seen in the example described in Chapter 7 with bidialectal children. When they are asked to repeat something that is presented to them in their less preferred dialect, they will, in their imitation, often translate the original model into their preferred dialect (Day, Boggs, Tharp, Gallimore, & Speidel, 1974). The example of the bilingual toddler saying "Ich love Du," when asked to say "I love you," shows that this "translation" phenomenon occurs already in very young children.

8.3 A Limited-Capacity Processing System and Implications for Imitation

Our capacity to take in information, the number of items to which we can attend at any one given moment, is limited—a phenomenon documented well, both by research (e.g., Baddeley, 1976, 1986; Miller, 1956) and by personal experience. Theories of how this limited-capacity system works abound (see Shiffrin and Schneider, 1977, for a review), and different names have been given to the limited processing-capacity phenomenon, such as attention span, working memory, short-term memory, and short-term store.

Shiffrin and Schneider (1977), like others, distinguish between two kinds of mental processes—controlled and automatic. Controlled processes require attention and therefore are capacity limited, whereas automatic processes are not. With practice and rehearsal, a skill requires less and less attention or control. As the skill becomes more automatic, processing capacity becomes available for attending to other things during its performance.

Bock (1982) has applied this view of mental processing to speaking. Her limited-capacity system is called *working memory*. She suggests that in mature speakers most of working memory's capacity is taken up by deciding on the content of the message or referential processes and relatively little by phonetic processes. Her referential and phonetic processes are roughly equivalent to the meaning and speech-planning networks in our own language-processing model, described in Section 8.2.

Bock speculates about changes in the allocation of working memory with development:

> Various linguistic subskills, including controlled articulation and word production, seem likely to require significant investments of processing capacity in early speech. For production abilities to go much beyond single words, children may have to automatize such lower level speech skills. The growth of automaticity in these components of language performance would permit allocation of processing resources to less predictable demands of utterance formulation. With further development, automaticity in performance may extend to higher levels in the hierarchy of language abilities. (p. 8)

The distinction between a behavior that is automatic and one that requires attention and control processes is relevant to the function of imitation. Bohannon and Stanowicz, Chapter 6, this volume, suggest that imitation is the result of priming and thereby reduces the load on working memory. The present study was conducted with a similar view of imitation in mind. In language learners the connections between the meaning and the speech-planning networks are not yet automatic: Therefore, much mental effort (i.e., control processes) will be required not only for activation of the meaning networks, but also for activation of units in the speech-planning network. Sentences would be expected to remain relatively short due to the limits of working memory. However, the use of words in speaking that have just been heard, as in immediate self-selected imitation, should require less effort than spontaneous production because the relevant speech-planning units have already been activated through the incoming speech-sound network. Consequently, the imitated portion should take up less working memory than spontaneous retrieval of those words (i.e., activation without support from the incoming speech-sound network), and the language learner should have more capacity left to be able to make longer sentences than without imitation.

8.4 Framework of the Study

For language learners the production of utterances requires much effort. Not only do they have to make decisions about what to say, but they also have to search for words and grammatical rules to match their thoughts. If one is able to incorporate a portion of what someone else has just said to expand one's utterance, this imitated portion should require less effort because it does not have to be retrieved. Therefore, there should be more processing capacity freed for the construction of the remainder of the utterance. Imitation, according to this reasoning, should help children make longer utterances.

This function of imitation was studied in an earlier era of language research through a comparison of children's spontaneous utterances with their ability to imitate utterances in elicited imitation. It was found that their performance on elicited imitation was no better than their spontaneous performance (Brown & Fraser, 1963; Ervin, 1964). Indeed, Slobin and Welsh (1974) found that Echo was unable to imitate a sentence as an elicited imitation task that earlier she had said spontaneously. From these early negative findings, the notion arose that imitation was not useful and did not help in the construction of longer utterances. These studies, however, were not based on very explicit theories of language processing. Since then we have come to see how many different forms and functions of imitation there are, and we recognize that *elicited imitation* is quite different from *self-selected imitation*. (From here on, unless otherwise mentioned, we mean self-selected imitation when we speak of imitation.)

The study below looks once again at the question of whether language learners use imitation in making longer utterances. The present approach to the problem is based on a combination of our three-network language-processing model with a limited-capacity information-processing system. The study provides information about the following set of predictions:

(1) If imitation reduces the load on the limited processing system in children when they are making utterances longer than their MLU (mean length of utterance), then utterances with imitation should be longer, in general, than utterances without imitation.

(2) More specifically, if imitation reduces the processing load on working memory, then (a) the longer utterances should contain more imitated words than the shorter utterances, and (b) the effects of imitation should be most pronounced on the longest utterances.

(3) With greater skill in speaking, there should be more automaticity in retrieval of many words and grammatical constructions. Therefore, children who are more advanced in speaking should show less imitation than children who are less advanced.

The study differs from earlier work in several ways: (1) the effect of self-selected imitation is studied; (2) the definition of imitation is very broad; (3) only utterances at and beyond the children's average speaking level are used as data; and (4) children of the same age, but at different levels of speaking skill, are compared in their use of imitation.

The subjects are also different from the usual 1½- to 3-year-old upper-middle-class children. They are older children, from families with Hawaiian backgrounds. One of the two groups of children is struggling with standard English and "school language," that is, with new forms of verbal expression and with putting more complex ideas into words. The selection of these children was not based on theoretical grounds. They were chosen because earlier observations had shown that the less advanced group used much repetition in their discussions during reading lessons. Up to half of the words in the children's speech had occurred previously during these discussions (Speidel, 1987a). Since these children's speech was generally not fluent, we suspected that this imitation helped them in constructing utterances.

8.5 Method

8.5.1 Subjects

Two groups of first graders enrolled in the Kamehameha Early Education Program, an educational program for children of Hawaiian ancestry (Speidel, 1981; Tharp, et al., 1984), took part in the study.

8.5.1.1 Low-MLU Group

One group consisted of six children who made up the lowest reading group in the class. They had difficulty with standard English as well as with verbal expression in general. Analysis of transcripts of the reading lessons showed that their average MLU during the discussions was 3.37. MLU was calculated in the manner recommended by Brown (1973) for older children. It was partly so low because there were many utterance fragments.

The children spoke Hawaiian English, a creole based on English and in the process of decreolization (Day, 1972). It is a language code that encompasses a range of forms from highly creolized to close approximations of English. As a language in flux, one can only characterize it in broad terms: It differs from standard American English in pronunciation and in grammar; as with other creole languages (Hall, 1966), many bound morphemes are expressed syntactically; there is much overlap between the Hawaiian-English and the English lexicon, but there are some differences in word usage and word meanings.

8.5.1.2 High-MLU Group

A group of four first graders in the top reading group of their class was the high-MLU comparison group. Their average MLU in the reading discussions was 4.54, one morpheme longer than that of the low-MLU children.

8.5.2 Setting

The Kamehameha Early Education Program is a language arts program for Hawaiian children (Speidel, 1981; Tharp et al., 1984). This program adjusts to the differences between the school language and the Hawaiian English spoken by the children in the following way: Rather than direct instruction in standard English grammar, many natural language-learning opportunities are provided in daily comprehension reading lessons (See Speidel, 1987a, b). During these lessons the teacher and the students discuss their readings or talk about other topics. The children use both standard English and Hawaiian English while they talk—often in the same utterance. The students participated daily for 20 min in such small group reading lessons of which at least 10 min were spent in discussions.

The low-MLU group was part of a longitudinal language development study (Speidel, 1987a). Their reading lessons were audiorecorded at approximately weekly intervals. During recording, each child wore a microphone that led into a separate tape recorder. The six tapes thus collected were transcribed onto a single master transcript. Three such transcribed lessons with approximately a monthly interval between them were the basis for the present data. The high-MLU group was not the focus of such intensive study, but one of their lessons was transcribed in the above manner in order to have a comparison group for the present study.

8.5.3 Analysis of Long Utterances

It is only in longer utterances that we would expect imitation to help noticeably by freeing processing space in working memory. Imitation in utterances shorter than the students' MLU does not address the issue. Therefore, only utterances that were at or beyond the children's MLU in these sessions were chosen for analysis.

8.5.4. Coding

A definition of imitation must describe at least two dimensions along which the imitated behavior is compared to its model source: similarity and elapsed time.

8.5.4.1 Similarity

The transcript below will help to clarify the coding system used. For purposes of clarity, the overlapping of speech is not marked, and many speech fragments are omitted. (T = Teacher; the other letters are initials of the children's names.)

139 T.   They found the plane crashed on the ground.
140 M.   Probably never have gas and drop . . . because . . .
143 J.   Maybe they was going.
144 T.   You think the plane might have crashed because it didn't have any gas?
150 J.   Maybe the wind . . .
151 J.   The wind wen go push 'om down.
152 S.   Maybe the guys that were 'pose to drive the plane.
153 L.   Maybe the wind . . .
156 J.   Maybe the wind wen push 'om down like inside the news.
158 L.   Maybe the wind wen go push 'om away.
160 T.   Like maybe the wind was too strong and pushed the plane down?
163 S.   Maybe the guys that sposed to drive the plane went to look at something . . .
164 S.   and then they felt the plane going down . . .
165 S.   and the plane was on the ground already.
170 T.   You mean that maybe the pilots weren't watching what they were doing?

The following three forms of repetition were *initially* coded:

(1) Either a part or all of someone else's utterance was incorporated into an utterance:
    150 J.   Maybe the wind . . .
    153 L.   Maybe the wind . . .
(2) Either a part or all of one's own utterance was included in a longer utterance (i.e., self-repetition):
    151 J.   The wind wen go push 'om down.
    156 J.   Maybe the wind wen push 'om down like inside the news.
(3) A mixture of (1) and (2):
    153 L.   Maybe the wind . . .
    156 J.   Maybe the wind wen push 'om down like inside the news.
    158 L.   Maybe the wind wen go push 'om away.

This last example, however, shows the difficulties we had in distinguishing between self-repetition and the repetition of others. Rather than a mixture of 153 and 156, L's utterance (158) could just as well have been seen as an imitation of J (156) only. Since J's and L's utterances were so close together in time, any distinction between the source of the imitation would have been most arbitrary.

Consequently, for the final analyses presented below, these *three types of repetitions were collapsed*. The collapse seemed valid because a preliminary analysis with the first coding system showed that each category was related to producing longer utterances. Furthermore, in both self-repetition and imitation of others the words are readily available to working memory. The effects of these two forms on the construction of longer utterances should therefore be the same. We view this collapse, however, not as the ideal. Whenever possible a distinction should be made between self-repetition and imitation (see Užgiris, Broome, & Kruper, Chapter 5, this volume, and Bohannon & Stanowicz, Chapter 6, this volume).

Grouping these three kinds of imitation together, every utterance four morphemes or longer was identified as either an utterance with imitation or without. This resulted in a highly reliable coding system. The agreement between two coders of the MLU without imitation was 97.5%, and of utterances with imitation, 95.3%.

In order to determine how many morphemes in an utterance were imitated, the source of imitation was critical. A single utterance with imitation was often based on several different sources, as we saw in the examples above. Moreover, since there was so much repetition, a particular imitated word or phrase could be found in several preceding utterances. The following priority guidelines were used in such a case:

(1) The utterance from which the greatest number of morphemes were incorporated as imitation was chosen as the source, that is, as the imitated model. For example, for L's utterance (158) "Maybe the wind wen go push 'om away," J's utterance (156) "Maybe the wen push 'om away" was chosen as the source rather than L's own earlier utterance.
(2) In all other instances, the utterance closest in time to the imitation was chosen as the model.

A reliability check on the number of imitated words was high. The agreement between two coders on the number of imitated words in an utterance was 94%.

8.5.4.2 Elapsed Time

The time interval between the source utterance and the imitation is very important for this study because we are hypothesizing that just having heard the words facilitates their use and frees working memory capacity for making longer utterances. Relevant processes involved in this imitation include *priming* (cf. Bohannon & Stanowicz, Chapter 6, this volume). In the lexical information-processing literature, priming is a very brief (a few seconds or less) facilitation of information retrieval, such as the observed facilitation on lexical decision-making tasks in reaction time experiments. But Bock (in press) finds syntactic priming effects over longer periods. We used a fairly long interval because we were trying to capture in our definition the experience we have all had: We can remember better the sound of a new word or name if we have recently heard it.

Because we could not measure elapsed time directly, we looked for the possible source of an imitation in the preceding 30 utterances. Calculation of 6 randomly chosen sequences of 30 utterances yielded an average sampling period of approximately 1 min.

8.6 Results

8.6.1 Are Utterances With Imitations Longer?

For each child, the utterances 4 morphemes or longer were categorized as either containing imitations or not. For this subset the mean length of utterances with and without imitation was obtained for each child. The utterances with imitation were longer in every child except one. Although the differences were not very large, they were very consistent. For the low-MLU group, the average length of utterances without imitation was 5.25, and with imitation, 5.86. For the high-MLU group, the average MLU of utterances without imitation was 6.13, and with imitation, 7.48. The Walsh Test for related samples shows that this effect was highly signification ($p < .01$) for the two groups combined.

8.6.2 Imitation and Very Long Utterances

If imitation helps to produce longer utterances by freeing processing space in working memory, then one would predict that it should have more impact in the production of very long utterances than in moderately long utterances. Therefore, the utterances four morphemes or longer were sorted into two categories: those that were moderately long, between 4 and 6 morphemes (the 4–6 category), and those that were very long, 7 morphemes or longer (the 7+ category). The effect of imitation was then studied on these two groups of utterances in three different ways.

First, a comparison between the length of utterances with imitation and without imitation showed according to the Walsh Test that the effects were moderately significant for the 4–6 category ($p < .051$; two-tailed), whereas the effect of imitation on utterance length was highly significant for the 7+ utterances ($p < .01$). Figure 8-1 shows this effect separately for the low- and high-MLU groups.

Second, a comparison of proportion of utterances with and without imitation showed that according to the Walsh Test there were significantly more utterances with imitation than without in both the 4–6 category ($p < .02$) and the 7+ category ($p < .01$). A direct comparison between the two utterance categories showed that the proportion of utterances with imitation to utterances without imitation was significantly higher in the 7+ category than in the 4–6 category ($p < .01$). Figure 8-2 shows these effects for the low- and high-MLU groups.

Finally, a comparison between the number of imitated morphemes in the 4–6 and 7+ categories was done. Figure 8-3 shows the results of this analysis. For the low-MLU group, the average number of imitated morphemes was 2.17 in the 4–6 category and 3.78 in the 7+ category; for the high-MLU group, it was 1.89 imitated morphemes per utterance in the 4–6 category and 2.73 in the 7+ category. The Walsh Test showed that significantly more words were imitated in the 7+ category than in the 4–6 category ($< .01$).

These three sets of findings all show that the effects of imitation are more pronounced in the very long than in the moderately long utterances. This suggests

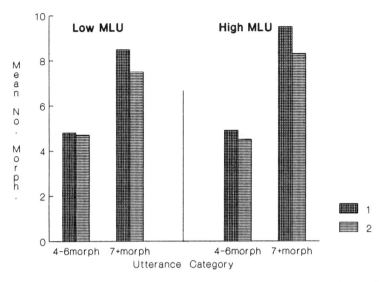

Figure 8-1. Mean number of morphemes in utterances with and without imitation for the moderately and the very long utterance categories. 1 = with imitation; 2 = without imitation.

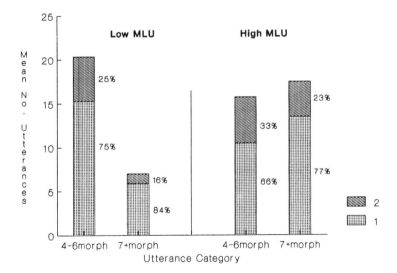

Figure 8-2. Mean number of utterances and the percentage of utterances with and without imitation for the moderately and the very long utterance categories. 1 = with imitation; 2 = without imitation.

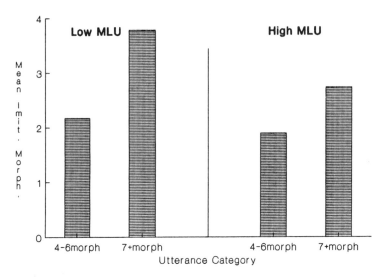

Figure 8-3. Mean number of imitated morphemes/utterance for the moderately and the very long utterance categories.

that imitation has a more pronounced effect on the very long than on the moderately long utterances in these children.

8.6.3 Do High- and Low-MLU Groups Use Different Amounts of Imitation?

A comparison between the skill groups of their moderately long and very long utterances showed that the advanced children had a higher proportion of 7+ utterances. Of the utterances four morphemes and longer, only 25% were 7+ utterances in the low-MLU group, whereas in the high-MLU group, 55% were 7+ utterances (see Figure 8-2). Each high-MLU child had a greater proportion of very long to moderately long utterances than any of the low-MLU children, and a Mann-Whitney U test for independent samples showed this difference between the groups was significant ($p < .01$). Thus, the linguistic advance of the high-MLU group was reflected in their special ability to put their thoughts into words using "very long" utterances.

Given the differences in skill, the high-MLU group should require less imitation. To test this prediction, the two groups were compared on the basis of their use of imitation.

(1) The proportion of utterances with and without imitation for the two skill groups is different. In the low-MLU group, the ratio of utterances with and without imitation in the 4–6 category was 3 : 1 and increased to nearly 6 : 1 for the 7+ category. In the high-MLU group, on the other hand, the ratio of utterances with and without imitation was only 2 : 1 for the 4–6 category and a little over 3 : 1 for the 7+ category (see Figure 8-2).

(2) A comparison of the number of imitated morphemes/utterance shows that the low-MLU children used more imitated morphemes in each utterance than the high-MLU children. A Mann-Whitney U test, however, revealed that this difference between the groups is statistically significant only in the very long (7+) utterances ($p < .05$; see Figure 8-3).

These two findings taken together suggest that the major difference between the two skill groups lies in their construction of 7+ utterances. These long utterances are still a challenge to the high-MLU group, as we saw in the findings above; but they are an even greater challenge to the low-MLU children, who not only infrequently produce these utterances, but also use significantly more imitation to produce them.

8.7 Discussion and Conclusion

The hypothesis that imitation could help children make longer utterances has been tested in prior work on the effects of imitation (Ervin, 1964; Slobin, 1968). The reasons for expecting such an effect, however, were not spelled out theoretically. Thus, it is not surprising that an unsuitable methodology was used in the early studies and the expected effects were not found. In this study, two models, a language-learning model and a limited-capacity processing model, gave us the rationale for the methodology used.

First, effects of imitation on utterance length needed to be studied with self-selected rather than elicited imitation. This is because the language-processing model suggests that the activation patterns among the networks are quite different in elicited and in self-selected imitation, as we described in Section 8.2. Since we wanted to see how imitation affects the making of long utterances in spontaneous speech, it was clear that we needed to look at self-selected imitation.

Second, we looked at imitations in the broadest sense of the word. This was partly dictated by our argument about self-selected imitation. An individual speaker has a message that he wishes to compose and he will select from previous utterances of others only those elements that help in the construction of the message. This means that at times only single words of preceding utterances may be usable. Another reason for the liberal definition was that the present group of children was older and their speaking and memory skills were further developed than those of toddlers, who are typically the focus of studies on imitation. Any effects of imitation would therefore be quite subtle.

Third, utterances primarily at and beyond the children's MLU (for the setting) were studed for imitation effects. This decision followed from the limited-capacity processing model. Imitation has many different functions, such as continuing the topic, confirmation, request for clarification (see Nelson et al., Chapter 13; Speidel & Nelson, Chapter 1, this volume; Užgiris, Broome, & Kruper, Chapter 5, this volume). Some of these utterances may be quite brief and put few demands on processing. From our limited-capacity processing model, we would expect imitation to help only in the production of utterances at the cutting edge of the children's skill.

Applying these methodological constraints, the predicted effects of imitation were obtained: (1) Utterances with imitation were significantly longer than utterances without imitation; (2) the effects of imitation were significantly more pronounced in the longest category of utterances, supporting the hypothesis that the effects of imitation on utterance length are to free processing capacity for making longer utterances; and (3) the two skill groups used different amounts of imitation. Even though the more advanced group had many more long utterances, they relied less on imitation: They had a smaller proportion of imitated to nonimitated utterances and used fewer imitated morphemes to construct their very long utterances.

The skill-group differences rule out alternative explanations of the findings, such as, given the liberal definition of imitation, the longer an utterance, the more repeated morphemes it could have due to chance alone. Or that, in order to be able to participate appropriately in a discussion, one has to repeat parts of the conversation: the longer the utterance, the more words must be borrowed from previous utterances to maintain cohesion. These two arguments cannot explain the differences in the use of imitation between the two groups of children.

The findings lend support to the processing models of speech production and limited capacity in working memory from which the predictions were derived. They show the significance of the memory component in speaking—the retrieval and maintenance in working memory of speech sounds and their arrangement to create words and grammatical order among those words may be strongly facilitated by imitation. Although Bloom, Miller, and Hood (1975) had a different frame of reference from the one presented here, they made a similar point:

> Linguistic competence entails the ability to access the linguistic code—*to remember the schema* [italics added]—relative to the child's attention to some element of experience.... Access to productive linguistic schemas...is a function of the relative strength of linguistic forms and structures in interaction with elements of content that are coded. Such relative strength is determined by...recency of learning, frequency of application, lexical familiarity. (p. 50–51)

The results also support the notion that, with increasing experience, retrieval becomes more automatic and thereby frees processing space in working memory: The more advanced children used less imitation, yet they simultaneously produced more "very long" utterances. In short, the ability to incorporate someone else's words into one's speech is most helpful in earlier stages of learning, where the activation of the speech-planning by the meaning networks is not yet automatic and therefore must draw heavily on working memory. As the access becomes more automatic with repeated experience, the involvement of working memory in this aspect of speaking gradually declines.

We adopted a rather broad definition of imitation for the reasons given above. The excerpted utterances show that, even in the low-MLU group, the use of imitation was often extremely creative. The incorporated portions of speech are intricately interwoven with speech produced independent of immediate models. Hearing the discussions (rather than inspecting the transcripts), one would probably not even notice the repetitiousness and would possibly consider it spontaneous speech. It could, therefore, be reasonably questioned whether the definition of imitation is too broad.

Finding support for each of our theoretically based predictions shows that the adoption of this lenient definition had sufficient power to distinguish the effects of imitation in each of the analyses we did. Particularly the differences in amount of imitation used by the two skill groups supports the appropriateness of our broad definition and suggests that imitation still has subtle effects in individuals who already have a fair degree of speaking skill.

A special feature of this study is the number of speakers—there were several speakers present throughout the sampled speech period rather than the dyadic arrangement that is typically the setting of this kind of study. This feature made for much overlapping speech so that one could not cleanly distinguish between self-repetition and imitation of others. Many utterances were combinations of both self-repetitions and imitation of the words of others. We hope in the near future to conduct a study on the nature of imitation in the low-MLU group in dyadic conversations with an adult. This should give use information about how situation specific the present findings are.

In conclusion, the data support our predictions about the role of imitation in helping language learners make longer utterances, but we must await further study before we can broadly generalize this outcome. Moreover, we hope to have succeeded in providing an example of how models of language processing can be used to make predictions about the functions of imitation and to guide the methods by which these functions are studied.

Acknowledgments. We wish to thank Keith Nelson for his valuable comments on earlier versions of this chapter, Janet Cooke for her excellent editorial assistance, and Toufiq Siddiqi for his help with the graphics.

References

Anderson, J.R. (1983). *The architecture of cognition*. Cambridge, MA: Harvard University Press.

Baddeley, A.D. (1976). *The psychology of memory*. New York: Basic Books.

Bloom, L., Miller, P., & Hood, L. (1975). Variation and reduction as aspects of competence in language development. In A. Pick (Ed.), *Minnesota Symposium on Child Psychology* (Vol. 9, pp. 3–55). Minneapolis: University of Minnesota Press.

Bock, J.K. (in press). Syntactic persistence in language production. *Cognitive Psychology.*

Bock, J.K. (1982). Toward a cognitive psychology of syntax: Information processing contributions to sentence formulation. *Psychological Review, 89,* 1–47.

Bowerman, M. (1977). The acquisition of word meaning: An investigation of some current concepts. In N. Waterson & C. Snow (Eds.), *Development of communication; Social and pragmatic factors in language acquisition*. New York: Wiley.

Brown, R. (1973). *A first language: The early stages*. Cambridge, MA: Harvard University Press.

Brown, R., & Fraser, C. (1963). The acquisition of syntax. In C.N. Cofer & B.S. Musgrave (Eds.), *Verbal behavior and learning*. New York: McGraw-Hill.

Carey, S. (1982). Semantic development. In E. Wanner & L.R. Gleitman (Eds.), *Language acquisition: The state of the art* (pp. 347–389). Cambridge, UK: Cambridge University Press.

Day, R.R. (1972). *Patterns of variation in copula and tense in the Hawaiian post-Creole continuum*. Unpublished doctoral dissertation. University of Hawaii, Honolulu, HI.

Day, R.R., Boggs, S.T., Tharp, R.G., Gallimore, R., & Speidel, G.E. (1974). A standard English performance measure for young children: The Standard English Repetition Test (SERT). *Working Papers in Linguistics, 6*, 73–85.

Edwards, M. (1984). *Disorders of articulation*. New York: Springer-Verlag.

Ervin, S. (1964). Imitation and structural change in children's language. In E.H. Lenneberg (Ed.), *New directions in the study of langauge* (pp. 163–189). Cambridge, MA: MIT Press.

Fodor, J.D. (1977) *Semantics: Theories of meaning in generative grammar*. New York: Crowell.

Hall, R.A. (1966). *Pidgin and creole languages*. Ithaca, NY: Cornell University Press.

Huttenlocher, J. (1974). The origins of language comprehension. In E.R. Solso (Ed.), *Theories in cognitive psychology: The Loyola Symposium* (pp. 331–368). Hillsdale, NJ: Erlbaum.

Johnson-Laird, P.N. (1987). The mental representation of the meaning of words. *Cognition, 25*, 189–211.

Leonard, L.B., Schwartz, R.G., Folger, M.K., & Wilcox, M.J. (1978). *Journal of Child Language, 5*, 403–415.

Liberman, A.V. & Mattingly, I.G. (1985). The motor theory of speech perception revised. *Cognition, 21*, 1–36.

Menyuk, P. (1971). *The acquisition and development of language*. Englewood Cliff, NJ: Prentice-Hall.

Miller, G.A. (1956) The magical number seven, plus or minus two: Some limits on our capacity for processing information. *Psychological Review, 63*, 81–97.

Oksaar, E. (1982). *Language acquisition in the early years*. New York: St. Martin's Press. Translated from the German. *Spracherwerb im Vorschulalter* (1977). Stuttgart: Kohlhammer.

Shiffrin, R.M., & Schneider, W. (1977). Controlled and automatic human information processing: II. Perceptual learning, automatic attending, and a general theory. *Psychological Review, 84*, 127–190.

Slobin, D.I. (1968). Imitation and grammatical development in children. In N.S. Endler, L.R. Boulter, & H. Osser (Eds.), *Contemporary issues in developmental psychology* (pp. 437–443). New York: Holt, Rinehart and Winston.

Slobin, D.I., & Welsh, C.A. (1974). Elicited imitation as a research tool in developmental psycholinguistics. In C.S. Lavatelli (Ed.), *Language training in early childhood education* (pp. 170–185). Urbana, IL: University of Illinois Press for ERIC Clearinghouse on Early Childhood Education.

Speidel, G.E. (Ed.). (1981). KEEP—The Kamehameha Early Education Program. *Educational Perspectives, 20.*

Speidel, G.E. (1987a). Conversation and language learning in the classroom. In K.E. Nelson & A. van Kleeck (Eds.), *Children's language,* (Vol. 6, p. 99–135). Hillsdale, NJ: Erlbaum.

Speidel, G.E. (1987b). Language differences in the classroom: Two approaches to language development. In E. Oksaar (Ed.), *Sociocultural perspectives of multilingualism and language acquisition* (pp. 239–259). Tübingen: Gunter Narr Verlag.

Tharp, R.G., Jordan, C., Speidel, G.E., Au, K.H., Klein, T.W. Calkins, R.P., Sloat, K.C.M., & Gallimore, R. (1984). Product and process in applied developmental research: Education and the children of a minority. In M. Lamb, A.L. Brown, & B. Rogoff (Eds.), *Advances in developmental psychology* (Vol. 3, pp. 91–141). Hillsdale, NJ: Erlbaum.

Whitehurst, G.J., & Vasta, R. (1975). Is language acquired through imitation? *Journal of Psycholinguistic Research, 4,* 37–59.

Winitz, H. (Ed.). (1984). *Treating articulation disorders: For clinicians by clinicians.* Baltimore, MD: University Park Press.

CHAPTER 9

A Biological Basis for Individual Differences in Learning to Speak

Gisela E. Speidel

Children go about learning language in different ways and at different rates. Brown's (1973) Eve had utterances averaging more than four morphemes when she was a little over 2 years old; Adam's utterances did not even quite reach that length when he was 3 years and 8 months old. Are such variations due to different neurological organization, different general cognitive ability, or different kinds and amounts of language input? Most likely, all three factors play a role in the variations observed in learning to speak and in the speaking skill eventually attained. Nevertheless, if the contribution of each could be isolated, it would help us to understand how language is acquired and help us to compare language learning to the learning of other cognitive skills.

Bretherton, McNew, Snyder, and Bates (1983) have drawn up a list of studies on the topic of language-learning styles. Among these studies is K. Nelson's (1973) classic one, in which she found differences in the kinds of words children learned first: Language learning in one group of children was object oriented; in the other, it was more self-oriented. In another well-known study on individual differences, Peters (1977) differentiated children according to predominant language-learning strategies (analytic or gestalt), while the work by Nelson, Baker, Denninger, Bonvillian, and Kaplan (1985) suggests that cognitive and emotional styles may affect learning. Several chapters in this book give us further examples of individual differences (Masur, Chapter 3; Snow, Chapter 4; Užgiris, Broome, & Kruper, Chapter 5; Nelson et al., Chapter 13).

In most of these studies, the effects of language input, cognitive ability, and constitutional factors cannot be disentangled. Although we can probably never exert enough control over these three variables to obtain precise findings, there are methodological approaches that can help us to understand more the contribution of each and how they interact with each other. One such approach is a longitudinal comparison on these variables between children who have a specific language disorder, such as developmental dysphasia, and children whose language develops normally (e.g., Grimm, 1983, 1984, 1986; Grimm & Weinert, 1987).

Another approach that may help in our search for causes of individual differences is to look at the simultaneous learning of two first languages. Bilingual language learning permits a comparison of the manner in which the learning of each of the two languages proceeds. For instance, if two children show little difference in the rate at which they learn one language, but a large difference in the rate at which they learn the other language, then one can possibly rule out biological and cognitive factors as the main causes of this difference (unless one believes that the two languages require different cognitive abilities). Environmental conditions in which the second language is learned, such as input, motivation, and so forth, would seem to be the most plausible cause in this case. On the other hand, if one child learns both languages more slowly than the other child, and the cognitive skills and language environments for the children are similar, then there is strong support for a biological basis of this difference in language learning.

This chapter describes a case study of two bilingual children, Mark and his sister, Sally, who is 2 years older. During their first 6 months of life, they were taken care of mainly by their German-speaking grandmother, who came to visit the family in the United States for the purpose of helping out with child care and who then returned to Germany. Since both parents were native speakers of German, the children heard only German in the home, unless English-speaking visitors came to the house or they listened to television. After the first 6 months, they went to baby-sitters who spoke only English. At age 2½ they were enrolled in an English-speaking Montessori preschool. At age 5 they began to attend an English-speaking elementary school.

After the first 6 months of life (during which they heard predominantly German), the amount of time exposed to the two languages was approximately the same: The children were away from their parents for approximately 8 to 9 hours during weekdays. However, the language-learning conditions for English and German differed: German was mainly heard from two adult models—the parents—whereas English was heard from many different adult and peer models.

The two children varied greatly in the ease with which they learned to speak the two languages. Sally learned to speak both languages quickly and rarely made errors. Mark, in contrast, had much difficulty in learning to speak both languages, and for a time it seemed as if he were reconstructing the language anew whenever he spoke.

9.1 Hypothesis

In Chapter 7, a model for language learning and processing was described. Briefly, language processes are viewed as partly simultaneous activity in three types of neural networks: a network for processing the incoming speech sounds, a network for processing the nonspeech-sound events accompanying speech, (i.e., the meaning aspects of language), and a network for planning and producing the speech sounds. Language learning is the development of these networks as well as their progressive integration with one another. Learning to *comprehend* language is viewed as the development of the incoming speech-sound and the meaning networks and their integration, whereas learning to *speak* is viewed as the development of the meaning and the speech-planning networks and their integration (see Figure 7-1). In bilingual subjects there are two incoming speech-sound networks and two speech-planning networks, one set for each language (see Figure 7-2). The meaning networks probably serve both language systems because they are developed mainly by nonspeech-sound events. (Although there may be separate meaning networks to the extent that children have had distinct experiences in the two languages. The distinction between compound or coordinate bilingualism is relevant here; e.g., Ervin & Osgood, 1954; Weinreich, 1953.)

It is thought that Mark's difficulty in learning to speak was due to neurological factors that slowed the development of the speech-planning networks. A sequence of events is suggested that links allergies and neurological differences to difficulties with articulation, short-term memory, speaking, and reading. In order to support the hypothesized events, this chapter deals with the following topics:

(1) a brief medical history of the two children;
(2) a comparison between Mark's and Sally's learning of the two languages;
(3) a comparison between Mark's and Sally's learning to read: This piece of information is included because Mark showed symptoms of dyslexia, and recent work in dyslexia and specific reading delay have shown that these difficulties are often preceded by difficulties in learning to speak;
(4) cognitive and linguistic test data on the two children;
(5) description of dysphasic children's language development and their difficulty with imitation and articulation; and
(6) recent work on autoimmune disorders and their relationship to language and reading difficulties.

Many of Mark's behaviors will seem normal to the reader. They will be seen as reflecting the old wisdom that boys are slower to mature than girls. In part, Mark fits these observations. Mark is normal, and there are many children who show some of the same kinds of behaviors that are described here as difficulties. However, he is very bright, at least as bright as his sister, yet he started speaking and reading significantly later than she. Although many of his skills were normally developed for his age, they were delayed with respect to his tested mental age; although many of his difficulties are not qualitatively different from those of other children, they are more predominant. To say that Mark and Brown's (1973) Adam were slower in learning to speak because they are boys or because they have a maturational lag is to offer very superficial explanations. We must begin to look more closely at what causes these developmental lags.

9.2 Medical History

Both Sally and Mark had recurrent bouts of otitis media, or middle-ear infections. Their infections were always treated immediately. However, Mark had more frequent infections and had to have tubes inserted to drain his middle ears when he was 2½ and again when he was 3½ years old. There is an association between middle-ear infections and language delay, but the causal connection is not clearly established (Feagans, 1986; Feagans, Blood, & Tubman, 1987; Feagans, Sanyal, Henderson, Collier, & Applebaum, in press; Finitzo & Friel-Patti, 1987; Friel-Patti, Finitzo-Heber, Conti, & Brown, 1982; Menyuk, 1980).

Developmental dyslexia, a form of specific reading delay associated with language difficulties (e.g., Bannatyne, 1976; Rawson, 1968, 1981; Vellutino, 1977) has recently been found to be related to immune disorders (Galaburda, 1986; Geschwind & Behan, 1984; Rosen, Sherman, & Galaburda, 1986) and to celiac disease. It is of interest to note that Mark suffered as a baby from a type of diarrhea that was finally diagnosed, when he was 1½ years old, as celiac disease, an intestinal allergy to certain grains. The mother had a history of allergies, which had been aggravated by her previous pregnancy with Sally, and she was receiving allergy shots during her pregnancy with Mark.

9.3 Language Development

The information in this section comes from two sources: longitudinal case-study observations for the first 7 years and speech samples.

9.3.1 Case-History Observations

9.3.1.1 Early Language Development: Ages 7 Months to 2 Years

Sally learned both languages readily without apparent effort. She began with repetitive babbling around 7 months and began to speak in words when she was a little over 1 year old. From the beginning her speech was fairly intelligible, and her language development followed the orderly progression described by Brown (1973), starting mainly with single referential words, then 2 words, and moving on to telegraphic-like speech and short sentences. At 18 months she had a vocabulary of over 25 German words. Her vocabulary in English was not recorded.

In contrast, Mark showed no repetitive babbling and spoke nearly unintelligibly until he was over 2 years old. He was not silent, but vocalized with the intonation contours of sentences, reminiscent of the language-learning strategy called *gestalt* by Peters (1977), which she characterized as learning "the tune before the words." (Peters's usage of the term *gestalt* must be differentiated from other usages of that term, such as Grimm's, which will be discussed later.) His mother was distressed that she did not understand him well enough to help him develop his speaking skills through expansions and recasts of his language.

Table 9-1. Sample of Mark's Actual German Sentences and His Intended Sentences[a]

Actual	Intended
Du mein Brot mach—in halb mach.	Mach mein Brot in halb.
All mein Speck ess hab.	Ich hab all meinen Speck gegessen.
Vermissen hab—Papa.	Ich hab Papa vermisst.
Sissi wehtut mir hat.	Sissi hat mir wehgetan.
Pappa aublas mir.	Pappa, blas mir das auf.
In Tidepool reingehn hab—Hos nass-macht hab.	Ich bin ins Tidepool reingegangen und hab die Hos nass gemacht.
Vergessen-Dein Brötchen—Du hast.	Du hast Dein Brötchen vergessen.
Mich auskratz kann?	Kann ich auskratzen?

[a] Age 3 years, 3 months, to 3 years, 6 months.

9.3.1.2 Age 2 to 4 Years

Sally continued to progress quickly in both English and German, separating the two languages astonishingly well. She had no obvious articulation or syntactical problems and made few speech errors and overgeneralizations. She rarely mixed German and English. Mark continued to show delayed intelligible speech. By 2½ years his speech had developed to the extent that a careful listener could guess what he was trying to say. Once his utterances could be understood, the dysphasic characteristics of his speech (Grimm, 1986; Menyuk, 1978; Menyuk and Looney, 1976)—articulation and word-order problems—became apparent in both languages. Table 9-1 shows how the word order in his sentences is very different from that for which he appeared to be striving. Mark's sentences were similar to those made by German children diagnosed as dysphasic (Grimm, 1983). He also had pronounced speech disfluencies and was beginning to stammer. A comparison of a sample of Mark's and Sally's speech during conversations when they were both approximately 4 years and 3 months old shows the difference in their skill in speaking German (see the Appendix).

Other features that indicated that Mark's language learning was different from Sally's were the following:

(1) Inattention to the sound of rhymes: For instance, he changed "See you later, alligator, after a while crocodile," to "See you later crocodile." Out of "Liar, liar, pants on fire," he created, "Lügner, Lügner, pants on fire." (*Lügner* means *liar* in German.) And he would say, "One, two, three, four, buckle my shoe," instead of "One, two, buckle my shoe; three, four, open the door."

(2) Difficulty with immediate imitation: When told to say, "I love you," he said "Ich love Du," as if it were easier for him to translate than to imitate. Another time when told to ask, "Willst Du zum Picnic kommen?" he said, "Du Picnic komm will?" changing the word order and dropping the inflections. In both

instances he understood the message, but found it easier to transform the message than repeat it the way it was said.

(3) He mixed the languages when speaking, although he virtually never received mixed input.

(4) He made many overgeneralizations.

In contrast to his difficulty with speaking, his comprehension of both English and German was good. Neither the parents, nor the babysitter, nor later the preschool teacher noticed that he had any difficulty understanding instructions, commands, comments, and so on.

When Mark was 3 years and 3 months old and had made little progress in speaking either German or English, he was seen for a speech and hearing evaluation in English. This evaluation confirmed the more informal observations: His comprehension was excellent, scoring at the 84th percentile on the Peabody Picture Vocabulary Test, and at the 98th percentile on the Screening Test for Auditory Comprehension of Language. In contrast, his expressive skills were 3 months below his age with difficulties in repeating digits and words and with word-order problems on the Sequenced Inventory of Communication Development. He also had numerous articulation difficulties, especially with consonants, on the Goldman Friscoe Test of Articulation.

9.3.1.3 Age 5 to 7 Years

Although English was becoming more and more the preferred language for Sally, she still separated the two languages perfectly and would speak German to her parents, although she began to speak more English to her brother. In both languages, she spoke fluently, had few hesitations and false starts, and made few grammatical errors.

Mark's speech became more intelligible. He continued to make many overgeneralizations: For a time he created a double past tense: *did came, did saw, did took*. In *cloze* tasks some of his overgeneralizations did not occur presumably because retrieval was made easier by most of the sentence being produced for him (see Bock, 1982; Bohannon & Stanowicz, Chapter 6, this volume; Speidel & Herreshoff, Chapter 8, this volume, on learning to speak and the limited-capacity processing system). Some of his overgeneralizations were very intricate and creative. A few examples of his use of analogies to create words whose sounds he did not remember are *firstdary* for *primary* (his teacher had talked about primary and secondary colors that day), *threeth* for *third* (analogy: *fourth, fifth*, etc.), *the continue* for *the continuation* (possible source: the nominalization of many verbs, *the talk, the walk, the smile, etc.*), and "The house should have been *solden*" (analogy: the cake should have been *eaten*). Another elegant example of his word creations was *Threesday*, when he reasoned, "Actually, *Threesday* should come after Tuesday."

He often forgot the exact sound of words, saying *excovery* for *discovery*, *matomic* for *atomic*, *illuminated* for *laminated*, and *gretzel* for *pretzel*. One of his most charming examples occurred when he said that he would vote for an individual as president of the United States, "because he has much *experiment*," meaning *experience*. (These examples are reminiscent of the child described by Peters [1977] who learned language so differently from most of the children described in the literature up to that time.)

Mark's articulation and syntactical difficulties decreased sharply during this period, so that his kindergarten teacher did not notice any speech difficulties until she was made aware of them. A speech assessment at age 5 ½ years described him as "having good expressive language and sentence formation skills and minimal misarticulations." Some misarticulations and syntactic problems, however, were still present at age 7. The most difficult sound for him then was *th*, for which he either substituted *t* or *f*, saying *Tanksgiving*, or *Fanksgiving* for Thanksgiving, and *forn* for *thorn*. He still created sentence anomalies, such as, "I don't think he lives in that house *any long more* "; "You can burp, but *no one can't hears* it"; and "You *shouldn't complainted*."

His learning to speak German went even more slowly. As his English-speaking skills developed, he spoke more and more English to his parents. A strange communication style evolved in which the parents spoke German to him and he replied in English. It was as if he were oblivious to their input. Yet this could not actually have been the case since his very appropriate answers to their German statements showed that he had understood them well. His understanding of German continued to grow, and he came to understand very complicated and abstract topics.

On those occasions, however, when he did speak in German he made overgeneralizations and word creations similar to those he would make when speaking English. He used many English words in his German, often adding German grammatical endings to English words, as in the following examples: "Ja, ich hab da ge*stung*en worden." ("Yes, I got stung there.") "Wie viele Jahre wird's *last*en?" ("How many years will it last?") Typical substitutions that he made were the English pronouns *he* and *she* for their German equivalents, for example, "*He* geht zur Schule; bevor *she* hat gekommen."

Upon return from a visit to Germany at age 6 (see also the next section), his mother wrote about his German:

> At times he gets out very nice phrases, then he has trouble with vocabulary and with grammar. He uses the English filler *like* nearly every third word, while speaking in German. He often uses English words. However, if he is stopped and asked for the German word, he can come up with it. It is as if the English words were more readily available.

With some effort he often could retrieve the German. For example, Mark had just finished brushing his teeth:

MARK. Daddy, want to smell me?
DAD. Oh, Du riechst so frisch. (*Oh, you smell so fresh.*)

MOM.   Mark, wie riechst Du? (*How do you smell?*)
MARK.   Very good.
MOM.   Sag's auf deutsch. (*Say it in German.*)
MARK.   Sehr gut. (*Very good.*)
MOM.   Was hat Pappa gesagt? (*What did Daddy say?*)
MARK.   So frisch. (*So fresh.*)

In sum, at age 7, his speech was still highly variable—at times fluent, at times full of hesitations and disfluencies, bordering on stammering. This variability seemed to be a function of the ideas he was expressing—how complex they were and how often he had already put them into words. Since he enjoyed speaking and delighted in talking about his abundant ideas, the difficulties were not so noticeable to the casual observer. Yet the analyses of the speech samples that follow show that he still had greater difficulty in putting his thoughts into words than his sister had at the same age.

9.3.1.4 Visits to Germany

Every other year the family went on visits to Germany. During these visits Mark's use of German increased markedly, especially on the trip just before his seventh birthday. On that trip it was noticed that within a 2-week period (1) he spoke mainly German to German people and adopted the dialect intonation spoken in the area (which differed from his parents' dialect); (2) his skill in speaking German was not obviously delayed compared to that of the other German children with whom he played; and (3) his use of English dropped markedly, and he spoke now in German to his parents and used English only to talk with his sister when they were not with other children. Upon returning to the United States, he took several months to revert to his old pattern of speaking mainly English to his parents while they spoke German to him. Interesting is the observation that he retained the dialect intonation, that is, the tune of the language, for a fairly long period of time.

Sally showed much less fluctuation in her language use than Mark. While in the United States, she responded in German when spoken to in German by her parents and their friends. On visits to Germany, she retained this pattern, merely extending it to her playmates. On her return to the United States, she would again continue speaking German when spoken to in German.

9.3.2 Speech Samples

Samples of the two children's speech in both of their languages were obtained when they were 6 years old—a time when Mark's obvious speaking difficulties in English had all but vanished. The setting for the samples in the two languages differed greatly. The English sample was obtained in school by the person who had administered many of the tests described in the next section. It was a relatively structured conversation in which, among other things, the children were asked to look at a wordless picture book, to describe the events, and then to retell the story. The German sample was obtained from taped breakfast conversations.

Table 9-2. Results of Language Samples[a]

	English		German	
	Sally	Mark	Sally	Mark
MLU (words)	6.9	5.6	5.8	4.9
Maze words/words	0.09	0.17	0.03	0.20
Grammatical errors/utterance	0.05	0.13	0.03	0.67

[a] Age 6 years.

Table 9-2 presents the results of the analyses. The measure of mean length of utterance (MLU) showed that Mark made somewhat shorter utterances than Sally in English. He used twice as many maze words—that is "ums," repetitions, and false starts—and made nearly three times as many grammatical errors. The pattern was identical in German, but more pronounced. Again Mark had shorter utterances, nearly 4 times as many maze words, and 20 times as many grammatical errors. Thus, although the interactions and the settings from which the samples in the two languages were taken differed greatly, Mark's difficulties with speaking them were identical.

9.4 Language and Cognitive Test Data

These observational data are supplemented by a number of language, memory, and cognitive ability tests. Unless mentioned, the tests were all given when the children were between the ages of 6½ and 7. Except for the paired-associate test, the tests have age norms, and the children's performance is presented as their relative standing within their age group. Theoretically this standing, such as the percentile rank, should not change greatly over time. Except for the German language test, the tests were administered individually in English by a psychometrist. The German test was administered by their mother.

9.4.1 Cognitive Ability Tests

Both children were given the Stanford Binet Intelligence Test, Sally when she was 4½ and Mark when he was 2½. Both scored in the superior range of intelligence. On the Raven's Progressive Matrices Test, a nonverbal reasoning test, both children performed at the 99th percentile. In short, they had similar levels of cognitive ability. Mark took the Goldschmid-Bentler Concept Formation Test, a test of Piagetian cognitive development, at age 5. He had a perfect conservation score, which according to Piagetian findings typically only happens around the ages 7 or 8.

9.4.2 Language Tests

The children were given the Illinois Test of Psycholinguistic Ability (ITPA) for their development of English and the Heidelberger Sprachentwicklungstest

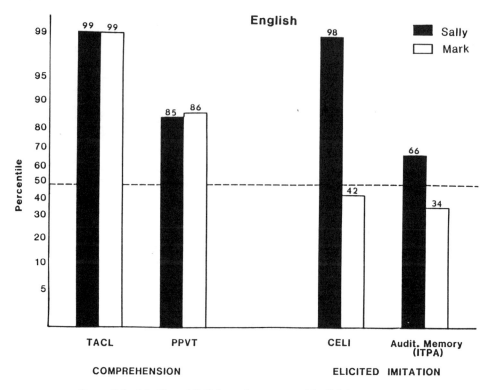

Figure 9-1. Mark's and Sally's performance on English language tests.

(H-S-E-T) for German. Both children performed well on the ITPA, obtaining language scores (averaged across subtests) above the 90th percentile. (Mark had been given the ITPA once before, when he was 4½. His percentile rank on that earlier testing was not significantly different from that on the later testing.) Their performance on the German test was lower, but still within the average range for their age. Thus, Sally and Mark did not differ greatly from each other when an average was taken of their performances across a series of different language tasks.

These results seem to contradict the observations above. However, the following, more fine-grained analysis will explain why the average performances were not different. Figure 9-1 shows their performance on two comprehension measures. On the Test for Auditory Comprehension of Language (TACL), both children obtained a score at the 99th percentile rank. On the Peabody Picture Vocabulary Test (PPVT), Sally performed at the 85th percentile, and Mark at the 86th percentile. Thus, there was no difference between them on these English comprehension tasks. The picture, however, is very different on elicited imitation on the Carrow Elicited Language Inventory (CELI). Sally was able to repeat

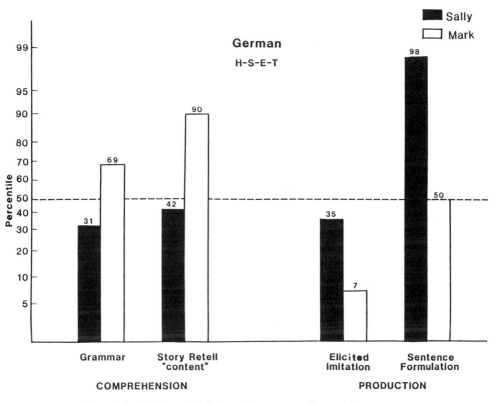

Figure 9-2. Mark's and Sally's performance on German language tests.

back the sentences accurately, obtaining a percentile rank score of 98. Mark, in contrast, had difficulty with such repetition and only obtained a percentile rank of 42. (Mark's percentile rank on this test at age 4½ was virtually identical to this later performance.)

Figure 9-2 shows the children's performance on similar language tasks in German. The H-S-E-T has a section on grammar comprehension similar to the TACL. On this test we see that Mark was actually better in comprehending German grammatical constructions than Sally. Similarly, when a story-retelling task is scored in terms of content units retold, Mark performed significantly better than Sally (90th vs. 42nd percentile, respectively). On a German elicited-imitation task, similar to the English CELI, both children had much more difficulty imitating the German than the English sentences when their performance is compared to German children of their age. Nevertheless, Sally was, as on the English test, significantly better than Mark. Her imitation performance was at the 35th percentile, whereas his performance only reached the 7th percentile. On the formulated sentences task, a task on which children are given two words and must compose a sentence using those words, Sally obtained a percentile rank of 98, while Mark scored in the average range.

The sharp contrast between Mark's language comprehension skills and his production skills is best shown on the story-retelling task on the H-S-E-T. Here Mark remembered the semantic content of the story extremely well; however, in his retelling of the story he used shorter sentences than Sally, he made many more grammatical errors per utterance — more than five times as many — and he used a high percentage of translated words, whereas Sally used none.

Mark's difficulty in retrieving the sounds of words is seen in his attempt at retelling this story. In recalling the different things that the protagonist found, he used five different forms for the same semantic concept, namely, *had found*, which in the German story version was always encoded as *hat gefunden* (the *u* pronounced as in *fool*). The first time he used appropriately *hat gefunden*. In the next utterance, he switched to *find* (the *i* pronounced as in *in*; this is the verb stem of the German present tense). The third time he created his own past tense, *gefinden*, (the *i* again pronounced as above). Then he created *fund* (the *u* as in *fool*), and finally he used the English word *found*. All of these forms he produced within two minutes, to describe what had been encoded each time in the story as *hat gefunden*.

9.4.3 Memory Tests

The difficulties with elicited imitation can be viewed as a difficulty with verbal short-term memory as verbal short-term memory is typically measured by performance on elicited repetition tasks (see Chapter 7). If this is indeed the case, then Mark should also have more difficulty on other tasks that tap verbal short-term memory.

9.4.3.1 Repetition of Unrelated Words

The children were given the Unrelated Words Repetition subtest of the Detroit Test of Learning Aptitude. On this test children hear strings of unrelated words of increasing length and have to repeat them back. Mark scored 8 months below his chronological age, whereas Sally scored 1 year and 9 months above her age.

9.4.3.2 Digit Span

Mark had much greater difficulty with the repetition of numbers on the ITPA than Sally. He obtained a percentile score of 34, whereas Sally obtained a percentile score of 66 (see Figure 9-1). On an earlier testing of the ITPA, at age 4½, Mark showed even greater difficulties with digit span, falling below the 20th percentile.

9.4.3.3 Paired-Associate Learning

Both children were given a paired-associate task when they were 6½. The task consisted of remembering five pairs of nonsense syllables. Mark remembered only one pair after the first presentation and took five trials to remember all five.

In contrast, Sally remembered three pairs after the first trial and all five after the second trial.

From the difficulties that Mark had on these verbal memory tests, we can conclude that his difficulty with elicited sentence imitation is not restricted to a specific difficulty with the grammatic-syntactic aspects of the elicited sentence-imitation task, but appears to be due to a more general memory problem which affects his ability to imitate series of speech sounds.

9.4.3.4 Visual Memory

To see whether Mark's memory problem was restricted to verbal items, or whether it was an even more fundamental memory problem, including visual processing, his performance on visual memory was assessed. He was given the Visual Sequential Memory Test from the ITPA. In this test the child is briefly shown a sequence of nonsense line drawings and is asked to reconstruct the sequence from memory by selecting chips that have the nonsense line drawings printed on them. Mark's visual memory was excellent. He obtained the top possible score for his age group. He was also given the Visual Motor Free Test. Again his performance was very high, obtaining the best possible score.

9.4.4 Summary of Test Findings

From the tests findings, we see that

(1) Mark and Sally have similar general intellectual abilities;
(2) Mark's comprehension of both English and German is excellent and comparable to Sally's;
(3) Mark has difficulty with certain aspects of speaking, and this difficulty is present in both languages;
(4) Mark's difficulty with language production seems to be associated with poorer short-term memory; and
(5) Mark's memory difficulty seems to be restricted to verbal content.

9.5 Reading Development

The preschool in which Mark and Sally were enrolled used the Montessori approach to reading, a very well-planned synthetic phonics program. Differences in the ease with which the children learned to read were already noticeable in their preschool report just before they were 5 years old. The preschool teacher wrote about Sally, "Sally has proceeded rapidly through the Moveable Alphabet exercises and made a smooth transition into reading." Two years later the same teacher wrote about Mark, "Work with the Moveable Alphabet continues to improve. He is able to compose three letter phonetic words by dictation or by using picture cards. His ability to isolate sounds in words has improved. He would benefit from continued auditory training in distinguishing beginning, medial, and final sounds in words."

Sally learned to read without difficulty and without the help of her mother. By the time she was 6½, she was reading books like *Charlotte's Webb* and *Pippi Longstocking* by herself, for pleasure. For Mark, on the other hand, learning to read was very arduous, bordering on painful. His mother tried to help him in different ways, but it seemed as if nothing worked. A diary report by the mother written when Mark was 6½ years old (an age at which his classmates were already reading well) reads:

> His performance is so varied. I really think that Mark shows us how reading is linked to the ease of accessing words. He is not good at articulating words properly. Important point though is that even though articulation may be a problem, it may not be the way to remedy the reading delay.

(Actually this report was written just at the beginning stages of an approach that in the end became very successful with Mark; see Speidel, in preparation.)

The children were given the Gates-McGinitie Reading Test, Level A, when they were 7 years old. Sally obtained the maximum score possible on that test, which translated into a reading performance typical of children at the middle of third grade. Her actual reading performance was probably a year higher as estimated by her performance on later administrations of tests with higher ceilings. Mark performed at the level typical of the middle of first grade. This was only ½ year below his chronological age, but more than 2 years below his mental age (if his approximate IQ of 130 at age 7 is converted to a mental age score).

The description of dyslexics by Critchley (1981) fitted Mark's reading behavior well: slow reading with hesitation in decoding unfamiliar or polysyllabic words, mirror letter confusions, omission of short words like articles, misreading *the* for *a* or *this* for *that*, substitution of words for words that appear similar, and substitution of words for other words that have more or less the same meaning. Mark showed the typical dyslexic symptoms of letter and word reversals, reading *left* for *felt*, *was* for *saw*, and *every* for *very*, and so forth. He would also substitute words for other words that had a similar meaning, but looked very different graphically, reading *fox* for *wolf*, *water* for *sea*, and *afraid* for *frightened*. *It was as if his visual memory of the graphic representation of the word was connected to its semantic representation without the phonetic representation.*

Several findings from reading research are relevant to Mark's situation. First, like Mark, children with reading delay have difficulty with elicited sentence imitation (e.g., Mann, 1984; Mann & Liberman, 1984; Speidel & Power, 1987). Second, children who have difficulty learning to read have trouble with phonemic awareness (e.g., Bradley & Bryant, 1983; Bryant, 1986; Stanovich, 1986; Stanovich, Cunningham, and & Cramer, 1984). Although the term *phonemic awareness* suggests an ability to process incoming speech sounds, the tasks that are actually used to assess it require highly developed and flexible speech-sound production skills. Phonemic-awareness tasks, for example, ask, "Listen to the word *ball*; if you take away the /b/ sound what word is left?" or, "Say the word *cat*;

now say the word *at*. What sound is missing from *at*?" Both the elicited sentence imitation and the phonemic-awareness task would seem to require facility in speech production, that is, in accessing the speech-planning networks.

Evidence for the involvement of articulatory processes in learning to read comes from the finding that direct articulatory training may help (Byrne, 1984; Lindamood, 1985; Lundberg, Frost, & Peterson, 1988). Relevant here is also Baddeley's (1976; 1986) work, which views short-term verbal memory, such as elicited verbal imitation, as requiring the operation of an *articulatory loop*. Not only can increased verbal memory span in children be traced to the development of articulatory skill, but also suppression of articulation will shorten verbal memory span (see Baddeley, 1986, for a review of relevant studies). With respect to reading, Baddeley (1986) brings evidence to support his hypothesis that in learning to read one must draw upon this short-term articulatory storage system. Reviewing a series of studies on short-term verbal memory problems of children with reading delay, he concludes that these children "may have an impairment of the functioning of the articulatory loop making it difficult to retain the sequence of sounds" (p. 218).

Even though Mark's articulation difficulties were no longer obvious at this age, the mother's diary report above suggests that they were not totally resolved. It is quite likely, therefore, that his difficulty with speech-sound retrieval and production is the basis of his problems with learning to read.

9.6 Developmental Dysphasia, Short-Term Verbal Memory, and Articulation Problems

Mark's difficulties in learning to speak were similar to those of children with developmental dysphasia, although much less pronounced. These children have no general intellectual problems, but their language is delayed. Like Mark, these children have difficulty with elicited sentence imitation (Menyuk & Looney, 1976). For instance, they will make the following errors in imitation:

Model	Imitation
How will he get there?	How he will get there?
When will he come?	When he will come?
They won't play with me.	They not play with me.
I can't sing.	I no can sing.

Menyuk and Looney (1976) argue that the kinds of errors these children make suggest that they "retain representations of the semantic aspects of these sentence types, how to express them, and little more." They hypothesize that this distorted decoding capacity is the result of limits on immediate memory.

> These limits do not allow time for storage of the complete phrase or sentence and a deeper analysis than that required to derive meaning-bearing elements.
> . . . One cannot even logically speculate about why these differences in language processing exist between the two groups of children, but can only state

that the differences must lie in their central nervous system functioning, and speculate that this functioning is specifically related to language, given their usual performance in other cognitive areas. The basis of this difference appears to be the functioning of memory in these children, but no evidence has been obtained about the possible anatomical and physiological reasons for this difference. (p. 278)

Grimm (1983, 1986), who studied German dysphasic children, wrote that it appeared as if they had to *reconstruct anew each sentence* and as if they had no patterns for sentences. This description is reminiscent of Mark's difficulty with speaking and suggests, once again, that there is poor memory for the sounds of speech. The deviant sentence patterns of the German dysphasic children are highly similar to sentence patterns used by Mark when he first began to produce utterances beyond two words.

Like Menyuk, Grimm's observations imply that these children have a problem with short-term verbal memory. She observed that normal children adopted larger units of maternal language, often imitating the complete utterance. This strategy was virtually absent in the dysphasic children, who use what she calls an "elementaristic" strategy of repeating single words. Grimm (1986) writes the following:

> The child memorizes to the best of his ability such language forms that he frequently hears, and which are important for his needs and desires, and then retrieves them in this remembered form. These longer units of speech thus have the status of internally represented models. . . . A strong argument that supports the concept of gestalt-like learning as a necessary condition for a normal acquisition of syntax, is the fact that D-children [dysphasic children] seldom make use of this learning strategy. I cannot yet explain why they do not do this . . . I would simply like to point again to the finding that the three most intelligent children primarily have syntactic problems and in the cognitive tasks investigated, they gave performances comparable to the N-children control groups. (pp. 13, 14)

There is another similarity between Mark and these dysphasic children—the presence of articulation problems. For instance, de Ajuriaguerra et al. (1976), Menyuk and Looney (1976), Menyuk (1978), and Morehead and Ingram (1976) all mention the presence of articulation problems in their language-delayed samples. Similarly, Grimm's (e.g., 1983, 1986) dysphasic children had articulation problems. The dysphasic children's poor performance on elicited imitation tasks may be related to these articulation problems. The previously cited work by Baddeley (1976, 1986) on the relationship between articulatory suppression and shortened verbal memory span also lends support to this notion.

To explain this point further, let us look at these children's difficulties using the three-network language-processing model (see Figure 7-1). The dysphasic children show by their repetitions that they have understood the syntax, and as Menyuk phrased it, their "meaning elements are in tact." This must mean that the incoming speech-sound and the meaning networks are appropriately developed.

The problem seems to lie in slower development and integration of the speech-planning networks, and/or in poorer transmission of signals between the incoming speech-sound or meaning networks and the speech-planning networks.

The articulatory difficulties of these children can be seen as an early reflection of the slower development of the speech-planning networks. In Chapter 7 it was suggested how the relationship between articulation and verbal short-term memory could come about: In children with articulatory problems, the acoustic trace in the incoming speech-sound networks may have faded before they are able to imitate much of the model due to their difficulty with articulation. This results in a poorer verbal imitation span, that is, poorer short-term verbal memory. Since immediate imitation can be seen as a form of rehearsal, children with articulation problems will have poorer rehearsal opportunities. This not only slows down their articulatory development, but also makes the retrieval of speech sounds from long-term memory, when speaking, more difficult. Moreover, if children are able to imitate only one or two words, they may not store into long-term memory longer phrases from which to build the syntactic patterns, as described in Chapter 7. This gives their speech the appearance of not using a gestalt strategy, which Grimm sees as being so necessary for the development of syntactic speech.

A look at the imitated sentences presented at the beginning of this section supports this hypothesis. These imitations are by no means unexplainable. Their origin is readily detectable. In the first two, the children use the most common word order *he will*, rather than *will he*; in the last two, the children adopt also the more frequent forms for expressing the negative — *not* and *no* are much more common in the speech usually addressed to them. Mark's syntactic errors can also be seen as the use of more frequent word order or combination of separate short phrases rather than whole or longer sentence frames. In English, for instance, he would say, "That's the only one *what I use* for my pets." "That's *what I use* . . ." is perfectly fine and probably more frequently heard by Mark than "That's the one *that I use*." Similarly, when he says, "How she should do it?" he is using the more typical word order *she should*.

It seems, therefore, that dysphasic children build their sentences from shorter and more frequent relationships between meaning units and units in the speech-planning network. This is a way of coping with their difficulty in storing the longer and/or more infrequent phrases such as "How will she . . ." or "I can't." This strategy, however, *gives the appearance* that they are using an analytic rather than a gestalt processing strategy. They may be using the same operations for building their utterances as normal children use, but they may have to apply them to shorter segments.

9.7 Biological Factors in Articulation and Verbal Memory

What could be the cause of the greater difficulty with articulation and verbal memory that we observed in Mark and in the developmentally dysphasic and dyslexic children? Does it have anything to do with the organization of the hemi-spheres of the brain? Although in adults there is evidence that different mental functions are localized in different parts of the two hemispheres, the theories on thinking modes of the hemispheres, such as *analytic* processing by the left hemisphere and *gestalt* processing by the right, receive little support (Corballis, 1980, 1983; Gazzaniga, 1987). According to Corballis (1983), the only verifiable differences between the hemispheres at the outset of development is that *the left hemisphere is better than the right at the motor planning/execution of small fine sequences of movements*. This advantage would make it the preferred hemisphere for the localization of speech.

> It seems likely that the origins of left-hemispheric specialization are motor rather than perceptual. Handedness itself is most obviously a motor phenome-non.... the common ingredient underlying speech and the dominant praxic functions of the left cerebral hemisphere appears to be *fine control over sequences of acts*. Speaking, writing, throwing, and actions commonly described as manipulative all require precise temporal coordination. (p. 62)

In Chapter 7 it was indicated how incredibly complex the neural activity for making speech sounds is, some sounds involving the coordination of 35 or more muscles (Hardcastle, 1976). Making speech sounds requires central spa-tial coordinate neural systems (Edwards, 1984; Kelso, Tuller & Harris, 1983; MacNeilage, 1970), or what is called here the speech-planning networks. If the neuromuscular processes for planning or making speech sounds are less efficient, or their access less available, then, it is argued, the development of the speech production system will be slower (given the same amount of input and practice). Another possibility, suggested by Liberman and Mattingly's (1985) work, is that the connections between the incoming speech-sound and the speech-planning networks are not as efficient and the activation of the incoming speech-sound networks cannot guide the development of the speech-planning networks as easily. Consequently, in children like Mark and in developmentally dysphasic children, there may be either some anomaly in the auditory/speech areas of the left hemisphere, or some factor that interferes with the usual dominance of the left hemisphere.

Recent research in developmental neurology and in dyslexia may throw some light on this issue. Postmortem anatomical examination of brains of individuals known to have been dyslexic has revealed that their brains are structured some-what differently from "normal" brains. Typically, the *planum temporale* – an area in the cortex in which language, particularly auditory functions, are localized – is larger in the left than in the right hemisphere. Galaburda (1986) has consistently found that in the brains of dyslexics the planum temporale is equally large in both hemispheres. Moreover, the planum temporale in these dyslexic brains had abnormalities, such as dysplasias and ectopias. These were usually found more often in the left planum temporale than in the right (Galaburda, 1986; Rosen, Sherman, & Galaburda, 1986). As Rosen et al. (1986) indicate, these kinds of anomalies are not unique to dyslexia; however, the time during development that they occur and their anatomical location may be. Such anomalies may interfere with the development of the usual cerebral dominance of the portion of the left hemisphere related to speech planning and thereby may slow the development of the speech motor-planning networks.

One theory links these neurological anomalies in dyslexics to immune disorders. Animal analogue research has shown that immune-mediated reactions during gestation may result in altered brain tissue resembling that found in the planum temporale of dyslexics (Galaburda, 1986; Rosen et al., 1986). Epidemiological findings support this notion: A fairly strong relationship between dyslexia and immune disorders as well as celiac disease has been observed (Geschwind & Behan, 1984).

Clearly, we are here on highly speculative ground. Articulatory problems may be caused by a variety of other environmental/constitutional problems. A prime candidate for such another factor in articulatory difficulties is otitis media, or middle-ear infection. These infections are related to language delay (e.g., Feagans et al., in press; Friel-Patti et al., 1982; Heath, Plett, & Tibbets, 1987; Menyuk, 1985). However, although it seems plausible to argue that ear infections cause language delay, it may be that the ear infections and language delay are connected in some other way. (See Feagans et al., in press, for a discussion of causation models.) That the relationship may not be a directly causative one in every case is supported by a report by Finitzo and Friel-Patti (1987), who found a group of children with severe otitis media histories, but no language delay. Moreover, the incidence of one or more episodes of otitis media in the infant population is high, around 75%, of which 50% to 75% can be without overt symptoms and can go unnoticed (Marchant et al., 1984; Schwartz, Stool, Rodriguez, & Grundfaster, 1981).

With Mark, the ear infections were probably secondary. His language delay was noticed before the ear infections began. Sally's series of ear infections, which occurred during her first 24 months of life, would seem to have occurred during a prime language-development time, and yet she did not show any signs of language delay. Moreover, Mark showed no comprehension problems or inattention to language, which Feagans (1986) suggests mediates the later speaking problems of children who have a history of previous media otitis. However, the ear infections cannot be ruled out as being the original cause in the slower development of Mark's speech.

9.8 Putting Together the Pieces of the Puzzle

Although this case study provides many interesting points for discussion of bilingual language learning, we will focus here on the different ways in which the two children's languages developed and on the possible reasons for these differences. From the diverse sources of information above, a rather clear picture emerges of how their language learning proceeded. Mark's comprehension proceeded well and was as good as, if not better than, Sally's. However, there were marked differences in the way their speaking developed. Mark did not show the typical repetitive babbling during his preword stage. Once he began to attempt words, he had very unclear articulation, which made the understanding of his speech most difficult. When his speech became intelligible, word-order problems became evident. His initial stammering then resolved itself into less pronounced speech disfluencies. He used many overgeneralizations and word creations. Sally, in contrast, did not show these difficulties to any noticeable degree. Mark's greater difficulty with speaking than with comprehension was evident in both of his languages.

Interpreting these observations in terms of the three-network language model, the fact that Mark's comprehension of the two languages developed as well as Sally's suggests that the incoming speech-sound networks for both languages and the meaning networks, as well as the interconnection between these two network systems, were developing at a similar rate in the two children.

Mark's difficulty with learning to speak must, therefore, reflect some kind of difficulty in the development of the speech-planning networks and/or their accessibility by the meaning networks. The lack of repetitive babbling in Mark can be seen as the first indication of this basic difficulty with the speech-planning networks. Once he began to attempt speech, he had trouble with articulation and stammered. His speech-evaluation report described his speech as "very small oral movements." Having difficulties with articulation, Mark may have had trouble producing speech sounds while the acoustic traces in the incoming speech-sound networks were still active. This, in turn, may have led to poorer immediate verbal imitation.

Mark was aware of his memory problem for finding the sounds of words. Once, their father suggested to Mark and Sally that they learn French. Mark answered immediately, "But then I'll forget my English. When I spoke English, I forgot German." Another time, his mother became frustrated by the fact that Mark would always reply in English when she spoke German to him, and she asked him why he didn't speak German to her. He answered that he had trouble remembering the German words and that if he had to speak German he would stutter. Another incident happened when Mark had made a print of the palm of his hand.

MARK.   They look like vines (*pointing to the lines on the print*).
MOTHER.   Veins, you mean? (*Mother responded in English because she was curious about this error.*)
MARK.   Yea, veins.
MOTHER.   Why did you say vines?
MARK.   Because they sound alike and I didn't remember.

The fact that Mark had difficulty with all kinds of short-term verbal memory tasks, that is, he had trouble not only with repeating back sentences but also repeating back digits and unrelated words and learning to pair nonsense syllables, suggests that his memory difficulty was not restricted to syntax, but that it involved anything in which he had to store, for a brief time, the sounds of speech. This interpretation is consistent with Baddeley and Hitch's (1974) and Baddeley's (1976, 1986) notion that short-term verbal memory span is a function of a working memory and an *articulatory rehearsal loop*, which acts as a "slave system" and supplements the limited capacities of working memory (cf. Speidel, Chapter 8 this volume).

To skirt his handicap in recalling or accessing the sounds of words, he used whatever other knowledge and cognitive skills he had at his disposal. He took advantage of the frequent features of language: *relying heavily on analogic reasoning*, he retrieved the most common sounds or forms for expressing the meaning elements of his thought. Consequently, he had many overgeneralizations in both bound morphemes and syntax. His word creations can also be seen as the use of analogy to find words when the exact sounds of the words could not be accessed in the speech-planning system. He truly at times "re-created" as Grimm said, the speech sounds from the pieces that were most readily accessible to him at the moment.

If, as a number of language researchers have suggested (e.g., Brown and Fraser, 1963; R. Clark, 1977; Grimm, 1986; Menyuk & Looney, 1976; Nelson, 1987; Speidel, Chapter 7, this volume), one needs a storehouse of remembered phrases for the induction of syntactic rules, then difficulty with immediate imitation means difficulty with developing this storehouse for building syntactic patterns. The strange syntax that Mark and developmentally dysphasic children show during learning can be seen as the result of the memory problem. Shorter phrases, frequency, analogy, saliency, and emotional/arousal level are probably some of the factors affecting these children's retrieval when speaking. Frequency in terms of identical repetition of a word or sentence is perhaps not as important as frequency by analogy, either in form of linguistic patterns, sound similarity, or their combination (see Moerk, Chapter 12, this volume).

Mark's seemingly strange way of responding in English when his parents spoke to him in German can be explained as follows: His German incoming speech-sound network and its integration with the meaning networks were well developed, so that his comprehension of German was high. However, either his speech-planning network for English speech sounds was much more developed than the equivalent network for German, or the English speech-planning network was more readily, more automatically accessible to the meaning networks. The truth may lie somewhere in between. The fact that on his visits to Germany he quickly began to speak German fairly well suggests that the many years of hearing German had helped to develop, at least to some extent, his German speech-planning network *without constant overt practice* (see activation Pattern 0, Chapter 7).

With time, with more input and more practice, Mark's English-speaking skill began to approximate his sister's. In other words, his speech-planning networks and their integration with the meaning networks developed to a point where speaking problems were not readily evident. The role of automaticity in this development is shown in his differential uses of English and German. The accessing (or retrieval) of the speech-planning networks by the meaning networks is not all-or-none, but is determined by other simultaneous events in the brain, such as the similarity between the cues during learning and retrieval and how much other work the limited processing system is doing (see Bock, 1982; Bohannon & Stanowicz, Chapter 6, this volume; Speidel & Herreshoff, Chapter 8, this volume). Thus, although by the time Mark was 6 his more automatic and effortless way of expressing his thoughts was in English, he was often capable of accessing the German equivalent when he attended to the task; that is, when his central processor—working memory—was focused on the retrieval task.

Mark's difficulties, we saw, next manifested themselves in his learning to read. In the way that children typically learn to read, print comes to be associated with the speech sounds of the language. Learning to read should therefore involve the speech-planning network, and one would expect that delay in the development of this network be reflected in slower reading acquisition.

Although by age 6 Mark's speech was fairly fluent, one reason for his reading difficulty may be that his speech-planning networks were not yet as automatic or as developed as his sister's. Some evidence for this is the fact that he still had some articulatory sound substitutions up to the age of 7. The diary report in which his mother was pondering his problems with reading also suggests that his articulatory system was not totally in place when he was learning to read. Finally, his elicited verbal imitation performance at age 6½ was still much lower than Sally's: A fact which, given Baddeley's (Baddeley, 1976, 1986; Baddeley & Hitch, 1974) work, probably reflects some form of difficulty with the articulatory system or its accessibility.

If we accept the hypothesis that the difference in the ease with which Mark and Sally learned to speak is due to some basic difficulty associated with the speech-planning networks, then the next question becomes, What might be the cause of this difficulty? The difficulty cannot be attributed to the following:

(1) differences in general cognitive ability, as they both had similar performances on intelligence tests and on nonverbal reasoning tests;
(2) bilingualism per se, because Sally had no special problems in learning to speak the two languages simultaneously; and
(3) language-input differences between the two children, at least not as the *primary* cause: It is highly unlikely that any difference in language input given to Mark and Sally was identical across both languages as the input conditions in the two languages were so different; yet, Mark showed in both languages the same pattern of high comprehension and relatively slower speech development.

It seems, therefore, that language input and intellectual factors are not the primary causes of the observed differences in how the two children learned to speak, and that we have fairly strong evidence for constitutional/neurological factors:

(1) The beginnings of Mark's difficulties can be traced to a very early age, when he showed no repetitive babbling. There is little reason to suspect that his environment at that early age was so different from his sister's, both being mainly cared for by their grandmother.

(2) Mark's articulation and verbal memory problems are similar to those of developmentally dysphasic children, although less pronounced. Constitutional factors have been implied to be a cause of dysphasic children's difficulties (Grimm, 1986; Menyuk & Looney, 1976).

(3) Mark's language and reading difficulties are similar to developmental dyslexics, and like many dyslexics, he had childhood celiac disease. Recent research on dyslexia points to a biological cause, namely, anomalies in the neural tissue of the language areas.

Although the pieces of the puzzle are clearly not cemented together with carefully controlled research, they do fit quite well and some pieces are already fairly well supported: (1) a biological basis for dyslexia, (2) the short-term verbal memory problem of dysphasic children, and (3) the short-term verbal memory and phonemic-awareness problems in reading delay. Bannatyne (1976) has already put the puzzle pieces together for developmentally dyslexic children in a way similar to how they have been put together in this study.

Moreover, we have followed one other boy from birth until age 7 — a boy with a background that differs in important ways from Mark's — a monolingual English- speaking, only child (Speidel & Brandt, 1987). This boy displayed the identical pattern: celiac disease, no repetitive babbling, unclear speech and speech therapy, strange syntax, word creations with a heavy reliance on analogical reasoning, and reading delay with dyslexic symptoms. Like Mark, he performed well on language comprehension tests, whereas on elicited sentence imitation he did very poorly.

If we look more carefully, we will probably see many more cases like Mark's. For example, among the expressive language-delayed children studied by Whitehurst and his associates (see Whitehurst & DeBaryshe, Chapter 11, this volume), there may some children like Mark. However, not all such children will show all of Mark's difficulties in the same way. Biological factors act in symbiosis with environmental and other constitutional factors. Thus, celiac disease may not appear if the child is not given the allergy-provoking foods. Dyslexia and its miserable consequences for schooling will only be manifest in societies in which there is an emphasis on literacy.

9.9 Factors Affecting Learning to Speak

The speed with which children learn to speak and the level of skill attained in speaking are a function of a number of factors, of which the degree of the initial difficulty involving the speech-planning networks is only one. Marks's longitudinal language development pattern shows that his initial difficulty with learning to speak decreases with age. By age 7 Mark's difficulty with English, his preferred language, was noticeable only through careful analysis of his speech. Although it is plausible that these improvements are due only to the *maturation* of his nervous system, another explanation, perhaps in conjunction with maturation, is the following: Because of his difficulty with the speech-planning networks, Mark needed more input and more practice opportunities than Sally for learning to speak.

It seems, therefore, that in the same way that normal children's ability to repeat back longer strings of words or sentences grows with more input and more practice (Baddeley, 1986), dysphasic children's memory capacity will increase. With time (more input and more practice), they should become able to store larger and larger chunks of language and eventually should be able to apply the gestalt-like language-learning strategy thought to be so important by Grimm (1986) and to develop relatively normal syntax.

If speaking is seen as requiring memory, then the shorter the delay between hearing a word and first using it, the more likely it is that it will be remembered and retrieved in the future. Immediate imitation can be viewed as immediate practice, as rehearsal without delay, making later retrieval more probable. It would seem, therefore, that children who have a difficulty, like Mark, would benefit from an imitative strategy (cf. Snow, Chapter 4, this volume). At first glance, however, Snow's data do not seem to provide strong evidence for such a benefit. In her sample, imitativeness (the extent to which an individual attempts to imitate models) and accuracy in imitation are at best moderately related: The accurate imitators are not always highly imitative.

However, the present hypothesis about initial differences in ability to imitate may show us why this relationship is not a perfect one. If there are constitutional differences in the efficiency with which the speech-planning networks develop (or in the efficiency of signal transmission between the incoming speech-sound networks and the speech-planning networks), then those children with the more efficient systems will learn to make the sounds of speech more quickly, and one could expect their speech also to become covert more quickly. Thus, even though they have good imitation ability and may be precocious in their speech development, they may not show much overt immediate imitation (see Snow, Chapter 4, this volume). Consequently, *it is possible that overt imitation is only important for learning to speak for children who have greater initial difficulty with making speech sounds.* The role that mothers appear to play in developing the imitativeness of their child (cf. Masur, Chapter 3, this volume; Užgiris et al., Chapter 5, this volume) may be particularly important for children who have difficulty with articulation and verbal memory.

Differences in intellectual ability will also affect the degree to which the initial difficulty with articulation affects the rate of learning to speak and final speech attainment. Derhulst-Schlichting, at the University of Utrecht, has worked with

Dutch language-delayed children and believes that there is a nonlinear relationship between intelligence and overt effects of language impairment: Children with average or low intelligence may not be able to compensate in the same way that children with high intelligence can (personal communication). Mark's creative word formations, based on pattern recognition, are suggestive of such compensatory strategies.

In short, as Galaburda (1986) has argued so well, the initial differences in brain organization may be accentuated or may become unnoticeable depending on other internal and external factors. Learning to speak is probably similar to other skill learning—a function of a number of constitutional differences, input, and practice. Thus, final attainment in speaking skill is probably the result of the initial degree of difficulty with articulation interacting with such secondary variables as intellectual abilities, quantity and quality of input, the imitativeness of the child, the quantity and quality of practice opportunities, and perhaps the demands of the language (German syntax may be initially more difficult, as it is quite variable). Children whose difficulty with articulation is very severe, who have low cognitive abilities, and little language input/practice may never attain flexible command of intricate syntactical constructions. On the other hand, children with the same initial articulatory difficulty may, on the basis of compensatory cognitive abilities, rich language input, imitativeness, and many speaking opportunities, come to have speaking skills that are not noticeably different from children who have not had those initial difficulties in learning to speak.

In closing this discussion about differences in learning to speak, an important methodological point is suggested by the above argument. The contributions of a specifically language-related biological factor will become less noticeable as the other variables necessary for learning to speak come into play. Differences in learning to speak due to neurological differences of the speech-planning networks will be most readily noticed early in the development of the child.

9.10 Conclusion

Research on memory, on normal and delayed speech development, and on delayed reading was brought to bear on understanding the different ways in which two bilingual children learned to speak and to read. Speaking, in contrast to speech comprehension, requires the development of an intricate motor skill—the articulation of words; it requires the smooth and rapid reproduction of sounds of words and their syntactic arrangement. Speaking, therefore, requires extensive short-term and long-term verbal memory, in other words, immediate and delayed verbal imitation. Findings with developmentally dysphasic children point out that a memory span of certain length may be necessary for learning to use correct word order. The development of verbal memory span is probably a function of articulatory skill.

One source of individual differences in learning to speak, therefore, is thought to be the rate or the nature of the development of central neural networks that organize and serve as plans for the complex neuromuscular chain of events required in articulation and in speaking. Research with developmentally dysphasic and dyslexic children suggests that the ease with which these speech-planning systems develop may have a biological basis. Initial differences in the ability to produce speech sounds will interact with differences in nonverbal cognitive ability, in imitativeness, and in the amount and kind of input/practice. In short, attained level of speaking skill is multidetermined.

Imitation (overt or covert) serves a memory function and should help to lay the foundations and to consolidate the neural planning systems for speech. If there are indeed individual differences in the ease with which these neural speech-planning networks develop, the role of overt imitation is more difficult to trace: Children who are more quick to develop speech-planning networks may also be the ones who are more quick to use covert speech. This would mean that those children who are precocious in learning to speak may early on begin to use covert imitation and show little overt imitation as a rehearsal mechanism.

Clearly, this model must still come under stringent testing. In the meantime it will hopefully serve as an impetus to integrate findings from the various disciplines that are presently only concerned with separate pieces of the language puzzle.

Acknowledgments. I wish to thank Keith Nelson and Madeleen Herreshoff for their insightful suggestions and Janet Cooke for her helpful editorial assistance and comments.

References

Baddeley, A. (1986). *Working memory.* Oxford: Clarendon Press.

Baddeley, A.D. (1976). *The psychology of memory.* New York: Basic Books.

Baddeley, A.D., & Hitch, G.J. (1974). Working memory. In G.H. Bower (Ed.), *The psychology of learning and motivation* (Vol. 12, pp. 47–90). New York: Academic Press.

Bannatyne, A. (1976). *Language, reading and learning disabilities: Psychology, neuropsychology, diagnosis and remediation.* Springfield, IL: Thomas.

Bock, J.K. (1982). Toward a cognitive psychology of syntax: Information processing contributions to sentence formulation. *Psychological Review, 89,* 1–47.

Bradley, L., & Bryant, P.E. (1983). Categorizing sounds and learning to read—A causal connection. *Nature, 301,* 419–421.

Bretherton, I., McNew, S., Snyder, L., & Bates, E. (1983). Individual differences at 20 months: Analytic and holistic strategies in language acquisition, *Journal of Child Language, 10,* 293–320.

Brown, R. (1973). *A first language: The early stages.* Cambridge, MA: Harvard University Press.

Brown, R., & Fraser, C. (1963). The acquisition of syntax. In C.N. Cofer & B. Musgrave (Eds.), *Verbal behavior and learning: Problems and processes* (pp. 158–201). New York: McGraw-Hill.

Bryant, P.E. (1986, April). *Phonological awareness, rhyme, and reading.* Symposium presentation at the Annual American Educational Research Association Meeting, Washington, DC.

Byrne, B. (1984). On teaching articulatory phonetics via an orthography. *Memory & Cognition, 12,* 181–189.

Clark, R. (1977). What's the use of imitation? *Journal of Child Language, 4,* 341–358.

Corballis, M. (1983). *Human laterality.* New York: Academic Press.

Corballis, M.C. (1980). Laterality and myth. *American Psychologist, 35,* 284–295.

Critchley, M. (1981). Dyslexia: An overview. In G.Th. Pavlidis & T.R. Miles (Eds.), *Dyslexia research and its applications to education* (pp. 1–34). New York: Wiley.

de Ajuriaguerra, J., Jaeggi, A., Guignard, F., Kocher, F., Macquard, M., Roth, S., & Schmid, E. (1976). The development and prognosis of dysphasia in children. In D.M. Morehead & A.E. Morehead (Eds.), *Normal and deficient child language* (pp. 345–385). Baltimore, MD: University Park Press.

Edwards, M. (1984). *Disorders of articulation.* New York: Springer-Verlag.

Ervin, S.M., & Osgood, S.E. (1954). Second language learning and bilingualism. *Journal of Abnormal and Social Psychology, 49,* 139–146.

Feagans, L. (1986). Otitis media in children: A model of effects and implications for intervention. In J. Kavanaugh (ed.), *Otitis media and child development* (pp. 192–208). Parkton, MD: York Press.

Feagans, L., Blood, I., & Tubman, J.G. (in press). Otitis media: Models of effects and implications for intervention.

Feagans, L., Sanyal, M., Henderson, F., Collier, A., & Appelbaum, M. (in press). Middle ear disease in early childhood and later language skills. *Journal of Pediatric Psychology.*

Finitzo, T., & Friel-Patti, S. (1987, April). *Assessment of hearing in infants and young children: The otitis media quandary.* Symposium presentation at the Biennial Meeting of the Society for Research in Child Development, Baltimore, MD.

Friel-Patti, S., Finitzo-Heber, T., Conti, G., & Brown, C.K. (1982). Language delay in infants associated with middle ear disease and mild, fluctuating hearing impairment. *Pediatric Infectious Disease, 1,* 104–109.

Galaburda, A.M. (1986, December). Keynote Address to the Convention of the Hawaii Dyslexia Association, Honolulu, HI.

Gazzaniga, M. (1987). *Thinking in the two cerebral hemispheres.* Plenary presentation at the Third International Conference on Thinking, Honolulu, HI.

Geschwind, N., & Behan, P. (1984). Laterality, hormones and immunity. In N. Geschwind & A.M. Galaburda (Eds.), *Biological foundations of cerebral dominance* (pp. 211–224). Cambridge, MA: Harvard University Press.

Grimm, H. (1983). *On the interrelation of internal and external factors in the development of language structures in normal and dysphasic preschoolers: A longitudinal study* (Occasional Paper No. 5). Honolulu, HI: The Kamehameha Schools.

Grimm, H. (1984). Zur Frage der spachlichen Wissenskonstruction. Erwerben dysphasische Kinder die Sprache anders? In E. Oskar (ed.), *Spracherwerb-sprachkontakt-Sprachkonflikt* (pp. 30–53). Berlin: de Gruyter.

Grimm, H. (1986). Developmental dysphasia: New theoretical perspectives and empirical results. *The German Journal of Psychology, 11*, 8–22.

Grimm, H., & Weinert, S. (1987, July). *Deviant language processing in dysphasic children*. Paper presented at the Fourth International Congress for the Study of Child Language, Lund, Sweden.

Hardcastle, W.J. (1976). *Physiology of speech*. New York: Academic Press.

Heath, R.W., Plett, J.D., & Tibbetts, K.A. (1987). *Some significant educational, ethnic, and social correlates of mild hearing dysfunction in preschoolers*. Honolulu, HI: Center for Development of Early Education, Kamhehameha Schools.

Kelso, J.A., Tuller, B., & Harris, K.S. (1983). A "dynamic pattern" perspective on the control and coordination of movement. In P.F. MacNeilage (ed.), *The production of speech* (pp. 137–173). New York: Springer-Verlag.

Liberman, A.V. & Mattingly, I.G. (1985). The motor theory of speech perception revised. *Cognition, 21*, 1–36.

Lindamood, P. (1985, December). *Cognitively exploring the speech-spelling-reading link*. Symposium presentation at the 35th Annual National Reading Conference, San Diego, California.

Lundberg, I., Frost, J., & Peterson, O. (1988). Effects of an extensive program for stimulating phonological awareness in preschool children. *Reading Research Quarterly, 23*, 263–284.

MacNeilage, P.F. (1970). Motor control of serial ordering of speech. *Psychological Review, 77*, 182–196.

Mann, V.A. (1984). Reading skill and language skill. *Developmental Review, 4*, 1–15.

Mann, V.A., & Liberman, I.Y. (1984). Phonological awareness and verbal short-term memory. *Journal Learning Disabilities,17*, 592–599.

Marchant, C.D., Shuring, P.A., Turczyk, V.A., Wasikowski, D.E., Tutihasi, M.A., & Kinney, S.E. (1984). Course and outcome of otitis media in early infancy: A prospective study. *The Journal of Pediatrics, 102*, 826–831.

Menyuk, P. (1978). Linguistic problems in children with developmental dysphasia. In M.A. Wyke (Ed.), *Developmental dysphasia*. London: Academic Press.

Menyuk, P. (1986). Predicting speech and language problems with persistent *otitis media*. In J.F. Kavanagh (Ed.), *Otitis media and child development* (pp. 83–96). Parkton: York Press.

Menyuk, P., & Looney, P.L. (1976). A problem of language disorder: Length versus structure. In D.M. Morehead & A.E. Morehead (Eds.), *Normal and deficient child language* (pp. 259–279). Baltimore, MD: University Park Press.

Morehead, D.M., & Ingram, D. (1976). The development of base syntax in normal and linguistically deviant children. In D.M. Morehead & A.E. Morehead (Eds.), *Normal and deficient child language* (pp. 209–238). Baltimore, MD: University Park Press.

Nelson, K. (1973). Structure and strategy in learning to talk. *Monographs of the Society for Research in Child Development, 48*(149).

Nelson, K.E. (1987). Some observations from the perspective of the rare event cognitive comparison theory of language acquisition. In K.E. Nelson & A. van Kleeck (Eds.), *Children's language* (Vol. 6, pp. 289–331). Hillsdale, NJ: Erlbaum.

Nelson, K.E., Baker, N.D., Denninger, M., Bonvillian, J.D., & Kaplan, B.J. (1985). *Cookie* versus *do-it-again*: Imitative-referential and person-social-syntactic-initiating language styles in young children. *Linguistics, 23*, 433–353.

Peters, A. (1977). Language learning strategies: Does the whole equal the sum of the parts? *Language, 53*, 560–573.

Rawson, M.B. (1968). *Developmental language disability: Adult accomplishments of dyslexic boys*. Baltimore, MD: John Hopkins University Press. (Reprinted in paperback, 1978, Cambridge, MA: Educators Publishing Service.)

Rawson, M.B. (1981). A diversity model for dyslexia. In G.T. Pavlidis & T.R. Miles (Eds.), *Dyslexia research and its applications to education* (pp. 13–34). New York: Wiley.

Rosen, G.D., Sherman, G.F., & Galaburda, A.M. (1986). *Biological interactions in dyslexia*. In J.R. Obrzut & G.W. Hynd (Eds.), *Child neurology, Vol. 1, Theory and research* (pp. 155–173). New York: Academic Press.

Rumelhart, D.E., & McClelland, J.L. (1987). Learning the past tenses of English verbs: Implicit rules or parallel distributed processing. In B. MacWhinney (Ed.), *Mechanisms of language acquisition* (pp. 195–248). Hillsdale, NJ: Erlbaum.

Schwartz, R.H., Stool, S.E., Rodriguez, W.J., & Grundfast, K.M. (1981). Acute otitis media: Toward a more precise definition. *Clinical Pediatrics, 20*, 549–554.

Speidel, G.E., & Brandt, B. (1987, April). *Individual differences in learning to speak and to read*. Paper presented at the Biennial Meeting of the Society for Research in Child Development, Baltimore, MD.

Speidel, G.E., & Power, M. (1987, April). *A cornucopia of language skills in learning to read*. Paper presented at the Biennial Meeting of the Society for Research in Child Development, Baltimore, MD.

Stanovich, K., Cunningham, A.E., & Cramer, B.B. (1984). Assessing phonological awareness in kindergarten children: Issues of task comparability. *Journal of Experimental Child Psychology, 38*, 175–190.

Stanovich, K.E. (1986). Matthew effects in reading: Some consequences of individual differences in the acquisition of literacy. *Reading Research Quarterly, 21*, 361–406.

Vellutino, F. (1977). Alternative conceptualizations of dyslexia: Evidence in support of a verbal-deficit hypothesis. *Harvard Educational Review, 47*, 334–354.

Weinreich, W. (1953). *Language in contact*. The Hague: Mouton.

Appendix

Conversation between Sally (approximate age: 4 years and 3 months) and her father about God, death, and paradise.

FATHER.   Und wo ist die Seele? (*And where is the soul?*)

SALLY.   Beim lieben Gott. (*With the dear God.*)

FATHER.   Ja, die ist beim lieben Gott, im Paradies. (*Yes, it is with the dear God in paradise.*)

SALLY.   Aber wo können sie schlafen, Pappa. (*But where can they sleep, Pappa?*)

FATHER.   Im Paradies kann man schlafen, wann man will. (*In paradise you can sleep whenever you want.*)

SALLY.   Wenn man tot ist, gel? (*When one is dead, yes?*)

SALLY.   Aber, als ich Paradies (*unclear target*)—und dann weg geht, dann brauchen die Leute schlafen und der liebe Gott auch, der muss auch schlafen, wenn es Schlafenzeit ist. (*But, when I paradise—and then go away, then the* people need to sleep and the dear God too, he too must sleep, if it is time for sleeping.)

FATHER. Der liebe Gott braucht nie zu schlafen. (*The dear God never has to sleep.*)

SALLY. Aber, der, der hat ein Bett. (*But he, he has a bed.*)

FATHER. Der schläft auf einer Wolke. Vielleicht hat er gar kein Bett sondern nur eine Wolke. Da ist es schön weich, da kann er auf 'ner Wolke schlafen. (*He sleeps on a cloud. Maybe he doesn't have a bed, but just a cloud. There it is nice and soft, and he can sleep on a cloud.*)

SALLY. Ich glaub der hat ein Wolkenkissen. (*I believe he has a cloud pillow.*)

FATHER. Ein Wolkenkissen, eine Wolkendecke, und ein Wolkenbett. (*A cloud pillow, a cloud cover, and a cloud bed.*)

SALLY. Sein Vater ist schon tot und seine Mama lebt noch ganz lange. (*His father is already dead, and his mother is still going to live for a long time.*)

FATHER. Der liebe Gott hat keinen Vater und keine Mutter. Der war schon immer da. (*The dear God doesn't have a father and a mother. He has always been there.*)

SALLY. Ich glaub, die Maria lebt im Paradies und sie hat ein Bett für ihn gekauft, im Paradies. (*I believe Mary lives in paradise and she has bought a bed for him, in paradise.*)

Conversation at breakfast between Mark (approximate age: 4 years and 3 months) and his mother. Incorrect features are underlined and, where necessary, described in brackets.

MARK Ich mag bei Onkel Eddie wohnen so he [English] kann Eis [Schnee] ma —haben [incorrect word order]. (*I want to live at Uncle Eddie's so he can ma-have Eis [meaning snow].*)

MOTHER. Im Winter wird's da auch kalt. (*In winter it gets cold there too.*)

MARK. Für mei' Schneehut [word creation]. (*For my snow hat.*)

MOTHER. Für Deinen Schneehut? Ach für Deine Mütze, die blaue. (*For your snow hat? Oh, for your cap, the blue one.*)

MARK. Ja . . . (*Yes . . .*)

MARK. Da gibt's Eis . . . im Winter . . . so, so ich kann mich hinaus gehen [inappropriate reflexive pronoun, incorrect pronoun] und, um, . . . und Mama soll mich [incorrect pronoun] ein [dropped inflection] Schlitten kaufen . . . und mei . . . und dann zieh ich mein Schneehut an, an, und dann geh ich Schli— und dann ma—wo ich kann drauf sitzen [incorrect word order] und dann fahren mit des [unclear target word] hinunter und—(*There is Eis . . . in winter . . . so, so I kann go me outside and, um, . . . and Mom should buy to me a sled . . . and my . . . and then I put on, on, my snow hat, and then I go sle—and then—where I can sit on and then ride down with the [unclear] and—*)

MOTHER. Hast Du denn das schon je gesehen? Warum kannst Du es so schön beschreiben? Hast Du es am Fernseh gesehen? (*Did you ever see that? Why can you describe it so well? Did you see it on TV?*)

MARK. Electric Company.

MOTHER. Und das hat Dir gefallen? (*And you liked that?*)

MARK. Und <u>das</u> [wrong article] <u>Mittmann</u> [word creation] <u>who</u> [English] is
... <u>hat de Schneehut</u> is in de Baum gefallen. Dann haben se de Baum [unclear target word]. (*And the middle man who is ... has the snow hat fell into the tree. Then they [unclear] the tree.*)

MOTHER. Der Baum is mit runtergerutscht? (*The tree slipped down with them?*)

MARK. 'Cause [English] ein Mittelmann ist ... in ... de Baum [unclear target]. (*'Cause the middle man is [unclear] the tree.*)

MOTHER. Ich versteh das nicht. (*I don't understand that.*)

MARK. Der ... der ... (*The one ... the one ...*)

MOTHER. Der Letterman oder wer? (*The Letterman or who?*)

MARK. Ein Mann. Der kleine Mann, der kleine ... der grosse is ... net der Lettermann, Mama! Mama ... der kleine Man ist der Lettermann, der kleine Mann ist der Lettermann ... und da war ein grosser Mann. (*A man. The little man, the little ... the big man is not Letterman, Mama! Mama --- the little man is Letterman, the little man is Letterman ... and there was a big man.*)

MARK. Und ich hab auch so ein Schli-Schlitten.

MARK. Mama ... ich mag, mag, mag ... wann ich ma-mal, ich mag mal wieder zu Onkel Eddie und da mal [unclear target word] runterkommen und da sollst Du mir so was kaufen, und, und, und ... (*Mama ... I want—want— want—when I a-again, I want to go to Uncle Eddie again and then once [unclear] come down and then you should buy me something like that, and, and ...*)

MOTHER. Aber zu Onkel Eddie gehen wir im Sommer.... Vielleicht können wir mal im Winter gehen. (*But we only go to Uncle Eddie in summer.... Maybe we can go once in winter.*)

MARK. Ja, dann sollst Du <u>mich</u> [incorrect pronoun] <u>vor</u> [incorrect preposition] de Wintertag so was kau—so ein, so ein, Schlitten und dann, und dann, und dann, und dann und da bleiben bis ... und Winter kommt ... und wenn Winter kommt da, da, da [target phrase unclear] Schneehut und de Schlitten. (*Yes, then you should before the winter day b—to me something like, like a sled, and then, and then, and then, and then stay there until ... and winter comes ... and when winter comes, then, then [unclear phrase] snow hat and the sled ...*)

CHAPTER 10

Phylogenetic Processes in Verbal Language Imitation

Roland G. Tharp and Caleb E.S. Burns

10.1 Introduction

Phylogenesis, culturogenesis, ontogenesis, and microgenesis all contribute to human phenomena. A complete account of the smallest grain of language behavior would require consideration of the social and historical forces affecting language and imitation, the individual ontogenetic variables in language development as they are expressed in imitation, and the microgenetic processes of rapid, small-unit acquisition of language as it is mediated by modeling and imitating.

It is appropriate to treat phylogenetic issues first, if only to honor this level by the order of its appearance. However, this chapter can have only the most modest goals, because it must be more speculative than demonstrative. Little work has directly addressed phylogenesis and language imitation, although there are hints of determinants and teasing possibilities for explanation. Such a discussion requires its authors to be intrepid more than prudent and wants readers willing to explore.

In that spirit, we will suggest certain phylogenetically determined processes, which, though they have been discovered and studied in other domains of behavior, may have some value in considering the roots and processes of language imitation. Evidence bearing directly on whether these processes operate in human language imitation is limited, and frequently circumstantial; there is at present no field of phylogenesis and language imitation to review. However, if scientists persevere, they will eventually discover phylogenetic preparations, processes, and mechanisms through which imitative language is expressed. Were it not so, imitative language behavior would be unique among human repertoires.

10.2 Levels of Genetic Analysis

Figure 10-1 displays the four levels of genetic analysis, distinguishing them by the nature of their characteristic processes and by the time spans ordinary for

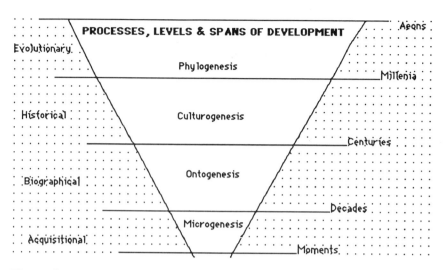

Figure 10-1. Levels of genetic explanation for human events. (Adapted from Tharp, 1987.)

their effects. The figure points to the interrelationships of the four levels, which are layered, simultaneous, and nonexclusive, but are open to separate discussion.

Phylogenesis, as a level of explanation, refers to processes that we call *evolutionary* and that ordinarily have their effects over periods of time *from aeons to millennia*. Figure 10-1 is introduced here to emphasize that the effects of phylogenetic processes may be altered, disguised, or emphasized by historical or biographical or acquisitional events; the obverse is that all other levels of genetic process are conditioned by phylogenetic events.

For example, cultural differences in patterns of language imitation can be easily noted when North American Indian speakers are compared with most nonnative speakers of the same area. These native Americans are accustomed to longer periods of turn taking in both formal and informal speech routines, leading to longer periods of delayed imitation. This is evident in classroom speech turns of early elementary Navajo children, who consequently imitate less often, and after longer delays, than do Hawaiian children of the same age (White, Tharp, Jordan, & Vogt, in press). These differences are attributable to historical processes and are accountable culturogenetically. However, these cultural expressions are laid down on common morphological and functional systems that are phylogenetically determined. Ontogenetically determined conditions are always conditioned by phylogenetic processes, which are inescapable in the human condition.

This is a more complex system of understanding than merely to contrast "innate" with "learned" behavior. Our understanding is not well served by continuing the argument of past decades as to whether language performance and language structures are "innate" or "learned," as has been characteristic of both the "nativist" and "behaviorist" camps. Indeed, we ill-treat ourselves by arguing whether imitation itself is innate or learned, as all human phenomena have their genesis in processes that operate interactively and simultaneously, processes that are phylo-, culturo-, onto-, and microgenetic.

10.3 Overview

The purpose of this chapter is only to discuss some phylogenetic processes in language acquisition. The domain for this demonstration is strictly verbal language and vocal imitation. Gestural or other symbolic languages in humans and primates are not treated here. There are books to be written on the phylogenesis of imitation and its relationship to the development of sign languages. That voluminous literature has not yet been arrayed, and the space available here would not allow it. We have chosen instead to illustrate the construction of phylogenetic arguments by concentrating on the limited domain of *verbal* language. This chapter will examine first some evidence for vocal imitation in subhuman species, evidence that suggests that both nativist and behaviorist views of language acquisition can profit from an incorporation of phylogenetic processes in their explanations. Then we will introduce the concept of neoteny, our candidate for the major phylogenic process most notable in early language acquisition. A brief survey of evidence concerning imitation and language in early infancy will be examined for consistencies with the neoteny hypothesis. Some arguments from collateral evidence will be adduced, principally from early imitation of facial gestures. The issue of critical or sensitive periods for language learning and for imitation will be discussed briefly. Some interesting possibilities for the implications of critical periods for developmental processes in (biological) morphology and these possibilities (principally arguments by analogy from visual-cortical systems) will be explored for the acquisition of verbal language.

10.4 Vocal Mimicry in Subhuman Species

The evolutionary presumptions of phylogenetic analyses lead us to search for precursors of human phenomena in subhuman species. Their presence or absence in birds or beasts is not the litmus test for phylogenesis, because behaviors that appears to be similar can arise from quite different historical sources. Nevertheless, the appearance of behaviors in the trunks and branches of the evolutionary line can illuminate both the history and current functions of human processes, and form part of our mosaic of understanding. As we will see, vocal imitation appeared early and has lasted long in the evolutionary line.

The capacity for "vocal mimicry" — as it is called in comparative psychology — has been often demonstrated in certain species of birds. Several adaptive functions of birds' vocal mimicry have been proposed: for example, pair bonding, "passwording" for territorial defense, and limiting outbreeding in populations (Kroodsma & Miller, 1982; Nottebohm, 1972; Richards, Wolz, & Herman, 1984). The range of mimicry is large, from the white-crowned sparrow, which generally learns only species-specific songs, to the gray parrot, which can imitate human speech.

Deferred imitation is also present in many birds and apparently plays as important a role for them as it does in human vocal development. Snow (1983) has presented an excellent discussion of deferred imitation's role in the acquisition of language by young children, and has amassed considerable evidence demonstrating that human young imitate complex speech, over considerable time delay and interpolated events, even prior to their ability to understand the utterances.

This complex and impressive repertoire is also present well below the human in the evolutionary ladder. Among many birds, complex deferred vocal imitation has been noted. Many sing duets with their mates in their habitats, male and female each producing its own separate notes with split-second timing. These duets are learned through practice and imitation. In one partner's absence, the other partner fills in sounds normally reserved for the first, resulting in the absent partner's instant return to the territory. Particularly for the male, hearing his own song coming from his territory is an imperious summons. Thorpe and North (1965) have reviewed this evidence (and produced much of it), concluding that vocal imitation is the basis for pair bonding. They suggest that evolutionary capacities in parrots and mynahs for complex imitation is not such an oddity as it seems: These, and many other species of birds, do use their complex vocal imitative abilities in the wild to acquire signature songs, to bond with a mate through duets, and to imitate the mate's songs to signal and call. Writing 25 years ago, Thorpe and North observed that this capacity seems to have appeared in birds, and not again in evolutionary time until humans.

More recent evidence demonstrates that far from an evolutionary oddity, vocal imitation has been found in several intermediate species. Members of the cetacean order have been extensively studied in this respect, perhaps because they are notably vocal. Among cetaceans, the vocal mimicry of the bottlenosed dolphin has been most studied. Little is known about the social use of dolphin vocalizations in the wild (Herman & Tavolga, 1980), but captive dolphins appear to mimic vocalizations spontaneously in about 1% of their responses (Gish, 1979; Herman, 1980). Richards, Wolz, and Herman (1984) suggest that the tendency to follow a model sound immediately with an imitation is to some degree an unconditioned response of dolphins. (This is in contrast to many birds, for whom teaching of vocal mimicry is more successful by manipulating eliciting social stimuli than by operant conditions. Parrots and mynahs, for example, can more often be induced to imitate by manipulating the people and conditions present during the presentation of the stimuli, than by manipulating the consequences of the imitation; see, e.g., Andrew, 1962.)

The plasticity of vocal responses into adulthood is of interest in mammalian species that exhibit vocal mimicry. Caldwell and Caldwell (1972) studied the ontogeny of the stereotyped signature whistle in young captive dolphins, along with observations of adult captives. They conclude that there is virtually no change in the vocal repertoire past infancy. However, this does not say that specific reinforcement programs cannot shape dolphin vocalizations. Using operant conditions, Richards et al. (1984) trained a bottlenosed dolphin to use the whistle mode of vocalization to mimic computer-generated sounds. They made no effort to duplicate natural social conditions, but rather mounted a sophisticated program of operant conditioning using food and social reinforcement to train a vocal repertoire in their dolphin, Akeakamai. This repertoire included the labeling of specific objects with specific vocalizations. Two years after the beginning of mimicry training, it was still possible to present new sounds to Akeakamai, and shape recognizable approximations in her vocalizations.

In dolphins, mimicry in the earliest years appears to establish a minimum vocal repertoire, including idiosyncratic "signature" whistles. While this level of verbal acquisition can be assured by phylogenetically established "infant" mimicry, more complex vocal behavior can be brought under reinforcement control. We do not know the degree to which mimicry continues to elaborate vocal repertories for dolphins in their own complex natural ecological niche. At the present time, there are available only suggestive data: For example, wild populations of various cetacean species appear to exhibit vocal dialects, indicating a flexibility of learning (see, e.g., Ford & Fisher, 1982, on killer whales).

The vocal mimicry of terrestrial mammals and in particular of the great apes is of interest for understanding the comparative phylogenesis of verbal behavior in humans. Vocal mimicry of human speech has proven virtually untrainable in the chimpanzee; it now seems obvious that this is attributable to vocal-tract limitations in the great apes (see Lieberman, 1968). However, evidence for vocal mimicry is not absent, and indeed is growing. For example, Haimoff (1981) has studied the "Great Songs" of the Siamang apes. These songs, often duetted, are appropriate for the study of imitation because they are flexible and nonstereotyped. Videotapes of these duets reveal clear imitation: Only short latencies (fractions of a second) for similar vocal behaviors intervened before they were echoed overtly by the listener apes.

The limited information available on vocal mimicry in nonhuman primates suggests that, in most species, vocalizations are highly patterned and little affected by ontogenetic or microgenetic processes. In the last decade, evidence for specific vocabularies (and for specific syntax) in several species has emerged; Snowden (1983) has presented an excellent short review. For Japanese macaques (Green, 1975) and for saddle-back tamarins (Hoden, Snowden, & Soini, 1981), locale-specific dialects have been noted. These dialects are comparable to those for cetacean populations discussed above, in that they provide suggestive evidence of a capability for vocal learning. This points to the possibility of historicogenetic processes in the vocal behavior of these species—adaptations that have operated across many generations.

Presumably the capacity to learn vocalizations could have survival value, on both an individual and a species level. This is well demonstrated in vervet monkeys, who label their common predators with a specific vocabulary of cries. That is, vervets issue one cry to one species of snake, and that is the python, the snake that regularly preys on them. Similarly they give the eagle cry only to the martial eagle, and the leopard cry only to the leopard.

Seyfarth and Cheney (1982) have discussed the ontogeny of this alarm calling in vervets. Young vervet monkeys give cries to categories of stimuli that are only generally correct. For example, a young monkey might give the eagle cry to some other bird, or even a falling leaf, and the snake cry to some sinuous-appearing object on the ground. Only gradually do the vervets come to the adult level of precision. Seyfarth and Cheney attribute this acquisition to imitation plus selective reinforcement by the adult monkeys. The status of this explanation is more hypothetical than evidential, but it is consistent with our suggestions throughout this chapter: Species with the capacity for vocal mimicry will acquire the "linguist" patterns of their community of speakers by that mechanism, and further ontogenetic modification of vocal behavior will occur through continued imitation plus selective reinforcement.

Research on subhuman species may further enlighten us as to the evolutionary relationships between mimicry and the gaining of full functional control of vocalizations. The appropriate methods for such research are under debate, and the issues are complex. Hill (1974) and Snowden (1983) are surely wise: Theories of the continuities of language evolution will be studied best in the natural ecological context of communication. For example, we may have been deceived for some years by the relative failure to establish vocal language in laboratory animals (Michael, 1984). This may well have been due to the lack of a vocal mimicking repertoire in the particular species examined, and to an insistence on training vocalizations inappropriate to the species' vocal tracts.

But experiments, too, have the potential for being informative. For example, there is evidence that early experience with vocal interaction is necessary for the normal development of vocalization in various primates (Newman & Symmes, 1982), including humans (Lieberman, 1984). This suggests a specific experiment: Would early deprivation of interaction in siamangs, who echo so elaborately, lead to impaired development of their later ability to sing?

Evidence continues to mount that the capacity for vocal imitation is widespread across species. We may suggest as an hypothesis that vocal imitation developed early in phylogenesis and has continued to be an operative process in further development, being functional in species that have the capacity for complex vocal articulation. That is, the capacity for vocalization is the limiting factor, not the phylogenetic process of imitation: Whatever can sing can imitate song.

10.5 Phylogenesis, Language, and Behaviorism

Behaviorist writers have set a trap for themselves by a relentless insistence on an exclusively ontogenetic interpretation of language behavior. For example, Vaughan and Michael (1982) noted a problem in their own explanations: Certain developments in language occur in the apparent absence of "obvious external reinforcement." In need of an additional explanatory concept, they propose "automatic reinforcement." Some behaviors are automatic in the sense that they do not involve the actions of another person, but nevertheless produce consequences that reinforce that behavior. In this explanation, complex verbal behavior is initially a function of contrived reinforcement and only through a rich conditioning history comes under the control of automatic reinforcement.

Skinner himself proposed an additional concept to account for the development of speech: the "echoic[1] repertoire":

> An echoic repertoire is established in the child through "educational" reinforcement because it is useful to parents, teachers, and others. . . . The educational reinforcement is usually supplied with the aid of mands of the type SAY "X" where the listener, becoming a speaker, is reinforced if his response yields the sound pattern "X". . . . It is essential, however, that specific reinforcements be entered in the paradigm. (1957, p. 56)

In the behaviorist account, the echoic, imitative response is founded on specific reinforcements just as is automatic reinforcement. In both instances, although immediate, specific reinforcement may be obscured, it is held to be present—either in automatic, unobservable processes and/or in relationship to imitation as a general repertoire.

However, it is important to recognize the many behaviors that are assumed even by behaviorists not to be acquired by ontogenetic learning processes. The congruence between behavioral functionalism and evolution-theory functionalism has been an enormous intellectual strength of behavior theory. The crucial problem for behaviorism has been to determine the differential contributions of phylogenic versus ontogenic functionalism.

Vaughan and Michael (1982) assembled a series of quotations that illuminate this issue.

> When a predator stalks its prey, the reinforcer seems to involve stalking and capturing. The mouse as food reinforcer precipitates out at some later point in its encounter with a cat. Prior to that, the mouse probably provides the occasion for reinforcers embodied in the cat's own behavior. (Herrnstein, 1977, p. 600)

In reply, Skinner (1977) argued that one need not explain behavior in terms of self-reinforcement when it is

> clearly traceable to natural selection. . . . The stalking behavior of a cat appears to be largely inherited, though the topography no doubt changes under reinforcement as a mouse is stalked. . . . Herrnstein wants to explain all the

---

[1]The term *echoic* will be restricted in this chapter to its Skinnerian meaning. We will sometimes later use *echoing* in its natural language sense, and indeed will later argue that echoing—in humans as well as some lower species—is a phylogenically determined emergent repertoire that is routinely observable from about 9 months to about 3 years.

> behavior as due to self-reinforcement – reinforcement not by the reactions of the
> mouse but by the very behavior itself. (p. 1011)

In 1966 Skinner contended that

> parts of the behavior of an organism concerned with the internal economy, as in
> respiration or digestion, have always been accepted as "inherited", and there is
> no reason why some responses to the external environment should not also
> come ready-made in the same sense. (p. 1205)

Skinner adds that behavior traceable to phylogenic contingencies may be recognized because it is too complex and occurs too rapidly to be generated by reinforcement contingencies.

Is language such a behavior? It is of interest that Skinner (1983) has recently modified his earlier position opposing the existence of innate imitation:

> In *Science and Human Behavior* I had said that an inherent reflex mechanism by
> which "a pattern of behavior in another organism elicits a series of responses
> having the same pattern . . . does not seem to exist." I had been misled by an
> early experiment at Indiana University. . . . An innate imitative repertoire was
> [now] obvious. (Skinner, 1983, p. 383, note 4)

Skinner referred here to his and Epstein's identification of "an innate imitative repertoire" in pigeons (Skinner, 1983, p. 383). Epstein (1984) has published the results of his study of imitative responses in pigeons and reported that the effect is a reliable one.

Specific, immediate, contingent ontogenic reinforcement is not and has never been convincing as the central mechanism for the development of verbal behavior – even to behaviorists, who have strained to retain that concept by introducing automatic reinforcement and the reinforced general repertoire of echoics. We suggest that the ultimate complete description of the evolution of humans into the culture-bearing, definitively verbal creatures that we have become will include phylogenetic processes operating on language acquisition. Both survival and differential reproducibility are mediated by the selection of adequate verbal behavior in humans, to a degree equal to that of stalking behavior in the cat.

10.6 Neoteny

In this section we consider one particular concept that offers some promise for bundling together a variety of hitherto unrelated observations about language development, particularly as it interacts with imitation. This concept allows us to see these phenomena as parts of a deep and powerful phylogenetic human process.

Homo sapiens has evolved from other primates in part due to a process known technically as *neoteny* ("holding youth"). As compared morphologically to other primates, Homo sapiens retains many juvenile features, including those below, originally listed by Bolk (1926), and then quoted and discussed by Gould (1977a):

> "1. Our rounded, bulbous cranium – house of our larger brain. Embryonic apes and monkeys have a similar cranium, but the brain grows so much more slowly than the rest of the body that the cranial vault becomes lower and relatively smaller in adults. . . .
> "3. Position of the foramen magnum – the hole in our skull base from which the spinal cord emerges. As in the embryos of most mammals, our foramen magnum lies underneath our skull, pointing downward. . . .
> "4. Late closure of the skull sutures and other marks of delayed calcification of the skeleton. Babies have a large 'soft spot', and the sutures do not fully close until well after adulthood. Thus, our brain can continue its pronounced postnatal expansion." (In most other mammals, the brain is nearly complete at birth and the skull is fully ossified). (pp. 64–65)

See DeBeer (1958) for a more extensive description of the role of neoteny in the evolution of various species. Also, see Gould (1977b) for an extended discussion of the role of neoteny in the development of Homo sapiens.

Harrison and Weiner (1964) also characterize the neoteny of Homo sapiens and add the following morphological characteristics: flatness of the face, the smallness of the face as compared with the braincase, and the hairlessness of the body. They also discuss the profound evolutionary consequences of neoteny:

> The evolutionary modification of ontogeny can . . . be effected by the abbreviation of development. All that is necessary before such abbreviation can happen is for sexual maturity to occur at progressively younger morphological stages; (neoteny) meant that an organism could escape adult specializations which, as a result of environmental change, had begun to limit its chances of survival. (p. 8)

From the point of view of evolution theory, the planetary consequences of neoteny cannot be exaggerated:

> Neoteny slows down the rate of bodily development in humans, giving them a longer childhood than their primate ancestors and a brain which grows in early life as fast as it grew in the womb. . . . The plasticity of the child's brain, its flexibility and redundancy, enabling it to shift and reorganize its resources to meet the needs of various modes of life, make the human species the least narrowly specialized of all animals. . . . No single evolutionary event has had such a transforming effect on the life of the planet; neoteny is the biological principle which made civilization possible. (Campbell, 1982, p. 143)

The processes of neoteny are observable in the course of ontogenetic development. For example, human neonates are not developmentally comparable to the newborn of other primates until some time has passed. Gould (1977a) writes,

> I will propose an answer to this question [of the helplessness of babies] that is bound to strike most readers as patently absurd: Human babies are born as embryos, and embryos they remain for about the first nine months of life. If women gave birth when they "should"—after gestation of about a year and a half—our babies would share the precocial features of other primates. (p. 72)

Gould based his estimate of the nine-month-old as equivalent to just-born primates on the basis of certain characteristics of growth, including bone development. Montagu (1961) cited quadruped locomotion as the marker of this equivalent development. Montagu noted that it takes about 9 months for quadruped locomotion to develop, and therefore,

> gestation, then, is not completed by the act of birth, but is only translated from gestation within the womb to gestation outside the womb [exteroception]. . . . According to this hypothesis, man spends the first half of his gestation period within the womb [uterogestation], and the second half of it outside the womb [exteroception]. (p. 156)

The processes of neoteny are manifested not only morphologically and biologically, but their inevitable behavioral consequences can also be observed, once the concept is grasped. Where would we expect to find behavioral manifestations of this phylogenic process? In those behaviors that are most complex; those most involved with central, brain mediation; those requiring the phylogenetically highest evolutionary apparatus; or those most definitive of Homo sapiens: Language. And indeed there is evidence for the nine-months-to-readiness pattern established morphologically by Montagu and Gould. That language is implicated deeply in neoteny is to be expected, if indeed neoteny is the evolutionary process "which has made civilization possible."

10.7 Relevant Data From the Study of Early Language Development

Most chapters in this book contain discussions of early language development. Here, we propose only the briefest recitation of data that bear on the neoteny/language-development/imitation complex.

At about 3 months, babbling begins. The absence of noncontingent controls in most infant "conditioning" studies has led to the general conclusion that increases in infant vocal responses cannot be attributed to conditioning processes. Wahler (1969) studied the vocalizations of an infant through the 1st year of life. Contingent reinforcement was able to increase and decrease targeted vocal behaviors. But new vocal behaviors were not under reinforcement control and not predictable by the experimenters. Wahler concluded that a reinforcement/shaping process was not responsible for the major vocal changes. Instrumental conditioning, it seems, does not appear to be the primary route for normal language acquisition.

This is not to say that infant vocalizations are not vulnerable to social influence and operant conditioning. During the babbling stage, social interaction has been shown to affect several aspects of infant vocalizations — rate, pause, patterns, and so forth. Operant conditionability of infant vocalizations has been demonstrated; for example, Routh (1969) produced a differential increase of vowellike sounds by 2- to 7-month-old babies. Bloom (e.g., 1977a, 1977b, 1979) has convincingly argued that failure to attend to adequate control procedures has led to spurious conclusions about infant capacities (Olson & Sherman, 1983).

> It must be emphasized that the present failure of the operant model in providing a convincing explanation in infant vocal behavior results from the unique elicitive tie between infant vocalization and adult social responsiveness and in no way refutes our knowledge of the infant's ability to learn contingent relationships. (Bloom, 1979, p. 68)

We may conclude that both processes — ontogenic adaptation and phylogenic adaptation — are present and interactive in infant language acquisition. No experimental evidence known to us even purports to implicate specific, contingent reinforcement in the emergence of linguistic-pattern repertoire, nor do we know of data that suggest the emergence of linguistic pattern behavior prior to about 9 months. It may be suggested that the neoteny process, at the 9-month point, produces the delayed maturation that allows the vocal imitative response through which linguistic patterns are acquired.

This pattern acquisition begins around 9 to 12 months of age, when babies' babbles come to resemble the intonational patterns of adult sentences (deVilliers & deVilliers, 1978). Nakazima (1962) has reported evidence that this is produced by imitation. During this period, children produce strings of utterances marked by intonation and stress, although they produce no clearly identifiable morphemes (Menyuk, 1971). During this same period — at about 9 months — the babblings of babies of English-speaking caretakers begin to lose their "German" gutturals and their "French" nasals. Some utterances are shortened to single syllables. The overall effect is that these utterances sound as if they are to be understood (Clark-Stewart, Friedman, & Koch, 1985).[2]

There does appear to be a tendency in humans, after an age of about 9 months, to echo the speech of others. This general response class of imitation does not require its own specific reinforcement, which is some evidence that the tendency is biologically emergent. In general, the general imitative response emerges prior to the capacity to control the production of more differentiated speech. This

---

[2]It is rather like learning to hum before learning to sing. Interesting parallels exist with the developmental course of written language. First productions of written text by young children clearly resemble the style of writing characteristic of that culture. Harste, Woodward, and Burke (1984, p. 82) have printed examples of the "writing" of 4-year-olds from the United States, Saudi Arabia, and Israel. Although no real letters appear in any of them, no one could fail to detect which was written by which.

seems to allow children "to learn the tune before the words," that is, to learn the sound patterns of language before understanding its meaning.

At about the age of 9 months, another significant language development stage can be observed to emerge: Children begin to name objects (e.g., Bates, Shore, Bretherton, & McNew (1983). There are very wide individual differences, but the most general statement is that the "holophrastic" phase, when production is most often of the one-word order, spans somewhere between 9 and 24 months.

Pertinent to our concerns here is that children, at about the age of 12 to 30 months, tend to immediately imitate items that appear at the end of the utterance addressed to them, or items that receive stress. It appears that the emergent repertoire of echoing must be coupled with emerging capacities of memory and attention; the "strategy" of imitating later or stressed items reduces the memory load (Reger, 1986; Rondal, 1985).

And so specific language imitation begins. Each chapter in this volume contains evidence and discussions for the role of imitation in language. This wealth of knowledge cannot be summarized in a few sentences, except for the most general observations. Certainly, the amount of spontaneous imitation of language varies from child to child. Imitation has been shown to be the source of both new vocabulary and new grammatical forms. At some point, for most children around the age of 3, spontaneous and immediate vocal "echoing" diminishes, and indeed becomes a rare event in mature speech. Other forms of imitation, expanded or partial, begin to function for a wide variety of communicative purposes – queries, comments, confirmations, matching claims and counterclaims, answers, and acquiescences. Echoing and mimicry are largely replaced by more flexible forms of imitation, which flow into the main stream of communicative competence.

10.8 Arguments by Analogy: Imitation of Facial Expressions and Gestures

It is of some interest to examine the development of other modalities of imitation in infants. We must not accept uncritically any arguments developed from data across modalities; there are undoubtedly differences in developmental histories and developmental processes in different performance systems. Nevertheless, in this effort to triangulate an unploughed field, we do well to note all observations.

For example, we have argued that the neoteny process provides for an emergence of a new form of imitative behavior at about the 9-month point. Might that apply to all imitative repertoires, or is it restricted to vocal imitation? Piaget's (1962) classic treatment distinguishes true imitation from various forms of pseudoimitation, which are attributable to other social learning processes. He asserts that a number of substantial skills are necessary to achieve true imitation of facial gestures, because the imitator cannot see the results of the imitative efforts, and thus corrective feedback is not produced. Piaget observed that true imitation, an important landmark of infant development, occurred late in the first year of life.

During the last decade a lively controversy about infant imitation has arisen. Meltzoff and Moore (1977) claimed to demonstrate that infants less than a week old can imitate the facial expressions of an adult. However, the phenomenon is somewhat fugitive; Hamm, Russell, and Koepke (1979), Hayes and Watson (1981), McKenzie and Over (1983), and Waite (1979), failed to replicate it. The evidential status of the Meltzoff and Moore data continues to be debated; for example, two chapters in the recent fourth edition of the *Handbook of Child Psychology* (Mussen, 1983) take views that are pro (Harris, 1983) and con (Olson & Sherman, 1983). Critics have argued that, whatever the infants are doing, it does not involve any cognitive matching of the features of the model (e.g., Kaye, 1982); infants are as likely to stick out their tongues to a protruding stick as to the stuck-out tongues of their mothers.

Bjorklund (1987), like the present authors, attempts a link to the phylogenetic explanatory level. He suggests that neonatal "imitation" is an altogether different process than later (post-9-month?) imitation; indeed neonatal "imitation" should be seen as a *transient ontogenetic adaptation* (Oppenheim, 1981), a process that has adaptation value in that it helps to maintain social interaction between mother and neonate. But, when infants are able to control their own mouth and head movements, and thus maintain social interaction, the reflexive "imitations" are no longer adaptive, and the process drops out.

However Meltzoff might respond to this interpretation, it is not inconsistent with recent data coming from his own laboratories. Meltzoff and Gopnik (Chapter 2, this volume) have pursued infant imitation along a new line—the differentiation of deferred imitation from immediate imitation. Facial gesture imitation deferred by 24 hours has been demonstrated by Meltzoff to occur in infants of 9 months. Meltzoff and Gopnik argue that language depends on deferred imitation in a fundamental way: There is no way a child can spontaneously generate the word *cat* in the presence of cats. Rather, having heard the word *cat* in the presence of cats, subsequent naming requires complex cognitive operations requiring that imitation be deferred until a cat appears again.

This new line of investigation is consistent with the hypothesis suggested in this chapter: that deferred imitation of facial gestures, like true imitation of language patterns, occurs only with the biological readiness that is delayed by neoteny until about 9 months.

10.9 Critical Period, Imitation, and Language Learning

For 2 decades the issue of "critical period" (Lenneberg, 1967) has been the primary phylogenetic concept used in discussions of language acquisition. More recently, the somewhat weaker hypothesis of "sensitive" period has replaced it.

The plasticity of spoken language development is clearly greater in childhood than in adulthood (Genesee, 1981; Patkowski, 1980). Although the response cost is greater than for children, adults do learn languages. Even adult developmentally delayed subjects can acquire language features (Rondal, 1985). Indeed, adults can learn new languages to a degree of proficiency virtually equal to that of childhood learners; the only aspect of verbal behavior that may be limited to a "sensitive period" is phonology (Oyama, 1976; Seliger, Krashen, & Ladefoged, 1975). It is generally accepted by psycholinguists that language acquired after "puberty" (about 14 years of age) will not be phonologically equivalent to native speech (e.g., Tahat, Wood, & Lowenthal, 1981).[3]

This appears to suggest a period of echoing competence that beings at 9 months, with a decline clearly evident by adolescence. But there is some evidence that the optimal period for acquiring phonological competence in a second language may end before 4 years of age; already by then there may be a loss in the ability to discriminate among nonnative speech sounds (Werker & Tees, 1983).

We may suggest that the critical period hypothesis should be rewritten to state that, in order for language to be acquired, the child must be exposed to *some* language during the critical period of (about) 9 months to (about) 3 years—a time span bounded at its beginning by the minimum neurological and anatomical maturation of the anatomical substrate required for deferred vocal mimicry, and bounded at its finish by the end of the period of biological plasticity of that substrate. This position may not be unacceptable to "critical period" theorists; Lenneberg (1967) has stated that the hypothesis is not troubled by second-language acquisition, so long as "the cerebral organization for language learning as such has taken place during childhood" (p. 176).

The principal appeal of such an hypothesis is its consistency with what is known about the contributions of use to morphology in other biological systems. The infant who hears no language and echoes no language may not form the functional "tracks" that lead to structural growth, in the way that the unused muscle atrophies and fails to develop. A nearer analogy is to that of the visual-cortical system. Experiments with kittens have shown that neonatal visual experience can lead to stabilization of corpus callosum neurons, which without stimulation do not survive; this produces a selective retention of connections that integrate the cortical fields in a particular way. Thus, the pattern of cortical tissue is affected by environmental interaction (Trevarthen, 1983). Lack of binocular vision during kittens' critical period results in a visual cortex that fails to develop normally.

The experimental literature for humans suggests that the critical period for binocular vision begins "several months" after birth and ends at about 3 years (Banks, Aslin, & Letson, 1975; Lieberman, 1984); that is, there must be exposure to normal, appropriate visual stimuli during that period or there will be behavioral deficits similar to those of the deprived cats. The apparent critical period for the visual-cortical system corresponds quite closely to the 9-months-to-3-years period suggested by the behavioral data for vocal imitation.

---

[3]A collateral line of evidence is of interest here. There are data (e.g., Crozier, Robinson, & Ewing, 1976/1977; and Ward, 1963) suggesting that a developed competence for Absolute Pitch is associated with early musical experience.

The various cortical systems may not develop simultaneously, but there is a period in infancy of neural plasticity, in which experience affects the structure of these systems. This period may be expected to be delayed and extended in humans as part of the neoteny process. But if the mimicking response is central to language acquisition, then the failure to develop the functions and structures of echoing may lead to a permanent lack of capacity for language acquisition.

This is consistent with the hypotheses of Netsell (1986), who also argues for a sensitive period, in the span of 3 to 12 months, during which "crucial anatomic developments" must occur in order for normal speech motor control to eventually develop. This general argument is also consistent with Speidel's (this volume, Chapter 7 & 9,) position that language acquisition is closely tied to the motoric, articulatory processes. Her position is allied to the motor theory of speech perception (See Eimas, 1974; Manyuk, 1977; Morse, 1974; Netsell, 1986), which suggests that

> through evolutionary development man has acquired the ability to detect phonetic feature distinctions in terms of distinct cortical motor commands that are realized as distinct articulatory movements within the vocal tract . . . . (Menyuk, 1977, p. 31)

If we assume that native-speaker phonological competence can only be acquired by quite young children, it can be argued that the vocal imitation of language, through its motoric, articulatory processes, has profound consequences for language acquisition. Our argument by analogy suggests that the acts of speaking might stimulate the development of the neural substrate of connections between hearing and speaking, and consequently allow imitation of language to continue throughout life. However speculative at this point, the position warrants some research: It may be that the critical period for language acquisition lies in its motoric aspects.

Whatever its detailed mechanisms, if there were no early imitation, would vocal speech development be forever precluded? Such speculations, of course, lead to thoughts of the "forbidden experiment," the nearest versions of which lie in the feral children chronicles. Nothing in that literature opposes our hypothesis, but the chronicles are woefully lacking in early-life details of the feral children. When restored to social life, learning of language by these children was slow, painful, and permanently inadequate. But no known circumstances of the feral children are clear tests of the hypothesis. For example, did the "wild boy of Aveyron" fail to learn to speak and understand language forever because he missed the (phylogenetically prepared) critical period stimulation of modeled human speech? The answer is beclouded by ontogenetic issues (Lane, 1976): The poor toddler may have been abandoned in the woods in the first place because he had a speech defect.

10.10 Conclusions

Our basic hypotheses are as follows: (1) A human repertoire of vocal mimicry is phylogenetically prepared; (2) this response of mimicry or echoing is not at an operative level of development until it emerges at about 9 months of age, due to the neoteny process; (3) aspects of verbal imitation can be illuminated by the concept of a critical or sensitive period; (4) the role of "echoing" is of early but declining importance in language acquisition through the course of development; and (5) although social reinforcement is also functional in verbal behavior throughout the life course, its role is more modest than heretofore assumed by behavior theory; whereas (6) the role of more complex forms of imitation is more central than generally suggested by nativists.

As promised at the beginning of this chapter, our reach has exceeded data that can be grasped. Our purpose has been to stimulate thought about the contribution of phylogenetic processes to language acquisition. Time after time, philosophy and science have erred by insisting on some human characteristic that is altogether unique and altogether discontinuous with lower or previous forms of life. Neither vocal language, nor imitation, nor the imitation of vocal language is such.

Eventually, phylogenesis will be seen to operate in general language acquisition, in ways more pervasive and more delicate than our preliminary suggestions here. The next order of inquiry should be to consider the vast literature in lower-species imitation, particularly appendage-movement imitation, its relationships to gestural languages in primates, and the relationship to human sign languages and other semiotic systems. This too-brief chapter has been able only to point toward phylogenetic inquiry as an area of great promise and great potential for understanding. Humankind will not be diminished by this understanding. It will be a finer wisdom to know those processes, begun aeons ago, through which children today come to say things the way we say them.

References

Andrew, R.J. (1962) Evolution of intelligence and vocal mimicking. *Science, 137,* 585–589.

Banks, M.S., Aslin, R.N., & Letson, R.D. (1975). Sensitive period for the development of human binocular vision. *Science, 190,* 675–677.

Bates, E., Shore, C., Bretherton, I., & McNew, S. (1983). Names, gestures, and objects: Symbolization in infancy and aphasia. In K.E. Nelson (Ed.), *Children's language* (Vol. 4, pp. 59–123). Hillsdale, NJ: Erlbaum.

Bjorklund, D.F. (1987). A note on neonatal imitation. *Developmental Review, 7,* 86–92.

Bloom, K. (1977a). Operant baseline procedures suppress infant social behavior. *Journal of Experimental Child Psychology, 23,* 28–132.

Bloom, K. (1977b). Patterning of infant vocal behavior. *Journal of Experimental Child Psychology, 23,* 367–377.

Bloom, K. (1979). Evaluation of infant vocal conditioning. *Journal of Experimental Child Psychology, 27,* 60–70.

Bolk, L. (1926). *Das Problem der Menschwerdung*. Jena: Gustav Fischer.

Caldwell, D.K., & Caldwell, M.C. (1972). Vocal mimicry in the whistle mode in the Atlantic bottle-nosed dolphin. *Cetology, 9*, 1–8.

Campbell, J. (1982). *Grammatical man: Information, entropy, language and life*. New York: Simon & Schuster.

Clarke-Stewart, A., Friedman, S., & Koch, J. (1985). *Child development*. New York: Wiley.

Crozier, J.B., Robinson, E.A., & Ewing, V. (1976/1977). [Etiology of absolute pitch.] *Bulliten de Psychologie, 30*, 792–803.

De Beer, G. (1958). Embryos and ancestors. Oxford: Clarendon Press.

deVilliers, P.A., & deVilliers, J.G. (1978). *Language acquisition*. Cambridge, MA: Harvard University Press.

Epstein, R. (1984). Spontaneous and deferred imitation in the pigeon. *Behavioural Processes, 9*, 347–354.

Ford, J.K.B., & Fisher, D. (1982). Killer whale (orcinus orca) dialects as an indicator of stocks in British Columbia. *Reports of the International Whaling Commision, 32*, 671–679.

Genesee, F. (1981). A comparison of early and late second language learning. *Canadian Journal of Behavioral Science, 13*(2), 115–128.

Gish, S.L. (1979). *Quantitative analysis of two-way acoustic communication between captive Atlantic bottlenose dolphins (Tursiops truncatus Montague)*. Unpublished doctoral dissertation, University of California at Santa Cruz.

Gould, S.J. (1977a). *Evern since Darwin: Reflections in natural history*. New York: Norton.

Gould, S.J. (1977b). *Ontogeny and phylogeny*. Cambridge, MA: Belknap Press.

Green, S. (1975). Dialects in Japanese monkeys: Vocal learning and cultural transmission of locale-specific vocal behavior? *Zeitschrift fur Tierpsychologie, 38*, 304–314.

Haimoff, E.H. (1981). Video analysis of siamang (Hylobates syndactylus) songs. *Behaviour, 76*, 128–151.

Hamm, M., Russell, M., & Koepke, J. (1979, March). *Neonatal imitation?* Paper presented at the Biennial Meeting of the Society for Research in Child Development, San Francisco, CA.

Harris, P.L. (1983). Infant cognition. In P.H. Mussen (Ed.), *Handbook of child psychology (4th ed.): Vol. 2. Infancy & developmental psychobiology* (pp. 689–782). New York: Wiley.

Harrison, G., & Weiner, J. (1964). Human evolution. In G. Harrison, J. Weiner, J. Tanner, & N. Barnicot (Eds.), *Human biology: An introduction to human evolution, variation, and growth*. New York: Oxford University Press.

Harste, J.C., Woodward, V.A., and Burke, C.L. (1984). *Language stories & literacy lessons*. Portsmouth, NH: Heinemann Educational Books.

Hayes, L.A., & Watson, J.S. (1981). Neonatal imitation: Fact or artifact? *Developmental Psychology, 17*, 655–660.

Herman, L.H. (1980). Cognitive characteristics of dolphins. In L.M. Herman (Ed.), *Cetacean behavior: Mechanisms and functions* (pp. 363–429). New York: Wiley-Interscience.

Herman, L.M., & Tavolga, W.N. (1980). The communication systems of cetaceans. In L.M. Herman (Ed.), *Cetacean behavior: Mechanisms and functions* (pp. 149–209). New York: Wiley-Interscience.

Herrnstein, R.J. (1977). The evolution of behaviorism. *American Psychologist, 32*, 593–603.

Hill, J.H. (1974). Possible continuity theories of language. *Language, 50,* 134–150.

Hoden, A., Snowdon, C.T., & Soini, P. (1981). Subspecific variation in the long calls of the tamarin, Saguinus fuscicollis. *A. Tierpscyhol., 57,* 97–110.

Kaye, K. (1982). *The mental and social life of babies: How parents create persons.* Chicago: The University of Chicago Press.

Kroodsma, D.E., & Miller, E.H. (Eds.). (1982). *Acoustic communication in birds.* New York: Academic Press.

Lane, H.L. (1976). *The wild boy of Aveyron.* Cambridge, MA: Harvard University Press.

Lenneberg, E. (1967). *Biological foundations of language.* New York: Wiley.

Lieberman, P. (1968). Primate vocalizations and human linguistic ability. *Journal of the Acoustical Society of America, 44,* 1574–1594.

Lieberman, P. (1984). *The biology and evolution of language.* Cambridge, MA: Harvard University Press.

McKenzie, B., & Over, R. (1983). Young infants fail to imitate facial and manual gestures. *Infant Behavior and Development, 6*(1), 85–95.

Meltzoff, A.N., & Moore, M.K. (1977). Imitation of facial and manual gestures by human neonates. *Science, 198,* 75–78.

Menyuk, P. (1971). *The acquisition and development of language.* Englewood Cliffs, NJ: Prentice-Hall.

Menyuk, P. (1977). *Language and maturation.* Cambridge, MA: MIT Press.

Michael, J.L. (1984). Verbal behavior. *Journal of the Experimental Analysis of Behavior, 42,* 363–376.

Montagu, A. (1961). Neonatal and infant maturity in man. *Journal of the American Medical Association, 178*(1), 56–57.

Morse, P. (1974). Infant speech perception: A preliminary model and review of the literature. In R. Schiefelbusch & L. Lloyd (Eds.). *Language perspectives: Acquisition, retardation and intervention* (pp. 19–54). Baltimore, MD: University Park Press.

Mussen, P.H. (1983). *Handbook of child psychology* (4th ed.). New York: Wiley.

Nakazima, S. (1962). A comparative study of the speech developments of Japanese and American English in childhood. *Studia Phonologica, 2,* 27–39.

Netsell, R. (1986). *A neurobiologic view of speech production and the dysarthrias.* San Diego, CA: College-Hill Press.

Newman, J.D., & Symmes, D. (1982). Inheritance and experience in the acquisition of primate acoustic behavior. In D.T. Snowden, C.H. Brown, & M.F. Peterson (Eds.), *Primate communication.* New York: Cambridge University Press.

Nottebohm, F. (1972). The origins of vocal learning. *American Naturalist, 106,* 116–140.

Olson, G.M., & Sherman, T. (1983). Attention, learning and memory in infants. In P.H. Mussen (Ed.). *Handbook of child psychology. Vol 2: Infancy and developmental psychobiology* (pp. 1001–1080). New York: Wiley.

Oppenheim, R.W. (1981). Ontogenetic adaptations and retrogressive processes in the development of the nervous system and behaviour: A neuroembryological perspective. In K.J. Connolly & H.F.R. Prechtl (Eds.), *Maturation and development: Biological and psychological perspectives.* Philadelphia, PA: International Medical Publications.

Oyama, S. (1976). A sensitive period for the acquisition of a nonnative phonological system. *Journal of Psycholinguistic Research, 5,* 261–283.

Patkowski, M. (1980). The sensitive period for the acquisition of syntax in a second language. *Language Learning, 30*(2), 449–472.

Piaget, J. (1962). *Play, dreams, and imitation in childhood.* New York: Norton.

Reger, Z. (1986). The functions of imitation in child language. *Applied Psycholinguistics*, 7, 323–352.

Richards, D.G., Wolz, J.P., & Herman, L.M. (1984). Vocal mimicry of computer-generated sounds and vocal labeling of objects by a bottlenosed dolphin, Tursiops truncatus. *Journal of Comparative Psychology*, 98, 10–28.

Rondal, J.A. (1985). *Adult-child interaction and the process of language acquisition*. New York: Praeger.

Routh, D.K. (1969). Conditioning of vocal response differentiation in infants. *Developmental Psychology*, 1, 219–226.

Seliger, H., Krashen, S., & Ladefoged, P. (1975). Maturational constraints in the acquisition of second language accent. *Language Sciences*, 36, 20–22.

Seyfarth, R.M., & Cheney, D.L. (1982). How monkeys see the world: A review of recent research on East African vervet monkeys. In C.T. Snowden, C.H. Brown, & M.R. Petersen (Eds.), *Primate communication*. New York: Cambridge University Press.

Skinner, B.F. (1957). *Verbal behavior*. New York: Appleton-Century-Crofts.

Skinner, B.F. (1961). *The technology of teaching*. New York: Appleton-Century-Crofts.

Skinner, B.F. (1966). The phylogeny and ontogeny of behavior. *Science*, 153, 1205–1213.

Skinner, B.F. (1974). *About behaviorism*. New York: Knopf.

Skinner, B.F. (1977). Herrnstein and the evolution of behaviorism. *American Psychologist*, 32, 1006–1012.

Skinner, B.F. (1980). *Notebooks*. (Edited by R. Epstein). Englewood Cliffs, NJ: Prentice-Hall.

Skinner, B.F. (1983). *A matter of consequences*. New York: Knopf.

Snow, C.E. (1983). Saying it again: The role of expanded and deferred imitations in language acquisition. In K.E. Nelson (Ed.), *Children's language* (Vol. 4, pp. 29–58). Hillsdale, NJ: Erlbaum.

Snowden, C.T. (1983). Ethology, comparative psychology, and animal behavior. *Annual Review of Psychology*, 34, 63–94.

Tahta, S., Wood, M., & Lowenthal, K. (1981). Age changes in the ability to replicate foreign pronunciation and intonation. *Language and Speech*, 24(4), 363–372.

Tharp, R.G. (1987, August). *Culture, cognition & education: A culturogenetic analysis of the wholistic complex*. A paper presented at the conference of the Institute on Literacy and Learning, University of California at Santa Barbara.

Thorpe, W.H., & North, M.E.W. (1965). Origin and significance of the power of vocal imitation: With special reference to the antiphonal singing of birds. *Nature*, 208, 219–222.

Trevarthen, C. (1983). Development of the cerebral mechanisms for language. In U. Kirk, (Ed.) *Neuropsychology of language, reading, and spelling*. New York: Academic Press.

Vaughan, M.E., & Michael, J.L. (1982). Automatic reinforcement: An important but ignored concept. *Behaviorism*, 10, 217–227.

Wahler, R.G. (1969). Infant social development: Some experimental analyses of an infant-mother interaction during the first year of life. *Journal of Experimental Child Psychology*, 7, 101–113.

Waite, L.H. (1979, March). *Early imitation with several models: An example of socio-cognitive and socio-affective development*. Paper presented at the Biennial Meeting of the Society for Research in Child Development, San Francisco, CA.

Ward, W.D. (1963). Absolute pitch: Part II. *Sound*, 2(4), 33–41.

Werker, J.F., & Tees, R.C. (1983). Developmental changes across childhood in the perception of non-native speech sounds. *Canadian Journal of Psychology*, 37, 278–286.

White, S., Tharp, R.G., Jordan, C., and Vogt, L. (in press). Cultural patterns of cognition reflected in the questioning styles of Anglo and Navajo teachers. In D. Topping, V. Kobayshi, & D.C. Crowell (Eds.). *Thinking: The Third International Conference*. Hillsdale, NJ: Erlbaum.

CHAPTER 11

Observational Learning and Language Acquisition: Principles of Learning, Systems, and Tasks

Grover J. Whitehurst and Barbara D. DeBaryshe

The thesis of this chapter is that language, like many other complex skills, is acquired in part through the process of observational learning. In observational learning, one person's behavior (the model's) is witnessed by a second person (the observer). Observational learning has occurred when some aspect of the model's behavior comes to control a related aspect of the second person's behavior. The observer's behavior may match the model's along the dimensions of topography, function, or discriminative context (Whitehurst, 1978). A topographical relation involves similarity of form. For example, a mother might say to her child, "You are incorrigible today," and the child replies, "I'm 'corrigbal." Matching along the functional dimension involves similarity between the outcome of the model's and observer's behavior. For example, a child might see people on a television commercial drinking bottles of soda; the child may then hurry into the kitchen to get a cup of juice. An example of observational learning of discriminative context (and topography) may be seen when a child is able to correctly name a real helicopter after having been exposed to pictures of helicopters and the word *helicopter* during picture-book reading with parents.

As these examples suggest, the observer's new response need not immediately follow the model's behavior, nor must it be an exact copy or even a close approximation of the modeled response. Observational learning theory allows for both *deferred* imitation, imitation that occurs long after the modeled example (e.g., Bandura, 1977), and *selective* imitation, imitation that incorporates some abstract dimension of the modeled response (Whitehurst & Vasta, 1975).

Existing theory and research on the role of imitation in language acquisition have focused on the prototypical case, involving a more or less exact and immediate topographical matching of an adult's verbalization by a child. In this context, when one asks about the role of imitation in language development, one is asking whether the child is helped or hindered in learning some aspect of language by the act of repeating adult examples. Although this is an important question, it should not be seen as the only question or even the principal question relating to imitation and language development.

One advantage of adopting a broader definition of imitation is that it is difficult to create an entirely satisfactory definition on the basis of a matching response. For example, must imitation be immediate in order to qualify? If a delay between the model and imitative behavior is allowed, how long may that delay be? What degree of overlap between the model and the imitative behavior must be achieved?

Whitehurst (1985) used transcripts of parent-child speech from a single dyad to illustrate how much information is lost by using a narrow definition of imitation. If both immediate and delayed responses, as well as exact and reduced imitations were counted, approximately 70% of the child's utterances were an imitation of parental speech. However, only 41% of the child's utterances were immediate matches, and only 39% were exact matches.

The questions posed in this chapter, then, do not deal with the effects of mimicking adult speech, but rather, they address the ways in which children come to learn language by observing others. The observational learning paradigm provides a parsimonious yet powerful system for conceptualizing such learning.

We will consider three classes of variables that affect the observational learning process. First, what are the *learning principles* that are relevant to observational learning of language? How might language models be presented in order to capitalize on general learning principles and make language learning most efficient? Second, any particular language form to which a child is exposed will affect the child differently depending on the degree and nature of the development of the child's linguistic and cognitive systems that are related to that stimulation. Thus, how are existing *systems of the child* related to what is acquired through observation of others? Third, any particular combination of learning mechanisms and systemic variables will lead to differential outcomes depending on the language forms, or *tasks*, to which the child is exposed. In summary, we are interested in how learning principles, the child's existing systems, and the structure of language tasks affect the child's acquisition of language through observation of others. (A diagram illustrating this approach is presented in Figure 11-1).

This chapter discusses each class of variables within the context of observational learning, using evidence from recent research conducted in our laboratory. We have limited our scope to a consideration of semantic and communicative development in preschoolers, primarily in the context of linguistic interactions with their caretakers. The same conceptual approach could be applied to other topics, for example, to syntactic development, to second-language acquisition, or to language in older children and adults.

As a final caveat, it should be noted that we are considering language-learning processes at a behavioral level. At this level, an explanation of learning processes entails the specification of predicted language outcomes given prior models and other observed historical events. Questions about learning processes may be

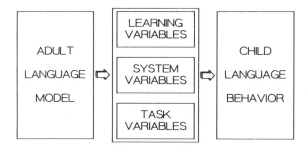

Figure 11-1. The role of learning, system, and task variables in the observational learning of language.

specified at other levels as well. For example, at the cognitive level, one might specify strategic encoding or retrieval processes (see Bohannon and Stanowicz, Chapter 6, this volume, for an information-processing model of imitation in language acquisition). Physiological processes or changes in neuronal activity and configuration could also be specified (e.g., Rumelhart and McClelland, 1986). The topic of language acquisition can be approached at many levels, and each contributes in an important way to a comprehensive understanding of this complex phenomenon.

11.1 Learning Principles

Learning principles are generalized descriptions of environmental relations that are functionally related to skill acquisition. There are two interdependent categories of learning principles to be considered: associative and operant.

11.1.1 Associative Principles

In associative conditioning, an organism learns a relationship between two or more events in the environment. One of those events is normally of significance to the organism, whereas the other is normally of less importance prior to learning. In the classic example of Pavlovian conditioning, the significant event is congenitally so, for example, food powder for a dog. However, studies in second-order conditioning have shown that associations may be learned among a wide variety of events whose significance to the organism is derived from experience (Rescorla, 1980).

Whitehurst and colleagues (Whitehurst, 1979; Whitehurst, Kedesdy, & White, 1982) have made the case that many variables that are important to the acquisition of language through observation are associative. In the case of early semantic development, for example, there are a wide variety of objects, events, and relations in the environment that are of significance for every child. Nelson

(1973) notes that foods are the most frequent category of referents in children's early vocabularies, followed by animals, clothes, toys, and vehicles. If events from categories in which the child has high interest (e.g., foods) are labeled by adults in the presence of the child, the child may associate the label with the event. The value of interpreting this process as an example of associative learning is that it allows contact with a large literature in which possibly relevant variables have been investigated systematically.

11.1.1.1 Attention

The study of attentional variables in associative learning has a long history, beginning with Pavlov (1927), who described the looking, listening, and autonomic responses that accompany the presentation of many stimuli as the investigatory reflex. These orienting responses are considered to be an important component of Pavlovian conditioning, one type of associative learning (Sokolov, 1960). Within the study of child-directed speech, or *motherese*, there are suggestions of the importance of the mother capitalizing on the child's attention when labeling or describing things for the child. For example, mothers often label objects their children are looking at (Collis, 1975, cited in Rondal, 1985) or pointing at (Masur, 1982). Tomasello and Todd (1983) found high correlations between the frequency of early interactions in which the mother maintains interactions by following the child's focus of attention and later vocabulary size.

This research suggests that the likelihood of a child learning the association between words used by an adult and the referents for those words is affected by momentary fluctuations in the child's attention to the potential referents of the adult's speech. Presumably an adult who timed instances of labeling for the child so as to follow the child's visible signs of attention to a shared event would induce more associative learning of vocabulary than an adult whose labeling was independent of the child's attention.

Valdez-Menchaca and Whitehurst (1988) investigated this hypothesis in an experimental design. Sixteen monolingual English-speaking 2-year-old children served as subjects. The referents were attractive toys, and the novel vocabulary items consisted of the appropriate Spanish names for the toys. Prior to training, each child's preference for the toys was assessed. Children were matched on the basis of toy preference and then randomly assigned to an experimental or yoked control group.

Experimental and control children were seen in separate sessions, with the experimental child always being seen first. During these sessions, the experimenter spoke to the child solely in Spanish. In the experimental condition, the adult would label a toy whenever the child expressed an interest in the toy, either by looking at the toy, pointing to it, or requesting it in English. In the control condition, Spanish labels were not provided contingent on the child's attention to the toy. Instead, the timing and content of the Spanish models presented to the control child were yoked exactly to the models presented to the corresponding child in the experimental group. Regardless of the experimental condition, the child was allowed to play with a toy for one minute if he or she requested it using the appropriate Spanish label. Thus, control-group and experimental-group subjects were exposed to identical reinforcement contingencies and identical models of the Spanish language. However, experimental subjects heard these models while attending to the referent (i.e., looking at it, pointing at it, or labeling it in English), whereas adult labeling in Spanish was randomly related to children's attention to the referent for control subjects.

Children's spontaneous language was tape-recorded during each session. At the conclusion of the study, formal tests of children's comprehension and production of the Spanish labels were conducted. The experimental group performed at a significantly higher level than the control group on production of Spanish labels during the training sessions as well as on the formal production posttest. Both groups performed equally well (and at above chance levels) on the formal comprehension task. These data demonstrate that an adult's ability to utilize visible signs of child attention to events as the occasion for labeling those events is an important variable in the child's ability to acquire productive vocabulary skills through observation. These data also demonstrate an interesting separation between variables that affect receptive skill, which was equivalent in the two groups, and expressive skill, which differed. We will return to the comprehension-production issue later.

11.1.1.2 Value

Value is a measure of the importance of an object or event to an organism. The prediction is that, when adults label a variety of objects or events, children will most quickly learn the labels for those objects or events that they value most highly.

Stewart and Hamilton (1976) found the expected relation between the a priori value of a set of referents and the extent to which children learned the labels for these referents from adult models. Acquisition of word-referent knowledge for expected valuables, such as food and manipulable toys, exceeded acquisition of labels for passive objects, such as a poster.

Whitehurst et al. (1982) examined the role of referent value experimentally. Six 2-year-olds were studied in a day-care center. Five novel objects were introduced, and the relative value of the objects for each child was measured in two ways: The first was the amount of time spent playing with each object when all the objects were freely available. The second was based on a forced choice procedure in which each child was asked which member among all possible pairings of five objects he or she preferred. The two scales of value were highly correlated (Kendall's $r = + .83$). After both measures of value had been taken, children were given training with word-referent relations. Each of the five referents was produced and labeled by an adult three times during each of three sessions. The child's visual contact with an object defined the onset of a labeling trial. A test of comprehension and production followed each session. The hypothesis that referent value would be related to observational learning was tested by correlating the time allocation scale of value with each child's combined comprehension and production scores. The mean correlation coefficient for the six subjects was + .64, demonstrating a significant relation between value and learning. Because labeling occurred only when children were attending to the relevant objects, this study demonstrates that referent value is a conceptually different variable than child attention (though one would expect the two to be highly correlated in every-day interactions between parents and children).

11.1.1.3 Informativeness

Modern approaches to associative learning have stressed that simple temporal contiguity between events is not sufficient for learning. Instead, a contingent, or informative, relation is required (Rescorla, 1980). For example, in Pav-lovian conditioning, imagine that meat powder in a dog's mouth is preceded on every occasion of presentation by both a tone and a light. Temporal con-tiguity would be high for both stimuli. Imagine further that the tone also occurs on other occasions when it is not followed by meat powder, although this is not the case for the light. The light would therefore convey more informa-tion to the dog about when meat powder was expected than would the tone. In these conditions, animals learn an association to the light, not the tone (Kamin, 1969), demonstrating that informativeness is a critical variable in associative learning.

Whitehurst et al. (1982) examined informativeness with six 2-year-olds. Chil-dren were shown a set of 15 novel objects, one at a time. Five objects were presented in each of three conditions. In the perfectly informative condition, the adult labeled each object every time it was presented and did not use the object's label on other occasions. In the extra thing condition, each object was also presented on two additional trials during which it was not labeled. In the extra word condition, each label was presented on two additional occasions without also presenting the object. Word-referent association was superior for objects presented in the condition of perfect informativeness. Children's comprehension scores (but not production scores) were significantly higher in the perfectly infor-mative condition than in the two conditions in which the informativeness of the relation between the adult label and the referent was degraded. Results are dis-played in Figure 11-2.

The role of informativeness may illuminate many phenomena involving the selectivity of children's observational learning. For example, the heavy prepon-derance of nouns in children's early vocabularies (Brown, 1973; Nelson, 1973) may be explained by considering the informativeness of parental language models. Although parents may use a variety of words in the presence of the child, some of those words, particularly nouns, are likely to be most informatively cor-related with objects and events of interest to the child. These will be imitated. Others, for example, articles, are likely to be nondifferentially and thus noninfor-matively associated with particular objects of value and will not be imitated.

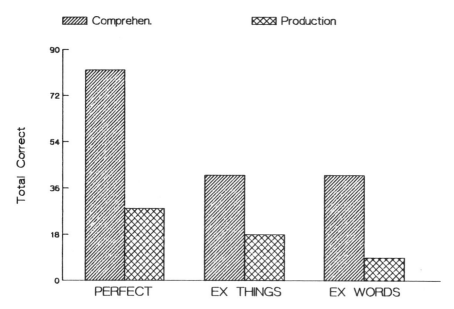

Figure 11-2. Comprehension and production scores as a function of whether referent and label were presented in a perfectly informative fashion, or with extra words or extra things.

An example of this is provided by Valdez-Menchaca and Whitehurst (1987), who exposed English-speaking 2-year-olds to an adult who modeled Spanish descriptions of attractive toys. Although two-thirds of the descriptions were in complete Spanish sentences, virtually none of the children's spontaneous Spanish usage consisted of other than the nouns that referred to the toys. Consider the Spanish phrase fragment "Este es el," which preceded many of the object labels, as in "Este es el payaso," "Este es el cuerno," "Este es el horno," "Este es el vaquero," and so forth. Although "Este es el" is highly correlated with referents, it carries little information about those referents, that information being much better conveyed by the nouns. Thus, children learn associations between nouns and their referents because nouns are highly informative.

11.1.1.4 Frequency

A final associative variable is the frequency with which adults model various relations between words and words, and words and referents. The frequency variable has been the source of considerable controversy. For example, in attempting to explain the order of emergence of various grammatical morphemes, Brown (1973, p. 364) says, "Thus far we have no evidence whatever that parental frequency of usage is a determinant of acquisition order." However, quite opposite conclusions have been drawn by others looking at much the same database:

[It] now appears safe to conclude that . . . frequency effects are obvious; obvious both as far as the theoretical conceptualization of skill learning is concerned and as far as the overwhelming factual evidence shows. (Moerk, 1986, p. 213)

We believe the data do not allow conclusions as strong as either those of Brown or Moerk, and that the effects of frequency of exposure on acquisition are likely to be both complicated and nonlinear. Certainly some frequency of exposure to elements of the language is necessary for children to acquire those elements. Research that has been interpreted as demonstrating the acquisition of syntactic skills in the absence of models (e.g., Goldin-Meadow, 1982; Goldin-Meadow & Feldman, 1977) does not hold up under close inspection (Whitehurst, 1982). Dollaghan (1985) presents evidence that children begin to make word-referent associations on the basis of very limited exposure. For example, following a single word-referent pairing, 81% of 2- to 5-year-olds could correctly select the requested novel referent from an array of objects, and 45% could name the novel referent with reasonable accuracy. We doubt that the effects of frequency of exposure to particular words and elements are linear across even a small range of frequencies. The effects of frequency will also be dependent on other variables we have discussed or will discuss. For instance, if a parent is not responsive to the child's attention when labeling, or if a word is modeled in the presence of many referents, or if the word for the referent is embedded in a complex sentence, or if the value of the referent to the child is low, or if the child has deficiencies in attentional skills, higher frequencies of exposure are likely to be necessary to obtain a given level of acquisition. Frequency is a variable that deserves more careful investigation within a multivariate perspective.

11.1.2 Operant Principles

Operant principles concern the social feedback functions for language use. Feedback for responding has at least three closely intertwined functions: motivation for talking, information concerning the correctness of the child's speech, and practice in talking. These are conceptually separable although they work in concert in natural settings. For instance, assenting nods from an adult conversational partner function to indicate that the child's message is understood (information). The motivational effect of this attention may vary with the adult's identity (e.g., mother vs. baby-sitter). This motivational variable will in turn affect the child's willingness to talk with that adult and to adopt characteristics of the adults' language (practice). This package of motivational, informational, and practice effects is called *reinforcement*.

11.1.2.1 Information Function of Reinforcement

The role of social feedback, or reinforcement, in language acquisition has been the source of considerable controversy for at least the last 25 years, since Chomsky (1959) challenged Skinner's (1957) assertion that language is operant behavior. Chomsky argued that normal children are able to acquire language through observation alone and that environmental reinforcement is not necessary. Given minimal exposure to examples of their native language, general cognitive and congenital linguistic mechanisms would ensure that learning occurs without the need for the environment to be responsive to children's attempts to use language. This same message has recently been presented in the context of the acquisition of language by chimpanzees (cf. Gardner & Gardner, 1988; Whitehurst & Fischel, 1988).

One piece of research (Brown & Hanlon, 1970) has contributed inordinately to scholarly consideration of the reinforcement issue. Based on correlational data from three children, these investigators concluded that parents give corrective feedback on the dimension of "truth value" rather than grammar. For example, the grammatically incorrect sentence, "He a girl," was accepted by a parent, whereas the grammatically correct sentence, "There's the animal farmhouse," was corrected because the building was actually a lighthouse. These results are usually interpreted as demonstrating that reinforcement is not important in grammatical development, and are often generalized to language development in general. For example, citing only the Brown and Hanlon (1970) results, Maratsos (1983, p. 767) says, "present findings do not indicate environmental contingencies that act directly on the child to shape the appropriate stimulus and response generalization and discrimination gradients."

Writers who are quick to cite the Brown and Hanlon (1970) work as demonstrating that reinforcement is unimportant in grammatical development virtually never draw the logically compelled symmetrical conclusion that reinforcement is important in semantic development. In addition, other investigators have found evidence that parents respond differentially to grammatical and ungrammatical child utterances (Bohannon & Stanowicz, Chapter 6, this volume; Hirsh-Pasek, Treiman, & Schneiderman, 1984; Penner, 1987). Such differential responding is typically of a more subtle form than overt correction (e.g., parents are more likely to repeat or expand ungrammatical utterances). Thus, children do receive potentially informative feedback.

11.1.2.2 Motivation Function of Reinforcement

Whitehurst and Valdez-Menchaca (1988) addressed the issue of the motivational role of feedback in an experimental design. Two- and 3-year-old children were exposed to elements of a foreign language over several weeks in a preschool setting. An adult model periodically labeled one of a set of attractive toys for the children using the foreign language. All other conversation with the children was also in the foreign language. The toys were placed on a shelf so as to be out of reach but visible to the children. A delayed treatment control design was used. Reinforcement contingencies for the experimental group remained constant over all treatment sessions. Experimental group subjects were allowed to obtain the toys only if the toys were requested in the foreign language. Thus, use of the foreign language was differentially reinforced. The delayed treatment control group was initially in a condition in which they could obtain toys through requests in the

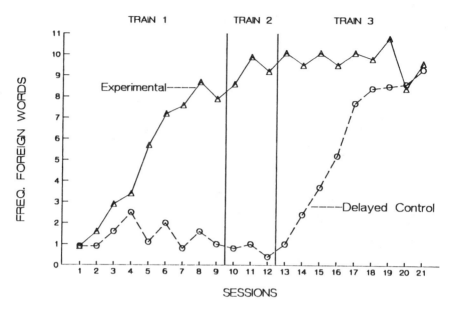

Figure 11-3. Mean frequency per session of use of foreign words by children in the experimental and control groups. The control group began to experience the differential reinforcement condition at Train 3, whereas the experimental group experienced it throughout the study.

native language or the foreign language. After several sessions, they were switched to the same differential reinforcement condition being experienced by the experimental group. The dependent variable of primary interest was the frequency of spontaneous requests for toys using the correct label in either the native language or the foreign language. This was measured by audiotaping interactions during training sessions. A second important set of dependent variables was obtained through formal tests of comprehension and production of vocabulary items in the second language conducted at two points during the course of training.

Results for the spontaneous production of foreign words by the two groups are displayed in Figure 11-3. Each group shows a highly significant increasing linear trend in the production of foreign words during the first period during which they were differentially reinforced (experimental group, Train 1; control group, Train 3).

Formal tests of production and comprehension of foreign language nouns occurred at the conclusion of the last session of Train 1 and the last session of Train 3. The production test involved showing the toys one at a time and asking the child (in his or her native language), "What did I call this when we were playing together?" The experimental group had significantly higher production scores than the control group on Test 1; this test followed the period when experimental group subjects had been differentially reinforced for spontaneous requests in the foreign language whereas the control group subjects were not. Group differences in foreign language production scores were eliminated on Test 2, at which point the control group had also been differentially reinforced. The same pattern of results was obtained for the comprehension measures; on this test children were asked to point to the correct referents for the foreign nouns. Children's comprehension scores were higher following periods of differential reinforcement for foreign language use. However, although the comprehension scores for the control group on Test 1 were lower than those of the experimental group, the control group subjects still showed comprehension performance that was significantly above levels expected on the basis of chance.

These results are consistent with the hypothesis that reinforcement is important in the acquisition of expressive vocabulary. When children were not differentially reinforced, they continued to use their native language. When they were differentially reinforced, they stopped using their native language and gradually began to use words in the foreign language. The results for the formal tests of comprehension and production also show clearly the effects of reinforcement. The control group's performance on the first test of comprehension also demonstrates that at least some level of receptive ability may be acquired through associative mechanisms alone, without overt practice and reinforcement.

11.1.2.3 Practice Function of Reinforcement

Practice, that is, overt production of to-be-learned behaviors, is important in theories of skill acquisition (e.g., Kaye, 1979), and language is among other things a skill (Moerk, 1986). Spontaneous imitation, in the prototypical sense of a more or less immediate and exact copy of an adult's language by a child, has often been conceptualized as serving a practice function. Snow (1981, 1983) has demonstrated that spontaneous reproductions of elements of adult speech by children may serve other than practice functions (e.g., as a signal of attention or comprehension, as a primitive conversational turn). If the primary function of exact imitation is to provide practice, one would expect the frequency of imitation to correlate with knowledge of the imitated form. However, measures of spontaneous imitation by 2-year-old children exposed to novel vocabulary words are highly variable across children and do not correlate significantly with formal measures of word comprehension or production (Whitehurst et al., 1982; but see Speidel, Chapters 7 & 9). It is possible, however, that spontaneous imitation serves a practice function for 1-year-olds.

Our research suggests that *directed practice*, as opposed to spontaneous imitation, may be more consistently useful in 2-year-olds. Directed practice is conceptualized as responding on the part of the child that takes advantage of an adult's model of appropriate usage and that is prompted and rewarded by the adult. Optimal directed practice will be sensitive to the child's zone of proximal development and to the child's interests in the selection by the parent of items to prompt. For example, a child in the initial stages of vocabulary acquisition might be prompted to imitate a particular word in a sentence the parent used, whereas the same child at a later point in development might be prompted to imitate a grammatical element of a similar adult sentence. Bohannon and Stanowicz (Chapter 6, this volume) have shown how parents use the pattern of a child's errors as a guide to the target of directed practice. In addition, in optimal directed practice, feedback will be naturally related to the language that the child is imitating. In these ways directed practice differs from the usual elicited imitation procedure that is employed in remedial language training. Elicited imitation typically involves adult presentation of models of language that someone has decided a child should learn, and involves reward for the child's imitation in some general form (e.g., praise). For example, the child might be shown a series of pictures of animals, told to imitate the adult's labeling of those animals, and be praised for successful mimicry. A contrasting example of directed practice might involve the adult saying the name of animals that a child is attending to spontaneously during picture-book reading, asking the child at some later point to name such animals, and rewarding correct delayed imitation by expanding the child's speech or telling the child something interesting about the animal whose name the child has imitated.

Directed practice is illustrated in a study by Whitehurst, Fischel, Caulfield, DeBaryshe, and Valdez-Menchaca (1988) involving children at the very beginning of the acquisition of expressive vocabulary. Parents of expressive language-delayed children were taught to use directed practice to teach specific vocabulary items. Children were 2- and 3-year-old boys with developmental expressive language delay (ELD). By definition, ELD children show normal auditory functioning, nonverbal intelligence, and receptive language ability, but are substantially delayed in expressive language skills. The diagnostic criteria used across our studies of ELD children include nonverbal IQ not more than 1 standard deviation below the mean on the Leiter International Performance Scale; receptive vocabulary score not more than 1 standard deviation below the mean on the Peabody Picture Vocabulary Test—Revised; and expressive vocabulary score at least 2.5 standard deviations below the mean on the Expressive One-Word Picture Vocabulary Test.

Parents were given a series of language stimulation exercises to practice with their child at home; the assignment described here was the second in a series of seven (see Whitehurst, Fischel, Caulfield, et al., 1989, for details on subject selection and parent-training procedures). Parents constructed a list of 20 words that their child did not currently say, whose referents were of considerable interest to the child, and whose referents were under the control of the parents. The parents would introduce the referent and direct the child to name it. For example, if a target word was *orange juice*, the parent would hold up a glass of juice at a time when the child was likely to be interested in it and say, "What do you want?" Pointing by the child led the parent to model the label, "Orange juice. Tell mommy what you want. Orange juice." The child would be given the juice only if he made some attempt at imitating the parent; the child did not have access to target items outside of the teaching context.

Samples of child speech were collected by having families make audiotape recordings of home mealtime conversation. Results for a subset of three subjects indicate an increase in children's use of the target words following the introduction of the directed practice assignment. Prior to the assignment, only 8% of the target words were said by the child on the audiotape. At the end of the assignment, 50% of the target words had been recorded. These data represented only a sample of child speech and were not taken from recordings of specific teaching sessions. Although practice, motivation, and other effects are confounded in this study, they are in all natural language interactions. The important role of directed practice, as defined above, is supported by comparing its effects to those of the spontaneous parental teaching strategy that it replaced. Prior to the introduction of the directed practice procedure, parents of ELD children engaged in a high rate of imitative directives, defined as occasions when the parent tells the child to imitate a parental model of language. Furthermore, ELD children were likely to imitate these imitative directives (Whitehurst, Fischel, Lonigan, Valdez-Menchaca, DeBaryshe, & Caulfield, 1988). However, little spontaneous language growth emerged from such prompts and imitations. Parents did not initially appreciate the difference between telling a child to say a word that the parents wanted the child to learn and rewarding him verbally or not at all for imitating (elicited imitation), versus asking the child to imitate the names of things the child was motivated to obtain and systematically rewarding the child with access to the things whose names were imitated (directed practice). The point is that there are many ways by which a child may be induced to imitate an adult's language. It is not so much the act of repeating an adult's language as it is the function that the imitation serves for the child that will determine whether the practice is a progressive influence in language acquisition.

Whitehurst, Falco, et al. (1988) also examined the role of parentally directed practice in children with normally developing language skills. The setting was picture-book reading to 27-month-old children in the home by parents. Families were randomly assigned to an experimental group and a control group. Both groups read at home to their children over a 4-week period. The control group of parents was instructed to read in a normal fashion. The parents in the experimental group participated in two training sessions in which they were instructed to increase the frequency of patterns of behavior that would lead to children talking more and parents talking less during story-reading sessions.

A major component of training was to encourage parents to increase the frequency of child practice at the expense of simple "reading." Parents were instructed to provide their child with more practice in answering *attribute questions* and *open-ended directives*. Attribute questions request information about characteristics of objects (e.g., "What color is the dog?", "What is the boy doing?"). Open-ended directives are nonspecific requests for spontaneous descriptions of the picture (e.g., "Tell me about this page."). Parents were instructed to follow the child's response to these prompts with contextually appropriate feedback, such as expanding the child's speech, or commenting on the themes and topics that the child introduced.

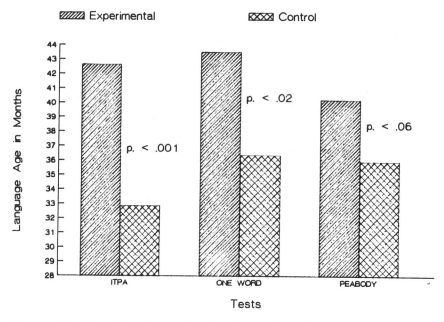

Figure 11-4. Comparison of experimental and control children on language scores on three tests of language ability following a 1-month at-home reading intervention for the experimental group.

The fidelity with which the intervention was implemented by parents in the home was investigated via audiotapes the parents had made of all reading sessions. It was clear that parents were successful in following instructions and altering how they read to their children. For instance, open-ended directives occurred in 32% of the intervals of observation during the 4th week of reading at home for the experimental group, but in only 1% of the intervals of observation for the control group. Control-group parents engaged in significantly higher rates of simple reading.

The provision of increased practice trials resulted in increased frequencies of child speech. Although experimental- and control-group children did not differ on rates of nonword vocalizations or single-word utterances during the story sessions, experimental-group children produced twice as many multiword utterances. Sequential analysis of parent-child conversation indicated that attribute questions and open-ended directives reliably evoked a verbal response by the child, whereas reading did not (Falco, 1986). Finally, mean length of utterance (MLU) was significantly longer for the experimental group, reflecting the children's more frequent use of phrases in preference to single-word responses.

Thus, the parental strategies led to increases in the frequency and complexity of child language in the story-time situation. More significantly, practice-intensive story-time sessions were also associated with increased language competence outside of the story-time setting. Posttest scores on standardized language tests showed consistent differences in favor of the experimental group. Figure 11-4 displays the mean language ages for the experimental group and the control group on the expressive subscale of the Illinois Test of Psycholinguistic Abilities (ITPA), the One-Word Expressive Picture Vocabulary Test, and the Peabody Picture Vocabulary Test. These differences are large and statistically significant on the ITPA and the One-Word; they are marginally significant on the Peabody. These results suggest that practice of a variety of linguistic forms strongly facilitates general language growth. Thus, practice should be reconceptualized to include a wider range of phenomena than immediate exact imitation of the form of a response. The two studies described above demonstrate particular benefit to the child for practice that involves selective imitation by the child of new forms, in circumstances in which the child must incorporate the new forms into appropriate contexts, and in circumstances in which the child's behavior will be rewarded by increased communicative effectiveness.

11.2 System Variables

System variables include those characteristics of the child that affect his or her ability to learn language from observation. It is necessary to know what skills and limitations the child brings to the learning situation because the efficacy of linguistic models depends in part on these child characteristics. Examples of system variables include the child's linguistic level, cognitive level, knowledge base, and individual experience. System variables affect language learning directly when they control what and how a child is able to learn. System variables have an indirect effect on language learning when adults tailor the form of the language models they provide in order to match their estimate of the child's processing abilities and constraints.

11.2.1 Child Effects on Adult Behavior

Bidirectional models of parent-child interaction draw attention to the fact that child characteristics play an important role in determining adult behavior (Bell, (1968). Both global (e.g., age, linguistic ability) and minute-by-minute (e.g., attention, eye contact, questioning intonation) child characteristics may cause parents to modify aspects of child-directed language. Thus, the child indirectly affects the language environment to which he or she is exposed.

For example, research by Bohannon and colleagues (Bohannon & Marquis, 1977; Bohannon & Stanowicz, Chapter 6, this volume; Stine & Bohannon, 1983) shows that adults adjust their speech on the basis of child behavior and comprehension. In their studies, adults immediately reformulated and shortened their utterances when children gave clear signals that they did not comprehend what was being said to them (e.g., saying "huh?"). Child comprehension has also been shown to control adult behavior in the context of joint picture-book reading (Ninio, 1983). When children failed to label a particular picture correctly, mothers would name it for the child the next time it was seen. In contrast, when a child had previously indicated knowledge of a particular referent (by correctly pointing to or naming a picture), mothers elicited child pointing or labeling and were less likely to label the referent themselves. Thus, mothers quizzed the child when they believed he or she knew the answer, but provided the answer themselves when they believed that the child could not.

Research from our laboratory has considered the role of children's language status in shaping adults' language models. This work compared parent-child language interaction in families of children who were developing language along a normal timetable with families of children exhibiting specific expressive language delay (ELD). Whitehurst, Fischel, Lonigan, et al. (1988), compared parent-child language interaction in three groups of children. Subjects were seventeen 28-month-old ELD children, fourteen 28-month-old normally developing children matched to the ELD subjects for chronological age and receptive language ability, and ten 16-month-old normally developing children matched to the ELD subjects for expressive vocabulary size. Samples of parent-child speech were collected in the home at mealtime. Twelve categories of parent speech were coded: Imitative directives, behavioral directives, yes/no questions, "what" questions, labeling, conversation, praise, correction, repetition, answer, other, and silence.

Results indicated that parent speech was highly similar in the ELD and expressive language-matched groups. Although parents of ELD children used more imitative directives (e.g., "Say milk") than parents of younger children with similar expressive skills, no significant group differences were found on the remaining parent behavior categories. In contrast, many group differences were found in the speech addressed to ELD versus receptive-language-matched children. Parents of ELD children used more imitative directives and were more likely to label objects for their child (e.g., "This is milk"), parents of receptive-age-matched children directed more speech toward their child overall, were more likely to answer the child's verbalizations, and were more likely to allow silent intervals to elapse.

These results provide strong evidence that parents adjusted their language input on the basis of their child's expressive language characteristics, rather than on the basis of the child's receptive abilities or chronological age. Although parents of ELD children provided language models that were appropriate for their child's expressive language skill, responsiveness to this single dimension could have negative long-term consequences for the child. ELD children were not receiving language models appropriate for their receptive language skills. There is substantial evidence that acquisition of particular language forms usually occurs first in the receptive mode (Whitehurst, 1977). We do not know the eventual effects of a widening gap between parental input level and child comprehension, and how this might relate to both expressive and receptive development.

In another study demonstrative of child effects, Falco (1986) presented evidence that parents' attempts to implement particular teaching strategies are shaped by child responsiveness. The setting was picture-book reading in the home. Subjects were 14 normally developing and 14 ELD 2-year-olds and their parents. Parents were instructed to increase their frequency of using complex "what" questions and open-ended directives. Parents of normally developing children increased these types of questions more than did the parents of ELD children. Normally developing children consistently responded to these questions with multiword utterances; ELD children did not. Thus, children of normal language ability responded appropriately to parental teaching attempts, which may have served to maintain this parental behavior. Presumably, parents of ELD children did not dramatically change their use of these teaching techniques because there was little reason to do so: Their children did not respond.

In summary, there is considerable evidence that parents' language models are often determined by child effects. Evidence for the role of child variables in the utilization of language models will now be considered.

11.2.2 Developmental Level and Forms of Stimulation

Older children may benefit from forms of stimulation that are simply inaccessible to younger children. Theories of vocabulary acquisition have posited developmental changes in the mechanisms through which children acquire new word meanings. Very young children are thought to rely on perceptual information. It is hypothesized that children first develop a preverbal understanding of a concept (e.g., for a ball as something to roll and throw) through perceptual experience, physical interaction, and other nonverbal cues. Only after a preverbal concept is formed can children learn a verbal label for that concept (Macnamara, 1972; Nelson, Rescorla, Grundel, & Benedict, 1978).

Over time, children increasingly rely on linguistic information. This reliance is central to the formal education system in which oral and written language models serve as the primary modes of knowledge transmission. Obviously, there is considerable developmental difference between a 1-year-old who learns that Mommy's label *cup* refers to a group of objects that she uses daily and a 12-year-old who is able to develop an accurate understanding of the word *justice* by reading a definition of the word and some examples of its use in an English workbook. This later-developing form of learning is called *intraverbal* learning. Intraverbal learning refers to a process in which language is used to acquire further language. Intraverbal learning is inherently efficient as it does not depend on direct experience. In addition, certain classes of abstract words, such as *justice* and *stepson*, can be verbally defined but are not easily demonstrated via concrete referents. Research in the Piagetian tradition (e.g., Werner & Kaplan, 1952) suggests that preoperational children are poor intraverbal learners because they lack requisite cognitive skills. Other research has demonstrated that younger children do show some intraverbal learning ability. For example, if a 5- to 7-year-old is told that "A *mib* is a bird", he or she can appropriately infer that *mibs* have wings (Harris, 1975).

Research from our laboratory has explored the early emergence of intraverbal learning in 3- and 4-year-old children (DeBaryshe & Whitehurst, 1986). Children were either shown pictures illustrating novel concepts (e.g., *kiwi*, *scythe*) or they were told verbal definitions of the concepts. The verbal definitions contained information about key physical and functional properties of the concepts. An additional manipulation consisted of including or omitting information about the superordinate category of the concept (e.g., "A *kiwi* is a kind of bird.").

Results indicated that young children can profit from intraverbal information. Children who heard verbal definitions could later recognize pictures of the novel concepts. The 4-year-olds could also make verbal inferences concerning superordinate category membership (e.g., they could infer that a *kiwi* is a bird); this was true even in the condition in which the verbal definition specifically omitted category information. Thus, intraverbal input augmented both perceptual and linguistic knowledge. In contrast, children who only saw pictures of the novel concepts did not show any cross-modal benefit. These children could identify new pictures of the same concepts, but could not make any verbal inferences about them.

The ability to gain conceptual knowledge from purely verbal sources is an important skill. Our research suggests that elementary forms of this ability appear by age 3. Gelman and Markman (1986) have demonstrated related abilities by at least age 4. Further research is needed to specify what characteristics of the child as a learning system are responsible for the increasing ability to abstract information from verbal models and to utilize this information in a variety of knowledge domains.

11.2.3 Developmental Level, Rule Knowledge, and Strategy Use

A large body of research on metacognition and metacommunication (e.g, Flavell, 1981) has considered the effects of system variables such as cognitive goals, knowledge base, strategy use, and metacognitive monitoring on children's cognitive and linguistic performance. The effects of system variables on learning language through observation are nowhere clearer than in studies in which children's existing knowledge of linguistic rules can be shown to interact with models of language use. Studies of children's referential communication skills provide excellent examples of this interaction.

In the referential communication paradigm, children attempt to describe a target object from an array with sufficient specificity to allow a listener to select that target object correctly. Whitehurst and Sonnenschein (1985) have summarized research showing that most preschoolers do not know the *difference rule* of referential communication. The difference rule states that a good message should describe how a referent is different from other objects with which it appears. When children do not know the difference rule, they are as likely to describe features that a referent and foils have in common, as they are to describe features that are unique to the referent. This, in turn, affects what the child learns from adult models of communication.

In a study by Whitehurst, Sonnenschein, and Ianfolla (1981), first graders were exposed to models of effective referential communication. After such exposure, children produced longer communications, but the features that they added to their description of referents were not more informative than would have been expected by chance. Thus, children who did not know the difference rule attended to the length and not to the informativeness of the model's communication.

These examples illustrate how the child's developing knowledge of rules and strategies for approaching learning tasks comes to play an increasingly large role in modulating and mediating the effects of associative and operant learning variables. However, systematic investigation of children's metalinguistic abilities has largely been limited to referential communication tasks; the role played by these variables (as well as system by learning variable interactions) across language tasks remains to be explored.

11.3 Task Variables

In our tripartite division of observational variables in language acquisition, we have considered learning variables and system variables. We now consider task variables. Unfortunately, there is a paucity of research comparing observational learning processes across different language tasks.

11.3.1 Reception and Expression

We wish to focus on one task variable that is particularly relevant to issues of observational learning and imitation: reception versus expression. Typically, comprehension and production tasks are viewed as tapping the same underlying conceptual knowledge. In contrast, we propose that it is more accurate to conceptualize comprehension and production as potentially overlapping, but separable skills (see also Speidel, Chapter 8). This raises a number of questions concerning whether different variables are important in the acquisition of receptive and expressive skills and the mechanisms through which children learn to coordinate knowledge from the two domains.

11.3.1.1 Variables in Reception and Expression

We have previously presented research suggesting that associative variables are more important in learning receptive skills and operant variables are more important in learning expressive skills. For example, in Whitehurst and Valdez-Menchaca's (1988) study of reinforcement in the acquisition of foreign vocabulary, essentially no expressive skills emerged in the absence of reinforcement for production. This was true for measures of spontaneous production during the training sessions as well as for formal tests of foreign word production. In contrast, performance on a formal receptive vocabulary test was above chance, even in the absence of reinforcement during training. In other words, simply hearing an adult label an object was sufficient for children to be able to point to that object when they later heard its label. But this did not lead to corresponding levels of expressive ability.

Similar effects were found in a study by Whitehurst et al. (1982) in which the temporal contiguity between novel words and their referents was varied. Tests of reception and production of the novel vocabulary items were conducted. In all conditions of contiguity, receptive performance was substantially above chance levels. Expressive abilities were substantially below receptive abilities for each word tested, and expressive abilities exceeded chance for only one of the conditions of contiguity. In other words, high levels of receptive skills occurred solely on the basis of optimal associative pairing. Expressive abilities did not emerge based on associative pairing, nor did receptive skill automatically lead to expressive skill.

That transfer between receptive skill and expressive skill is not automatic is illustrated dramatically by the existence of significant numbers of children with specific expressive-language delay. These are children, as described previously, who have age-appropriate receptive skills, but who have minimal to nonexistent expressive skills. When these children begin to develop expressive skills, as nearly all do at some point during the preschool years, their development of these skills is gradual rather than immediate (Whitehurst, Fischel, Caulfield, et al., 1988). This phenomenon conflicts with the unitary competence model in which reception and expression are seen as reflecting the same underlying knowledge.

In the normal course of language acquisition, receptive skills emerge before corresponding expressive skills, particularly at younger ages (Fraser, Bellugi, & Brown, 1963; Lovell & Dixon, 1967; McCarthy, 1954; Whitehurst, 1977). Evidence from training studies in which new vocabulary items are introduced also suggests an asymmetry between the comprehension and production domains.

For example, Ruder, Hermann, and Schiefelbusch (1977) trained first- and second-grade children to a criterion of 100% correct responding on comprehension trials for initially novel vocabulary items; even at this high level of comprehension performance; however, children responded correctly to only 25% to 50% of verbal production probe trials. However, Cuvo and Riva (1980) found that normally developing 5-year-olds and mentally retarded adolescents who demonstrated perfect performance on a trained comprehension task also achieved a 75% correct performance on a production. Outcome differences may lie in the procedures; Ruder et al.'s subjects were prevented from engaging in spontaneous verbal rehearsal during comprehension training, and Cuvo and Riva's subjects were exposed to hundreds of comprehension training trials. In contrast to the Ruder et al. and the Cuvo and Riva works, the strong lack of expressive transfer found in our own studies is probably related to both the younger age of our subjects and to the smaller number of training trials.

Thus, we suggest that age and exposure are related to children's ability to integrate receptive and expressive knowledge. Younger children should have more difficulty with this task, and require more exposure before transfer can be achieved. Cuvo and Riva (1980) also suggest that task difficulty affects coordination of receptive and expressive skills. In a discussion of unpublished data from their laboratory, generalization from comprehension to production was reported for one-syllable but not for two-syllable responses. Nelson (1982) and Leonard & Schwartz (1985) have discussed other variables that may help explain the substantial variation that obtains across studies and subjects in comprehension-versus-production levels.

Our position is that receptive skill and expressive skill for language are at the outset largely independent for most children. At some point normal children learn to utilize receptive knowledge in expression, and vice versa. This development may well be a product of learning history rather than an automatic process. For example, Valdez-Menchaca and Whitehurst (1987) have shown that the length of the delay that adults interpose between asking a child a *wh-* question and providing the answer for that question is strongly related to expressive skill, with longer delays associated with more spontaneous expression by the child. We believe that substantial dividends will be paid by attending to the experiential precursors and prerequisites of receptive-expressive transfer.

11.4 Final Discussion

We have presented a conceptual approach in which language development is viewed as one instance of the observational learning of a complex skill. Three important classes of relevant variables were defined. Learning variables are those principles of associative and operant conditioning that describe how environmental conditions affect the acquisition of new language skills. Adult language models have been shown to be most beneficial to children when they are presented in a fashion that optimizes conditions of associative and operant learning. System variables refer to those characteristics of the child that affect his or her success at observational learning from language models. Some system variables are developmental in origin, whereas others are due to individual difference factors or result from learning history. Finally, task variables refer to characteristics of different language skills that make them more or less easily learned.

For purposes of clarity, we presented learning, system, and task variables as if they were separable entities. In reality, these variables are intertwined and influence each other reciprocally. We have given several examples of interaction between these classes of variables. A comprehensive account of in vivo language acquisition and language use must take a dynamic point of view even though components of a more complex whole may be individually examined for heuristic reasons.

Although the topic of this volume is the role of imitation in language development, we have chosen to avoid the problems associated with a response-based definition of imitation in favor of framing the more general question of how children learn language from others. We have argued that conceptualizing imitation as a functional relation between a modeled behavior and a subsequent response opens the possibility of explaining a wider range of linguistic achievements as well as a wider range of acquisition paths.

This strategy requires an experimental rather than a descriptive approach. Instead of looking at the child's response and asking whether or not it is imitative, controlled language models are presented to the child in order to determine if the child's language changes as a result. If it does, as determined through comparison with a control condition, we can say that the child has learned through imitation (or, as we prefer to say, through observational learning). Experimental manipulation of individual learning, system, and task variables may be used to verify each component of the overall model. This approach is promising, as we believe the research reviewed above demonstrates, because it allows the application of simple but powerful explanatory principles to the complex and little-understood phenomenon of language acquisition.

We are reminded of the old joke about there being two theories of language acquisition: one making the process a mystery, and the other making it impossible. We expect that most readers would place our treatment in the category of the impossible theory because of the relative simplicity of the variables on which we call and because we do not build our explanations on rule-based cognitive processes in the head of the child. If the reader is not convinced of the power of explanations based on "simple" associative and feedback mechanisms from the preceding review of our own research, we invite consideration of the successes of related lines of research and theory: Rumelhart and McClelland (1986) have demonstrated that the developmental data involving children's acquisition of the past tenses of English verbs (such as initial acquisition of irregular verbs and subsequent overregularization of regular verbs) can be reproduced in a simple pattern associator neural network model. Input to the model consists of naturally occurring frequencies of regular and irregular verbs (e.g., irregular verbs are fewer in number but occur more frequently than individual regular verbs). Output from the pattern associator is compared with an ideal model of performance, and connection strengths within the neural model are adjusted incrementally to minimize errors. The model learns gradually, goes through a stage of overregularization, and can eventually provide correct past-tense endings for regular verbs that were never encountered in training. There are no rules of any type to be found anywhere within the neural model. We do not propose that children actually learn past-tense endings in the form of the particulars of Rumelhart and McClelland's neural model. For example, the network includes no mechanism for external feedback and incorporates a perfect representation of correct forms against which output can be compared. Children, however, do receive feedback in acquiring grammar, as we have reviewed previously, and there is no evidence that their acquisition of productive competence depends on a perfect internal standard of performance. These details aside, the Rumelhart and McClelland work demonstrates convincingly that complex linguistic phenomena can be modeled by simple associative mechanisms.

A related line of work involves Bates and MacWhinney's (1987) Competition Model. Here the child's use of words in their correct syntactic roles is a combinatorial function of the strength of various stimulus cues within the sentences to which the child is exposed. For instance, in learning to decline the German definite article, young children have available a number of probabilistic cues to the gender, number, and case of the words to which they are exposed, for example, words ending in -e tend to be of feminine gender. However, these cues are seldom perfectly reliable, are sometimes not available, and may be in conflict. In the Competition Model, the strength of individual cues is a function of their validity (i.e, the proportion of time a cue is present and provides correct information). There have been a number of demonstrations that naturalistic data on acquisition of complex linguistic abilities, such as declension of the German definite article, can be accounted for within the Competition Model (Bates & MacWhinney, 1987). Note that the mechanisms within the Competition Model are entirely associative and depend on an informational analysis of stimulus functions that is very similar to the one to which we have appealed in our model of observational learning.

The principles involved in the observational learning of language are simple, but life and language are not. The challenge, which we believe is characteristic of the scientific enterprise, is to make the mysterious understandable in terms that are mundane.

Acknowledgments. This work has been supported by Grand HD19245 from the National Institute of Child Health and Human Development to the senior author, and by grants of equipment from NEC Telephones, Inc.

References

Bandura, A. (1977). *Social learning theory.* Englewood Cliffs, NJ: Prentice-Hall.

Bates, E., & MacWhinney, B. (1987). Competition, variation, and language learning. In B. MacWhinney (Ed.), *Mechanisms of language acquisition* (pp. 157–193). Hillsdale, NJ: Erlbaum.

Bell, R.Q. (1968). A reinterpretation of the direction of effects in studies of socialization. *Psychological Review, 75,* 81–95.

Bohannon, J.N., III, & Marquis, A.L.(1977). Children's control of adult speech. *Child Development, 48,* 1002–1008.

Brown, R. (1973). *A first language: The early stages.* Cambridge, MA: Harvard University Press.

Brown, R., & Hanlon, C. (1970). Derivational complexity and order of acquisition in child speech. In J.R. Hayes (Ed.), *Cognition and the development of language* (pp. 155–207). New York: Wiley.

Chomsky, N. (1959). [Review of B.F. Skinner's *Verbal Behavior*]. *Language*, *35*, 26–58.

Cuvo, A.J., & Riva, M.T. (1980). Generalization and transfer between comprehension and production: A comparison of retarded and nonretarded persons. *Journal of Applied Behavior Analysis*, *13*, 315–331.

DeBaryshe, B.D., & Whitehurst, G.J. (1986). Intraverbal acquisition of semantic concepts by preschoolers. *Journal of Experimental Child Psychology*, *42*, 169–186.

Dollaghan, C. (1985). Child meets word: "Fast mapping" in preschool children. *Journal of Speech and Hearing Research*, *28*, 449–454.

Falco, F.L. (1986). *Social linguistic determinants of language development and delay*. Unpublished doctoral dissertation. State University of New York at Stony Brook.

Flavell, J.H. (1981). Cognitive monitoring. In W.P. Dickson (Ed.), *Children's oral communication skills* (pp. 35–60). New York: Academic Press.

Fraser, C., Bellugi, U., & Brown, R. (1963). Control of grammar in imitation, comprehension, and production. *Journal of Verbal Learning and Verbal Behavior*, *2*, 121–135.

Gardner, R.A., & Gardner, B.T. (1988). Feedforward vs feedbackward: An ethological alternative to the law of effect. *Behavioral and Brain Sciences*, *11*, 429–430.

Gelman, S.A. & Markman, E.M. (1986). Categories and induction in young children. *Cognition*, *23*, 183–209.

Goldin-Meadow, S. (1982). The resilience of recursion: A study of a communication system developed without a conventional language model. In E. Wanner & L. Gleitman (Eds.), *Language acquisition: The state of the art*. Cambridge; MA: Cambridge University Press.

Goldin-Meadow, S., & Feldman, H. (1977). The development of language-like communication without a language model. *Science*, *197*, 401–403.

Harris, P. (1975). Inferences and semantic development. *Journal of Child Language*, *2*, 143–152.

Hirsh-Pasek, K., Treiman, R., & Schneiderman, M. (1984). Brown and Hanlon revisited: Mother's sensitivity to grammatical forms. *Journal of Child Language*, *11*, 81–88.

Kamin, L.J. (1969). Predictability, surprise, attention and conditioning. In B.A. Campbell & R.M. Church (Eds.), *Punishment and aversive behavior* (pp. 279–296). New York: Appleton-Century-Crofts.

Kaye, K. (1979). The development of skills. In G.J. Whitehurst & B.J. Zimmerman (Eds.), *The functions of language and cognition* (pp. 23–55). New York: Academic Press.

Leonard, L.B., & Schwartz, R.G. (1985). Early linguistic development of children with specific language impairment. In K.E. Nelson (Ed.), *Children's language* (Vol. 5, pp. 291–318). Hillsdale, NJ: Erlbaum.

Lovell, K., & Dixon, E.M. (1967). The growth of the control of grammar in imitation, comprehension, and production. *Journal of Child Psychology and Psychiatry*, *8*, 31–39.

Macnamara, J. (1972). Cognitive basis of language learning in infants. *Psychological Review*, *79*, 1–13.

Maratsos, M. (1983). Some current issues in the study of the acquisition of grammar. In P. H. Mussen (Ed.), *Handbook of child psychology* (4th ed., pp. 707–786). New York: Wiley.

Masur, E.F. (1982). Mothers' responses to infants' object related gestures: Influences on lexical development. *Journal of Child Language*, *9*, 223–230.

McCarthy, D. (1954). Language development in children. In L. Carmichael (Ed.), *Manual of child psychology* (2nd ed., pp. 492–630). New York: Wiley.

Moerk, E.L. (1986). Environmental factors in early language acquisition. In G.J. White-hurst (Ed.), *Annals of child development* (Vol. 3, pp. 191–236). Greenwich, CT:JAI Press.

Nelson, K. (1973). Structure and strategy in learning to talk. *Monographs of the Society for Research in Child Development, 38*, (Serial Nos. 1–2).

Nelson, K., Rescorla, L., Grundel, J.M., & Benedict, H. (1978). Early lexicons: What do they mean? *Child Development, 49*, 960–968.

Nelson, K.E. (1982). Experimental gambits in the service of language-acquisition theory: From the Fiffin project to operation input swap. In S. Kuczaj (Ed.), *Language development. Vol. 1: Syntax and semantics* (pp. 159–199). Hillsdale, NJ: Erlbaum.

Ninio, A. (1983). Joint book reading as a multiple vocabulary acquisition device. *Developmental Psychology, 19*, 445–451.

Pavlov, I.P. (1927). *Conditioned reflexes.* Oxford: Oxford University Press.

Penner, S.G. (1987). Parental responses to grammatical and ungrammatical utterances. *Child Development, 58*, 376–384.

Rescorla, R.A. (1980). *Pavlovian second-order conditioning.* Hillsdale, NJ: Erlbaum.

Rondal, A.J. (1985). *Adult-child interaction and the process of language acquisition.* New York: Praeger.

Ruder, K.F., Hermann, P., & Schiefelbusch, R.L. (1977). Effects of verbal imitation and comprehension training on verbal production. *Journal of Psycholinguistic Research, 6*, 59–72.

Rumelhart, D.E., & McClelland, J.L. (1986). On learning the past tenses of verbs. In J.L. McClelland, D.E. Rumelhart, & the PDP Research Group (Eds.), *Parallel distributed processing: Explorations in the microstructure of cognition. Volume 2: Psychological and biological models* (pp. 216–271). Cambridge, MA: The MIT Press.

Skinner, B.F. (1957). *Verbal Behavior.* New York: Appleton-Century-Crofts.

Snow, C.E. (1981). The uses of imitation. *Journal of Child Language, 8*, 205–212.

Snow. C.E. (1983). Saying it again: The role of expanded and deferred imitations in language acquisition. In K.E. Nelson (Ed.), *Child language* (Vol. 4, pp. 29–58). New York: Gardner Press.

Sokolov, E.N. (1960). Neuronal models and the orienting reflex. In M.A.B. Brazier (Ed.), *The central nervous system and behavior.* New York: Josiah Macy, Jr., Foundation.

Stewart, D.M., & Hamilton, M.L. (1976). Imitation as a learning strategy in the acquisition of vocabulary. *Journal of Experimental Child Psychology, 21*, 380–392.

Stine, E.L., & Bohannon, J.N., III (1983). Interaction, imitations, and language acquisition. *Journal of Child Language, 10*, 589–603.

Tomasello, M., & Todd, J. (1983). Joint attention and lexical acquisition style. *First Language, 4*, 197–212.

Valdez-Menchaca, M.C., & Whitehurst, G.J. (1987). *The role of time delay in spontaneous language production.* Unpublished manuscript. State University of New York at Stony Brook.

Valdez-Menchaca, M.C., & Whitehurst, G.J. (1988). The effects of incidental teaching on vocabulary acquisition by young children. *Child Development, 59*, 1451–1459.

Werner, H., & Kaplan, E. (1952). The acquisition of word meanings: A developmental study. *Monographs for the Society for Research on Child Development, 15* (Serial No. 51).

Whitehurst, G.J. (1977). Comprehension, selective imitation, and the CIP hypothesis. *Journal of Experimental Child Psychology, 23*, 23–38.

Whitehurst, G.J. (1978). Observational learning. In A.C. Catania & T.A. Brigham (Eds.), *Handbook of applied behavior analysis: Social and instructional processes* (pp. 142–178). New York: Irvington.

Whitehurst, G.J. (1979). Meaning and semantics. In G.J. Whitehurst & B.J. Zimmerman (Eds.), *The functions of language and cognition* (pp.115–139). New York: Academic Press.

Whitehurst, G.J. (1982). Language development. In B.B. Wolman (Ed.), *Handbook of developmental psychology* (pp. 367–386). Englewood Cliffs, NJ: Prentice-Hall.

Whitehurst, G.J. (1985, April). The role of imitation in language learning by children with language delay. In G.E. Speidel (Chair), *The many faces of imitation.* Symposium conducted at the biennial meeting of the Society for Research in Child Development, Toronto, Canada.

Whitehurst, G.J., Falco, F.L., Fischel, J.E., Lonigan, C., Valdez-Menchaca, M.C., DeBaryshe, B.D., & Caulfield, M.B. (1989). Accelerating language development through picture book reading. *Developmental Psychology, 24,* 552–559.

Whitehurst, G.J., & Fischel, J.E. (1988). Feedback in the acquisition of language and other complex behavior. *Behavioral and Brain Sciences, 11,* 478–479.

Whitehurst, G.J., Fischel, J.E., Caulfield, M., DeBaryshe, B., & Valdez-Menchaca, M.C. (1989). Assessment and treatment of early expressive language delay. In P. Zelazo & R.Barr (Eds.), *Challenges to developmental paradigms. Implications for theory, assessment and treatment.* Hillsdale, NJ: Erlbaum.

Whitehurst, G.J., Fischel, J.E., Lonigan, C.J., Valdez-Menchaca, M.C., & DeBaryshe, B. D., & Caulfield, M.B. (1988). Verbal interaction in families of normal and expressive language delayed children. *Developmental Psychology, 24,* 690–699.

Whitehurst, G.J., Kedesdy, J., & White, T.G. (1982). A functional analysis of meaning. In S.A. Kuczaj (Ed.), *Language development. Volume 1: Syntax and semantics* (pp. 397–427). Hillsdale, NJ: Erlbaum.

Whitehurst, G.J., & Sonnenschein, S. (1985). The development of communication: A functional analysis. In G.J. Whitehurst (Ed.), *Annals of child development* (Vol. 2). Greenwich, CT: JAI Press.

Whitehurst, G.J., Sonnenschein, S., & Ianfolla, B.J. (1981). Learning to communicate from models: Children confuse length with information. *Child Development, 52,* 507–513.

Whitehurst, G.J., & Valdez-Menchaca, M.C. (1988). What is the role of reinforcement in early language acquisition? *Child Development, 59,* 430–440.

Whitehurst, G.J., & Vasta, R. (1975). Is language acquired through imitation? *Journal of Psycholinguistic Research, 4,* 37–59.

CHAPTER 12

The Fuzzy Set Called "Imitations"

Ernst L. Moerk

> The mere fact that the child learns the language of
> his environment is evidence of the importance of
> imitation.
>
> (McCarthy, 1954, p. 517)

This chapter has two goals, one major and one ancillary: First, it will share in the endeavors of the other contributors to this book by analyzing and crystallizing the concept of "imitation" that was taken over as an "unexamined concept" (Kaplan, 1964) from everyday language. It is hoped that the combined conceptual analyses will differentiate and precisely specify the domain. In addition to this attempt at conceptual clarification, brief selections from parent-child interactions will demonstrate the usefulness of some of the differentiations and distinctions suggested. Neither conceptual nor factual exhaustiveness in the treatment of this complex topic can be the goal of a single essay. Such a result might be attained by the integration of all the contributions of this book, which in their diversity and broad range are more than the sum of their parts.

12.1 A Set-Theoretical Conceptualization of Imitation

The conceptual domain of imitation in its relationship to other domains can advantageously be represented by a Venn diagram (see Figure 12-1).

Imitation encompasses, obviously, a perceptual and a behavioral aspect. Incorporating some restrictions of the domain, namely, to areas of learning, these aspects are referred to in Figure 12-1 as "perceptual learning" and "learning through doing." Both of these large domains require a few words of highly selective comments.

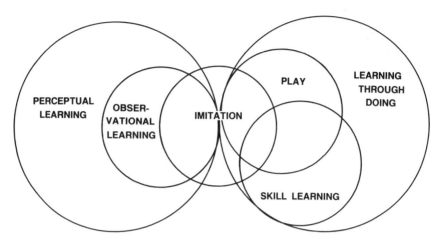

Figure 12-1. A Venn diagram of psychological processes involved in imitation.

12.1.1 Perceptual Learning

The innovative proposals of James and Eleanor Gibson, especially their emphasis on "affordances" (e.g., E.J. Gibson, 1969; J.J. Gibson, 1966, 1982) appear to offer conceptual bases for the analysis of "imitational" phenomena. In brief, the argument of the Gibsons that appears to have great value for the field of language acquisition, including the processes of imitation, is the following: Almost all the environmental givens are structured, that is, they entail information. If the organism explores and understands these environmental givens, it necessarily has to absorb this information and the environmental structures. The Gibsons have pointed out in detail how information-rich the environment is—if it is conceived correctly, that is, relationally. They also have shown that all observational learning inevitably involves pattern abstraction. Their emphasis can, therefore, provide a valuable counterpoint to the argument about the presumably degenerate input that was so fashionable recently among psycholinguists. It also suggests that the abstraction of structures, whether syntactic or otherwise, is far less extraordinary than often asserted and that imitation will largely be structural, whether it pertains to the structure of a single act, of a single word, or of an entire sentence.

12.1.2 Learning Through Doing

The term *enactive learning* might have expressed this aspect more elegantly, but this term has been preempted by Bandura (1986) for the behavioristic approach. As the two subsets of "learning through doing" in Figure 12-1 indicate, the emphasis in the present discussion is quite different. Both play and skill learning are generally more complex than the behavioristic stimulus-response learning;

they proceed largely without direct reward; finally, they are quite often spontaneous and not reactive. A good deal of creativity and flexibility is entailed in both.

The skill-learning aspect in its relationship to language acquisition has recently been discussed in detail by Moerk (1986). The function of play in language has received wide attention. Articles by Kuczaj (1982), Cazden (1976), and Garvey (1977) are more recent examples. But the extensive descriptions of language play provided by Weir (1962) and by Chukovsky (1963) are especially noteworthy. They provide ample evidence that language play is largely derived from input fragments that have been stored and are replayed with variations on the theme. The same applies to most social play of animal and human offspring (cf. Bruner, Joley, & Sylva, 1976; Tizard & Harvey, 1977). A careful integration of research on play and verbal imitation will need to explore the many commonalities of both fields.

One aspect of imitation deserves special emphasis because it has often been neglected. Whether it is the evidence from skill learning, the old saying that one learns best by teaching something, or the diverse drills employed in all training endeavors, all suggest that *doing* something has a special value in *learning* something. Whether it contributes to more refined mastery of the skill, to longer-lasting retention, or to its increasing automaticity and economy, the contribution is important indeed. Snow (1983) reported an intriguing pertinent finding: If her subject immediately imitated a maternal utterance about a picture book, he uttered the same statement in 51.7% of the instances when the same picture was viewed again later. If he did not immediately imitate, he only mentioned it later in 23.1% of the cases. A strong impact upon long-lasting retention is suggested by this report. Besides Snow's report, relatively little research exists on these special effects of productive use on first language acquisition, and much of it (e.g., Schwartz & Leonard, 1985) is marred by the problem of how to define *imitation* and to differentiate it from *spontaneous productions*. Depth of processing, that is, the fact that production generally involves both semantic/structural and detailed phonological processing, compared with more superficial processing in comprehension, might be the main causal factor. Yet, the involvement of different brain structures in knowledge acquisition, and therewith of different types of learning and memory (i.e., procedural vs. declarative knowledge), as elaborated by Tulving (1984), certainly needs to be considered too.

The enactive aspect of imitation seems to have additional and essential functions in language acquisition. Spoken language is an extremely fleeting and transient stimulus; even in the nursery, considerable intervals between adult displays of the same stimulus, whether a word or a specific sentence, are common. Often only one model is available in echoic or short-term memory for possible analysis. For a child to analyze new and unknown aspects of an utterance during the very brief interval while it is perceived would mean that complex abstraction processes have to be performed within seconds and on the basis of one exemplar. However, immediate imitation of the acoustic stimulus will keep it available for a longer interval. This will also contribute to the storage of the stimulus for somewhat delayed comparisons and will, in both instances, make it available for deeper processing, whether on the semantic or the syntactic level. Examples of these almost indispensable contributions of imitation will be presented in a later section.

12.1.3 Observational Learning

Returning to the Venn diagram of Figure 12-1, a few further remarks are required pertaining to the relationship of imitation to observational learning. The theory of observational learning, or "modeling," as elaborated by Bandura (e.g., 1986) can provide several contributions to the explanation of first language acquisition. Observational learning mainly pertains to observations of the actions of cospecies members. Those actions are necessarily patterned. Gibson's argument regarding the wealth of information in the structure of environmental stimuli therefore also applies to these behavior patterns. The learner, in observing and understanding these actions, must therefore learn to abstract their structures.

Another important aspect, elaborated in the field of observational learning, is Bandura's careful distinction between the acquisition of a modeled act and its possibly very delayed performance. A range of studies has shown that an act can be imitative even in the absence of an immediate model and even if it does not exactly match the temporally remote model. These findings provide close analogies to *delayed imitations* in language acquisition and to the incorporation of these verbal imitations in productions of increasing spontaneity.

Furthermore, a systematic contrast in language has to have important consequences for observational language learning: With the possible exception of a very limited number of rigid formulas, at any stage of learning the input frequency of individual utterances will be much lower than the frequency of the underlying pattern, such as the S-V-O pattern, reflected in most of these utterances. It should therefore be considerably easier to learn the common pattern than individual behavioral strings through observational learning. In the same manner, a melody, which remains the same over stanzas, is learned more easily than any or all the stanzas of a song, which change. Refrains are learned earlier than the changing texts of stanzas. Note also the structural regularities of the metric verse and the standing, often repeated, formulas that served as productive props for ancient bards, as in Homeric verse (Kirk, 1976). Similar findings are commonly reported with respect to first language learning: Infants reproduce intonational contours (cf. Peters, 1983) before they have learned a single multiword utterance. Later, patterned constructions, such as the so-called Pivot-Open constructions, appear early and are used as molds for an increasing range of specific utterances.

12.1.4 The Overlapping Sets

A final glance at Figure 12-1 can summarize the argument presented: Imitation is a subset of behaviors that derives from the intersection with a perceptual and an enactive set. On the enactive side, skill learning and play have been explored in considerable detail. On the perceptual side, Bandura's social learning theory has been applied consistently to language acquisition (e.g., Bandura, 1986; Bandura & Harris, 1966). Yet the Gibsons' lucid analyses of the relational nature of information and the wealth of the quite directly discernible information have been only minimally applied to the conceptualization of language acquisition. All of these fields, and possibly more, will have to be integrated for a fuller understanding of imitation.

Having sketched out the conceptual relations of imitation to other domains of psychological functioning and research, I will focus on the phenomenon of imitation itself. With a phenomenon as complex as imitation, a choice between breadth of coverage and depth of analysis has to be made. I will emphasize detailed analyses, although this delimits the scope of the domain. I will only focus on verbal imitation and will only analyze *filial* imitations. This excludes the broad range of parental imitations and their function in language transmission and in filial language acquisition.[1]

Even within filial imitations, the motivational aspects as well as the pragmatic aspects will be neglected in order to concentrate fully on informational aspects. Admittedly, the borderline between informational and pragmatic functions is not fully definitive. As Bohannon and Warren-Leubecker (1985) have pointed out, filial imitation is often a signal of only partial comprehension and serves thereby a pragmatic function. Considering that children often imitate new and unknown words (Brown, 1973; Ryan, 1973), imitation seems to serve, in certain cases, as a signal for complete lack of comprehension. This signal is then mostly responded to by parents in performing the repair sequences needed to clarify the new items. The conversational and pragmatic use of imitations leads, therefore, in this case often to the acquisition of new information. Partial, partially incorrect, or uncomprehending imitations by children could mainly serve a pragmatic function for the children; that is, they could serve as a placeholder in the turn-taking sequence of discourse. Yet, they could be taken by the parent as a signal that repair processes and further clarifications are required. In brief, the emphasis of the present analysis will be on how imitations contribute to new learning and rehearsal of learned items, although this emphasis is not intended to denigrate pragmatic and conversational aspects.

12.2 Developmental and Process-Based Aspects of Imitation

12.2.1 Changes in the Product

It is known since Valentine's (1930) report that imitation is subject to a process of learning, that is, change. Piaget (1951) argued that it differs qualitatively at

---

[1]The term *filial* will be generally employed instead of the Saxon Genitives *the child's* and *the children's* or the prepositional phrases *of the children*. *Filial* matches not only etymologically the terms *parental*, *maternal*, and *paternal*, it also better fits its three-syllable counterparts stylistically and rhythmically.

diverse levels of development, depending partially on maturational factors, and on adult modeling of this strategy and adult feedback to earlier imitations. Lewis (1936) has indicated the same conceptualization, arguing that early imitation is only rudimentary and that linguistic imitation grows and changes while language itself grows. He saw this change proceeding from mere echoing to the establishment of templates for the creation of new utterances, a conceptualization that closely matches more recent "depth-of-processing" formulations.

Findings presented by Meltzoff and Moore (1977) and research derived from the subsequent controversy about the earliest appearance of imitation, has contributed some evidence about the preverbal development of imitation. A brief consideration of the contrast between Piaget's (1951) conceptualization of imitation and Meltzoff and Moore's (1977) finding, integrated with Lewis's (1936) descriptions, suggests differences not only in time of appearance, but also in the character of imitation. A "levels of processing" conceptualization would capture these differences and could be applied fruitfully to various forms of imitation in language development. At one extreme, mere superficial processing could focus on the stimulus that results in more or less reflexive sound productions of newborns. During later periods and after the beginning of language acquisition, templates or structures could be abstracted in the process of imitation, reflecting several advances in depth of processing.

12.2.2 Changes in the Process

For verbal imitation four major levels of processing seem to be implied by the diverse studies:

(1) on the phonetic/phonemic level without any deeper processing;
(2) on the semantic/formulaic level, which includes at least partial comprehension, for example, of the function of a phrase in a context;
(3) on the level of morphology, involving the distinct comprehension and full reproduction of free morphemes and increasingly some bound ones; and
(4) on the level of syntax, involving the analysis of underlying syntactic structures and the grasp of grammatical principles.

Bloom, Hood, and Lightbown (1974) and Clark (1977) have reported that children are especially prone to imitate those linguistic items that they only partly understand (level (2)). Additionally, Brown (1973) and Ryan (1973) reported that children preferentially imitated unknown items (level (1)). Kagan, Kearsley, and Zelazo (1978) suggested cognitive discrepancy as the underlying motivational principle, a suggestion that is well supported by the report of Watson and Fischer (1977). Their subjects imitated pretend behavior (levels (2) or (3)) at or near their highest cognitive capacity and ignored those they had long mastered.

Because cognitive mastery, and therewith cognitive discrepancy, changes with development, the types of predominant imitation would be expected to change too. In the course of language development, level (1) imitations would, necessarily, have to be more predominant during the early stages, and level (3) and (4) imitations would appear later. Moreover, the processes underlying imitation of the same item could also change microgenetically. At any age, imitation might be employed first to retain a new model in short-term memory (level (1)) and then to analyze it further (levels (3) and (4)). Examples that suggest such progressive changes will be provided when the temporal dimension of imitation is discussed below.

It follows from these considerations that different learning consequences would derive from the diverse levels of imitation. Anderson's (1983) report from his child and his computer program provides support for these diverse consequences. In both cases "initial utterances are repeats of sequences in the adult model; only later do they [the child and the program] come up with novel utterances" (Anderson, 1983, p. 294), that is, learning proceeds from rote to creative. These complex developmental and microgenetic aspects will be touched upon and exemplified later in this essay. The analyses will suggest that imitation might be a strategy that is acquired and applied by children as a learning tool for increasingly varied domains. It might, therefore, entail a considerable variety of processing levels (Moerk, 1985b).

12.3 Major Dimensions of Imitation

Whether it is Clark (1977), Snow (1981), Kuczaj (1983), Speidel and Herreshoff (1985; Chapter 8, this volume), or many others, all recognized that the so-called imitations often vary on two dimensions: (1) the dimension of similarity and (2) the temporal dimension. Imitations can be topographically identical or almost identical (a distinction that will be clarified below); they can differ to varying degrees from the model, and they can follow immediately after the model(s) or be delayed for considerable periods.

12.3.1 The Temporal Dimension

Although the focus will be on the varying degrees of similarity between model and matching response, a brief consideration of the temporal dimension is necessary because of frequent relationships between similarity and temporal lag of imitations.

The temporal dimension entails in itself several aspects:

(1) It will happen only rarely that a modeled item will have been produced for the very first time within earshot of the child. In most cases, it will be a repetition of previously produced models. Their number and presentation, whether in massed or spaced form, and the intervals between lags will be important.
(2) In the same manner, the child's repetition of a specific modeled item will, with the exception of the very first attempt, always be a repetition of previous trials. Again, the temporal patterning of these learning trials needs to be

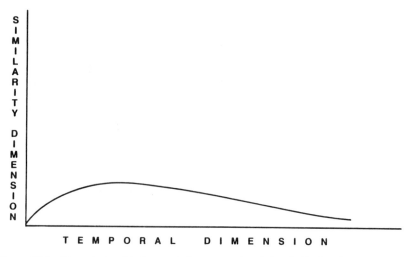

Figure 12-2. The relationship between the temporal and the similarity dimension of imitation.

explored. The effects of both the multiple models and multiple trials are reflected in the third aspect of the temporal dimension.

(3) The third aspect is the lag between one specific instance, or the last instantiation of a model, and the child's imitation. This aspect has received most attention. Several authors (e.g., Kaye & Marcus, 1978, 1981; Valentine, 1930) have reported a relationship between this interval and the degree of topographical similarity between model and imitation. Figure 12-2 represents the general trend of this relationship.

A gradual increase in similarity with increasing lag is suggested by Figure 12-2, followed by a period of maximum similarity, and then by an even more gradual decline in similarity over an extended period. Multiple specifications of this interdependency need, however, to be added: The early increase in similarity depends often on repeated attempts at mastering the modeled act, that is, a gradual "working up to" the standard set by the model. The slope of this ascending leg will partly depend on the "readiness" of the subject. The period of maximum similarity should depend on the degree of learning and on the types of item acquired. In the case of fixed routines, an asymptotic trend toward complete matching would be expected, and the formula would be retained permanently in unchanged form. In contrast, most other items are expected to decline in similarity. This decline would be either due to simple forgetting and could, therefore, serve to measure the degree of learning. Or it could be due to flexible adaptation of the new skill to changing communicational situations.

Several examples will suggest the interactional dynamics of these relationships, although detailed studies will be required to explore them fully. These examples provide suggestions about levels of processing and about the relationship between imitation and memory. They also indicate how fruitless it would be to dissect to continuous dimensions of time and learning into a dichotomy of immediate versus delayed imitation.

Table 12-1 provides one example from each of two children, Brown's Adam and Eve. Eve encounters for the first time the observer, Fraser. As an unknown person, he attracts her attention. His name is mentioned twice, and Eve responds with a distorted repetition: "Fraydiy." After two maternal corrective models, Eve improves in utterance 21 by changing the last vowel. Note that in all three maternal models, the word *Fraser* is in the recency position in the sentence, a fact that should simplify reception and short-term storage. Eve's improvement is rewarded with double praise, which leads to another try and another improvement: The consonant *s* is added. Another corrective feedback from the mother follows. Finally, after one page of intervening text, Eve utters twice "Fraser" with correct enunciation. Two accepting maternal imitations and a conditioned reward, "Yes," inform Eve of her success. Some 30 utterances later, Eve tests her newest acquisition, receives the needed feedback, and proceeds to incorporate the acquired element into a syntactic construction.

A fascinating sequence is encountered in this brief episode of around 120 utterances. First, we find a progress in imitation from inexact to exact, while Eve works up to this goal (cf. Kaye, 1982, for similar reports for younger ages). This is in contrast to the previous, often implicit assumption that immediate imitations would always be exact and delayed ones would entail changes. Second, we find Eve's progress from the mastery of the single element to its syntactic use; and this progress, in turn, is achieved through a double imitation: In the maternal utterances 112 and 113, the words *Fraser* and *water* are found in recency position and these two recently modeled words are combined by Eve into a two-word sequence, which is interpreted by her mother meaningfully as a subject-object construction. Briefly afterwards, the partners progress to "Fraser coffee," modeled first by the mother and imitated with reduction by Eve. Faulty imitation has, therewith, progressed to "exact imitation" and to "substituting imitation"; that is, the level of processing has changed in addition to the level of achievement.

The dynamics might, however, be even more entangled than suggested by Table 12-1. Briefly before this sequence, Eve's mother had uttered the following four syntactic constructions: "We . . . have lunch," "You . . . eat cracker," "You . . . want milk?," and "You had . . . juice." All four model the subject-object construction and the topic of eating/drinking, which Eve—according to the mother's interpretation—produced in "Fraser water." The dynamics might consequently include a case of "structural" and semantic imitation, although this could not be firmly asserted on the basis of one example.

Adam's interaction with his mother, in Table 12-1b, indicates complex interactions of diverse memory stores, as they affect the process of imitation. The mother models the words *diesel locomotive* and invites Adam to imitate her

Table 12-1. Processing in Short-Term Memory and Transition to Long-Term Storage

	Eve: Sample 1, Hour 1	
Utterance	Mother	Child
	(The name "Fraser" is mentioned twice.)	
14		Fraydiy
15	I think that was "Fraser."	
16		Fraydiy
17/18/19	What? Are you saying "Fraser?" "Mr. Fraser?"	
21		Fraydae
22/23	Yes, that's much better.	
24		Fraydsay
25	"Mr. Fraser?"	
	[*One page of text intervening*]	
67		There, Fraser
80		Fraser [*correct enunciation*]
81	Mr. Fraser, yes. Mr. Fraser.	
110		That?
111	What is that?	
112	That's Mr. Fraser.	
113	There, drink the water.	
114		Fraser water?
115/6	No, I don't think Mr. Fraser wants any water.	
117		(Oh) Fraser
123		Fraser water.
124/5	Will you ask Mr. Fraser if he'd like a drink of water?	
126		Fraser water.
128	Mr. Fraser has coffee.	
133		Coffee.
134/5	Yes, he's drinking his coffee.	
136		. . . Fraser coffee.
137/8	Right. That's Mr. Fraser's coffee.	

Table 12-1. *Continued.*

Adam: Sample 2, Hour 1	
Mother	Child
This is a diesel locomotive. Can you say that?	
	Diesel motor. No no moto.
[*Eight utterances intervening*] Modern steam locomotive	
	Motor.
Electric locomotive	
	(yeltric tomomotor);
[*Approximately 20 min*]	
	Motor. Boot [*meaning caboose*]
Locomotive?	
	Yeah, motor boot.
	Adam motor boot. Adam motor.

model. Whereas Adam has no problem with the word *diesel*, problems arise with his production of *locomotive*. Adam, with his great interest in everything even remotely resembling a car or truck, knows the word *motor*. Now, when he tries to imitate *locomotive*, an item from his long-term store interferes, and the result is *diesel motor*. This outcome is in conflict with the model to be imitated and Adam produces, therefore, a repair attempt. The elements added to the first product "diesel motor," namely, "no no moto," match the model "locomotive" in number of syllables, and the first three vowels are reproduced correctly, all being *o*s. The last vowel is assimilated to the item *motor* from long-term memory. These brief examples of filial imitations demonstrate the interaction between echoic store and long-term memory, and acoustic and rhythmic analysis, dynamics that can only be ascertained in microanalyses.

Eight utterances later, Adam's mother models "modern steam locomotive" and Adam's imitation is now exclusively shaped by his long-term store, although it was triggered by the maternal model. With three quite rare words, the model was probably too difficult for Adam to process. Yet, the following maternal model, "Electric locomotive," containing the more familiar word *electric* is imitated quite adequately by Adam as "(yeltric tomomotor)." This response entails multiple aspects: The parentheses indicate that it was not very loud and clear, suggesting processing problems; the repeated vowel *e* in the maternal model has been simplified, as has the triple consonant cluster *ctr*. Turning to the word of special interest, *locomotive*, conflicting process-approaches are noticeable again. The impact of the sensory input is reflected in the syllabic match of the first three vowels, *o*. Only in the unstressed final syllable does the effect of the long-term store surpass the effect of the immediate model from the sensory register. And the first *t* of *tomomotor* is probably the result of a reduplication of the *t* in *electric*.

Without any further massing, that is, intensive training within a brief time interval, the new item is insufficiently stored, it seems, and the next maternal input of "locomotive," around 20 minutes later, is overwhelmed by items from long-term memory: "motor" and "boot" (meaning "caboose"). Note here the predominance of Adam's spontaneously produced "motor boot," which seems to interfere even with the full sensory processing of the input because Adam in his answer "Yeah, motor boot . . . " does not seem to notice the discrepancy between the model and his production, which could barely be called an imitation in this case. The principles of *priming* and *cueing* (both through their phonetic similarity, i.e., "locomotive" vs. "motor," and semantic relatedness, i.e., pertaining to trains) would probably describe the dynamics better than the term *imitation*.

These examples from microanalyses of Eve's and Adam's imitations, respectively, can serve several functions:

(1) They indicate the complex processing that can be captured when careful attention is given to the temporal dimension of imitation.
(2) They demonstrate how misleading it would be to employ a simple dichotomy of *immediate* versus *delayed* imitation. Because time, learning, and forgetting are continuous dimensions, an arbitrary dissection would distort the data and present an incorrect picture of the processes involved.
(3) They exemplify, most of all, the close interdependency of the temporal and the similarity dimension, which will be the main focus of the final section of this chapter.

12.3.2 The Similarity Dimension

The ideal instance of imitation has always been considered as the topographically exact and temporally immediate repetition of a modeled behavior. Even a brief consideration of the facts indicates that this ideal was basically never met and, as I will argue, could not be met in principle during the early stages of language acquisition. When young children imitate parental verbal models, the first obstacle to exact imitation lies in the differences in the vocal apparatus between adult and child. Phonetic/phonemic differences follow necessarily from these physiological differences. It is also well known that children generally omit functors and change vocabulary items or the syntactic structure if the adult model is of any complexity. What is generally labeled *imitation* is based on certain resemblances, not in surface details, but in patterns between model and imitated utterance.

A brief consideration of neurological aspects that are most generally agreed on suggests that such differences in topography are based on necessity. Stimuli transmitted by the sensory organs convey the model to the brain where they are represented — even if only briefly — in a neural pattern, and from where they are conveyed by means of patterned neural responses to the motor organs. Estes (1976) summarized this principle concisely in reporting about "the increasing understanding that information stored in memory generally does not take the form of a replica of some experience but rather involves various levels of recoding the information" (p. 6). Or, "Even at the lowest levels of processing, what enters into, for example, short-term auditory memory is not a faithful representation of an acoustic signal, but rather a representation of what the individual perceived in terms of critical features or higher order units" (p. 9). Certainly, imitation is based on storage of input in memory. The principles underlying memory storage must therefore also underlie imitation. Applying Estes's argument concerning storage, all imitation involves abstraction from the almost infinite number of stimuli that could be attended. It will, of necessity, reflect more stringent abstraction the lower the information processing capacities or the more intense the new input (Werner's [1957] "orthogenetic law"). An abstracting and economizing procedure will therefore be most important for infants and young children, who are constantly confronted with novel information and whose memory capacity can easily be overtaxed.

The conclusion that imitation is based on pattern abstraction and pattern reconstruction reverses the entire problem of language acquisition: Language skills, instead of resulting from exact surface replications, would first derive from replications of the underlying patterns. That is, some forms of deep structures are necessarily learned first. The imitation of underlying syntactic patterns was most clearly captured in Whitehurst's (1977) "selective imitation," wherein only syntactic patterns are imitated, but the vocabulary items that fill the syntactic slots can be exchanged. More generally, the conceptualization of imitation in all its forms changes from a passive echoing to an active process of abstraction and reconstruction. To quote again from Estes, "What is retrieved from human memory is not specific items entered, but rather the product of an interaction of the individual's memory system with the original input" (1976, p. 9). This product can certainly differ in the balance between previously stored items and the modeled input. Either contribution can vary by minute degrees. Any dichotomy between spontaneous and imitative productions is precluded by the principles of neurological functioning.

Up to now, the analysis has been mainly theoretical: First, references were presented arguing that imitations could vary along several dimensions. Then it was shown logically and neurologically that exact imitation is impossible. Arguments from observational learning and memory research supported the point that, on all levels involved, phenomena of pattern abstraction are encountered. The abstracted patterns vary with context and with the experience of the child who performs the abstractions.

In the following sections, findings from interactional analyses will substantiate the theoretical points. First, finer differentiations of the general set of imitation will be made, and relationships between the resulting subsets and phenomena of language teaching and learning will be explored. Then, interactional sequences will be presented that exhibit additional effects of verbal priming by a partner than can not easily be labeled imitation. Finally, the interactional functions of the various subsets of imitation will be clarified and demonstrated.

12.3.2.1 Subsets Varying in Degree of Similarity

In the context of a more encompassing analysis of language teaching and learning in mother-child interactions (Moerk, 1983), 10 subsets of imitational phenomena were differentiated, both in maternal instructional techniques and filial learning strategies. Table 12-2 presents a brief label for each subset, its definition, and the frequencies with which these subsets were employed by two children, Adam and Eve, who are well known from Brown's analyses. Only their ages and mean lengths of utterances (MLUs) for those parts of the transcripts that were analyzed will be presented. They are, for Adam, 27 to 35 months and an MLU between 2.0 and 2.5 and, for Eve, 18 to 25 months and an MLU between 1.5 and 4.0. Eighteen hours of interaction were analyzed for Adam, and 20 for Eve. Imitations in their various forms were defined for an interval of one page of the transcripts. Therefore, an utterance did not need to follow the model immediately to be categorized as imitation. But the relatively brief interval chosen for the definition suggests that more delayed imitations, as discussed by Moerk and Moerk (1979) and by Snow (1983), will have been missed. the inclusion of longer-interval imitations would increase the frequencies, change the weights of the frequencies, and possibly lead to new subsets of imitation.

The various subsets in Table 12-2 are presented largely in a sequence approximating gradual decreases in similarity. Because no established similarity metric exists, this arrangement is certainly not definitive. Additionally, items within the last two subsets, "Imitative self-repetition" and "Quotations," can vary widely in similarity. These two subsets entail new factors: self-repetition and literary models. Because definitions of each of the subsets of imitation are provided in Table 12-2, few further clarifications are needed. For the more unfamiliar categories, verbatim examples will be given of one or two interaction episodes for each child.

Identical imitations, the first category in Table 12-2 and the presumed focus of many past discussions, are obviously not very frequent, appearing only five times or less per hour of interaction.

The well-known *reduced imitations*, which are almost identical but entail omissions, as described extensively by Brown and associates (e.g., Brown & Fraser, 1963), are predominant. They indicate the children's difficulty in handling and reproducing all the incoming information. It is known, from Brown's and other research, that children omit mostly minor functions in this case and retain the major content words and the overall syntactic structure; that is, they abstract from the input and assimilate it to the semantic relations they understand. Certainly much structural learning could derive from these imperfect repetitions because the stable meaning elements stand starkly apart from minor varying functors. The relationships between the contentives, such as Agent-Action-Object, remain also the same.

Substituting imitations represent instances of exercises of the *slot and filler principle*, that is, instances wherein the underlying syntactic structure is ab-

Table 12-2. Ten Subsets of Imitation

Label	Definition	F/Adam[a]	F/Eve
Simple imitation	Identical imitation with at most pronominal substitution	80	103
Reduction, reduced imitation	Minor syntactic elements, i.e., functors are deleted while retaining others	502	395
Substituting imitation	Most words and the structure are retained, one or a few items are substituted	180	140
Combinatory imitation	Combines items from two or more model utterances in own utterance	18	27
Chaining imitation	Combines items from model with own newly produced or repeated items	217	100
Integrative imitation	A sentence fragment of the child completes a preceding fragment of the model	29	36
Structural imitation	Retained unusual structures of model while changing all or most words	10	6
Incorporating imitation	Subsumes single constituent utterance of model into own longer utterance	0	9
Imitative self-repetition	Imitation of model, being also a repetition of own preceding utterance	113	104
Quotation	Items from books, stories, or songs	45	63
Total		1,194	983

[a] The frequencies are derived from 18 h of interactions of Adam and from 20 h of interaction of Eve with their respective mothers/fathers and, to a certain extent, the observers.

stracted from the surface string. Because the child retained the underlying structure without change, while substituting words, it is obvious that the input was processed on a deeper level than the mere acoustic one. The model provides support for the syntactic structure, the substitution results in communicational flexibility, and subsequent parental feedback provides information on whether or not the children were on track or made a mistake in their linguistic/communicational contribution, as in the following example:

MOTHER. That's Eve's plate.
EVE. (This) Mom plate.
MOTHER. (That's) Mom's plate. Right.
EVE. (That Pop) plate.

This subset of imitations was excluded by definition in many previous studies that required topographical identity for inclusion of a repetition as imitation.

Combinatory imitation is somewhat rare in both children, probably because it requires relatively complex processing. One example will demonstrate this:

MOTHER.   Will you please sit on your stool. You're in my way. Please sit on your stool.

EVE.   (On) stool Mommy way.

The child takes constituents from two separate maternal utterances, often those in the recency position, and combines them into a relatively meaningful utterance. Both memory and integrative processes would seem to be involved to attain this, but no new elements are added by the child.

Chaining imitations and *integrative imitations*, in contrast, proceed one step further in the child's creative use of models. Parts recently primed through an adult model are combined with productions derived from long-term memory. Depending on the number of items derived from each source, they vary on the similarity dimension. Clark (1977) has discussed those imitations in detail. Therefore, only a few major aspects need to be elaborated. Common evidence and the reports of Clark indicate that the new products are mostly meaningful and communicatively successful. This suggests that children process them on the semantic and also partly on the syntactic level. The difference between chaining imitation and integrative imitation is relatively minor: In chaining imitation the emphasis lies only on the imitated fragments that are absorbed in a quite spontaneous syntactic construction of the child. In integrative imitation the child utilizes not only a sentence fragment of the model verbatim, but also relies on the syntactic structure of the model's utterance. Two examples shall demonstrate this difference, although it has to be admitted that it is sometimes very tenuous.

When Adam employed one or two words of the model with barely a trace of syntactic influences, it was labeled *chaining imitation*:

MOTHER.   Oh, that would be an awfully clever baby.

ADAM.   Adam baby. 'at Adam baby.

In contrast, when Eve employed additionally almost exactly the maternal syntactic model, it was coded as *integrative imitation*.

EVE.   S. [*name of the mother*], I want to blow this up.

MOTHER.   See if I can get it off the stick.

EVE.   See if I can blow it up.

In both instances, by utilizing the recently primed elements, the children have changed the underlying task of linguistic production: Instead of needing to rely fully on spontaneous recall from long-term memory of often rare syntactic constructions, they can recall parts from short-term memory that were modeled by the parents. As Kirsner and Smith (1974) have shown experimentally, priming of vocabulary items, if performed through the auditory channel, retains its facilitating effects at least up to 270 s, that is, 4½ min, after presentation. After a sharp drop in facilitating effects during the first 20 s, probably the interval affected by mere sensory processing, these authors found only minimal decay during the next minutes in spite of extensive interference due to new item presentations. The time span of 4 to 5 min is closely equivalent to the interval of one page of transcripts used in the present study to delimit imitations.

Having reduced the task demands, because not all elements need to be recalled from long-term memory, the child has more free information-processing capacity available and can construct longer and more complex utterances than he or she could construct spontaneously (see also Speidel & Herreshoff, 1985; Chapter 8, this volume). These forms of imitation would have been by definition eliminated in most previous studies, although they must be very beneficial for language learning and although they illustrate fascinating processing strategies used by children.

The *structural imitations* and *incorporating imitations* in Table 12-2 are most remote on the similarity dimension. They were mainly employed by adults and will therefore not be discussed here.

Imitative self-repetition is of special interest as far as definitional problems are concerned. These imitations are mostly similar to the preceding model and to the original production of the child. They reveal the redundancy of the interactions between mothers and young children. Redundancy, in addition to lowering the information-processing load, implies massed repetitions of the linguistic terms involved. This massed rehearsal will be discussed in Sections 12.3.2.2 and 12.3.2.3. Frequent instances suggest that the self-repetitions are not exact repetitions either, but that the repeated form is somewhat superior to the original form; that is, it has incorporated linguistic information from the intervening model.

This subset represents a close analogue to interaction structures and training/learning strategies commonly found in other domains. Repeated cycles of trials, followed by feedback and improved trials are extremely common in most forms of skill learning. The trainer-coach provides feedback to an imperfect performance of a learner, and the learner tries to improve his performance based on this modeled feedback of the more perfect form and also on his earlier attainments. Fine calibrations of the performance are achieved in these cases. Similar interactional phenomena will be more extensively demonstrated later in Tables 12-3 and 12-4.

The last subset, *quotations*, could be of great importance, as the studies of Moerk and Moerk (1979), Ninio and Bruner (1978), Ninio (1980, 1983), and Snow and Goldfield (1983) suggest. Moerk (1985a) has recently summarized the research on the probable impact of picture-book reading and the child's use of literary models. Quotations can be employed in a great variety of ways and are more frequent than the numbers in Table 12-2 suggest. The low frequencies recorded were partly an artifact of the lack of complete evidence for the use of picture books. As Moerk and Moerk (1979) and Snow and Goldfield (1983) have suggested, such quotations occur often in highly transformed utterances and might not easily be recognized without encompassing knowledge of all the input derived from picture books (see Moerk & Moerk, 1979, for specific examples). Additionally, overlearned quotations are minimally susceptible to forgetting so that the interval between model and quotation could almost be unlimited. These

Table 12-3. The Most Frequent Digram Structures of the Pattern: Mother–Child[a]

Eve		
Maternal technique	Filial strategy	Frequency
Vocabulary perseveration	Vocabulary perseveration	160
Morpheme perseveration	Vocabulary perseveration	99
Morpheme perseveration	Morpheme perseveration	89
Replacement sequence	Reduced imitation	80
Frame variation	Reduced imitation	76
Frame variation	Vocabulary perseveration	75
Morpheme perseveration	Description	69
Replacement sequence	Vocabulary perseveration	66
Vocabulary perseveration	Reduced imitation	61
Description	Reduced imitation	58
Total		833
Adam		
Maternal technique	Filial strategy	Frequency
Vocabulary perseveration	Vocabulary perseveration	176
Morpheme perseveration	Morpheme perseveration	169
Morpheme perseveration	Reduced imitation	138
Morpheme perseveration	Vocabulary perseveration	122
Morpheme perseveration	Substituting imitation	100
Frame variation	Reduced imitation	95
Optional transformation	Reduced imitation	86
Morpheme perseveration	Break-down sequence	78
Replacement sequence	Reduced imitation	73
Morpheme perseveration	Description	67
Total		1,104

[a] Digrams wherein the child's response was not codable within the system employed are excluded.

quotations occur with considerable frequencies in some homes and may have strong impact on language progress (see Carlson & Anisfeld, 1969; Katz, 1927; Moerk, 1985a; White, 1954; Wyatt, 1969).

A final aspect of Table 12-2 deserves brief discussion and evaluation in its relation to theoretical questions: the overall frequency of imitation. Table 12-2 shows that each child exhibited approximately 1,000 instances of imitation in 18 to 20 hours of interaction. This is around 50 imitations per hour and almost 1 per minute. This is a low estimate because the counted imitations did not capture those with intervals of more than one page. It has to be concluded even from this preliminary evidence that the two children utilized quite extensively the linguistic cues entailed in preceding adult utterances. More intense utilization will be demonstrated when Table 12-3 is discussed. Because all forms of imitation

Table 12-4. The Most Frequent Digram Structures of the Pattern: Mother–Child, Wherein the Child Imitates Part or All of the Maternal Utterance[a]

Eve		
Maternal technique	Filial strategy	Frequency
Morpheme perseveration	Substituting imitation	32
Vocabulary perseveration	Imitative self-repetition	29
Replacement sequence	Substituting imitation	22
Frame variation	Chaining imitation	21
Replacement sequence	Chaining imitation	20
Morpheme perseveration	Chaining imitation	20
Expansion	Imitative self-repetition	20
Vocabulary perseveration	Substituting imitation	18
Frame variation	Substituting imitation	18
Imitative self-repetition	Imitative self-repetition	17
Total		217

Adam		
Maternal technique	Filial strategy	Frequency
Morpheme perseveration	Chaining imitation	66
Optional transformation	Chaining imitation	36
Morpheme perseveration	Substituting imitation	34
Replacement sequence	Chaining imitation	33
Frame variation	Chaining imitation	31
Replacement sequence	Substituting imitation	29
Simple imitation	Imitative self-repetition	29
Vocabulary perseveration	Imitative self-repetition	25
Optional transformation	Substituting imitation	25
Vocabulary perseveration	Chaining imitation	24
Total		332

[a] Reduced imitations, which are most frequent, are not included.

involve repetition, that is, rehearsal — which does not need to be intentional or be performed with metalinguistic awareness — it has to be concluded that the two children studied, and others known from the literature, rehearsed the linguistic input they received quite consistently. The next section illustrates that rehearsals also are encountered in connection with other interactional phenomena.

12.3.2.2 Minimal Matching

Imitation, in all its forms, is by definition an interactional phenomenon. Imitation is a response to the input provided by a conversation partner. Yet, in this essay and in much of the past literature, imitation has been discussed largely as isolated from the flow of discourse acts. The following two tables will partly counteract this tendency. Tables 12-3 and 12-4 will relate antecedents and consequent filial utterances in regard to the elements the latter incorporate from the former.

The structure of both Tables 12-3 and 12-4 is relatively straightforward: Each row in the tables represents one interactional sequence, initiated by a maternal *technique* and responded to by a filial *strategy*. The techniques display linguistic information, while the strategies are employed by children to utilize the displayed information; whether intentionally or unintentionally is of no concern. (Obviously, much information about environmental circumstances is used quite unintentionally in our daily coping behaviors.) The frequencies in the right column specify how often each specific pattern occurred in the 18 and 20 hours of interaction between the mothers and Adam and Eve, respectively. To evaluate these frequencies, it has to be taken into account that almost 40 strategies and almost 40 techniques were differentiated. The resulting number of possible different digrams of the form, maternal technique followed by a filial strategy, is therefore 40^2 that is, 1,600. Whereas the frequency of each specific digram can, consequently, not be very high in restricted samples such as those available, the patterns common to many digrams are cumulative in their possible effects. In Table 12-3, for example, maternal vocabulary and morpheme modeling is predominant, followed by filial perseverations and reduced imitations (i.e., by repetitions).

The patterns of digrams, that is, sequences encompassing two turns, are derived from a matrix of transitional probabilities. Transitional probabilities between all maternal teaching techniques and all filial learning strategies were computed for each two-step sequence and the most significant patterns, that is, those most clearly deviating from chance co-occurrences and occurring frequently enough to contribute potentially to learning, are presented. The exact details of the computations and additional categories are presented in Moerk (1983).

Table 12-3 presents the 10 most frequent digram structures in which the child's turn was codable as a learning strategy. Cases where no learning strategy could be discerned, coded as 0 = uncodable, are omitted from the presentation. These were instances of nonverbal responses, simple "what" questions or a "Hmmm?," "Yes," and so forth. For both Adam and Eve, five sets of the first 15 most frequent digram sets had a 0, or "Uncodable" second element. The remaining 10 patterns reveal the full complexity of the problem of imitation. In their digram structures, both Eve and Adam exhibit rehearsals, that is, several forms of redundancy similar to imitation, in addition to the redundancy that was discussed in Table 12-2 and specified under the various subsets of imitation. The most frequent nonimitative rehearsal was a repetition of new or rare vocabulary items, specified as *Vocabulary perseveration* in the tables. *Morpheme perseveration*, that is, the repetition of bound morphemes that were employed before by the mother and/or the child, is also quite high in the rank order for both children. Several subsets of imitative rehearsals follow in order of frequency in Table 12-3. Reduced imitation is more common for Eve, the younger child, whereas Adam appears more often involved in syntactic exercises, such as *substituting imitations* and *breakdown sequences*, that is, syntactic abstractions and analyses of longer strings into their elements.

These interactional phenomena make the continuity of the similarity dimensions and, consequently, the fuzziness of the set of imitation obvious. Enormous redundancy exists in mother-child interactions in the nursery, as is widely reported. There are, therefore, few filial utterances, whose number will vary from dyad to dyad and with the age of the child, that are not related partially to a preceding maternal utterance; that is, they could have been primed. If primed, they would fall under a broad category of *partial imitation*. It follows from these two premises that the sets of filial verbal behavior and of verbal imitation would almost be coextensive, as some critics observed. Such findings and conclusions stand in clear contrast to the fashionable exclusive emphasis on the child's linguistic creativity. Therefore, they invite a reconsideration and a tempering of the dogma. Yet, reliance on priming does not exclude creative use of the primed items.

12.3.2.3 Subsets of Imitation Seen in Interactional Perspective

It will be noted that several forms of imitation, as specified in Table 12-2, do not appear in the digram structures in Table 12-3. Before a fuller interpretation of the patterns is attempted, Table 12-4 is added to provide evidence as to the use of the other forms of imitation. Table 12-4 contains those digrams, subsequent to the first 15, that had an imitation in the child's turn. This table is intended to demonstrate how the more rare and complex imitations were utilized by the children. The frequent form of reduced imitation that was already encountered in Table 12-3 is therefore omitted.

Predominantly substituting imitations and chaining imitations are encountered in these instances. Both entail relatively complex syntactic activities, as argued in Section 12.3.2.1 and both are responses to highly complex syntactic exercises of the mother as indicated by the first column of the table. The predominant forms of imitation that appear important for language progress involve much flexibility and even "creativity." An oxymoron of "creative imitation" could be coined to focus attention on this apparent contrast. Yet, considered more broadly, all creative art is based on the achievements of predecessors and in some sense is imitative.

Imitative self-repetition is the only subset not to reflect this creativity. Table 12-4 suggests the reason for this exception: Imitative self-repetitions often follow *expansions*, and train thereby the improved model (cf. Slobin, 1968). The same probably applies when they follow simple imitations, because these almost always entail phonetic and other minor improvements. Imitative self-repetitions also follow maternal imitative self-repetitions and vocabulary perseverations. In these instances massive rehearsals are encountered, whether of new or rare vocabulary items or of other linguistic aspects, whether accompanied by metalinguistic awareness or not. The importance of such massed training has been argued in another study (Moerk, 1986, 1989) and is known from memory research. Considering the large number of vocabulary items children need to learn and the ease of forgetting them, these rehearsals would appear to be necessary for long-term storage.

Although any conclusions must be preliminary and can only serve a hypothesis-generating function, fascinating patterns are suggested in Tables 12-3 and 12-4: Massed rehearsals are predominant because the items in the maternal column are, almost without exception, repetitions as well. For vocabulary training and learning, multiple repetitions are most obvious as seen in the sequences vocabulary perseveration–vocabulary perseveration, which entail at least three repetitions. When the mother models syntactic transformations, the most common filial response is a simplified repetition, that is, reductions or imitations with reduction. This lowers information-processing demands, but is also a rehearsal. Yet, both Adam and Eve respond to maternal syntactic transformations also quite often with syntactic exercises of their own, using either the underlying syntactic pattern of the model or parts of the surface string of the model. They hereby use imitation in order to be creative. Longer strings would need to be analyzed, and the verbatim interactions would have to be scrutinized in order to specify exactly what and how much the children learned from each of these "imitative exercises." Such extended microanalyses could then further demonstrate the differential use of the diverse subsets of the overall "fuzzy set of imitation."

12.4 Summary and Discussion

Due to space limitations, the discussion will have to be restricted to the major points only. Any integration of the present arguments with the wealth of controversy in the field cannot even be attempted.

I have argued and partially demonstrated that so-called imitations can vary on several dimensions: (1) the temporal dimension and (2) the dimension of similarity between model and production. Developmental evidence suggests that it can also (3) vary in level of processing. Within this three-dimensional space, specific forms of imitation can occur anywhere; that is, the dimensions appear to be orthogonal to each other. Specific interdependencies are due to particular aspects of processing. As demonstrated in Section 12.3, Table 12-1, in some cases temporal delay involves repeated trials and this "working up to" results in closer and closer similarity between model and production. In the absence of repeated trials, temporal delay mostly leads to greater dissimilarity, either due to simple forgetting or to better mastery and, therefore, greater flexibility in the use of an acquired skill. Deeper processing generally results in longer retention but, often, also in lowered surface similarity because the "imitation" pertains mainly to the content or structure of the modeled act, whereas the specific vocabulary items can be supplied creatively.

It is certainly possible that some of the dimensions could still be further differentiated. Similarity can vary, for example, due to omission of elements, distortion of the input through lack of processing skills, or creative addition of new elements. I do not know of any systematic study of the dimension that results from differences in levels of processing. Processing variations can occur at the sensory level, at the central level, or at the motor-output level. In many analyses such finer distinctions will be important.

The main conclusion to be drawn from the above analyses is the following: It is suggested that the controversy about imitation derives largely from terminological ambiguities. The term *imitation* was taken over from lay language without much conceptual analysis. Then followed reification, and the term was presumed to refer to a class variable that involves distinctly distributed differences in kind, leading to a differentiation of imitative speech and productive speech as dichotomous opposites. Imitative speech has, however, to be considered as a dimensional variable that involves continuously distributed differences in degree. Or, in more psychological parlance; imitation is a dependent variable that varies quantitatively on the dimensions of productivity, that is, of similarity, of delay, and of level of processing.

Such a conceptualization of the domain entails many scientific advantages: First of all, the strengths of scientific quantitative methodology can be utilized. Based on this, functional relationships between a range of independent variables and varying dependent measures, such as the intervals between model and production, amount and type of omissions, degree of innovation, and aspects of the model employed, can be established. Once the independent and dependent variables are clearly conceptualized and means to measure them have been established, the independent variables can be experimentally and systematically manipulated. For example, sensory processing can easily be influenced by the speed and clarity of enunciation—as demonstrated in *motherese*. Storage processes are influenced by the number of rehearsals (see Tables 12-1 to 12-4), as shown in memory research. In brief, language teaching and learning can be conceived as a set of functional relationships: $l = f(tr)$. That is, language is a function of training, where the training can be varied on one or more continuous dimensions and where concomitant variations in the learning variables can be measured.

If this argument appears plausible, then it has to be concluded that the unexamined concept of imitation is a misnomer. Being originally employed to designate an ideal prototype of almost identical and immediate matching, it cannot reflect the many differences in forms of imitation. Thus, we can see that the term and domain stand in a one-to-many relationship and the use of the term cannot differentially specify which subset of phenomena is designated. Just because the domain of phenomena is so important (cf. Bandura's [1986] Social Learning Theory) and in spite of often close family resemblances between the many faces of imitation, clear differentiations are needed. As it has proven functionally and pragmatically necessary in all cultures to differentiate members of a family, so the many aspects of learning from models must be differentiated (cf. Moerk, 1977; Snow, 1981; Stine & Bohannon, 1983). A verb form, for example, matching, might prove more conducive to differential descriptions. Verbs can easily be supplemented by a variety of arguments, mirroring the fact that imitation, that is, matching, can be immediate or delayed to varying degrees, can be identical or differ in surface or underlying features, can refer to various contents (vocabulary items, intonation contours, underlying syntax, etc.), and can also be more or less successful.

Considered in such a differentiated way, *matching* fits easily into the Venn diagram of Figure 12-1. What has been labeled "imitation" is a form of information processing that is special due to two features: First, the source of the information is generally the behavior of members of the same species. Second, the information processing is externalized to a considerable degree, which presents a unique opportunity for the researcher. Instead of needing to rely on inferences, drawn from indirect relations between input and behavior, as to what information was processed, some of the processed information is rendered directly through matching.

Because it is correct, as some critics have argued, that, in the limit, all of language is imitation, and most of nonverbal social behavior too, the domain of imitation is in some sense coexistensive with language and social behavior. If we continue to refer to the domain of imitation by a single technical term, the category will be too global and diffuse, and this will be detrimental to finer conceptual and scientific analysis.

The first goal therefore has to be a differential designation of the "many faces of imitation." This was attempted by suggesting the three dimensions along which "imitational" phenomena vary. Yet, differing from the metaphorical use of the family concept with its cardinal or, at most, ordinal scale for siblings ("Quintus, Sextus, ..., Decimus," in ancient Rome), the differentiated dimensions suggest that it might prove possible to employ interval or even ratio scales in the analysis of imitational phenomena. Then, in accordance with Werner's (1957) orthogenetic law, a hierarchic integration of the domain can be attempted. The Venn diagram, sketched out in the beginning of this chapter, is a first attempt. The entire book, of which this chapter is a part, represents a more encompassing step in this endeavor.

Acknowledgments. The final drafts of this article were written while the author was supported by a grant from the Spencer Foundation. This support greatly facilitated concentration upon this research. The author also wants to thank Professor A. Bandura and Dr. G. Speidel for suggestions and critical feedback to preliminary drafts of this article.

References

Anderson, J.R. (1983). *The architecture of cognition.* Cambridge, MA: Harvard University Press.

Bandura, A. (1986). *Social foundations of thought and action.* Englewood Cliffs, NJ: Prentice-Hall.

Bandura, A., & Harris, M.B. (1966). Modification of syntactic style. *Journal of Experimental Child Psychology*, *4*, 341–352.

Bloom, L., Hood, P., & Lightbown, P. (1974). Imitation in language development. If, when, and why? *Cognitive Psychology*, *6*, 380–420.

Bohannon, J., & Warren-Leubecker, A. (1985). Theoretical approaches to language acquisition. In J.B. Gleason (Ed.), *The development of language* (pp. 173–217). Columbus, OH: Merrill.

Brown, R. (1973). *A first language*. Cambridge, MA: Harvard University Press.

Brown, R., & Fraser, C. (1963). The acquisition of syntax. In C.N. Cofer & B. Musgrave (Eds.), *Verbal behavior and learning: Problems and processes* (pp. 158–201). New York: McGraw-Hill.

Bruner, J., Jolly, J., & Sylva, K. (Eds.). (1976). *Play: Its role in development and evolution*. New York: Basic Books.

Carlson, P., & Anisfeld, M. (1969). Some observations on the linguistic competence of a two-year-old child. *Child Development*, *40*, 569–576.

Cazden, C.B. (1976). Play with language and metalinguistic awareness: One dimension of language experience. In J. Bruner, J. Jolly, & K. Sylva (Eds.), *Play: Its role in development and evolution* (pp. 603–608). New York: Basic Books.

Chukovsky, K. (1963). *From two to five*. Berkeley, CA: University of California Press.

Clark, R. (1977). What's the use of imitation? *Journal of Child Language*, *4*, 341–358.

Estes, W.K. (1976). Introduction to Volume 4. In W.K. Estes (Ed.), *Handbook of learning and cognitive processes: Vol. 4. Attention and memory* (pp. 1–16). New York: Wiley.

Garvey, C. (1977). Play with language. In B. Tizard & D. Harvey (Eds.), *Biology of play* (pp. 74–99). Philadelphia, PA: Lippincott.

Gibson, E.J. (1969). *Principles of perceptual learning and development*. New York: Appleton-Century-Crofts.

Gibson, J.J. (1966). *The senses considered as perceptual systems*. Boston, MA: Houghton-Mifflin.

Gibson, J.J. (1982). Notes on affordances. In E. Reed & R. Jones (Eds.), *Reasons for realism: Selected essays of James J. Gibson* (pp. 401–418). Hillsdale, NJ: Erlbaum.

Kagan, J., Kearsley, R.B., & Zelazo, P.R. (1978). *Infancy. Its place in human development*. Cambridge, MA: Harvard University Press.

Kaplan, A. (1964). *The conduct of inquiry*. San Francisco: Chandler.

Katz, R. (1927). Beobachtungen an Kindern beim Marchenerzahlen. *Zeitschrift fur angewandte Psychologie*, *28*, 140–143.

Kaye, K. (1982). *The mental and social life of babies: How parents create persons*. Chicago, IL: University of Chicago Press.

Kaye, K., & Marcus, J. (1978). Imitation over a series of trials without feedback: Age six months. *Infant Behavior and Development*, *1*, 141–155.

Kaye, K., & Marcus, J. (1981). Infant imitation: The sensory-motor agenda. *Developmental Psychology*, *17*, 258–265.

Kirk, G.S. (1976). *Homer and the oral tradition*. Cambridge, MA: Cambridge University Press.

Kirsner, K., & Smith, M.C. (1974). Modality effects in word recognition. *Memory & Cognition*, *2*, 637–640.

Kuczaj, S.A. (1982). Language play and language acquisition. In H.W. Reese (Ed.), *Advances in child development and behavior* (Vol. 17, pp. 197–232). New York: Academic Press.

Kuczaj, S.A. (1983). *Crib speech and language play*. New York: Springer-Verlag.

Lewis, M.M. (1936). *Infant speech*. New York: Humanities Press.

McCarthy, D. (1954). Language development in children. In L. Carmichael (Ed.), *Manual of child psychology*. New York: Wiley.

Meltzoff, A.N., & Moore, M.K. (1977). Imitation of facial and manual gestures by human neonates. *Science, 198*, 75–78.

Moerk, E.L. (1977). Processes and products of imitation: Additional evidence that imitation is progressive. *Journal of Psycholinguistic Research, 6*, 187–202.

Moerk, E.L. (1983). *The mother of Eve—as a first language teacher*. Norwood, NJ: Ablex.

Moerk, E.L. (1985a). Picture-book reading by mothers and young children and its impact upon language development. *Journal of Pragmatics, 9*, 547–566.

Moerk, E.L. (1985b, July). *Interactional/instructional principles and learning processes in the course of first language acquisition*. Paper presented at the Eighth Biennial Meeting of the International Society for the Study of Behavioral Development, Tours, France.

Moerk, E.L. (1986). Environmental factors in early language acquisition. In G.J. Whitehurst (Ed.), *Annals of child development* (Vol. 3, pp. 191–236). Greenwich, CT: JAI Press.

Moerk, E.L. (1989). *Memory and the matching response*.

Moerk, E.L., & Moerk, C. (1979). Quotations, imitations, and generalizations: Factual and methodological analyses. *International Journal of Behavioural Development, 2*, 43–72.

Ninio, A. (1980). Ostensive definition in vocabulary teaching. *Journal of Child Language, 7*, 565–573.

Ninio, A. (1983). Joint book reading as a multiple vocabulary acquisition device. *Developmental Psychology, 19*, 445–451.

Ninio, A., & Bruner, J. (1978). The achievement and antecedents of labeling. *Journal of Child Language, 5*, 1–15.

Peters, A. (1983). *The units of language acquisition*. New York: Cambridge University Press.

Piaget, J. (1951). *Play, dreams, and imitation in childhood*. New York: Norton.

Ryan, J.F. (1973). Interpretation and imitation in early language development. In R. Hinde & J.S. Hinde (Eds.), *Constraints on learning: Limitations and predispositions* (pp. 427–443). New York: Academic Press.

Schwartz, R.G., & Leonard, L.B. (1985). Lexical imitation and language acquisition in language-impaired children. *Journal of Speech and Hearing Disorders, 50*, 141–149.

Slobin, D.I. (1968). Imitation and grammatical development in children. In N.S. Endler, L.R. Boulter, & H. Osser (Eds.), *Contemporary issues in developmental psychology* (pp. 437–443). New York: Holt, Rinehart & Winston.

Snow, C.E. (1981). The uses of imitation. *Journal of Child Language, 8*, 205–212.

Snow, C.E. (1983). Saying it again: The role of expanded and deferred imitations in language acquisition. In K.E. Nelson (Ed.), *Children's language*. (Vol. 4, pp. 29–58). Hillsdale, NJ: Erlbaum.

Snow, C.E., & Goldfield, B. (1983). Turn the page please: Situation-specific language learning. *Journal of Child Language, 10*, 551–569.

Speidel, G.E., & Herreshoff, M.J. (1985, April). Imitation and learning to speak standard English as a second dialect. In G.E. Speidel (Chair), *The many faces of imitation*.

Symposium conducted at the biennial convention of the Society for Research in Child Development, Toronto.

Stine, E.L., & Bohannon, J.N. (1983). Imitations, interactions, and language acquisition. *Journal of Child Language, 10*, 589–603.

Tizard, B., & Harvey, D. (Eds.). (1977). *Biology of play.* Philadelphia, PA: Lippincott.

Tulving, E. (1984). Multiple learning and memory systems. In K.M.J. Lagerspetz, & P. Niemi (Eds.), *Psychology in the 1990's* (pp. 163–184). Amsterdam: North-Holland.

Valentine, C.W. (1930). The psychology of imitation with special reference to early childhood. *British Journal of Psychology, 21*, 105–132.

Watson, M.W., & Fischer, K.W. (1977). A developmental sequence of agent use in late infancy. *Child Development, 48*, 828–836.

Weir, R. (1962). *Language in the crib.* Mouton: The Hague.

Werner, H. (1957). The concept of development from a comparative and organismic point of view. In D.B. Harris (Ed.), *The concept of development* (pp. 125–148). Minneapolis, MN: University of Minnesota Press.

Whitehurst, G.J. (1977). Imitation, response novelty, and language acquisition. In B.C. Etzel, J.M. LeBlanc, & D.M. Baer (Eds.), *New developments in behavioral research: Theory, method, and application. In honor of Sidney W. Bijou* (pp. 119–132). Hillsdale, NJ: Erlbaum.

White, D. (1954). *Books before five.* New York: Oxford University Press.

Wyatt, G.L. (1969). *Language learning and communication disorders in children.* Glencoe, IL: The Free Press.

CHAPTER 13

Implications for Language Acquisition Models of Childrens' and Parents' Variations in Imitation

Keith E. Nelson, Mikael Heimann, Lutfi Abuelhaija,
and Roberta Wroblewski

In the course of this chapter, we consider evidence from three countries, Sweden, Jordan, and the United States. Individual differences between children and also between parents in their imitation tendencies will be examined through a series of questions concerning imitation at different ages and in different cultures. It will be possible to both summarize important research findings on imitation and to discuss theoretical implications of these research findings.

13.1 How Extensive Are Individual Differences in Children's Imitation in the First 60 Months of Life?

A good starting point for this inquiry is Gothenburg, Sweden. Swedish babies were examined for their imitation tendencies at 3 days, 3 weeks, and 3 months of age (Heimann, Nelson, & Schaller, in press). These Swedish infants showed very strong differences in imitation tendencies. The most sensitive index was imitation of tongue protrusion, when an adult stuck out his or her tongue and the infant imitated by sticking out his or her own tongue. Imitation of these kinds of simple actions is more frequent at 3 days of age and 3 weeks of age than at 3 months of age. In addition, in this project there is some stability between infants' tendencies to be high imitators or low imitators at 3 days and also at 3 weeks, but limited stability after 3 weeks of age. In line with research by Heimann and Nelson (1986), Heimann and Schaller (1985), Field, Woodson, Greenberg, and Cohen (1982), Meltzoff and Moore (1985), and others, these results indicate that even in the first month of life children approach social interaction with quite varied tendencies to imitate or not to imitate the actions of other people. Many of these imitated actions can be assumed to lead into and affect children's processing of adults' speech-related and sign-language-related productions.

In contrast to research in areas such as personality development, there has been relatively little theoretical sophistication in accounting for individual differences in infants, toddlers, and preschool children in their language behavior and in various social and cognitive behaviors that may interface with the acquisition of language. However, whenever language acquisition has gone beyond the traditional tendency to study one to four children as the basic sample for reported study, there have been strong clues that individual differences are rampant in language-related factors such as temperament (Plomin & Dunn, 1986), imitation tendencies, and imitation skills and play skills (Fischer & Pipp, 1984), as well as in varied aspects of language behavior (e.g., Bates, Benigni, Bretherton, Camaioni, & Volterra, 1979; Bonvillian & Nelson, 1982; Braine, 1976; Clark, 1982; K. Nelson, 1981; K. E. Nelson, 1977a; Obler, 1988; Obler & Menn, 1982).

Children's imitations can present the face of clues to what the children have processed from immediately preceding adult utterances. But children's imitations can also present many other faces in the complex arena of language acquisition. Accordingly, what we shall investigate below is a series of related questions on how information processing by the child may be influenced by the child's own imitations and also by various kinds of imitations and reformulations made by conversational partners.

13.2 How Do Imitations Directly Affect Immediate and Subsequent Information Processing by the Child?

In the above Swedish sample (Heimann et al. in press), it was extremely interesting to discover that what young infants (at 3 days or 3 weeks of age) typically did was to observe an adult who modeled a gesture such as sticking out his or her tongue, and then, after the modeling period was over, to show imitation of that tongue protrusion gesture. In short, children seemed to be encoding information about the adult behavior while the adult behavior was in progress. Seconds or minutes subsequent to the adult modeling period, children tended to retrieve whatever encodings they had made and to produce tongue protrusions of their own. For different children, the tendency to encode tongue protrusions effectively and to plan their own tongue protrusions was dramatically higher than the same tendency would be for other children. At these early ages, it remains quite unclear whether the children who show high imitative tendencies of tongue protrusions, mouth openings, and similar gestures differ in their ability to encode and to retrieve actions modeled by adults, or whether the individual differences between babies rest in differential motivation or tendencies to produce actions that the children have seen modeled and are capable of producing (see also, Meltzoff & Gopnik, Chapter 2, this volume).

Within the first 3 months of life, however, there are clues that children who have more opportunities for observing adult behavior may be better at imitating particular gestures modeled by adults. Expressed simply, infants who tended to have only limited periods when they were averting their gaze away from adults tended to be better at imitating adult actions (Heimann, 1988). In terms of nonverbal imitation, children's substantial increases in tolerating model complexity and delays since model presentation indicate increasingly sophisticated analysis, storage, and retrieval abilities in the period between 6 and 18 months of age (Meltzoff & Gopnik, Chapter 2, this volume). In related work, Mannle and Tomasello (1978), Baldwin and Markman (in press), and Lock (in press) stress how attention deployment may be critical in the young child's mapping of words and sentences to referents.

At older ages as well, children's immediate imitations of adults needs to be considered in terms of attention and processing. Even when children are 18, 24, or 30 months of age, the processing of what adults have just presented in terms of a model may be enhanced, paradoxically, by delaying any productions on the children's part. Just as we have seen in the first 3 months of infancy, children may be limited to selective processing at 18 to 30 months, and when something new comes along in interaction that could be learned, it may be better to devote processing capacity to analyzing these new examples rather than immediately imitating them. Thus, children may show a tendency to selectively imitate those vocabulary items and those gestures that they have recently acquired, rather than those that they are in the process of acquiring. Results from Bloom, Hood, and Lightbown (1974), K. E. Nelson and Bonvillian (1973, 1978), and Bates, Bretherton, and Snyder (1988) are all convergent with results by Leonard and Schwartz (1985). Particularly when noun examples, such as *beaver*, *cookie*, and *fiffin* are examined, children who overall tend to be high imitators in the period between 18 and 30 months may show a relative advantage in terms of acquiring new concepts and new semantic labels for these concepts. However, information processing associated with the acquisition of new concepts and new semantic labels may be concentrated in analysis windows following salient and easy-to-process models in conversation, without accompanying immediate imitation by the children. Leonard and Schwartz (1985), Bates et al. (1988), and K. E. Nelson and Bonvillian (1973, 1978) all found that immediate imitation of a concept name was not strongly associated with successful acquisition of that concept and subsequent comprehension of the name for that concept. What these results suggest is that, even though children do sometimes imitate adult language production, their immediate imitations of new concept names will fail to contribute on some occasions to mapping concepts to concept labels and in other instances may actually interfere with the acquisition of the category-word connections. Again, children have limited processing capacities and may need the time and space to accommodate novel concepts and novel mapping between words and concepts.

In contrast, once children have entered into their language system a new structural relationship between a concept and a semantic term, as in the case of the connection between the concept of a lobster and the word *lobster*, some but not all children will use imitation as a selective tool for consolidating and rehearsing the tentative mapping of this new term. The results of Bloom et al. (1974), Leonard and Schwartz (1985), and K. E. Nelson and Bonvillian (1978) are particularly informative in this regard.

13.3 How Do Children's Imitations Indirectly Affect the Information Available to the Child and How the Child Processes This Information?

On the average, children who imitate quite a lot relative to other children at 18 to 24 months of age are likely over the next 6 to 12 months to make more rapid progress in terms of lexical acquisition. This observation may at first appear to be in contradiction to the above conclusions on the effects of imitation on immediate processing. The resolution of this apparent conflict lies in the eliciting effects of children's imitations on what adults do around children. These eliciting effects, as described by Shatz (1987), among others, include a greater tendency on the part of adults to supply linguistic descriptions for objects and events to children who relatively often imitate the adults' language expressions for objects and events. Children are most likely to imitate those terms that are already part of their language system. But adults typically are not experts in monitoring which terms are already in the child's language system and which terms are novel to the child's language system. Therefore, adults may respond to young children who seem to be very interested in imitating by supplying them (vs. other children) more examples of names in general and more frameworks that make the interrelations of concepts and names obvious to the child.

A related phenomenon is the production of relatively long utterances by children. Speidel and Herreshoff (Chapter 8, this volume) show that children often produce longer utterances in turns in which they imitate preceding utterances by others as compared with turns in which they initiate new, nonimitative utterances. In such cases it appears that children's speech mechanisms rely on a kind of shortcut by utilizing elements that have just been accessed and stored from the speakers' preceding turn in combination with additional elements that are patterned into new sentence production.

It is fundamental to see also that in reports by Cross (1977, 1978), K. E. Nelson and Bonvillian (1973, 1978), Pye (1986), Schieffelin (1979), and Wells (1980), among others, that many children succeed in acquiring language despite extremely limited reliance on imitation of any immediately preceding utterances by adults or other children who are fluent in the language they are acquiring. Thus, it is important to consider the indirect effects of *not* imitating as well. Some of the conversational circumstances that arise when children do not imitate may facilitate the child's processing of new structures and the acquisition of new structures. Precisely such an argument was made by K. E. Nelson, Baker, Denninger, Bonvillian, and Kaplan (1985) in reference to the superior long-term language skills of children who at 22 and 27 months of age tended to be low imitators with high social and formulaic uses of language. For example, significantly more effective referential sentences at age 4½ years were generated by the low imitators early on. In many rounds of conversations over many years, these children who rely relatively little on imitation may acquire more complex discourse and sentences from others as compared with children who continue to depend heavily on imitation after 27 months of age.

13.4 How Do Differences in Temperament Between Children Relate to Imitative Differences in Children's Language Behavior?

Only recently have psychologists and linguists incorporated a measurement of children's personality and temperament into studies of language acquisition. K. E. Nelson, Baker, Denninger, Bonvillian, and Kaplan (1985) argued that around 22 months of age children can make excellent progress in language acquisition by relying either on a high-imitative–high-referential style or on a low-imitative–high-social-syntactic style in language acquisition. Moreover, depending on conversational partners and routines, a child between birth and about 24 months may on some occasions be low and on others high in the relative frequency of imitative utterances (Bates, Bretherton, & Snyder, 1988; Heimann, 1988; K. E. Nelson et al., 1985; Užgiris, Broome, and Kruper, Chapter 5, this volume). As the child matures and acquires greater experience in language between 2 and 5 years of age, however, the typical pattern is for imitative tendencies to decline in language. The implication is that the impact of language-learning style on language progress must always be adjusted for the period of language acquisition under discussion. Future work should contrast alternative ways of characterizing children's styles and the manner in which imitative skills and imitative tendencies contribute (cf. Dunn, 1986).

13.5 How Can a Process-Oriented Model Incorporate Imitative and Temperament Differences Between Children?

Language acquisition models need to consider what happens in working memory as well as what happens in the storage and retrieval of information from long-term memory. As we have argued elsewhere (K. E. Nelson, 1980, 1987, 1989), children in the course of acquiring language only acquire new structures when these structures are present in input, observed and engaged by the processor, and given adequate processing by the child's system. Among other factors that affect these steps, children's imitative tendencies and their temperament influence what will be processed and how it will be processed. Even though nearly all children may bring some biological, physiological mechanisms to bear on their language and the interactions they enter, children are highly selective processors of the interactions they enter. This runs counter to assumptions of theorists as diverse as Wexler and Cullicover (1980), MacWhinney (1986, 1987), McClelland and Rumelhart (1986), Pinker (1985), and Rumelhart and McClelland (1986a) that

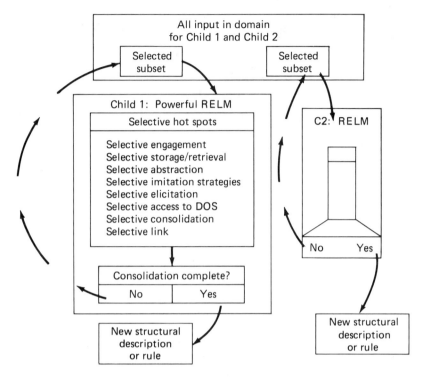

Figure 13-1. The Rare Event Learning Mechanism (RELM) model of language processing and acquisition.

children process each example that comes along in input. It is far more likely that
children selectively engage and process only a small portion of exemplars that
occur in input to them. Accordingly, a sensitive process-oriented model should
specify which conditions in conversation lead a particular child with particular
imitative and temperament tendencies to engage, process, and store relevant
exemplars. Similar questions arise in relation to how early temperament influe-
ences selective construction of social schemata such as those involved in attachment to adults and in peer relations (cf. Buss & Plomin, 1986; Dunn, 1986).

The RELM model, capturing a rare-event learning mechanism account of language acquisition, gives attention to the above factors. As Figures 13-1 and 13-2
show, the child's engagement, analysis, storage, and retrieval of all relevant information for the acquisition of new semantic or syntactic structures is both highly
selective and highly modulated by individual differences. Children do not concentrate their limited processing capacities on all exemplars that come along in
input. Instead, they form selective focus points or "hot spots" of engagement and
analysis that lead to a heavy concentration of available processing capacity on
highly relevant exemplars for stage-relevant acquisition.

(1) Engagement/attention

    HI: OK in thin context or independent learning
    LO: Need redundant, rich context

(2) Abstracting from comparison set assembled in working memory

    HI: Rapid; few exemplars
    LO: Slower; need more and more varied exemplars

(3) Selective storage and retrieval

    HI: Good tags; active parallel search; revisit prior pathways
    LO: Incomplete tags; narrow search; may fail to revisit successful pathways

(4) Imitative contributions

    HI: Tendency + high imitative skill—large role for unanalyzed chunks
    LO: Tendency + low imitative skill—RELM proceeds without reliance on
        imitative material

(5) Going far beyond given information

    HI: Ready invention of new tentative rules; ready generation of hypotheses
        across domains (link) and across subdomains; high reliance on varied
        divergent and convergent modes
    LO: Conservative bias; bias toward convergent and subdomain-specific
        rules; low reliance on link

(6) Monitoring and consolidation

    HI: Efficient consolidation of current hypotheses frees processing for
        next stages
    LO: Some incomplete consolidation; some overkill leading to plateau
        before new stages

(7) Relative sociability

    HI: Active elicitor of complex language; most efficient processing
        with moderate arousal
    LO: More reactive role in conversation; most efficient processing with
        low arousal

Figure 13-2. Hot spot selective processing: Individual differences.

One implication of individual differences in children's selective processing tendencies is that there will be high impact of a good correspondence between the child's approach to selective processing and the approach of parents and other relevant conversational partners. As Clark (1982), Lieven (1978, 1984), K. Nelson (1973), and K. E. Nelson et al. (1985) have argued, children are more likely to make rapid progress in language acquisition if there is a good match between their particular styles in processing language information and the strategies of parents and other frequent conversational partners in approaching discourse with the language learner.

13.6 How Extensive Are Parental Individual Differences in Language Imitation When Their Children Are Developing During the First 60 Months of Life?

In this volume there is no doubt about the data on maternal imitations. Mothers of language-learning children differ dramatically in their imitation tendencies according to Snow (Chapter 4, this volume) and Užgiris, Broome, and Kruper (Chapter 5, this volume). These strong differences in maternal imitation during conversations with the language-learning children match very well indeed with reports by Barnes, Gutfreund, Satterly, and Wells (1983), Wells (1980), Cross (1977, 1978), and Liebergott, Menyuk, Schultz, Chesnick, and Thomas (1984) and a broad-based review by K. E. Nelson et al. (1984). Within the American culture, the English culture, the Australian culture, and other Western technological cultures, it is clear that there are extremely wide-ranging differences in how often mothers, fathers, and other adults use imitation as a strategy of replying to what a child has just said. Cross-cultural work by Pye (1986) in Guatemala and by Schieffelin (1979) in New Guinea further underline this point. In these two cultures, it appears that imitation by adults of what children say is extremely infrequent by comparison with the most frequently reported dyadic situations in children's language investigations in other cultures. Nevertheless, the full range of variation within Western technological societies overlaps with results to date from village cultures in Guatemala, New Guinea, and elsewhere. As in the case of children's widespread variation in imitativeness, theories of language acquisition must find a place for children who succeed in successfully working out a language system when adults and children as conversational partners rely heavily on imitation, when they rely moderately on imitation, and when they rely almost entirely on new spontaneous utterances rather than on any imitations of what the child has just said in conversation.

13.7 How Do Parental Differences in Various Forms of Imitation Affect the Child's Immediate and Subsequent Information Processing of Language Examples?

As Bohannon and Stanowicz report in Chapter 6, this volume, one possible effect of parental immediate, exact imitation may be to confirm or to acknowledge for the child that the child's prior utterance was well formed. When parental utterances are selectively patterned so that exact, immediate imitation occurs exclusively or primarily for well-formed utterances, then this is a definite possible influence on the child's interpretation and processing of the parental utterances.

Another possibility, however, is that, when the full range of opportunities for replying to children's utterances is considered, parents who rely extensively on immediate imitation may limit the child's opportunity to analyze and learn new and more challenging structures that are beyond the children's current language system. Thus, it is not surprising that K. Nelson (1973, 1981) and K. E. Nelson et al. (1984), among others, have reported that, within the period between 15 and 30 months of age, mothers who rely relatively heavily on imitative tendencies tend to have children who make relatively slow progress overall in the acquisition of language. This kind of overall result definitely needs to be further analyzed according to the kinds of imitation that occur and the levels of language development that are impacted by the parental imitative reply strategies. Nevertheless, these studies send up a danger signal indicating that nonselective, exact, immediate imitation of children's utterances may limit rather than enhance children's opportunities for processing new language structures. Speidel (1987) also considers possible drawbacks as well as contributions of exact imitation.

Differentiation is needed. In a recent analysis completed by K. E. Nelson et al. (in preparation), there are indications that during the period between 15 and 18 months of age there may be an important influence of maternal imitation on certain children's language gains. For 24 children observed at 15 months of age, the children were divided into two groups according to the rate of vocabulary explosion between 15 and 18 months. Some "low-growth" children acquired between 2 and 35 words during this period, and other "high-growth" children acquired more than a median number of items—between 35 and an astonishing 303 words during this brief period of 3 months. These vocabulary explosion differences were not closely related to the children's initial levels of vocabulary at 15 months or to nonverbal imitation tendencies at 15 months. However, a high rate of vocabulary explosion was related to frequent maternal imitation of the children's utterances at 15 months, whereas a low rate of vocabulary explosion was related to a relatively low (below median) tendency on the part of mothers to imitate their babies or toddlers ($X^2 = 16.19$; 1 d.f.; $p < 001$).

These children at 15 months were primarily in the one-word stage, and all were potentially in the position of acquiring vocabulary rapidly during the period between 15 and 18 months. It may be when the child has just produced a single word and the mother produces a single word or several words by way of imitation of the 15-month-old's utterance that the child has an opportunity to compare his or her one-word utterance with the relatively simple utterance given in reply by the mother. At this point the child as a processor of language may be able primarily to abstract new lexical items or new phonological refinements of lexical items already in the child's system but with deviant phonology. A child who says "Bea" to "Ball" pronounced by the mother may be working toward perfect pronunciation of *ball*, and in addition the child may learn many new lexical items from the immediate imitations provided by his or her mother. Later on in the child's development, there will be more maternal imitations and a wider variety of relations between the child's utterances and the mother's partly or wholly imitative replies to the children's utterances. But at this early period the child may have direct processing advantages in the sense of seeing new information presented immediately after his or her own attempts at encoding events in the environment. There may be indirect effects in that mothers who imitate their 15-month-olds relatively frequently may set up conversational frames and routines in which it becomes easier for the child to devote limited processing capacity to the analysis in the maternal-imitation reply of new lexical information. This account also fits data for 12-month-olds (Hardy-Brown, Plomin, & DeFries, 1981).

In relation to these findings for children between 12 and 30 months of age, note that there may not be a reciprocal advantage in learning new lexical items or new syntactic structures for the child to immediately imitate the adult imitation of the child. In order to address this question thoroughly, we would need sophisticated, differentiated analyses in which cycles of utterances are analyzed, such as a child's utterance, followed by an adult utterance, followed by a child's utterance, followed by an adult utterance, and so forth. To date we have few such analyses as related to children's progress in lexical acquisition, in syntax, or in discourse (for beginnings, see Bohannon & Stanowicz, Chapter 6, this volume; Moerk, Chapter 12, this volume; Messe, 1982; Speidel, 1987). These differentiated multilayered analyses of conversational sequences are very much needed for the refinement of theory and intervention, as K. E. Nelson (1980, 1988) has argued. In any consideration of language acquisition models, variations in processing across individual children also must be kept in mind. So far, theoretical models have provided only modest accommodation to such individual differences. Referring back to the cross-cultural observations mentioned above, it would appear that New Guinea children are asked to imitate and do imitate adult utterances on the average much more frequently than we see in Western technological societies. On the other hand, the acquisition of Quiché in Guatemala children appears to rely very infrequently indeed on imitations of what adults have just said. Accordingly, a processing model should allow for the attention to utterances, engagement of analytic mechanisms with particular utterances, the storage and retrieval of related utterance examples, and the abstraction of similarities and differences between assembled sets of utterances—with all processing steps detailed both when imitation is involved and when absolutely no imitation by the child is employed.

Another related consideration is that, even when children do not show any imitation, acquisition of new lexical items and new syntactic structures on many occasions can occur very rapidly indeed. This process has been described variously as "fast mapping" or "rare-event learning." As Bates et al. (1988), Carey (1978), K. E. Nelson (1982), K. E. Nelson and Bonvillian (1973, 1978), Rice (1987), and Rice and Woodsmall (1989) all demonstrate, in a matter of minutes or hours of encounters with new language structures children are often able to abstract, store, and employ productively new language structures that have been given only one or two or a handful of exposures in the input. Children can deal with rare events and can rapidly map new language events or structures into their own systems even when there is no direct teaching of these structures and when the child attempts no immediate imitation of these structures during exposure of the exemplars in input on television, in stories, or in live conversation. Children have powerful abilities in focusing their mechanisms on particular language structures, in storing and retrieving relevant examples that are a focus of analysis, and in abstracting new structures from a very small set of exemplars or even in some cases from a single exemplar (see K. E. Nelson, 1982).

13.8 How Do Parental Variations in Imitations Affect the Child's Temperament and the Child's Own Imitative Tendencies?

In this volume, Chapters 3, 4, and 5, by Masur, Snow, and Užgiris et al., respectively, all indicate that mothers who show high imitative tendencies in language may sometimes influence children's own tendencies toward high imitative tendencies. Snow argues that this effect is very domain specific. That is, children do not develop high tendencies to imitate in every domain, either on the basis of modeling or on the basis of other factors. K. E. Nelson et al. (1985) similarly reports that mothers' imitative tendencies in the period between 22 and 27 months of age may influence children's own imitative tendencies in language. In recent longitudinal work, Heimann and Nelson (1986) and Nelson, Heimann, Garber, and Pemberton (in preparation) investigate more systematically the relationship between imitation in nonverbal behavior of children and in children's language imitations.

13.9 How Can a Process-Oriented Model Incorporate Parental Differences in Various Kinds of Imitations of Utterances?

An essential condition for the child abstracting new language structures is that the child assemble and analyze in working memory a set of related exemplars that include a definite challenge to the child's current language structure. What is important is that the child find some strategies for limiting other processing demands so that language structures on some occasions can be given considerable processing engagement. Different children obviously manage these demands in contrasting ways. Some children rely much more heavily on comprehension without production, whereas other children rely on a mix between production and comprehension. And some children rely extensively on immediate imitation, while other children rely virtually nil on immediate imitation. Thus, it is important in a theory like RELM to fit in children who assemble and analyze needed exemplar sets while being relatively quiet or limited contributors to conversation, and at the same time to accommodate children who imitate what fluent language users have just produced on more than 50% of opportunities that arise.

Granted that individual-difference characteristics must be accommodated within any adequate acquisition model for language, there remains the question of variations in processing across different language acquisition levels or stages. When children are roughly between Brown's Stage 1 and fluent acquisition of first language, there is considerable evidence that particular kinds of adult-modified imitations of children's own utterances can set up excellent processing and learning opportunities for the children. Investigations by Barnes et al. (1983), Cross (1977, 1978), Pemberton and Watkins (1987), Speidel (1987), and Wells (1980), and a series of studies by Nelson and his colleagues (Baker & Nelson, 1984; K. E. Nelson, 1977b, 1980, 1987, 1989; K. E. Nelson, Carskaddon, & Bonvillian, 1973) provide converging methods, samples, and outcomes showing *growth recasts* may be strong facilitators of children's acquisition of new language structures. Growth recasts are replies that keep the basic meaning and reference of a child's prior utterance, but that build in a growth opportunity because there is a more complex language structure in the reply than in the child's prior utterance. These growth opportunities are growth "recasts" because by keeping the same meaning but displaying a more complex structure the adult effectively recasts the child's meaning into a new language structure. Processing may be enhanced because the child, after producing his or her own utterance, has already activated phonological, semantic, and syntactic representations for his or her own utterance that are also relevant to the closely related growth recasts provided by the adult. To the extent that comparisons occur between the child's own utterance and the growth recast, the analysis therefore may proceed efficiently to abstract structural differences between the child's utterance and the growth recast. Many further differentiations are needed in future research. Nevertheless, it is rewarding to see that there is already differentiated evidence in the literature indicating that not just any imitation by adults provides beneficial processing opportunities for children. Instead, very particular kinds of replies like growth recasts have been demonstrated in both naturalistic and experimental studies to play a role in children's enhanced processing and acquisition of new language structures.

At very early language-learning stages, as during the period between 9 months and the onset of combinatorial speech or sign-language utterances, it appears that adults' exact imitations of what children have said and relatively simple modifications of what children have just said may provide important and beneficial processing opportunities. For example, when the child's language is very simple there is the possibility that children's vocabulary explosions may be triggered by straightforward adult imitation. Exactly this result was shown in the study described above. Similarly, in acquisition of early components of syntax, children may use their processing system more efficiently when the comparison opportunities between the child's own utterance and adult imitations provide very modest challenges to the child's current language system. Much more experimental work needs to be done to test out these latter speculations, but naturalistic results from Bohannon and Stanowicz (1989; Chapter 6, this volume), K. E. Nelson et al. (1984), and Speidel (1987) are favorable to these ideas.

Table 13-1. Frequencies and Percentages of Reply Types by Jordanian and United States Parents

| | Jordan | | United States | |
| Parental reply type | ($n = 8$; Ages 1.6 to 4.6) | | ($n = 9$; Ages 2.3 to 3.7) | |
	Frequency	Percentage	Frequency	Percentage
(1) Close imitations	32	34.8%	83	26.2%
(2) All simple recasts	14	15.2%	45	14.2%
(a) Expansions	9	9.8%	17	5.4%
(b) Reductions	2	2.2%	4	1.3%
(c) Other simple recasts	3	3.3%	24	7.5%
(3) All complex recasts	46	50.0%	189	59.6%
(a) Expansions	8	34.8%	66	20.8%
(b) Reductions	0	0.0%	30	9.5%
(c) Other complex recasts	13	14.1%	93	29.3%
(4) Total adult close imitations and recasts	92	100.0%	317	100.0%

Here we look at two new samples of child–adult speech, one from Jordan and another for a similar age range from a United States preschool. Exactly the same coding system was used for both cultures to determine the relative frequencies of adult close imitations and of two broad and six differentiated subcategories of adult recasts. Results were very similar across the Jordanian Arabic sample and the United States (Pennsylvania) sample. As indicated in Table 13-1, the two most frequently used parental categories of reply were complex recasts (two or more major sentence constituents changed) and close imitations—accounting for 85% to 86% of Table 13-1 replies in each culture. The remaining replies were simple recasts. For the six differentiated subcategories of recasts, in both cultures simple reduction recasts were infrequent, and the two most frequent subtypes were complex expansion recasts and complex recasts involving rearrangements or expansion/reduction combinations. By looking at pooled data across eight to nine children in each culture, highly similar adult reply strategy patterns thus emerge. Of course, these clues of cross-cultural similarity in input/interaction must be balanced with other clues that also indicate that a persuasive account of language will need to accommodate many individual differences both within and across cultures and languages (K. E. Nelson, 1977a, 1980; K. E. Nelson et al., 1984; Pye, 1986; Slobin, 1985).

For the more extensive American data, a further analysis was done to allow comparison with some of the results of Bohannon and Stanowicz (Chapter 6, this volume) on adult replies to error-free and error-containing child utterances. As Table 13-2 demonstrates, United States parents show a *selective* pattern of using recasts and close imitations. Parental close imitations are heavily skewed (71.1%)

Table 13-2. American Parents' Differential Use of Exact Imitation and Recast Strategies to Contrasting Children's Sentence Types

	One phonological error only	One syntactic error only	Two or more errors of any kind	No error	All
Close imitation	22.9%	3.6%	2.4%	71.1%	100%
Simple recast	6.7%	20.0%	13.3%	60.0%	100%
Complex recast	10.1%	15.3%	13.2%	57.4%	100%

to follow errorless sentences by the children. Most of the remaining close imitations (22.9%) follow child utterances with just one word mispronounced (one phonological error); all of these "close imitations" use the child utterance as a close model for the meaning and syntax expressed, but all but one of them also *correct* the child's mispronunciation error. Less than 6% of all close imitations are allocated to follow children's sentences with a syntax error or with more than one error of any type. This selective pattern of use of close imitation may help some children notice and process phonological differences between a single mispronounced word of their own and an adult reply with correct pronunciation but with none of the additional structural contrasts that recast replies carry.

Table 13-2 also reveals a different pattern for recasts: replies with essential meaning maintained, but with syntactic expansion and/or reduction and/or rearrangement. Adult recasts to error-containing child sentences more often followed single syntactic errors or multiple-error sentences than they followed single pronunciation/phonological errors. As we saw above, close imitations instead were associated with children's single phonological errors. Bohannon and Stanowicz report similar patterns of results. This new sample thus converges with their results in indicating that following children's syntactic errors close imitations are relatively rare, but that syntactic recasts are more frequent and may provide children with opportunities to compare and analyze syntactic differences between child and adult language systems.

Similarly, we should look at relatively late stages and the child's piecing together of a mature language system. It remains to be seen which kind of adult imitations or other replies may be useful to the child's mechanism in working out refinements of his or her language system. Bowerman (1985) has shown that in late stages children often reanalyze and reconsider structures that may have appeared to be consolidated earlier in development. It would be fascinating to discover what conversational circumstances may trigger the onset of new analyses, the assembly in working memory of new exemplar sets for comparison, and the abstraction of new and more complete systems of language.

13.10 Conclusions

In this chapter we have argued both for children and for their conversational partners that there are enormous variations in how frequently imitation occurs and its impact on the child's processing of language exemplars. Wide variations occur also in the interrelations between imitation and other components of children's cognitive and social styles. We can hope theories of language acquisition increasingly will take into account a mix of relevant possible mechanisms or sub-mechanisms in acquisition—language-specific mechanisms, general cognitive mechanisms, and mechanisms that involve analyses and integration of language, cognition, emotion, and personality. Similarly, we can hope that language acquisition models take seriously the task of accounting in detail for the course of successful language acquisition for children who imitate very little, for children who imitate moderately, and for children who imitate very extensively during the first 5 years of life. Throughout these endeavors it will be essential to provide differentiated considerations of the kinds of imitations that occur. In agreement with the basic lines of argument made by Bohannon and Stanowicz in Chapter 6 of this volume, we would like to stress that imitations by the child and imitations by his or her conversational partners should not be presented just in overall terms. Instead, the most informative analyses will be those that show whether the child's imitation in an immediate conversational opening contributes to acquisition of new structures over the longer term and also whether adult variations in imitation do or do not incorporate challenges to the child's current level of language structure. All imitations do not present the same opportunities for processing. Studies that will take us closer to refined models at the level of theory and refined models at the level of intervention will be those that provide related differentiations of the child's level of language, the level of language challenge in adult imitations of various kinds, and children's imitations that bear differential relations to what adults have provided in their conversational turns. As this chapter has shown, when such differentiations are provided there are some striking similarities and clues about how children process and learn language across cultures as diverse as Jordan, the United States, Sweden, Guatemala, New Guinea, Australia, and England, to name just a few. And, at the same time, the evidence of this chapter indicates that, within any culture that has been examined in detail, there are very striking individual differences. Different faces of imitation are shown both by different children and by their multiple conversational partners. Persuasive language acquisition theories and powerful intervention models are likely to depend on energetic accommodation of the full range of imitation skills in children, imitation tendencies in children, imitation types in children, and imitation types and tendencies in children's conversational partners.

Acknowledgments. Preparation of this report and conduct of reviewed studies were supported in part by Grant 1 R03 MH37803-01 from the National Institute of Mental Health and by National Science Foundation Grant BNS-8013767 to Keith Nelson, and by research grants to Mikael Heimann from The First of May Flower Annual Campaign for Children's Health, Gothenburg, Sweden, and from the Royal Swedish Academy of Science, Stockholm, Sweden.

Sincere thanks to Joy Struble for assistance on the manuscript and to Soonwha Kim and Amy Luther for research assistance.

References

Baker, N., & Nelson, K.E. (1984). Recasting and related conversational techniques for triggering syntactic advances by young children. *First Language*, *5*, 3–22.

Baldwin, D.A., & Markman, E. (in press). Establishing word-object relations; A first step. *Child Development*.

Barnes, S., Gutfreund, M., Satterly, D., & Wells, G. (1983). Characteristics of adult speech which predict children's language development. *Journal of Child Language*, *10*, 65–84.

Bates, E., Benigni, L., Bretherton, I., Camaioni, L., & Volterra, V. (1979). *The emergence of symbols: Cognition-communication in infancy*. New York: Academic Press.

Bates, E., Bretherton, I., & Snyder, L. (1988). *From first words to grammar: Individual differences and dissociable mechanisms*. New York: Cambridge University Press.

Bloom, L., Hood, H., & Lightbown, P. (1974). Imitation in language development: If, when, and why. *Cognitive Psychology*, *6*, 380–420.

Bock, K. (1982). Toward a cognitive psychology of syntax: Information processing contributions to sentence formulation. *Psychological Bulletin*, *89*, 1–47.

Bohannon, J.N., & Stanowicz, L. (1988). The issue of negative evidence: Adult responses to children's language errors. *Developmental Psychology*, *24*, 684–689.

Bonvillian, J.D., & Nelson, K.E. (1982). Exceptional cases of language acquisition. In K.E. Nelson (Ed.), *Children's language, vol. 3* (pp. 322–391). Hillsdale, NJ: Erlbaum.

Bowerman, M. (1985). Beyond communicative adequacy: From piecemeal knowledge to an integrated system in the child's acquisition of language. In K.E. Nelson (Ed.), *Children's language* (Vol. 5, pp. 369–398). Hillsdale, NJ: Erlbaum.

Braine, M.D.S. (1976). Children's first word combinations. *Monographs of the Society for Research in Child Development*, *41*, 1–104.

Buss, A.H., & Plomin, R. (1986). The EAS approach to temperament. In R. Plomin & J. Dunn (Eds.), *The study of temperament: Changes, continuities, and challenges* (pp. 67–80). Hillsdale, NJ: Erlbaum.

Camarata, S., & Nelson, K.E. (1988). Remediating language disorders: Treatments and targets. Paper presented at the University of Wisconsin-Madison Symposium on Research in Child Language Disorders, Madison, WI.

Carey, S. (1978). The child as word learner. In M. Halle, J. Bresnan, & G.A. Miller (Eds.), *Linguistic theory and psychological reality*. Cambridge, MA: MIT Press.

Clark, R. (1982). Theory and method in child-language research: Are we assuming too much? In S.A. Kuczaj (Ed.), *Language development: Syntax and semantics*. Hillsdale, NJ: Erlbaum.

Cross, T.G. (1977). Mother's speech adjustments: The contribution of selected child listener variables. In C.E. Snow & C.A. Ferguson (Eds.), *Talking to children*. Cambridge, MA: Cambridge University Press.

Cross, T.G. (1978). Mothers' speech and its association with rate of linguistic development in young children. In N. Waterson & C. Snow (Eds.), *The development of communication*. New York: Wiley.

Cross, T.G., Nienhuys, T.G., & Kirkman, M. (1985). Parent–child interaction with receptively-disabled children: Some determinants of maternal speech style. In K.E. Nelson (Ed.), *Children's language, vol. 5* (pp. 247–290). Hillsdale, NJ: Erlbaum.

Dunn, J. (1986). Commentary: Issues for future research. In R. Plomin & J. Dunn (Eds.), *The study of temperament: Changes, continuities, and challenges* (pp. 163–172). Hillsdale, NJ: Erlbaum.

Field, T.M., Woodson, R., Greenberg, R., & Cohen, D. (1982). Discrimination and imitation of facial expressions by neonates. *Science, 218*, 179–181.

Fischer, K.W., & Pipp, S.L. (1984). Processes of cognitive development: Optimal level and skill acquisition. In R.J. Sternberg (Ed.), *Mechanisms of cognitive development* (pp. 45–80). New York: Freeman.

Hardy-Brown, K., Plomin, R., & DeFries, J.C. (1981). Genetic and environmental influences on the rate of communicative development in the first year of life. *Developmental Psychology, 17*, 704–717.

Heimann, M. (1988). *Imitation in early infancy: Individual differences among infants 0–3 months of age*. Unpublished doctoral dissertation, The Pennsylvania State University, University Park, PA. University Microfilm #0000061.

Heimann, M., & Nelson, K.E. (1986). The relationship between nonverbal imitation and gestural communication in 12 to 15 month old infants. *Göteborg Psychological Reports, 16*, 2:1–2:20.

Heimann, M., & Schaller, J. (1985). Imitative reactions among 14–21 days old infants. *Infant Mental Health Journal, 6*, 31–39.

Heimann, M., Nelson, K.E., & Schaller, J. (in press). Neonatal imitation of tongue protrusion and mouth opening: Methodological aspects and evidence of early individual differences. *Scandinavian Journal of Psychology*.

Leonard, L.B., & Schwartz, R.G. (1985). Early linguistic development of children with specific language impairment. In K.E. Nelson (Ed.), *Children's language* (Vol. 5, pp. 291–318). Hillsdale, NJ: Erlbaum.

Liebergott, J., Menyuk, P., Schultz, M., Chesnick, M., & Thomas, S. (1984, April). *Individual variation and the mechanisms of interaction*. Paper presented at the Southeastern Conference on Human Development, Athens, GA.

Lieven, E.V.M. (1978). Conversations between mothers and young children: Individual differences and their possible implications for the study of language learning. In N. Waterson & C. Show (Eds.), *The development of communication*. New York: Wiley.

Lieven, E.V.M. (1984). Interactional style and children's language learning. *Topics in Language Disorders*, 15–23.

Lock, A. (in press). The interactive nature of language acquisition. In N. Krasnegor, D. Rumbaugh, & R. Schiefelbusch (Eds.), *The biobehavioral foundations of language development*.

MacWhinney, B. (1986). Hungarian language acquisition as an exemplification of a general model of grammatical development. In D.I. Slobin (Ed.), *The crosslinguistic study of language acquisition* (Vol. 2, pp. 1069–1156). Hillsdale, NJ: Erlbaum.

MacWhinney, B. (1987). Competition, variation, and language learning. In B. MacWhinney (Ed.), *Mechanisms of language acquisition*. Hillsdale, NJ: Erlbaum.

McClelland, J.L., & Rumelhart, D.E. (1986). *Parallel distributed processing* (Vol. 2). Cambridge, MA: MIT Press.

Mannle, S., & Tomasello, M. (1978). Fathers, siblings, and the bridge hypothesis. In K.E. Nelson & A. vanKleeck (Ed.), *Children's language, volume 6.* (pp. 23–42). Hillsdale, NJ: Lawrence Erlbaum Associates.

Meltzoff, A.N., & Moore, M.K. (1985). Cognitive foundations and social functions of imitation and intermodal representation in infancy. In J. Mehler & J.R. Fox (Eds.), *Neonate cognition: Beyond the blooming, buzzing confusion* (pp. 139–156). Hillsdale, NJ: Erlbaum.

Messe, M. (1982). Individual and dyadic differences and developmental change in mother–child conversational styles. Unpublished master's thesis, The Pennsylvania State University, University Park.

Nelson, K. (1973). Structure and strategy in learning to talk. *Monograph: The Society for Research in Child Development* (Serial No. 149).

Nelson, K. (1981). Individual differences in language development. *Developmental Psychology, 17,* 170–187.

Nelson, K.E. (1977a). Aspects of language acquisition and use from age two to age twenty. *Journal of the American Academy of Child Psychiatry, 16,* 584–607. Also printed in S. Chess & A. Thomas (Eds.), *Annual progress in child psychiatry and child development* (Vol. 11). New York: Bruner/Mazel.

Nelson, K.E. (1977b). Facilitating children's syntax acquisition. *Developmental Psychology, 13,* 101–107.

Nelson, K.E. (1980). Theories of the child's acquisition of syntax: A look at rare events and at necessary, catalytic, and irrelevant components of mother–child conversation. *Annals of the New York Academy of Sciences, 345,* 45–67.

Nelson, K.E. (1982). Experimental gambits in the service of language acquisition theory: From the Fiffin Project to operation input swap. In S.A. Kuczaj (Ed.), *Language development: Syntax and semantics* (pp. 159–199). Hillsdale, NJ: Erlbaum.

Nelson, K.E. (1987). Some observations from the perspective of the rare event cognitive comparison theory of language acquisition. In K.E. Nelson & A. van Kleech (Eds.), *Children's language, vol. 6* (pp. 289–322). Hillsdale, NJ: Erlbaum.

Nelson, K.E. (1989). Strategies for first language teaching. In M. Rice & R.L. Schiefelbusch (Eds.), *Teachability of language* (pp. 263–310). Baltimore, MD: Pan Brookes.

Nelson, K.E. (in press). On differentiated language learning models and differentiated interventions. In N. Krasnegor, D. Rumbaugh, & R. Schiefelbusch (Eds.), *The biobehavioral foundations of language development.* Hillsdale, NJ: Erlbaum.

Nelson, K.E., Baker, N.D., Denninger, M., Bonvillian, J.D., & Kaplan, B.J. (1985). *Cookie* versus *do-it-again*: Imitative-referential and personal-social-syntactic-initiating language styles in young children. *Linguistics, 23,* 433–454.

Nelson, K.E., & Bonvillian, J.D. (1973). Concepts and words in the two-year-old: Acquisition of concept names under controlled conditions. *Cognition, 2,* 435–450.

Nelson, K.E., & Bonvillian, J.D. (1978). Early semantic development: Conceptual growth and related processes between 2 and 4½ years of age. In K.E. Nelson (Ed.), *Children's language* (Vol. 1, pp. 467–556). New York: Gardner Press.

Nelson, K.E., Carskaddon, G., and Bonvillian, J.D. (1973). Syntax acquisition: Impact of experimental variation in adult verbal interaction with the child. *Child Development 44,* 497–504.

Nelson, K.E., Denninger, M.M., Bonvillian, J.D., Kaplan, B.J., & Baker, N.D. (1984). Maternal input adjustments and non-adjustments as related to children's linguistic advances and to language acquisition theories. In A.D. Pellegrini & T.D. Yawkey

(Eds.), *The development of oral and written languages: Readings in developmental and applied linguistics*. New York: Ablex.

Nelson, K.E., Heimann, M., Garber, B., & Pemberton, E.V. (in preparation). Developmental tapestries: How different children weave communicative skill and style from cognitive, temperament, and linguistic threads.

Obler, L.K., & Fein, D. (Eds.) (1988). *Neurolinguistic aspects of language development*. New York: The Guilford Press.

Obler, L.K., & Menn, L. (1982). *Exceptional language and linguistics*. New York: Academic Press.

Pemberton, E.F., & Watkins, R.V. (1987). Language facilitation through stories: Recasting and modeling. *First Language, 7*(1), 1–15.

Pinker, S. (1985). Language learnability and children's language: A multifaceted approach. In K.E. Nelson (Ed.), *Children's language* (Vol. 5, pp. 399–442). Hillsdale, NJ: Erlbaum.

Plomin, R., & Dunn, J. (Eds.). (1986). *The study of temperament: Changes, continuities, and challenges*. Hillsdale, NJ: Erlbaum.

Pye, C. (1986). Quiché Mayan speech to children. *Journal of Child Language, 13*, 85–100.

Rice, M.L. (1987, July). *Preschool children's fast mapping of words: Robust for most, fragile for some*. Paper presented at the Fourth International Congress for the Study for Child Language, Lund, Sweden.

Rice, M.L., & Woodsmall, L. (in press). Lessons from television: Children's word learning when viewing. *Child Development*.

Rumelhart, D.E., & McClelland, J.L. (1986a). On learning the past tenses of English verbs. In J.L. McClelland & D.E. Rumelhart (Eds.), *Parallel distributed processing, volume 2*. Cambridge, MA: MIT Press.

Rumelhart, D.E., & McClelland, J.L. (1986b). *Parallel distributed processing* (Vol. 1). Cambridge, MA: MIT Press.

Schieffelin, B.B. (1979). Getting it together: An ethnographic approach to the study of the development of communicative competence. In E. Ochs & B. Schieffelin (Eds.), *Developmental pragmatics*. New York: Academic Press.

Shatz, M. (1987). Bootstrapping operations in child language. In K.E. Nelson & A. van Kleeck (Eds.), *Children's language* (Vol. 6). Hillsdale, NJ: Erlbaum.

Slobin, D.F. (Ed.). (1985). *The crosslinguistic study of language acquisition Volume 2*. Hillsdale, NJ: Erlbaum.

Speidel, G.E. (1987). Conversation and language learning in the classroom. In K.E. Nelson (Ed.), *Children's language, volume 6* (pp. 99–136). Hillsdale, NJ: Erlbaum.

Wells, G. (1980). Apprenticeship in meaning. In K.E. Nelson (Ed.), *Children's language* (Vol. 2, pp. 45–126). Hillsdale, NJ: Erlbaum.

Wexler, K., & Cullicover, P.W. (1980). *Formal principles of language acquisition*. Cambridge, MA: MIT Press.

Author Index

Subject Index

Imitations specifically related to adults are found under "Adult Imitation." Otherwise, specific types and characteristics of imitation are entered in alphabetical order.

Springer Series in Language and Communication

Continued from page ii